Ethics and Professional Practice for Paralegals

THIRD EDITION

S. Patricia Knight

2015
Emond Montgomery Publications
Toronto, Canada

Emond Montgomery Publications Limited
60 Shaftesbury Avenue
Toronto ON M4T 1A3
http://www.emp.ca/highered

Printed in Canada.

We acknowledge the financial support of the Government of Canada through the Canada Book Fund for our publishing activities.

Publisher: Mike Thompson
Managing editor, development: Kelly Dickson
Director, editorial & production: Jim Lyons
Developmental editor: Sarah Fulton
Production & copy editor: Cindy Fujimoto
Proofreader: Laura Bast
Permissions editor: Bradley Myles
Indexer: Paula Pike
Text designer: Shani Sohn
Cover designer: Tara Wells
Cover image: OJO Images Ltd / Alamy

Library and Archives Canada Cataloguing in Publication

Knight, S. Patricia, author
Ethics and professional practice for paralegals / S. Patricia Knight.—3rd edition.

Originally published under title: Ethics and practice management for paralegals.
Toronto : Emond Montgomery Publications, 2006.
Includes index.
ISBN 978-1-55239-597-4 (pbk.)

1. Legal assistants—Ontario. 2. Legal assistants—Professional ethics—Ontario. 3. Practice of law—Ontario. I. Title.

KEO168.L43K55 2015   340.023'713   C2014-905330-4
KF320.L4K55 2015

In memory of Martha Schuler Higgins,
Terence Higgins, and Lloyd Higgins.

Contents

Preface

Welcome to the third edition of *Ethics and Professional Practice for Paralegals*. This book is designed to assist students and others to understand the principles of legal ethics and professional conduct, and the application of those principles. In each chapter, rules are discussed in conjunction with the applicable guideline(s) and other relevant material. Class activities, problems, and fact situations give readers an opportunity to consider and analyze the Rules, and apply them appropriately in order to comply with their ethical and professional obligations.

To ensure the text continues to be a valuable resource to instructors and students, the third edition has been updated to address significant changes to the *Paralegal Rules of Conduct*, as outlined in the paragraphs that follow.

Since May 1, 2007, paralegals—that is, non-lawyers who provide legal services in Ontario—have been regulated by the Law Society of Upper Canada. The *Law Society Act* provides the framework for governance of the legal and paralegal professions. The *By-Laws*, *Paralegal Rules of Conduct*, and *Paralegal Professional Conduct Guidelines* implement that framework. Licensing categories, requirements, and exemptions are governed by the *Law Society Act* and By-law 4.

The *Paralegal Rules of Conduct* set standards for professional conduct for paralegal licensees. In the years since regulation was implemented, those standards have evolved, and over time the Rules and Guidelines have been amended accordingly. Most recently, extensive changes to the Rules and the Guidelines were triggered by a Canada-wide initiative to implement standard rules of professional conduct for lawyers in all provinces and territories based on the *Model Code of Professional Conduct* (2012) of the Federation of Law Societies of Canada. These changes to the rules of professional conduct for both lawyers and paralegals in Ontario came into effect on October 1, 2014.

The October 1, 2014 amendments to the Rules include many significant changes and clarifications. For example, the definition of "client" in Rule 1.02 now states specific criteria for determining whether a person is a client or a non-client. Under the new definition, either a person is a client to whom a paralegal owes all of the duties set out in the Rules, or a person is a non-client to whom a paralegal may owe only certain duties, such as the duty of confidentiality. Rule 1.02 now contains a definition of "conflict of interest" that replaces the previous standard of "likely to affect adversely a paralegal's judgment … or loyalty" with a standard of "substantial risk" and "genuine, serious risk" to the duty of loyalty or to client representation. Rule 3, Duty to Clients, has been extensively revised.

That said, a paralegal's duty to provide legal services and discharge all responsibilities to clients, tribunals, the public, and other members of the legal professions honourably and with integrity remains unchanged.

Acknowledgments

I would like to thank Kelly Dickson and Anthony Rezek for their encouragement and support as we went forward with the third edition of this textbook; Sarah Fulton for her painstaking efforts to prepare the text for production; Cindy Fujimoto for her excellent advice and suggestions for improvements to the contents; my family for their understanding and support as this edition went through several revisions; and my students in the paralegal program at Sheridan Institute—my partners in teaching and learning.

Thank you also to the reviewers of the third edition: Adriana Melo, Algonquin College, and Deirdre Way, Loyalist College.

S. Patricia Knight, November 2014

Paralegal Governance in Ontario 1

LEARNING OBJECTIVES

After reading this chapter, you will understand:

- Paralegal governance in Ontario.
- Who must be licensed.
- Permitted areas of practice for P1 licensees.
- The licensing process.
- The good character requirement.
- Exemptions from licensing.

Background

paralegal
in Ontario, a non-lawyer agent who provides legal services to the public and who must be licensed to do so unless he falls within one of the categories of exemptions; the paralegal profession is governed by the Law Society of Upper Canada

In Ontario, **paralegals** have been practising as independent, non-lawyer agents providing paid legal services to the public for several decades. In many cases, the legal services offered by independent paralegals were authorized by statute. For example, paralegals were authorized to appear before various courts and tribunals by statutes that expressly permitted a defendant or accused in a quasi-criminal or criminal proceeding, or a party in a civil or administrative proceeding, to be represented by counsel or "an agent." Prior to April 30, 2007, the *Courts of Justice Act*, the *Statutory Powers Procedure Act*, and the *Provincial Offences Act* all contained such provisions.

Because of their affordability, a demand developed for paralegal services. In response to this demand, and in the absence of any form of governance prescribing the role of paralegals, independent paralegals began providing legal services in areas of law where there was no statutory or other legal authority for them to do so. These areas included family law, corporate law, wills and estates, and real estate. From the outset, the legal profession opposed this practice. However, the public needed affordable legal services, and independent paralegals met that need. Independent paralegals were inexpensive, and therefore accessible to people who did not have a lot of money to spend on legal services.

Many independent paralegals were honest and competent, and handled their clients' cases to a professional standard. They formed professional associations, complied voluntarily with good character requirements and professional codes, and carried errors and omissions insurance. **Errors and omissions insurance** is a form of liability insurance that is intended to reimburse clients for loss or damage suffered as a result of negligence or wrongdoing by a legal representative.

errors and omissions insurance
insurance intended to reimburse clients for loss or damage suffered as a result of negligence or wrongdoing by a legal representative

In the absence of any legislated form of professional governance, membership in paralegal professional associations and compliance with their requirements was voluntary. In reality, anyone could set up an office and provide legal services to the public as an independent paralegal. Independent paralegals were not required to have any formal legal training. They were not required to be of good character, to comply with a code of professional standards, or to carry errors and omissions insurance. If a paralegal firm was not insured, a client who had suffered damage as a result of a paralegal's incompetence or negligence could not look to an insurer for compensation. Instead, the complainant would be forced to sue the defendant paralegal firm for redress. Many independent paralegals incorporated their businesses. A successful plaintiff often found himself or herself trying to enforce a judgment against a shell corporation—that is, a business with no assets to enforce a judgment against.

Law Society of Upper Canada
a self-governing body that regulates the legal and paralegal professions in Ontario in the public interest, according to Ontario law and the rules, regulations, and guidelines of the Law Society

This situation raised issues of consumer protection with the Ministry of the Attorney General and the **Law Society of Upper Canada**, which governs the legal profession in Ontario in the public interest. In the absence of regulatory legislation, the Law Society had been confined to prosecuting paralegals on a case-by-case basis, as complaints came to its attention, for offences contrary to the *Law Society Act* and the *Solicitors Act*. This ad hoc approach to disciplining rogue paralegals was not a very effective way of protecting the public interest. As the Ontario Court of Appeal noted in a much-quoted passage from *R v. Romanowicz* (at paragraph 88):

> A person who decides to sell t-shirts on the sidewalk needs a licence and is subject to government regulation. That same person can, however, without any form of government regulation, represent a person in a complicated criminal case where that person may be sentenced to up to 18 months imprisonment. Unregulated representation by agents who are not required to have any particular training or ability in complex and difficult criminal proceedings where a person's liberty and livelihood are at stake invites miscarriages of justice. Nor are *de facto* attempts to regulate the appearance of agents on a case-by-case basis likely to prevent miscarriages of justice.

Romanowicz was a criminal matter. There were similar concerns about the potential for harm if uneducated, uninsured, and unregulated persons continued to be permitted to provide legal services to the public in other areas of law.

Regulation by the Law Society of Upper Canada

On May 1, 2007, the *Law Society Act* was amended to make the Law Society of Upper Canada the regulator of the paralegal profession in Ontario. The following is an overview of some key features of paralegal regulation in Ontario.

How Did the Law Society of Upper Canada Become the Regulator?

In 2001, then Ontario Attorney General David Young advised the Law Society that the Ministry of the Attorney General was interested in developing a framework for paralegal regulation. By that time, paralegals had been providing legal services in Ontario for roughly two decades without regulation. Two things were clear:

- there was public demand for paralegal services, and
- some form of regulation was urgently required if paralegals were to continue to provide legal services to the public.

Although the Law Society had previously resisted invitations to regulate the paralegal profession, in response to the Attorney General's invitation it formed a working group of legal organizations, including advocacy groups for lawyers and paralegals. In 2002, the Working Group on Paralegal Regulation published a consultation paper, whose recommendations elicited a storm of protest from paralegals and lawyers alike.

In the absence of consensus, the government took no further action on paralegal regulation. Then, in January 2004, at the invitation of then Attorney General Michael Bryant, the Law Society set up a Task Force on Paralegal Regulation. In its September 2004 *Report to Convocation*, the Task Force made its final recommendations for paralegal regulation. Most of the essential points outlined in the 2004 Report were incorporated (some in modified form) into Schedule C of Bill 14, the *Access to Justice Act, 2005*, an omnibus bill that was introduced to the legislature on October 27,

2005 by then Attorney General Michael Bryant. The rationale for Schedule C was that regulation of paralegals would improve access to justice by giving consumers more choice in qualified legal services while protecting people who seek legal services from non-lawyers. The *Access to Justice Act, 2005* became law on May 1, 2007, amending the *Law Society Act* to establish the Law Society as the regulator of the legal and the paralegal professions in Ontario.

Among the amendments to the *Law Society Act* were a new definition of the Law Society's function (s. 4.1) and a statement of its principles (s. 4.2). Pursuant to s. 4.1, it is the Law Society's function to ensure that:

(a) all persons who practise law or provide legal services in Ontario meet standards of learning, professional competence and professional conduct that are appropriate for the legal services they provide; and

(b) the standards of learning, professional competence, and professional conduct for the provision of a particular legal service in a particular area of law apply equally to persons who practise law in Ontario and persons who provide legal services in Ontario.

Section 4.2 states that, in carrying out its functions, duties and powers under the *Law Society Act*, the Law Society shall have regard to the following principles:

1. The Society has a duty to maintain and advance the cause of justice and the rule of law.
2. The Society has a duty to act so as to facilitate access to justice for the people of Ontario.
3. The Society has a duty to protect the public interest.
4. The Society has a duty to act in a timely, open and efficient manner.
5. Standards of learning, professional competence and professional conduct for licensees and restrictions on who may provide particular legal services should be proportionate to the significance of the regulatory objectives sought to be realized.

How Does Paralegal Regulation Affect the Role of Paralegals in Ontario?

In some Canadian jurisdictions (British Columbia, for example), a paralegal's role is very similar to that of a legal office assistant or a law clerk in Ontario. In those jurisdictions, a paralegal may perform a wide range of law-related tasks—some very complex—but may not give legal advice to a client or provide other legal services to a client for a fee. The paralegal's work is always done under the supervision of a lawyer, who is accountable for that work.

The role of paralegals in Ontario was, until 2007, unique, with paralegals assuming a wide range of roles depending on the nature of their work. Some worked as independent paralegals—that is, non-lawyer agents who provided legal advice and other legal services (including appearances before courts, statutory boards, and tribunals) to the public for a fee. Others worked as supervised paralegals in roles similar or identical to those of legal office assistants or law clerks. Supervised paralegals worked under the supervision and direction of lawyers or other managers, who were accountable for the quality of their work, in a range of law-related venues, including law firms, court offices, Crown offices, municipal prosecutions, government ministries, children's aid societies, and legal aid clinics.

Effective May 1, 2007, both lawyers and non-lawyer agents who provided legal services to clients for a fee were required to be licensed. The *Law Society Act* establishes the framework for governance of the legal and paralegal professions, while the By-Laws, the Rules of Conduct, and the Guidelines implement that framework. Licensing categories, requirements, and exemptions are governed by the *Law Society Act* and By-law 4.

The licensing model established by the *Law Society Act* and By-law 4 abolishes the old distinction between independent (unsupervised) paralegal advocates and supervised paralegals. You cannot assume, because you are working under the supervision of a lawyer, that you are exempt from the licensing process. To determine whether you are providing legal services—and therefore need a licence—you must refer to the *Law Society Act*, By-law 4, and any relevant information in the "For Paralegals" section of the Law Society website (http://www.lsuc.on.ca). Providing legal services to the public without a licence is an offence contrary to s. 26.1 of the *Law Society Act*.

In the unregulated environment, paralegals provided legal assistance in any area of law where there was a demand for their services. Effective May 1, 2007, a P1 (paralegal) licensee is authorized to provide legal services only in areas of law authorized by the by-laws for that class of licence (*Law Society Act*, s. 26.1(3)). Providing legal services that are not authorized for the holder of a P1 licence is an offence.

Licensing

A **paralegal licensee** is a person who is licensed to provide legal services in Ontario. A person **provides legal services** if she engages in conduct involving the application of legal principles and legal judgment to the circumstances or objectives of another person (*Law Society Act*, s. 1(5)). By-law 4, s. 5 establishes the P1 (paralegal) class of licence, which allows P1 licensees to provide legal services in Ontario.

paralegal licensee
a person licensed to provide legal services in Ontario

provide legal services
to engage in conduct involving the application of legal principles and legal judgment to the circumstances or objectives of another person

Requirements for Issuance of a P1 Licence

The following are the requirements for the issuance of a Class P1 licence for an applicant who applies for the licence after June 30, 2010 (By-law 4, s. 13(1)):

1. The applicant must have graduated from a legal services program in Ontario that was, at the time the applicant graduated from the program, an accredited program.
2. The applicant must have successfully completed the applicable licensing examination or examinations set by the Society by not later than two years after the end of the licensing cycle into which the applicant was registered.

Section 13(2) sets out a list of persons who are exempt from the education requirement:

Exemption from education requirement

(2) An applicant is exempt from the requirement mentioned in paragraph 1 of subsection (1) if,

(a) for an aggregate of at least 3 years, the applicant has exercised the powers and performed the duties of a justice of the peace in Ontario on a full-time basis; or

(b) the applicant is mentioned in subsection (4) and,

(i) has provided legal services, that a licensee who holds a Class P1 licence is authorized to provide, on a full-time basis for a total of three years in the five years immediately prior to her or his application for a Class P1 licence,

(ii) has provided written confirmation from two persons, from a list of persons and in a form provided by the Society, verifying that the applicant meets the requirement mentioned in subclause (i), and

(iii) has successfully completed a professional conduct and advocacy course conducted by the Society by not later than two years after the end of the licensing cycle into which the applicant was registered;

(c) the applicant is a member in good standing of the Human Resources Professionals Association of Ontario, the Ontario Professional Planners Institute, the Board of Canadian Registered Safety Professionals or the Appraisal Institute of Canada and,

(i) has been a member in good standing of the organization for a total of three years in the five years immediately prior to her or his application for a Class P1 licence,

(ii) has carried on the profession or occupation represented by the organization, including engaging in activities related to the provision of legal services that a licensee who holds a Class P1 licence is authorized to provide, on a full-time basis for a total of three years in the five years immediately prior to her or his application for a Class P1 licence, and

(iii) has successfully completed a professional conduct and advocacy course conducted by the Society by not later than two years after the end of the licensing cycle into which the applicant was registered;

(d) the applicant is registered and in good standing as a collector under the Collection Agencies Act and,

(i) has been registered and in good standing as a collector under the Collection Agencies Act for a total of three years in the five years immediately prior to her or his application for a Class P1 licence,

(ii) has acted as a collector, including engaging in activities related to the provision of legal services that a licensee who holds a Class P1 licence is authorized to provide, on a full-time basis for a total of three years in the five years immediately prior to her or his application for a Class P1 licence, and

(iii) has successfully completed a professional conduct and advocacy course conducted by the Society by not later than two years after the end of the licensing cycle into which the applicant was registered;

(e) the applicant was previously licensed to provide legal services in Ontario and applied for that licence prior to July 1, 2010;

(f) for an aggregate of at least 5 years, the applicant has, on a full-time basis, exercised the powers and performed the duties of a member of one or more [of the boards and tribunals listed in s. 13(2)(f)]; … or

(g) for an aggregate of at least 5 years, the applicant has, on a full-time basis, exercised the powers and performed the duties of an Appeals Resolution Officer at the Workplace Safety and Insurance Board.

BOX 1.1 What Is an Accredited Legal Services Program?

An **accredited legal services program** is defined at By-law 4, s. 7 as a legal services (paralegal) program in Ontario that is approved by the Ministry of Training, Colleges and Universities and accredited by the Law Society. The curriculum of accredited programs must, at a minimum, include at least 18 courses, the majority of which must cover areas within the **permitted scope of paralegal practice**, include a course or courses on professional responsibility and ethics, and include a field placement component of no less than 120 hours. The program content must cover and evaluate all of the competencies established by the Law Society for a paralegal education program.

All applicants who apply for a Class P1 (paralegal) licence after June 20, 2010 must be graduates of an accredited paralegal program. A list of accredited paralegal programs can be found on the Law Society website in the "For Paralegals" section.

By-law 4, s. 8(1) outlines the basic procedures and requirements for the issuance of a P1 licence under the *Law Society Act*:

> 8(1) The following are the requirements for the issuance of any licence under the Act:
>
> 1. The applicant must submit to the Society a completed application, for the class of licence for which application is made, in a form provided by the Society.
> 2. The applicant must pay the applicable fees, including the applicable application fee.
> 3. The applicant must be of good character.
> 4. The applicant must take the applicable oath.
> 5. The applicant must provide to the Society all documents and information, as may be required by the Society, relating to any licensing requirement.

accredited legal services program
a paralegal program in Ontario that is approved by the Ministry of Training, Colleges and Universities and accredited by the Law Society of Upper Canada

permitted scope of paralegal practice
areas of law in which licensed paralegals may provide legal services, as prescribed by the Law Society and the By-Laws

The Licensing Process Policies—Paralegal (Licensing Policies) at the Law Society website provide supplementary rules and procedures for licensing applications. They should be read in conjunction with By-law 4. The following is a brief discussion of some key points.

False or Misleading Representations

A **misrepresentation** is a statement or conduct by a person that is misleading or false, and that is intended to deceive another person. A deliberate failure to disclose accurate information is also misrepresentation.

misrepresentation
a statement or conduct by a person that is misleading or false, and that is intended to deceive another person; includes a deliberate failure to disclose correct information

It is essential that applicants be truthful and forthright, and comply with the Licensing Policies when completing the various steps in the licensing process. A person who makes a false or misleading representation or declaration by commission or omission in connection with (1) the application for a paralegal license; (2) an examination application; and/or (3) the registration into the paralegal licensing process is deemed not to meet the requirements for that step in the process, and that step plus any previously completed steps will be deemed to be void (By-law 4, s. 8(2); Licensing Policies, Part V).

Good Character Requirement

Under the *Law Society Act*, an applicant for a licence must be of good character (s. 27(2)).

The Licensing Process Policies authorize the Law Society to require applicants to provide information and/or supporting documentation regarding good character. As an applicant, you must disclose any of the following if they apply to you. Part VI of the Licensing Process Policies states:

> **6. Good Character Requirement**
>
> 1. An applicant for a paralegal licence shall be of good character.
> 2. In order to determine whether a person is of good character, the Society may require the person to provide information and/or supporting documentation regarding good character. This information and supporting documentation may include but is not limited to information and documentation with respect to whether the person:
>   i. has been found guilty of, or convicted of, any offence under any statute;
>   ii. is the subject of criminal proceedings;
>   iii. has had judgment rendered against him or her in an action involving fraud;
>   iv. has any outstanding civil judgments against him or her;
>   v. has ever disobeyed any order of any court requiring the person to do any act or to abstain from doing any act;
>   vi. has been discharged from any employment where the employer has alleged that there was cause;
>   vii. has been suspended, disqualified, censured or otherwise disciplined as a member of any professional organization;
>   viii. has been denied a licence or permit or had any licence or permit revoked for failure to meet good character requirements;
>   ix. has been refused admission as an applicant or member of any professional body;
>   x. has had allegations of misconduct made against him or her while attending a post-secondary institution or has been suspended, expelled or penalized by a post-secondary institution for misconduct while attending that institution;
>   xi. is subject to a petition or assignment in bankruptcy or a proposal to creditors under the *Bankruptcy and Insolvency Act* (Canada) or has been bankrupt or insolvent under any statute;
>   xii. has been disciplined by an employer or been a respondent in proceedings in relation to a Human Rights Code violation; and
>   xiii. has been sanctioned or had a penalty imposed upon him or her by a court, an administrative tribunal or a regulatory body.

If one or more of the above applies to you, you must make the appropriate disclosure on the Paralegal Application Form in the good character section. The Law

Society will then conduct an investigation. If the investigation reveals that there are grounds for concern with regard to your character, the matter will be referred to the Law Society Hearing Panel for consideration. Section 27(4) of the *Law Society Act* states that a person may not be refused a licence without a hearing before the Hearing Panel.

If an application for a licence is refused, another application may be made at any time, based on **fresh evidence** or a **material change in circumstances** (s. 27(6)). Fresh evidence is evidence of something that has happened since the first hearing, or has come to the applicant's knowledge since the hearing and could not by reasonable means have come to her knowledge before that time. A material change in circumstances is a change in the applicant's circumstances since the first hearing that may justify a variation of the original order.

fresh evidence
evidence of something that has happened since the first hearing, or that has come to the knowledge of the applicant since the hearing and could not by reasonable means have come to her knowledge before that time

material change in circumstances
a change in the applicant's circumstances that has occurred since the the previous hearing and that may justify a variation of the original order

BOX 1.2 What Needs to Be Disclosed in the Good Character Section of the Paralegal Application Form?

Fact Situation

During Samuel Brown's first semester in an accredited paralegal program, he was discovered using unauthorized materials on a final exam. After an investigation, Samuel's professor was satisfied that a breach of academic integrity had taken place. It was Samuel's first offence. Samuel received zero on the exam, and a breach of academic integrity letter was put on his file. In accordance with the policies and procedures of the educational institution he attended, nothing appeared on his transcript. He passed the course with a D.

Samuel is now in his third semester of the program. He has committed no further breaches of academic integrity. He is applying to the Law Society to write the Paralegal Licensing Exam. He has read the Licensing Policies and understands their contents.

When completing the good character section of the application, Samuel does not disclose the breach of academic integrity. He figures that there is no way the Law Society will ever find out that he cheated on an exam in first year because there is nothing on his transcript.

Questions for Discussion

1. Has Samuel made a false or misleading representation to the Law Society?
2. If Samuel has made a false or misleading representation, what are the consequences if it is discovered?
3. What would be the consequences if Samuel had disclosed the breach of academic integrity?
4. Why does disclosure matter here, since it is unlikely that the Law Society will ever learn of Samuel's omission?

Provision of Legal Services

A person who provides legal services in Ontario must be licensed in accordance with the *Law Society Act* and the By-Laws. A person provides legal services if she engages in conduct involving the application of legal principles and legal judgment to the circumstances or objectives of another person (*Law Society Act*, s. 1(5)). Section 1(6) further defines what constitutes the provision of legal services. The excerpt below has been edited to reflect activities that fall within the permitted scope of paralegal practice:

1. Advising a person about the legal interests, rights, or responsibilities of the person or another person;
2. Selecting, drafting, completing, or revising, on behalf of a person,
   i. a document that affects a person's interests in or rights to or in … personal property,

   . . .

   vi. a document that affects the legal interests, rights, or responsibilities of a person in areas of law authorized for paralegals, or
   vii. a document for use in a proceeding before an adjudicative body;
3. Representing a person in a proceeding before an adjudicative body; or
4. Negotiating the legal interests, rights, or responsibilities of a person.

adjudicative body
a body—such as a federal or provincial court, an administrative tribunal, a statutory board, or an arbitrator—that hears evidence or legal argument and makes a decision affecting the legal interests, rights, or responsibilities of a person (*Law Society Act*, s. 1)

representing a person in a proceeding
representation includes making decisions about service and filing of documents relating to a proceeding; deciding what persons to serve a document on or with whom to file a document; deciding when, where, or how to serve or file a document; and/or engaging in any other conduct necessary to the conduct of the proceeding

person
any entity that is recognized by law as the subject of legal rights and obligations, including the right to sue and be sued

An **adjudicative body** is defined in s. 1(1) of the *Law Society Act* as a body that hears evidence or legal argument, and makes a decision affecting the legal interests, rights, or responsibilities of a person, including (a) a federal or provincial court, (b) an administrative tribunal, (c) a statutory board, and (d) an arbitrator.

Conduct that is deemed to be **representing a person in a proceeding** includes (*Law Society Act*, s. 1(7)):

1. Determining what documents to serve or file in relation to the proceeding, determining on or with whom to serve or file a document, or determining when, where or how to serve or file a document.
2. Conducting an examination for discovery.
3. Engaging in any other conduct necessary to the conduct of the proceeding.

An examination for discovery is a disclosure process available in civil proceedings in the Superior Court of Justice.

BOX 1.3 What Is a "Person"?

Ordinarily, the word "person" means a human being. For legal purposes, a **person** is any entity that is recognized by law as the subject of legal rights and obligations, including the right to enter into contracts, and the right to sue and be sued. For example, a corporation is a legal person.

By-law 4, s. 6(2) sets out permitted practice for paralegals. At present, P1 licensees may do any of the following:

1. Give a party advice on his, her or its legal interests, rights or responsibilities with respect to a proceeding or the subject matter of a proceeding.
2. Represent a party before,
   i. in the case of a proceeding in the Small Claims Court, before the Small Claims Court,
   ii. in the case of a proceeding under the *Provincial Offences Act*, before the Ontario Court of Justice,
   iii. in the case of a proceeding under the *Criminal Code*, before a summary conviction court,

iv. in the case of a proceeding before a tribunal established under an Act of the Legislature of Ontario or under an Act of Parliament, before the tribunal, and
v. in the case of a proceeding before a person dealing with a claim or a matter related to a claim, before the person.
3. Anything mentioned in subsection 1(7) of the Act, provided the activity is required by the rules of procedure governing a proceeding.
4. Select, draft, complete or revise, or assist in the selection, drafting, completion or revision of, a document for use in a proceeding.
5. Negotiate a party's legal interests, rights or responsibilities with respect to a proceeding or the subject matter of a proceeding.
6. Select, draft, complete or revise, or assist in the selection, drafting, completion or revision of, a document that affects a party's legal interests, rights or responsibilities with respect to a proceeding or the subject matter of a proceeding.

In summary conviction court (s. 6(2)2(iii)), a P1 licensee may not represent a party in matters where the maximum penalty is a fine of more than $5,000 and/or imprisonment for a term of more than six months.

For purposes of s. 6(2)2(v), "claim" means a claim for statutory accident benefits within the meaning of the *Insurance Act*, excluding a claim of an individual who has or appears to have a catastrophic impairment within the meaning of the Statutory Accident Benefits Schedule.

Immigration Law

On June 30, 2011, Bill C-35, *An Act to Amend the Immigration and Refugee Protection Act* came into force. Section 91 of the *Immigration and Refugee Protection Act* was amended to state the following:

Representation or Advice

Representation or advice for consideration

91(1) Subject to this section, no person shall knowingly, directly or indirectly, represent or advise a person for consideration—or offer to do so—in connection with a proceeding or application under this Act.

Persons who may represent or advise

(2) A person does not contravene subsection (1) if they are

(a) a lawyer who is a member in good standing of a law society of a province or a notary who is a member in good standing of the Chambre des notaires du Québec;

(b) any other member in good standing of a law society of a province or the Chambre des notaires du Québec, including a paralegal; or

(c) a member in good standing of a body designated under subsection (5).

Paralegals who are licensed by the Law Society fall within subparagraph 2(b) as "other member[s] in good standing of a law society of a province," and are therefore exempt from the general prohibition in s. 91(1) against knowingly, directly or indirectly, representing or advising a person for consideration or offering to do so in an application under the Act.

The Law Society's position is that paralegal licensees may represent clients before the Immigration and Refugee Board and may provide legal services to clients in matters related to Immigration and Refugee Board hearings. Giving advice, preparing documents or providing other legal services in areas not related to Immigration and Refugee Board matters is outside the permitted scope of practice for paralegals licensed by the Law Society. A paralegal licensee who wishes to provide a full range of immigration services must be registered with the Immigration Consultants of Canada Regulatory Council and accredited as a Regulated Canadian Immigration Consultant.

client
a person who consults a paralegal and on whose behalf the paralegal provides or agrees to provide legal services; or, having consulted the paralegal, reasonably concludes that the paralegal has agreed to provide legal services on his or her behalf; includes a client of the firm of which the paralegal is a partner or associate, whether or not the paralegal handles the client's work

Disclosure to Client

A **client** is a person who (Rule 1.02):

> (a) consults a paralegal and on whose behalf the paralegal provides or agrees to provide legal services; or
> (b) having consulted the paralegal, reasonably concludes that the paralegal has agreed to provide legal services on his or her behalf
>
> and includes a client of the firm of which the paralegal is a partner or associate, whether or not the paralegal handles the client's work.

retainer agreement
a written agreement between the client and the paralegal that confirms that the paralegal has been hired to provide legal services to the client, and confirms the terms upon which she has been hired

engagement letter
a letter to the client from the paralegal that confirms the retainer and the terms of the retainer

non-engagement letter
a letter written by a paralegal to a client confirming that the paralegal will not be providing legal services to the client in a particular matter

At the initial consultation, you should identify yourself as a paralegal licensee to the client and determine whether the client's matter falls within an area of permitted practice for P1 licensees. If you are retained by a client, this discussion should be confirmed in writing in the **retainer agreement** or **engagement letter**. A retainer agreement is a contract between the client and the paralegal confirming that the paralegal has been hired (retained) to provide legal services to the client, and outlining the terms upon which she has been hired. It is signed back to the paralegal by the client. An engagement letter (also called a retainer letter) is a letter to the client from the paralegal that confirms the retainer and the terms of the retainer. It is not signed back to the paralegal by the client.

If a client's matter falls outside the permitted scope of paralegal practice, you shall decline the retainer. You should confirm that you have declined the retainer, and your reasons for doing so, in writing in a **non-engagement letter** directed to the client. A non-engagement letter is written confirmation that a paralegal has declined to represent a client in a particular client matter, or that the client has declined to hire the paralegal. If you decline the retainer because the client matter falls outside of the permitted scope of paralegal practice, the non-engagement letter should recommend that the client seek the assistance of a lawyer.

It has been recommended that, at the initial consultation with a client, paralegals be required to obtain and file on record the client's written acknowledgment of disclosure of the scope of the paralegal's services and legal advice.

Offences

If you do not have a P1 licence in Ontario, s. 26.1 of the *Law Society Act* prohibits you from:

1. providing legal services in Ontario (s. 26.1(1)), and/or
2. holding yourself out or representing yourself to other persons as someone who may provide legal services in Ontario (s. 26.1(2)).

If you possess a P1 licence in Ontario, s. 26.1 prohibits you from:

1. providing legal services that are not prescribed for your class of licence by the *Law Society Act* or the By-Laws (s. 26.1(3)), and/or
2. holding yourself out or representing yourself to others as a person who may provide legal services without specifying the restrictions on the areas of law in which you are authorized to provide legal services and the legal services that you are authorized by law to provide (s. 26.1(4)).

Failure to comply with s. 26.1 is an offence that is punishable upon conviction with a fine of not more than $25,000 for a first offence, and not more than $50,000 for each subsequent offence (s. 26.2(1)).

If a person is convicted of an offence contrary to s. 26.1, the court may make it a condition of a probation order that the person pay compensation or make restitution to any person who suffered a loss as a result of the offence (s. 26.2(3)). The court that convicts a person of an offence contrary to s. 26.1 may also prescribe as a condition of a probation order that the person shall not contravene section 26.1 (s. 26.2(4)).

Exemptions from Licensing

Persons Deemed Not to Be Practising Law or Providing Legal Services

The general rule is that anyone who practises law or provides legal services in Ontario must be licensed. Section 1(8) of the *Law Society Act* states that certain categories of persons are deemed not to be practising law or providing legal services, and accordingly are not required to be licensed. They include:

1. a person who is acting in the normal course of carrying on a profession or occupation governed by another provincial or federal statute that regulates specifically the activities of persons engaged in that profession or occupation;
2. an employee or officer of a corporation who selects, drafts, completes, or revises a document for the use of the corporation or to which the corporation is a party;
3. an individual who is acting for herself or himself, whether in relation to a document, a proceeding or otherwise;
4. an employee or a volunteer representative of a trade union who is acting on behalf of the union or a member of the union in connection with a

grievance, a labour negotiation, an arbitration proceeding, or a proceeding before an administrative tribunal; and

5. a person or a member of a class of persons prescribed by the By-Laws, in the circumstances prescribed by the By-Laws.

Section 28 of By-law 4 prescribes persons or members of a class of persons who are deemed not to be practising law or providing legal services and accordingly are not required to be licensed.

> **Not practising law or providing legal services**
>
> 28. For the purposes of this Act, the following persons shall be deemed not to be practising law or providing legal services:
>
> **Aboriginal Courtwork Program**
>
> 1. A person who delivers courtworker services to Aboriginal people through an Aboriginal delivery agency that has contracted with the Government of Ontario or the Government of Canada to deliver courtworker services as part of the Aboriginal Courtwork Program.
>
> **Other profession or occupation**
>
> 2. A person whose profession or occupation is not the provision of legal services or the practice of law, who acts in the normal course of carrying on that profession or occupation, excluding representing a person in a proceeding before an adjudicative body.
>
> **Committee of adjustment**
>
> 3. A person whose profession or occupation is not the provision of legal services or the practice of law, who, on behalf of another person, participates in hearings before a committee of adjustment constituted under section 44 of the Planning Act.

Persons Providing Legal Services Who Are Exempt from Licensing

By-law 4, ss. 30, 31, and 32 (excerpted below) set out additional classes of persons who may provide legal services without a licence.

> **Providing Class P1 legal services without a licence**
>
> 30(1) Subject to subsection (2), the following may, without a licence, provide legal services in Ontario that a licensee who holds a Class P1 licence is authorized to provide:
>
> **In-house legal services provider**
>
> 1. An individual who
>   i. is employed by a single employer that is not a licensee or a licensee firm,
>   ii. provides the legal services only for and on behalf of the employer, and
>   iii. does not provide any legal services to any person other than the employer.

Legal clinics

2. An individual who,
    i. is any one of the following:
        A. An individual who is enrolled in a degree program at an accredited law school and volunteers in or is completing a clinical education course at a clinic, within the meaning of the *Legal Aid Services Act, 1998*, that is funded by Legal Aid Ontario,
        B. An individual who is employed by a clinic, within the meaning of the *Legal Aid Services Act, 1998*, that is funded by Legal Aid Ontario,
        C. An individual who is enrolled in an accredited program and is completing a field placement approved by the educational institution offering the program at a clinic, within the meaning of the *Legal Aid Services Act, 1998*, that is funded by Legal Aid Ontario,
    ii. provides the legal services through the clinic to the community that the clinic serves and does not otherwise provide legal services, and
    iii. has professional liability insurance coverage for the provision of the legal services in Ontario that is comparable in coverage and limits to professional liability insurance that is required of a licensee who holds a Class L1 licence.

Student legal aid services societies

3. An individual who,
    i. is enrolled in a degree program at an accredited law school,
    ii. volunteers in, is employed by or is completing a clinical education course at a student legal aid services society, within the meaning of the *Legal Aid Services Act, 1998*,
    iii. provides the legal services through the clinic to the community that the clinic serves and does not otherwise provide legal services, and
    iv. provides the legal services under the direct supervision of a licensee who holds a Class L1 licence employed by the student legal aid services society.

Student *pro bono* programs

3.1 An individual who,
    i. is enrolled in a degree program at an accredited law school,
    ii. provides the legal services through programs established by Pro Bono Students Canada, and
    iii. provides the legal services under the direct supervision of a licensee who holds a Class L1 licence.

Not-for-profit organizations

4. An individual who,
    i. is employed by a not-for-profit organization that is established for the purposes of providing the legal services and is funded by the Government of Ontario, the Government of Canada or a municipal government in Ontario,

ii. provides the legal services through the organization to the community that the organization serves and does not otherwise provide legal services, and

iii. has professional liability insurance coverage for the provision of the legal services in Ontario that is comparable in coverage and limits to professional liability insurance that is required of a licensee who holds a Class L1 licence.

Acting for friend or neighbour

5. An individual,

i. whose profession or occupation is not and does not include the provision of legal services or the practice of law,

ii. who provides the legal services only for and on behalf of a friend or a neighbour,

iii. who provides the legal services in respect of not more than three matters per year, and

iv. who does not expect and does not receive any compensation, including a fee, gain or reward, direct or indirect, for the provision of the legal services.

Acting for family

5.1 An individual,

i. whose profession or occupation is not and does not include the provision of legal services or the practice of law,

ii. who provides the legal services only for and on behalf of a related person, within the meaning of the *Income Tax Act* (Canada), and

iii. who does not expect and does not receive any compensation, including a fee, gain or reward, direct or indirect, for the provision of the legal services.

Member of Provincial Parliament

6. An individual,

i. whose profession or occupation is not and does not include the provision of legal services or the practice of law,

ii. who is a member of Provincial Parliament or his or her designated staff, and

iii. who provides the legal services for and on behalf of a constituent of the member.

Other profession or occupation

7. An individual,

i. whose profession or occupation is not the provision of legal services or the practice of law,

ii. who provides the legal services only occasionally,

iii. who provides the legal services as ancillary to the carrying on of her or his profession or occupation, and

iv. who is,

A. a member of the Human Resources Professionals Association of Ontario in the Certified Human Resources Professional category,

B. a member of the Board of Canadian Registered Safety Professionals, or

C. a member of the Appraisal Institute of Canada in the designated membership category.

Individuals intending to apply or who have applied for a Class P1 licence

8. An individual,
   i. whose profession or occupation, prior to May 1, 2007, was or included the provision of such legal services,
   ii. who will apply, or has applied, by not later than October 31, 2007, to the Society for a Class P1 licence,
   iii. who has professional liability insurance for the provision of the legal services in Ontario that is comparable in coverage and limits to professional liability insurance that is required of a holder of a Class L1 licence, and
   iv. who complies with the Society's rules of professional conduct for licensees who hold a Class P1 licence.

• • •

Office of the Worker Adviser

31(2) An individual who is a public servant in the service of the Office of the Worker Adviser may, without a licence, provide the following legal services through the Office of the Worker Adviser:

1. Advise a worker, who is not a member of a trade union, or the worker's survivors of her or his legal interests, rights and responsibilities under the *Workplace Safety and Insurance Act, 1997.*
2. Act on behalf of a worker, who is not a member of a trade union, or the worker's survivors in connection with matters and proceedings before the Workplace Safety and Insurance Board or the Workplace Safety and Insurance Appeals Tribunal or related proceedings.

Office of the Employer Adviser

(3) An individual who is a public servant in the service of the Office of the Employer Adviser may, without a licence, provide the following legal services through the Office of the Employer Adviser:

1. Advise an employer of her, his or its legal interests, rights and responsibilities under the *Workplace Safety and Insurance Act, 1997* or any predecessor legislation.
2. Act on behalf of an employer in connection with matters and proceedings before the Workplace Safety and Insurance Board or the Workplace Safety and Insurance Appeals Tribunal or related proceedings.

Injured workers' groups

(4) An individual who volunteers in an injured workers' group may, without a licence, provide the following legal services through the group:

1. Give a worker advice on her or his legal interests, rights or responsibilities under the *Workplace Safety and Insurance Act, 1997.*
2. Act on behalf of a worker in connection with matters and proceedings before the Workplace Safety and Insurance Board or the Workplace Safety and Insurance Appeals Tribunal or related proceedings.

. . .

Trade unions

32(2) An employee of a trade union, a volunteer representative of a trade union or an individual designated by the Ontario Federation of Labour may, without a licence, provide the following legal services to the union, a member of the union, a former member of the union or a survivor:

1. Give the person advice on her, his or its legal interests, rights or responsibilities in connection with a workplace issue or dispute.
2. Act on behalf of the person in connection with a workplace issue or dispute or a related proceeding before an adjudicative body other than a federal or provincial court.
3. Despite paragraph 2, act on behalf of the person in enforcing benefits payable under a collective agreement before the Small Claims Court.

In *LSUC v. OPSEU et al.*, the Ontario Superior Court of Justice held that the exemptions in subsections 31(2) and 31(3) of By-law 4 do not apply to employees of the Office of the Worker Advisor and employees of the Office of the Employer Advisor who provide legal services to the public pursuant to 2011 amendments to the *Occupational Health and Safety Act*. Employees of the Office of the Worker Advisor and the Office of the Employer Advisor who provide such services must be licensed by the Law Society. The Paralegal Standing Committee has created a new process to facilitate the licensing process for persons wishing to obtain a Class P1 licence in such circumstances.

Section 34.1 allows paralegal students to provide legal services without a licence if they are completing field placement with a Class P1 or Class L1 licensee, a legal services firm or a law firm, a professional corporation established by Class P1 licensees, Class L1 licensees, or both, or the federal or provincial government or a municipal government, under the direct supervision of a Class P1 licensee or a Class L1 licensee, but the legal services provided must be those authorized for holders of a Class P1 licence.

Paralegal student completing a field placement

34.1 A student enrolled in an accredited program and completing a field placement approved by the educational institution offering the program may, without a licence, provide legal services in Ontario that a licensee who holds a Class P1 licence is authorized to provide if the student,

(a) is completing the field placement with a licensee who holds a Class P1 licence or a Class L1 licence, a legal services firm, a law firm, a professional corporation described in clause 61.0.1(1)(c) of the Act, the Government of Canada, the Government of Ontario or a municipal government in Ontario;

(b) provides the legal services,

(i) where the student is employed by a licensee, through the licensee's professional business,

(ii) where the student is employed by a legal services firm or a law firm, through the legal services firm or the law firm,

(iii) where the student is employed by a professional corporation described in clause 61.0.1(1)(c) of the Act, through the professional corporation, or

(iv) where the student is employed by the Government of Canada, the Government of Ontario or a municipal government in Ontario, only for and on behalf of the Government of Canada, the Government of Ontario or the municipal government in Ontario, respectively; and

(c) provides the legal services,

(i) where the field placement is with a licensee, under the direct supervision of the licensee,

(ii) where the field placement is with a legal services firm, under the direct supervision of a licensee who holds a Class P1 licence who is a part of the legal services firm,

(iii) where the field placement is with a law firm, under the direct supervision of a licensee who holds a Class L1 licence who is a part of the law firm,

(iv) where the field placement is with a professional corporation described in clause 61.0.1(1)(c) of the Act, under the direct supervision of,

(A) a licensee who holds a Class P1 licence who provides legal services through the professional corporation, or

(B) a licensee who holds a Class L1 licence who practises law as a barrister and solicitor through the professional corporation, or

(v) where the field placement is with the Government of Canada, the Government of Ontario or a municipal government in Ontario, under the direct supervision of a licensee who holds a Class L1 licence or a Class P1 licence and who works for the Government of Canada, the Government of Ontario or the municipal government in Ontario, respectively.

The Law Society recognizes the principle that the number of exemptions should be reduced over time where possible. It has been recommended that the Law Society continue to pursue elimination of exclusions to its regulation that cannot be justified in terms of facilitating access to justice and/or protection of the public interest. In its progress report on paralegal regulation to Convocation presented on February 27, 2014, the Paralegal Standing Committee noted (at paragraph 20):

> The Committee has continued work on the reviewing of the licensing exemptions in By-law 4, in keeping with Convocation's policy that exemptions should be reduced where possible. To facilitate this policy, the Law Society developed and conducted a successful "Integration Process," providing a facilitated route to licensing for previously exempted persons. Over 420 persons applied through this process, of whom 207 have been licensed so far. There has been progress towards recognition of the advantages of licensing, even in settings where this is not mandatory.

BOX 1.4 Do You Need a Licence?

If you are a non-licensee working under the supervision of a Class L1 or Class P1 licensee, you may require a Class P1 licence in some circumstances. To determine whether you are providing legal services and therefore may require a Class P1 licence, ask yourself the following questions.

Question: Are you providing legal services?

Discussion: To determine whether you are providing legal services, begin with the definitions of provision of legal services at ss. 1(5) and (6) of the *Law Society Act*.

Question: Do you advise clients with respect to the legal interests, rights, or responsibilities of that client or another person?

Discussion: If the answer is yes, then you are providing legal services, and require a Class P1 licence. Non-licensees are not permitted to give legal advice to clients.

Question: Do you select, draft, complete, or revise, on behalf of a client, a document that affects the client's legal interests, rights, or responsibilities, or a document to be used in a proceeding before a court or tribunal?

Discussion: If the answer is yes, then you are providing legal services, and require a Class P1 licence. Non-licensees are permitted to draft routine correspondence and documents only. All other correspondence and documents shall be reviewed by a licensee.

Question: Do you represent clients in proceedings before an adjudicative body? That is, do you:

- determine what documents to serve or file in relation to the proceeding?
- determine on or with whom to serve or file a document?
- determine when, where, or how to serve or file a document?
- engage in any other conduct necessary to the conduct of a proceeding?

Discussion: If the answer to one or more of the above questions is yes, then you are providing legal services, and require a Class P1 licence. Particular tasks and functions assigned to non-licensees by licensees are subject to the licensee's direct supervision and review. Non-licensees are permitted to appear before tribunals on routine scheduling and other administrative matters only.

Question: Are you responsible for negotiating a client's legal interests, rights, or responsibilities?

Discussion: Non-licensees are permitted to carry out routine negotiations only, with the client's consent and subsequent review by a licensee. In any other circumstances, you are providing legal services, and require a Class P1 licence.

Exemptions

Question: Does your role fall within any of the exceptions or exemptions set out in the *Law Society Act*, s. 1(8) or By-law 4?

Discussion: If your conduct is captured by s. 1(8) of the *Law Society Act* or s. 28 of By-law 4, then you are deemed not to be providing legal services and therefore do not require a Class P1 licence. If your conduct is captured by one of the exemptions at By-law 4, ss. 30 to 34.1, then you may continue to provide legal services without a licence so long as you meet the conditions of the applicable exemption.

Other Features of Paralegal Governance

Continuing Professional Development

continuing professional development the maintenance and enhancement of a licensee's knowledge, skills, attitudes, and professionalism throughout the licensee's career

Rule 3.01(4)(j) of the *Paralegal Rules of Conduct* requires that a competent paralegal pursue appropriate training and development to maintain and enhance knowledge and skills. By-law 6.1, which governs **continuing professional development** (CPD), requires that a paralegal licensee shall complete one hour of eligible activities for each calendar month in the year during which the licensee provides legal services in Ontario for any amount of time. Twenty-five percent of the total required hours shall consist of eligible activities that are accredited by the Law Society covering ethics, professionalism, or practice management topics (By-law 6.1, s. 2(2)). An "eligible activity" is an activity that serves to maintain or enhance a licensee's professional knowledge, skills, attitudes, or ethics, as determined by the Law Society (By-law 6.1, s. 1).

In other words, in her first full year of providing legal services on full-time basis, a paralegal licensee is required to complete a minimum of 12 CPD hours—that is, one CPD hour for each month of providing legal services—consisting of at least three hours on topics related to professional responsibility, ethics, and/or practice management ("Professionalism Hours," which must make up 25 percent of the total required hours) and at least nine hours on topics related to substantive or procedural law, or related skills ("Substantive Hours"). New licensees who provide legal services are required to meet the CPD requirement on a pro rata basis, to be determined starting with the month after the month in which they become licensed.

A fee is charged to licensees who fail to meet the annual CPD reporting deadline of December 31, and/or for failing to complete the annual CPD requirement by December 31.

The CPD requirements for licensees have changed and evolved over time. For current, detailed information about the CPD requirement, go to the Law Society website (http://www.lsuc.on.ca).

Convocation

The benchers, sitting as **Convocation**, govern the affairs of the Law Society. Under the *Law Society Act*, as amended by Bill 111, the composition of the **elected benchers** sitting on Convocation is as follows:

1. Forty lawyer licensees (s. 15), and
2. Five paralegal licensees (s. 16, as amended).

In addition, there may be eight lay benchers, who are appointed by the Lieutenant Governor in Council (s. 23). A **lay bencher** is a non-licensee who sits on Convocation.

Convocation
the governing body of the Law Society of Upper Canada

elected bencher
a licensee who is elected to sit on Convocation

lay bencher
a non-licensee who sits on Convocation

Paralegal Standing Committee

The **Paralegal Standing Committee** is established by Convocation and is responsible for developing, for Convocation's approval, policy options on matters relating to the regulation of P1 licensees in the public interest (*Law Society Act*, s. 25.1).

The composition of the Paralegal Standing Committee is as follows (s. 25.1(3)):

(a) five paralegal licensees, who are elected benchers;
(b) five lawyer licensees, who are elected benchers; and
(c) three lay benchers.

Pursuant to By-law 3, s. 130, the Paralegal Standing Committee is responsible for developing policy options on the following:

Paralegal Standing Committee
a committee of five paralegal licensees who are benchers, five lawyer licensees who are benchers, and three lay (non-licensee) benchers, which is responsible for developing policy on all issues affecting paralegal practice in Ontario

1. the classes of licence for the provision of legal services in Ontario issued under the Act, the scope of activities authorized under each class of licence, and the terms, conditions, limitations, or restrictions imposed on each class of licence;
2. the licensing of paralegals in Ontario, including the qualifications and other requirements for licensing and the application for licensing;
3. the regulation of paralegal licensees with respect to the handling of money and other property, and the keeping of financial records;
4. the rules of professional conduct applicable to paralegal licensees;
5. the requirements to be met by paralegal licensees with respect to indemnity for professional liability;
6. the professional competence of paralegal licensees, including
   i. the requirements to be met by such persons with respect to continuing legal education, and
   ii. the review of the professional business of such persons;
7. guidelines for professional competence applicable to paralegal licensees;
8. the provision of legal services through professional corporations;
9. the provision of information to the Society, and the filing of certificates, reports, and other documents relating to the Society's functions under the Act, by paralegal licensees;
10. the election of five paralegal licensees who are benchers as members of the Committee;
11. the election of five paralegal licensees as benchers; and
12. the appointment of the chair of the Committee.

See also *Law Society Act* ss. 16(1) and 25.1(3)(b).

Legal Needs Analysis

As discussed above, s. 4.2 of the *Law Society Act* sets out the principles to be applied by the Law Society when exercising its regulatory function. These include facilitating access to justice for the people of Ontario, protecting the public interest, and ensuring that licensees are suitably trained and competent to meet the needs of their clients.

In 2010, the Law Society committed to reviewing the scope of paralegal practice. In 2011, the Law Society commenced a series of small group consultations with lawyers and paralegals to obtain their views on access to justice in Ontario. A theme that emerged in these consultations was the evolution of the paralegal profession, and how barriers to access to justice might be addressed by clarification of the role of paralegals and/or expansion of the scope of paralegal practice. Participants expressed the view that a precondition to expansion of the scope of paralegal practice should be careful consideration of what further education, competencies, and credentialing would be required of paralegals as part of a properly managed integration of the paralegal profession into new practice areas.

Themes that emerged from the initial round of consultations were as follows (at paragraph 9 *et seq.* of the April 2012 *Treasurer's Report to Convocation: Update on the Law Society's Legal Needs Analysis*):

> 9. First, there was the clear indication that there are "foundational" issues, or those [that] lie at the heart of any future advancement in access to justice and the ability of the professions to provide solutions for legal needs. These foundational issues include:
>   a. competency of legal services providers (both new and experienced practitioners and both lawyers and paralegals);
>   b. underlying systemic issues in the administration of justice;
>   c. barriers to access to justice;
>   d. public awareness with respect to the justice system and service providers; and
>   e. evolution and maturation of the paralegal profession.
> 10. Second, there was a belief that the foundational issues may have to be addressed in advance of potential modifications to scope of practice. For example, there were views expressed that what is needed to improve or enhance access to justice is access to qualified legal services, and that as part of addressing the maturation of the regulated paralegal profession, before expansion of the scope of practice is considered, further education, training and credentialing is required.
> 11. Third, the suggestion was that addressing these issues will assist in setting the stage for an expansion of practice activities for paralegals, improve access to courts by members of the public and increase access to and use of legal professionals by the public.

The report recommended that the analysis go forward (at paragraph 13):

> 13. … More particularly, using the foundational issues as a guide,
>   a. considering how to address the systemic deficiencies in the justice system and barriers to access would involve examining solutions that cut across access, procedural, technological and training issues;
>   b. ensuring competency among paralegals would require a review of the prelicensing and licensing requirements, ensuring they are sufficiently robust and an exploration of the merits of limited licensing or credentialing;
>   c. ensuring competency among lawyers would require examining solutions to address how to maintain competence through targeted initiatives and measurements, including the merits of limited licensing or credentialing;
>   d. addressing public awareness around legal service providers would require consideration of measures to improve public knowledge and how to demonstrate and reinforce the value of using either a lawyer or a paralegal; and
>   e. a focused examination of the need for additional trained service providers to assist the public primarily in advocacy areas and the necessary training for that purpose would be required as a necessary component of addressing the [*sic*] how the need should be met.

Five-Year Review of Paralegal Regulation in Ontario

As part of the process of implementing paralegal regulation in Ontario, the *Law Society Act* required the Law Society to carry out a five-year review of paralegal regulation. Specifically, the Law Society was required to

- review the manner in which paralegal licensees providing legal services in Ontario have been regulated under the Act during the five-year period covered by the review;
- review the effect that regulation has had on paralegal licensees and on members of the public;
- prepare a report of the review, ensuring that a portion of the report is authored by the Paralegal Standing Committee; and
- give the report to the Attorney General for Ontario within three months after the end of the review period.

The five-year review of paralegal regulation required by the *Law Society Act* was delivered to the Attorney General on June 28, 2012.

As required by the *Law Society Act*, upon receipt of the review, the Attorney General appointed a non-licensee, David J. Morris, to

- review the manner in which paralegal licensees in Ontario have been regulated under the Act during the review period;
- review the effect that regulation has had on paralegal licensees and on members of the public;
- prepare a report of the review; and
- give the report to the Attorney General for Ontario within six months after the end of the review period.

The Morris Report made the following recommendations:

> **Recommendation 1:** That the Law Society continues to pursue elimination of exclusions to its regulation that cannot be justified in terms of facilitating access to justice and/or protection of the public interest.
>
> **Recommendation 2:** That the *Law Society Act* be amended to provide for proportionally equal representation of lawyers and paralegals in its governance structure.
>
> **Recommendation 3:** That language in statutes that serves to exclude paralegals, when that exclusion cannot be justified in the interest of facilitating access to justice or protecting the public interest, is amended so as to include paralegals.

Recommendation 4: That the Law Society undertakes a comprehensive review of the paralegal training and examination regime, beginning with a re-assessment of the competency profile that is appropriate for the legal services that are permissibly offered by newly-licensed sole practitioners.

Recommendation 5: That the Law Society considers implementation of subclasses of paralegal licences and/or other forms of accreditation to which, following specialized and substantive training, is attached the right to practice in specific areas of law (e.g. Small Claims Court).

Recommendation 6: That the Law Society undertakes a public education program that raises awareness of the legal services options available to Ontarians and the protection offered its consumers.

Recommendation 7: That the Law Society allocates the necessary resources to actively enforce within the paralegal sector adherence to its standard of professional conduct.

Recommendation 8: That paralegal licensees of the Law Society are required to include a Law Society-authorized description of their licence class (e.g. "Paralegal") and/or subclass in all marketing and communications materials.

Recommendation 9: That paralegals are required at their first meeting with a client to obtain and file on record the client's acknowledgement of disclosure of the scope of the paralegal's services and legal advice.

Recommendation 10: That the Law Society continues to actively pursue opportunities to facilitate greater access to justice through broadening of the scope of permissible paralegal practice, but that such broadening is directly linked to the recommendations above with respect to paralegal education and training and professional conduct.

Recommendation 11: Consistent with Recommendation 5 above, that the Law Society considers implementation of sub-classes of paralegal licences and/or other forms of accreditation to which, following specialized and substantive training, is attached the right to practice in specific areas of law that might currently fall outside of the scope of permissible paralegal practice.

Many of the recommendations in the Morris Report are consistent with positions that the Law Society has already taken on these issues, notably in the April 2012 *Report to Convocation: Update on the Law Society's Legal Needs Analysis.*

CHAPTER SUMMARY

On May 1, 2007, the *Law Society Act* was amended to make the Law Society of Upper Canada the regulator of the paralegal profession in Ontario.

The governance model established by the Act and the By-Laws requires that any person who provides legal services in Ontario be licensed to provide those services. Providing legal services includes (1) advising a person about the legal interests, rights, or responsibilities of the person or another person; (2) drafting documents on behalf of a person that affect that person's legal interests, rights, or responsibilities; (3) drafting documents on behalf of a person for use before a court, tribunal, board, or arbitrator; (4) representing a person in a proceeding before a court, tribunal, board, or arbitrator; and (5) negotiating the legal interests, rights, or responsibilities of a person.

Paralegal licensees are permitted by By-law 4 to:

1. give a party advice on legal interests, rights, or responsibilities with respect to a proceeding;
2. represent a party in Small Claims Court, provincial offences court, summary convictions court, before statutory boards and tribunals, or in Statutory Accident Benefits Schedule claims under the *Insurance Act*;
3. make decisions about service and filing of documents relating to a proceeding (including deciding what persons to serve a document upon or with whom to file a document, and deciding when, where, or how to serve or file a document); conduct an examination for discovery; and/or engage in any other conduct necessary to the conduct of a proceeding, pursuant to the *Law Society Act*, s. 1(7);
4. select, draft, complete, or revise a document for use in a proceeding, or help someone else to do so;
5. negotiate a party's legal interests, rights, or responsibilities with respect to a proceeding; and
6. select, draft, complete, or revise a document that affects a party's legal interests, rights, or responsibilities in a proceeding, or help someone else to do so.

Certain classes of persons who are not licensed are permitted by the *Law Society Act* and By-law 4 to provide legal services in Ontario. It has been recommended that the Law Society continue to pursue elimination of exclusions to its regulation that cannot be justified in terms of facilitating access to justice and/or protection of the public interest.

If you are not a P1 licensee, you shall not provide legal services or represent yourself to other persons as someone who may provide legal services in Ontario.

If you are a P1 licensee, you shall not provide legal services that are not prescribed by the *Law Society Act* or the By-Laws, and, in offering legal services, you shall specify what legal services you are authorized by law to provide.

Failure to comply with the above requirements is an offence. You are liable upon conviction to a fine of up to $25,000 for a first offence and up to $50,000 for a subsequent offence.

KEY TERMS

accredited legal services program, 7
adjudicative body, 10
client, 12
continuing professional development, 20
Convocation, 21
elected bencher, 21
engagement letter, 12
errors and omissions insurance, 2
fresh evidence, 9
Law Society of Upper Canada, 2
lay bencher, 21
material change in circumstances, 9
misrepresentation, 7
non-engagement letter, 12
paralegal, 2
paralegal licensee, 5
Paralegal Standing Committee, 21
permitted scope of paralegal practice, 7
person, 10
provide legal services, 5
representing a person in a proceeding, 10
retainer agreement, 12

REFERENCES

Courts of Justice Act, RSO 1990, c. C.43, as amended.

Immigration and Refugee Protection Act, SC 2001, c. 27.

Insurance Act, RSO 1990, c. I.8.

Law Society Act, RSO 1990, c. L.8, as amended.

Law Society of Upper Canada, *By-Laws* (2007), as amended ("the By-Laws"), http://www.lsuc.on.ca/with.aspx?id=1070.

Law Society of Upper Canada, Paralegal Licensing Process, http://www.lsuc.on.ca/licensingprocessparalegal.

Law Society of Upper Canada, Licensing Process Policies—Paralegal (November 2007), http://www.lsuc.on.ca/licensingprocessparalegal.aspx?id=2147495377.

Law Society of Upper Canada, *Paralegal Professional Conduct Guidelines* (October 2014) ("the Guidelines"), http://www.lsuc.on.ca/paralegal-conduct-guidelines.

Law Society of Upper Canada, *Paralegal Rules of Conduct* (October 2014) ("the Rules"), http://www.lsuc.on.ca/paralegal-conduct-rules.

Law Society of Upper Canada, Paralegal Standing Committee, *Report to Convocation* (April 25, 2013), http://www.lsuc.on.ca/WorkArea/DownloadAsset.aspx?id=2147494497.

Law Society of Upper Canada, Paralegal Standing Committee, *Report to Convocation*, at Tab 5.3.2, Progress Report on Paralegal Regulation (February 27, 2014), http://www.lsuc.on.ca/uploadedFiles/For_the_Public/About_the_Law_Society/Convocation_Decisions/2014/convfeb2014_PSC.pdf.

Law Society of Upper Canada, *Report to the Attorney General of Ontario on the Implementation of Paralegal Regulation in Ontario Pursuant to Subsection 63.0.1(2) of the Law Society Act* (January 2009), http://www.lsuc.on.ca/media/mar3009_paralegal_regulation_en.pdf.

Law Society of Upper Canada, Task Force on Paralegal Regulation, *Report to Convocation* (September 23, 2004), http://www.lsuc.on.ca/media/convsept04_paralegal_report.pdf.

Law Society of Upper Canada, Treasurer's Report, *Report to Convocation: Update on the Law Society's Legal Needs Analysis* (April 26, 2012), http://www.lsuc.on.ca/WorkArea/DownloadAsset.aspx?id=2147487345.

LSUC v. OPSEU et al., 2014 ONSC 270, [2014] OJ no. 1949.

Morris, David J., *Report to the Attorney General of Ontario: Report of Appointee's Five-Year Review of Paralegal Regulation in Ontario Pursuant to Section 63.1 of the Law Society Act* (2012), Queen's Printer for Ontario, http://www.attorneygeneral.jus.gov.on.ca/english/about/pubs/paralegal_review/default.asp.

Occupational Health and Safety Act, RSO 1990, c. O.1.

Provincial Offences Act, RSO 1990, c. P.33, as amended.

R. v. Romanowicz, 1999 CanLII 1315, 45 OR 506, [1999] OJ no. 3191 (CA).

Solicitors Act, RSO 1990, c. S.15.

Statutory Powers Procedure Act, RSO 1990, c. S.22.

REVIEW QUESTIONS

1. What are the functions of the Law Society of Upper Canada, as set out in the *Law Society Act*? Provide the statutory authority for your answer.
2. What principles must the Law Society have regard to when carrying out its functions, duties, and powers, according to the *Law Society Act*? Provide the statutory authority for your answer.
3. Define "person who is authorized to provide legal services in Ontario." Provide the statutory authority for your answer.
4. Define "provision of legal services" and give five examples. Provide the statutory authority for your answers.
5. What is the permitted scope of practice for P1 licensees? Provide the statutory or other authority for your answer.
6. You are a librarian. Your mother's best friend asks you to help her draft simple wills for her and her husband. She says she phoned some lawyers, but the lowest fee quoted was $1,000. You have known her all your life, and have always called her and her husband "aunt" and "uncle." You obligingly draft up wills and powers of attorney. You and your mother witness their signatures on the wills. You don't charge them anything.

   When answering the following questions, give reasons for your answers, referring to the *Law Society Act* and By-law 4.

   a. Are you providing legal services when you draft the wills and powers of attorney?

   b. Have you committed an offence? If yes, what are the penalties?
7. You are a P1 licensee. Your mother's best friend asks you to help her draft simple wills for her and her husband. She says she phoned some lawyers, but the lowest fee quoted was $1,000. You've known her all your life, and have always called her and her husband "aunt" and "uncle." You obligingly draft the wills and the powers of attorney. You and your mother witness their signatures on the wills. You don't charge them anything.

   When answering the following questions, give reasons for your answers, referring to the *Law Society Act* and By-law 4.

   a. Are you providing legal services when you draft the wills and power of attorney?

   b. Have you committed an offence? If yes, what are the penalties?

Professionalism

2

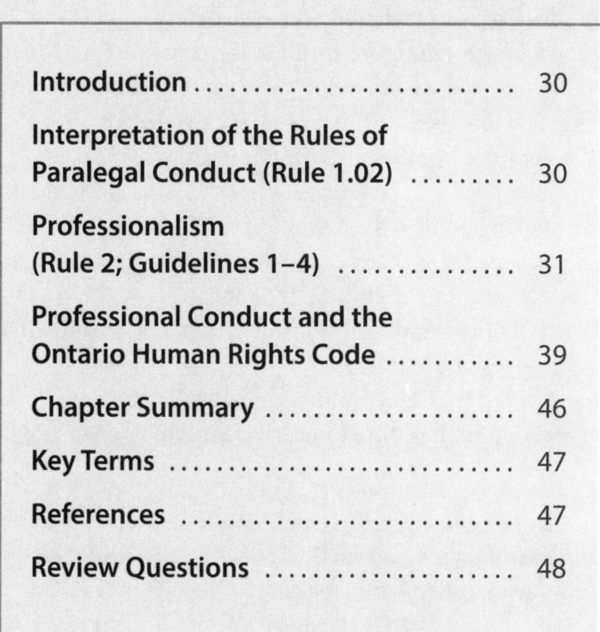

LEARNING OBJECTIVES

After reading this chapter, you will understand:

- How to read the *Paralegal Rules of Conduct*.
- How to use the *Paralegal Professional Conduct Guidelines*.
- The general duty of integrity and civility.
- Management of outside interests and public office.
- The role of the paralegal as mediator.
- The obligation to fulfill undertakings.
- Harassment and discrimination.
- The role of the Discrimination and Harassment Counsel.

Introduction

The *Paralegal Rules of Conduct* ("the Rules"), which establish standards of professional conduct for paralegals in Ontario, were approved by Convocation on March 29, 2007. As a paralegal, you shall know the Rules and shall comply with the Rules. Non-compliance may result in disciplinary action by the Law Society. More importantly, unprofessional conduct may bring the reputation of the paralegal profession in Ontario into disrepute.

Interpretation of the Rules of Paralegal Conduct (Rule 1.02)

When reading and interpreting the Rules, you shall refer to the definitions set out in Rule 1.02. The definitions tell you what certain terms mean in the context of the Rules and of professional practice. Some terms (such as "client" or "consent") may have different meanings in other contexts. However, for purposes of compliance with the Rules, your starting point is the definition of the term set out in Rule 1.02.

If you are trying to determine whether a paralegal–client relationship exists between a person and you, your starting point is the definition of "client" in Rule 1.02. If you are considering whether you are in a position of conflict of interest, your starting point is the definition of "conflict of interest" in Rule 1.02. If you are seeking a client's consent to a certain arrangement, you shall consult Rule 1.02 first to ensure that any consent given is valid for purposes of the Rules.

The Rules should be read and interpreted in conjunction with the *Paralegal Professional Conduct Guidelines* ("the Guidelines"). See the Introduction to the Guidelines at paragraph 2:

> The *Paralegal Professional Conduct Guidelines* ("Guidelines") have been created to assist paralegals with the interpretation and application of the *Paralegal Rules of Conduct* ("*Rules*"). The Guidelines should be considered along with the *Rules*, the *Law Society Act* (the "*Act*"), the By-Laws made under the *Act* and any other relevant case law or legislation. Neither the *Rules* nor the Guidelines can cover every situation; they should be interpreted and applied with common sense and in a manner consistent with the public interest and the integrity of the profession. It is expected that a paralegal will exercise his or her professional judgment in interpreting the Guidelines, keeping in mind the paralegal's obligations to the client, the court or tribunal and the Law Society.

When interpreting the Guidelines, keep the following principles from the Introduction to the Guidelines in mind:

- The terms "shall" or "must" are used in those instances where compliance is mandated by either the by-laws made pursuant to the *Law Society Act* or the *Rules*.
- The term "should" and the phrase "should consider" indicate a recommendation. These terms refer to those practices or policies that are considered by the Law Society to be a reasonable goal for maintaining or enhancing professional conduct.

- The term "may" and the phrase "may consider" convey discretion. After considering suggested policies or procedures preceded by "may" or "may consider," a paralegal has discretion whether or not to follow the suggestions, depending upon the paralegal's particular circumstances, areas of professional business or clientele, or the circumstances of a particular client or matter.

When assessing a situation in which ethical or professional issues arise, consider taking the following steps:

1. Identify the ethical or professional issue or issues.
2. Consider any law that may apply, including but not limited to the *Law Society Act*, the By-Laws, and/or tribunal decisions such as Law Society discipline decisions.
3. Review the applicable rule(s) and guideline(s).
4. Assess the fact situation with reference to the rule(s) and guideline(s).
5. Determine what action is necessary in order to comply with both the spirit and the letter of the Rules. Observing the Rules in both the "spirit" as well as the "letter" means conducting yourself in a manner that complies with both the intent or purpose of the Rules and the words on the page.
6. Consider whether the action required by the rule is mandatory (you "shall" do something), or discretionary (you "may" do something).
7. Be circumspect if you are in a "grey area"—that is, a situation where there is no clear language in the Rules, the Guidelines, or other resources directing you toward a particular course of action.
8. If, after the above steps, you are still unsure about what action to take,
   - consult with another paralegal or a lawyer to secure legal advice about your proposed conduct (see Rule 3.03(8)),
   - check the Resources for Paralegals at the Law Society website if you have not already done so, and/or
   - contact the Practice Management Helpline for assistance.
9. Keep a written record of your analysis and any steps you took to deal with the situation.

Professionalism (Rule 2; Guidelines 1–4)

General

With respect to professionalism generally, Guideline 1 states:

> 1. A paralegal should inspire the respect, confidence and trust of clients and the community.
> 2. Public confidence in the administration of justice and in the paralegal profession may be eroded by a paralegal's unprofessional conduct. A paralegal's conduct should reflect favourably on the legal professions, inspire the confidence, respect and trust of clients and of the community, and avoid even the appearance of impropriety.
> 3. A paralegal has special responsibilities by virtue of the privileges afforded the paralegal profession and the important role it plays in a free and democratic

> society and in the administration of justice. This includes a special responsibility to recognize the diversity of the Ontario community, to protect the dignity of individuals and to respect human rights laws in force in Ontario.

Integrity and Civility

Integrity

A paralegal has the following duties (Rules 2.01(1), (2)):

> (1) [T]o provide legal services and discharge all responsibilities to clients, tribunals, the public and other members of the legal professions honourably and with integrity.
>
> (2) [T]o uphold the standards and reputation of the paralegal profession and to assist in the advancement of its goals, organizations and institutions.

Acting with integrity means being honest and conducting yourself in accordance with high ethical and moral principles. Guideline 1 states:

> *Integrity* is the fundamental quality of any person who seeks to provide legal services. If integrity is lacking, the paralegal's usefulness to the client and reputation within the profession will be destroyed regardless of how competent the paralegal may be.

BOX 2.1 Integrity

Fact Situation

You are a paralegal licensee. One of your clients is the defendant in a Small Claims Court proceeding. On the morning of the date set for trial you are waiting at the courthouse for your client when she phones to tell you that something urgent has come up and she cannot attend at court that day. You advise your client that in the circumstances the judge may order that the trial proceed in her absence or, if the judge grants an adjournment, she may be required to pay costs to the plaintiff, who is also represented, for inconvenience and delay. "Oh, just tell the judge that the baby's got colic and I can't get a sitter. That'll break his heart," your client says, and terminates the call. You happen to know that she has no children.

Question for Discussion

Can you follow your client's instructions?

Civility (Rule 2.01(3))

In *Principles of Civility for Advocates* (2006), the Advocates Society notes that

> [c]ivility amongst those entrusted with the administration of justice is central to its effectiveness and to the public's confidence in that system. Civility ensures matters before the court are resolved in an orderly way and helps preserve the role of counsel in the justice system as an honourable one.

> Litigation, however, whether before a court or tribunal is not a "tea party." Counsel are bound to vigorously advance their client's case, fairly and honourably. Accordingly, counsel's role is openly and necessarily partisan and nothing which follows is intended to undermine those principles. But counsel can disagree, even vigorously, without being disagreeable. Whether among counsel or before the courts, antagonistic or acrimonious behaviour is not conducive to effective advocacy. Rather, civility is the hallmark of our best counsel.

Rule 2.01(3) requires that a paralegal shall be courteous and civil, and shall act in good faith toward all persons with whom he has dealings in the course of his practice. **Acting with civility** means that a paralegal shall communicate politely and respectfully and act in a manner that does not cause unnecessary difficulty or harm to another. The obligation to be polite, respectful, and considerate of others extends to clients, opposing parties, other paralegals and lawyers, support staff, court and tribunal officers, court and tribunal staff, and Law Society representatives. The obligation applies regardless of the formality or informality of the venue, or the stage you are at in a matter (Guideline 1).

acting with civility being polite, respectful, and considerate of others

Acting in good faith means making legitimate and honest efforts to meet your obligations in a given situation, without trying to mislead other persons or parties, or attempting to gain an unfair advantage over others, through legal technicalities or otherwise.

acting in good faith making legitimate and honest efforts to meet your obligations in a given situation, without trying to gain an unfair advantage over or mislead other persons or parties through legal technicalities or otherwise

Paralegals shall make their legal services available to the public in a way that commands respect and confidence, and is compatible with the integrity and independence of the paralegal profession.

BOX 2.2 Courtesy, Civility, and Good Faith

Fact Situation

You run a small paralegal practice that consists of yourself and a part-time legal assistant, Christopher, who has been working with you for four months.

One afternoon, you have a meeting with a client to review her evidence in a matter that is going to a hearing the following week. You are in court that morning longer than you expected, and return to your office an hour late. The client is waiting for you in the reception area.

When you go into your office, the client file is not on your desk. You go back out to reception and say, "Where's the file?" Christopher gives you a panicky look and says, "The file? I don't think I've seen it."

While the client waits, Christopher starts going through everything on his desk and in his filing cabinet, looking for the file. You smile apologetically at the client, and say to Christopher, "I might be able to get stuff done around here if you got organized." Then you go back into your office, where you check your file trays and the filing cabinet. Finally, you find the file under some papers on your desk, where you must have left it the last time you phoned the client.

You go out to the reception area and tell Christopher, "It's okay, I found it where you buried it." You look at the client, shake your head, and say, "You can't count on anyone, can you? He's new. I guess he'll learn."

You've been so busy that you haven't had time to review the file. You quickly go through it, making notes. By the time you ask the client into your office, she has been waiting almost 45 minutes.

Question for Discussion

Have you complied with Rule 2.01? When answering this question, please consider your conduct toward both Christopher and the client.

Outside Interests and Public Office (Rules 2.01(4), (5); Guideline 2)

outside interest
any profession, business, occupation, or other outside interest, including holding public office, engaged in by a paralegal concurrently with the provision of legal services

A paralegal who engages in another profession, business, occupation, or other **outside interest**, or who holds public office at the same time as she is providing legal services, shall not allow the outside interest or public office to jeopardize the paralegal's integrity, independence, or competence (Rule 2.01(4)). A paralegal shall not allow involvement in an outside interest or public office to impair the exercise of her independent judgment as a paralegal on behalf of a client (Rule 2.01(5)). The question of whether and to what extent it is proper for the paralegal to engage in the outside interest will be subject to any applicable by-law or rule of the Law Society.

1. The term "outside interest" covers the widest range of activities. It includes activities that may overlap or be connected with provision of legal services, for example, acting as a director of a corporation or writing on legal subjects, as well as activities less connected such as, for example, a career in business, politics, broadcasting or the performing arts.
2. When participating in community activities, a paralegal should be mindful of the possible perception that the paralegal is providing legal services and a paralegal–client relationship has been established. A paralegal should not carry on, manage or be involved in any outside interest in such a way that makes it difficult to distinguish in which capacity the paralegal is acting, or that would give rise to a conflict of interest or duty to a client.
3. It is the paralegal's responsibility to consider whether the outside interest may impair his or her ability to act in the best interest of his or her client(s). If so, the paralegal must withdraw, either from representation of the client or from the outside interest.
4. When acting in another role, the paralegal must continue to fulfill his or her obligations under the *Rules*, for example, to
   - act with integrity,
   - be civil and courteous,
   - be competent in providing legal services,
   - avoid conflicts of interest, and
   - maintain confidentiality (Guideline 2).

conflict of interest
an interest, financial or otherwise, that may negatively affect a paralegal's ability to fulfill her professional and ethical obligations to a client

A **conflict of interest** arises when there exists a substantial risk that a paralegal's loyalty to or representation of a client would be materially and adversely affected by the paralegal's own interest or the paralegal's duties to another client, a former client, or a third person. The risk must be more than a mere possibility. There must be a genuine, serious risk to the duty of loyalty or to client representation arising from the retainer (Rule 1.02 definitions).

A paralegal who finds herself in a situation where her involvement in an outside interest gives rise to a substantial risk that her loyalty to or representation of a client will be adversely affected shall decide whether she will withdraw from representation of the client or cease her involvement in the outside interest.

When contemplating involvement in an outside interest, a paralegal shall also consider whether involvement in the outside interest will adversely affect her professional competence by, for example, taking up so much of her time that she is unable to attend properly to her clients' interests.

BOX 2.3 Outside Interests

Fact Situation

You have been a member of the board of directors of a small, publicly funded community organization for two years. The organization consists of a general manager, four full-time staff, and a part-time office assistant. You are the only licensee on the board. During the course of your directorship, the general manager and you have become friendly.

Over the past few months, the general manager has begun calling you at your office more frequently. She is unhappy with the performance of Gloria, one of the full-time staff. Gloria has begun to take a lot of sick days. She takes long lunches, and does not always complete the tasks assigned to her, placing an extra burden on the other staff. She is rude to her co-workers. Her conduct has caused resentment, disruption and inconvenience. The general manager is at a point where she would like to terminate Gloria's employment. She wants your advice about how to manage the situation.

Question for Discussion

What are your obligations in these circumstances?

Acting as a Mediator (Rule 2.01(6))

Mediation is a non-adversarial process in which a qualified and impartial third party (the **mediator**) helps the parties to a dispute resolve their differences. A mediator has a duty to be neutral in relation to the participants in the mediation—that is, the mediator must have no preconceived opinions or biases in favour of or against one party or another.

mediation
a non-adversarial process in which a qualified and impartial third party (the mediator) helps the parties to a dispute resolve their differences

mediator
a qualified and impartial third party who helps the parties to a dispute resolve their differences through mediation

A paralegal mediator does not provide legal services to either party in the mediation. A paralegal who acts as a mediator shall, at the outset of the mediation, ensure that the parties to the mediation understand that the paralegal is not acting as a representative for either party, but, as mediator, is acting to assist the parties to resolve the issues in dispute (Rule 2.01(6)). In other words, a paralegal–client relationship does not exist between a paralegal mediator and the parties whose dispute is being mediated. This does not preclude the paralegal mediator from providing information to the parties about the consequences if the mediation fails (Guideline 2).

When acting as a mediator, a paralegal should guard against potential conflicts of interest. Neither the paralegal mediator nor the paralegal mediator's partners or associates should provide legal services to the parties whose dispute is being mediated. A paralegal mediator should suggest and encourage the parties to seek the advice of a qualified licensee before and during the mediation process if they have not already done so (Guideline 2). The commentary to s. 5.7 of the *Rules of Professional Conduct* for lawyers recommends that if, in the course of a mediation, a mediator prepares a draft settlement for the parties to consider, the mediator should expressly (that is, in writing) advise and encourage the parties to seek separate independent legal representation for purposes of reviewing the draft contract. A paralegal mediator shall also advise the parties that he cannot represent either or both of them in any subsequent legal matter related to the issues mediated.

Undertakings and Trust Conditions (Rules 2.02, 6.01; Guideline 3)

Undertakings

undertaking
an unequivocal, personal promise by a paralegal to perform a certain act

An **undertaking** is a promise to carry out specific tasks and/or fulfill specific conditions (Guideline 3). Undertakings given by licensees are "matters of the utmost good faith and must receive scrupulous attention" (*Towne v. Miller*, at paragraph 11).

Rule 2.02(1) states that a paralegal shall fulfill every undertaking given, and shall not give an undertaking that cannot be fulfilled. Except in exceptional circumstances, undertakings shall be made in writing at the time they are given, or confirmed in writing as soon as possible thereafter (Rule 2.02(2)). Unless the language of the undertaking clearly states otherwise, a paralegal's undertaking is a personal promise, and it is the paralegal's personal responsibility to fulfill the undertaking (Rule 2.02(3)).

The language of undertakings should be clear and unambiguous. If a paralegal giving an undertaking does not intend to accept personal responsibility, this should be clearly stated in the undertaking. Documents that are to be produced should be described with a reasonable degree of specificity. Tasks to be performed should be clearly described. Deadlines for completion of undertakings are recommended, and should be stated in writing. If performance of the undertaking depends on certain events, the undertaking should clearly state what those events are, and what will happen if they do not occur—for example, does the obligation become null and void, or does it continue to exist, in a modified form? Licensees who give undertakings should identify themselves as licensees on the undertakings.

fulfill (or answer) an undertaking
to complete the requirements of the undertaking

diarize
to note a deadline or other important date in your tickler system, along with a series of bring-forward dates to remind you that the deadline is approaching

tickler system
a paper or electronic system that gives notice of upcoming deadlines (including limitation periods) or tasks to be completed

If you receive written undertakings from others, you should review them carefully to ensure that they reflect your understanding of what you asked for. If they do not, clear up any discrepancies as soon as possible, and confirm any revisions in writing.

Diarize for any deadlines for completing undertakings, including undertakings to be completed by other parties. To **fulfill (or answer) an undertaking** means to complete the requirements of the undertaking. To **diarize** means to note a deadline or other important date (for example, a date set for a motion or a hearing) in your tickler system, along with a series of bring-forward dates to remind you that the deadline is approaching. A **tickler system** is a paper or electronic system that gives you notice of upcoming deadlines (including limitation periods) or tasks to be completed.

It is good and courteous professional practice to fulfill your own undertakings as soon as possible after they are given. If other parties fail to fulfill their undertakings by a stated deadline (or, where there is no stated deadline, in a timely fashion), you should follow up with them immediately in writing.

Do not give an undertaking that you cannot perform. If you know that you cannot fulfill an undertaking, because it is unreasonable or for some other reason, do not give the undertaking.

BEST EFFORTS UNDERTAKINGS

Sometimes you will be asked for an undertaking that is reasonable, but is not in your power to fulfill. An example would be a request by another party for documents that are relevant to issues in the matter and that may be available to your client, but have not been produced to you. You cannot take personal responsibility for production of the documents, because their production is not in your control—it is in your client's control.

Guideline 3 states that a person who accepts a paralegal's undertaking is entitled to expect the paralegal to carry it out personally. Using the phrase "on behalf of my client," even in an undertaking itself, may not release the paralegal from the obligation to honour the undertaking. If you do not intend to take personal responsibility for fulfilling the undertaking, the language stating this in the undertaking should be clear and unequivocal. In such a case, where honouring the undertaking depends on the actions of another person, you should undertake to make best efforts. **Best efforts** means that you will make good-faith efforts to see that the undertaking is fulfilled, but you will not assume personal responsibility for answering it.

best efforts
a paralegal's effort to do what he can to ensure that an undertaking is fulfilled, without assuming personal responsibility

BOX 2.4 What Are a Paralegal's Responsibilities in a "Best Efforts" Undertaking?

Giving another party a best efforts undertaking does not absolve a paralegal from making a good-faith effort to ensure that the undertaking is fulfilled. As the court noted in *Gheslaghi v. Kassis* (at paragraph 7):

> A promise to use one's best efforts ... is an undertaking which a court will enforce and, in appropriate cases, apply sanctions for non-performance where serious efforts have not been undertaken. "Best efforts" mean just what one would expect the words to mean. The words mean that [a licensee] and his/her client will make a genuine and substantial search for the requested information and/or documentation. The undertaking is not to be taken lightly—a cursory inquiry is not good enough. ... If a party and/or [licensee] is/are not able to discover the subject of the undertaking, [the part and/or licensee] must be able to satisfy a court that a real and substantial effort has been made to seek out what is being requested by the other party.

Undertakings may be enforced by a court or a tribunal. A paralegal may be required to appear before a court or tribunal to explain why an undertaking was not fulfilled, and may be ordered to take steps to fulfill the undertaking and/or pay any damages resulting from the breach of undertaking (Guideline 3). A **breach of undertaking** is a failure to fulfill an undertaking.

breach of undertaking
failure to fulfill an undertaking

Failure to fulfill an undertaking is a breach of Rule 2.02, and may result in another party making a complaint to the Law Society about you. The Law Society will review the situation, and may discipline you for a breach of undertaking, which may result in a finding of professional misconduct. This is why it is very important to have clear language in an undertaking about who is to fulfill the undertaking, what action is to be taken or documents produced, deadlines for completion, and so on.

Undertakings Given to the Law Society (Rules 6.01(8), (9))

In certain circumstances, a paralegal or a non-licensee may be required to give an undertaking to the Law Society.

A paralegal whose licence to provide legal services is suspended may be required to give an undertaking to the Law Society not to provide legal services. In this case, the paralegal shall not (Rule 6.01(8))

(a) provide legal services, or
(b) represent or hold himself or herself out as a person entitled to provide legal services.

A paralegal required to give an undertaking to the Law Society to restrict his or her provision of legal services shall comply with the undertaking (Rule 6.01(9)).

Failure to comply with undertakings given to the Law Society could result in disciplinary action.

Trust Conditions

trust condition
a condition or conditions that must be performed before a paralegal may release certain documents and/or property held in trust by the paralegal

legal practitioner
a person who is a member of the bar in a Canadian jurisdiction other than Ontario, and is authorized to practise law as a barrister and solicitor in that jurisdiction; a lawyer

In certain circumstances, a paralegal may be required to hold documents and property in trust until certain conditions have been performed. The conditions pursuant to which the documents and property are held are called **trust conditions** (Guideline 3). A paralegal shall honour every trust condition once accepted (Rule 2.02(4)).

Once a trust condition is accepted, it is binding upon a paralegal, whether it is imposed by another legal practitioner or by a layperson. A **legal practitioner** is a person (Rule 1.02):

(a) who is a licensee;
(b) who is not a licensee but who is a member of the bar of a Canadian jurisdiction, other than Ontario, and who is authorized to practise law as a barrister and solicitor in that other jurisdiction.

Guideline 3 states that:

7. Trust conditions should be clear, unambiguous and explicit and should state the time within which the conditions must be met. Trust conditions should be imposed and accepted in writing. Trust conditions may be varied with the consent of the person imposing them, and the variation should be confirmed in writing.
8. A paralegal should not impose or accept trust conditions that are unreasonable, nor accept trust conditions that cannot be fulfilled personally. When a paralegal accepts property subject to trust conditions, the paralegal must fully comply with such conditions, even if the conditions subsequently appear unreasonable.

9. A paralegal may seek to impose trust conditions upon a non-licensee, but great caution should be exercised in so doing since such conditions would be enforceable only through the courts as a matter of contract law.

Professional Conduct and the Ontario Human Rights Code

Harassment and Discrimination (Rule 2.03; Guideline 4)

General (Rules 2.03(1), (2))

Rule 2.03(1) incorporates the principles of the Ontario *Human Rights Code* ("the Code") and related case law into the interpretation of Rule 2.03. This means that Rule 2.03, the *Human Rights Code*, and any relevant case law applying and interpreting the Code must be read together. A term used in Rule 2.03 that is defined in the *Human Rights Code* has the same meaning as in the Code (Rule 2.03(2)).

The Ontario Human Rights Code

The Ontario *Human Rights Code* gives every person equal rights and opportunities without discrimination in the following areas:

- services, goods, and facilities;
- accommodation (housing);
- contracts;
- employment; and
- membership in trade or vocational associations, trade unions, and self-governing professions.

PROHIBITED GROUNDS

The Code prohibits discrimination or harassment of persons with respect to activities in any of the above areas on any of the following **prohibited grounds**:

- *Race or colour*. There is an exemption for special service organizations.
- *Ancestry and place of origin*. **Ancestry** refers to family descent. **Place of origin** means country or region of birth, and includes regions in Canada.
- *Ethnic origin*. **Ethnic origin** relates to cultural background.
- *Citizenship*. Citizenship refers to citizenship status, including landed immigrant, refugee, or non-permanent resident. Discrimination on the basis of citizenship is allowed in the circumstances set out in s. 16 of the Code.
- *Creed*. **Creed** means religion or faith. The Code prohibits a person from trying to force another person to accept or conform to a particular religious belief or practice. As well, it may require an employer to make a reasonable accommodation for the religious beliefs and practices of an employee, such as allowing breaks for prayer at certain times. An **accommodation** is an action taken or a

prohibited grounds
grounds upon which discrimination is prohibited by the Ontario *Human Rights Code* (s. 1)—race or colour, ancestry, place of origin, ethnic origin, citizenship, creed, sex, sexual orientation, gender identity, gender expression, age, marital or family status, or disability; for purposes of employment, record of offences is also a ground of discrimination

ancestry
family descent

place of origin
for purposes of the Ontario *Human Rights Code*, a person's country or region of birth, including a region in Canada

ethnic origin
cultural background

creed
religion or faith

accommodation
an action taken or a change made to allow a person or group protected by the Ontario *Human Rights Code* to engage in any of the activities covered by the Code—for example, employment

change made to allow a person or group protected by the Code to engage in any of the activities covered by the Code—for example, employment.

- *Sex*. For a woman, the right to equal treatment on this ground includes the right to equal treatment without discrimination in the event that she is or may become pregnant (Code, s. 10(2)).
- *Sexual orientation*. Sexual orientation includes heterosexual, lesbian, gay, bisexual, transgendered, transsexual, and intersexed people.
- *Gender identity or gender expression*.
- *Age*. Age means 18 years or more.
- *Record of offences* (in the context of employment only). A **record of offence** is a *Criminal Code* conviction that has been pardoned, or a provincial offence (Code, s. 10(1)). Discrimination against a person with a criminal offence for which no pardon has been granted is legal.
- *Marital status or family status*. **Marital status** refers to the status of being married, single, widowed, divorced, separated, or living with a person in a conjugal relationship outside marriage (Code, s. 10(1)). **Family status** means parent and child relationships (Code, s. 10(1)). A parent may be a biological parent, an adoptive parent, or a legal guardian.
- *Disability*. The definition of disability in s. 10(1) of the Code encompasses a broad spectrum of conditions, including (a) any degree of physical disability, infirmity, malformation, or disfigurement that is caused by bodily injury, birth defect, or illness and, without limiting the generality of the foregoing, includes diabetes mellitus, epilepsy, a brain injury, any degree of paralysis, amputation, lack of physical coordination, blindness, or visual impediment, deafness or hearing impediment, muteness or speech impediment, or physical reliance on a guide dog or other animal or on a wheelchair or other remedial appliance or device; (b) a condition of mental impairment or a developmental disability; (c) a learning disability, or a dysfunction in one or more of the processes involved in understanding or using symbols or spoken language; (d) a mental disorder; and (e) an injury or disability for which benefits were claimed or received under the insurance plan established under the *Workplace Safety and Insurance Act, 1997* ("handicap"). It includes past and presumed disabilities (Code, s. 10(3)) and, in the context of housing only, receipt of public assistance (O. Reg. 290/98, s. 4).

record of offence
for purposes of the Ontario *Human Rights Code*, a *Criminal Code* conviction that has been pardoned, or a provincial offence

marital status
for purposes of the Ontario *Human Rights Code*, the status of being married, single, widowed, divorced, separated, or living with a person in a conjugal relationship outside of marriage

family status
parent and child relationships (*Human Rights Code*, s. 10(1)); a parent may be a biological parent, an adoptive parent, or a legal guardian

Paralegals provide legal services to the public. Paralegal firms provide employment to other persons. Paralegals shall ensure that no one is denied services or receives inferior service on the basis of any of the prohibited grounds (Rule 2.03(6)). Paralegals shall ensure that their employment practices do not offend Rule 2.03 (Rule 2.03(7))—in other words, that their employment practices comply with the Code.

Discrimination (Rules 2.03(4), (5))

discrimination
unfair treatment by one person of another person or group on any of the prohibited grounds under the *Human Rights Code*

Discrimination means treating a person or group differently or negatively based on a prohibited ground of discrimination under the Code. When determining whether discrimination has occurred, an objective standard is used. A person who makes discriminatory comments or engages in discriminatory conduct may not consciously intend to be discriminatory. However, if they ought reasonably to have known that their conduct would not be welcomed by the recipient, their conduct is discriminatory.

Discrimination includes **constructive discrimination** (sometimes referred to as **adverse impact discrimination**), defined in the Code as "a requirement, qualification, or factor that is not discrimination on a prohibited ground but that results in the exclusion, restriction, or preference of a group of persons who are identified by a prohibited ground of discrimination" (Code, s. 11(1)).

constructive discrimination
a requirement, qualification, or factor that is not discrimination on a prohibited ground but that results in the exclusion, restriction, or preference of a group of persons who are identified by a prohibited ground of discrimination (*Human Rights Code*, s. 11(1)); also known as adverse impact discrimination

adverse impact discrimination
see constructive discrimination

Rules 2.03(4) and (5) state the general duty of a paralegal to respect the requirements of human rights laws in force in Ontario:

> **Discrimination**
>
> (4) A paralegal shall respect the requirements of human rights laws in force in Ontario and without restricting the generality of the foregoing, a paralegal shall not discriminate on the grounds of race, ancestry, place of origin, colour, ethnic origin, citizenship, creed, sex, sexual orientation, gender identity, gender expression, age, record of offences, marital status, or disability with respect to the employment of others or in dealings with other licensees or any other person.
>
> (5) The right to equal treatment without discrimination because of sex includes the right to equal treatment without discrimination because a woman is or may become pregnant.

The exclusion of family status from the prohibited grounds in Rule 2.03(4) complies with the nepotism policy exemption in s. 24(1)(d) of the Code. **Nepotism** is favouritism based on family relationships. This exemption in the Code permits a paralegal employer who prefers not to have closely related employees in the workplace to implement hiring practices that prohibit spouses, children, or parents of employees from being hired. Without the exemption, such hiring practices would be discriminatory.

nepotism
favouritism based on family relationships

Paralegals shall take reasonable steps to prevent or stop discrimination by any staff or other person who is subject to their direction and control.

Harassment (Rule 2.03(3))

Rule 2.03(3) states:

> **Harassment**
>
> (3) A paralegal shall not engage in sexual or other forms of harassment of a colleague, a staff member, a client or any other person on the ground of race, ancestry, place of origin, colour, ethnic origin, citizenship, creed, sex, sexual orientation, gender identity, gender expression, age, record of offences, marital status, family status or disability.

The Code defines **harassment** as "engaging in a course of vexatious comment or conduct that is known or ought reasonably to be known to be unwelcome" (s. 10(1)). Harassment is a form of discrimination. It includes unwelcome comments or behaviour that might reasonably be expected to cause insecurity, discomfort, offence, or humiliation to another person. Harassment includes, but is not limited to, behaviours such as name calling, racial or religious slurs and jokes, sexual slurs and jokes, sexually suggestive conduct, and demands for sexual favours.

harassment
engaging in a course of vexatious comment or conduct that is known or ought reasonably to be known to be unwelcome (*Human Rights Code*, s. 10(1))

The definition in the Code speaks to a "course of vexatious comment or conduct." Guideline 4 notes that:

> 6. ... Generally speaking, harassment is a "course of conduct" or a pattern of behaviour where more than one incident has occurred. Even one incident however, may constitute harassment if the incident is serious in nature.

SEXUAL HARASSMENT

The Code prohibits harassment in the workplace based on sexual orientation or gender identity, and sexual solicitation (ss. 7(2) and (3)).

> **Harassment because of sex in workplaces**
>
> (2) Every person who is an employee has a right to freedom from harassment in the workplace because of sex, sexual orientation, gender identity or gender expression by his or her employer or agent of the employer or by another employee.
>
> **Sexual solicitation by a person in position to confer benefit, etc.**
>
> (3) Every person has a right to be free from,
>
> (a) a sexual solicitation or advance made by a person in a position to confer, grant or deny a benefit or advancement to the person where the person making the solicitation or advance knows or ought reasonably to know that it is unwelcome; or
>
> (b) a reprisal or a threat of reprisal for the rejection of a sexual solicitation or advance where the reprisal is made or threatened by a person in a position to confer, grant or deny a benefit or advancement to the person.

Note that there are two parts to the test for sexual harassment at s. 7(3)(a). First, a tribunal must consider whether the person engaging in the harassment knew that his or her behaviour was unwelcome. Second, a tribunal must consider whether the person engaging in the harassment ought to have known that his or her conduct was unwelcome—in other words, how would a reasonable person have perceived the impugned conduct in the circumstances?

In its "Policy on preventing sexual and gender-based harassment," the Ontario Human Rights Commission offers guidance on this topic. Gender-based harassment is any behaviour, usually including bullying, that reinforces traditional heterosexual gender norms. It may be used to force people to conform to traditional gender stereotypes. It may be, but is not generally, motivated by sexual interest or intent.

Sexual harassment is generally motivated by sexual interest or intent. Sexual harassment may include some or all of the following behaviours:

- sexual solicitation and advances (your manager asks for sex in exchange for a promotion);
- a poisoned environment (inappropriate comments and pornographic images in the workplace);
- gender-based harassment (targeting someone for not following sex-role stereotypes);
- violence (if inappropriate sexual behaviour is not dealt with, it may move to more serious forms, including sexual assault and other violence).

Some examples of sexual and gender-based harassment include:

- demanding hugs;
- invading personal space;
- making unnecessary physical contact, including unwanted touching, etc.;
- using language that demeans others, such as sex-specific derogatory comments and/or sex-specific derogatory names;
- leering or inappropriate staring;
- making gender-related comments about someone's physical characteristics or mannerisms;
- making comments or treating someone badly because he or she doesn't conform with sex-role stereotypes;
- showing or sending pornography, sexual pictures, or cartoons, sexually explicit graffiti, or other sexual images (including online);
- sexual jokes, including passing around written sexual jokes (for example, by email);
- rough and vulgar humour or language related to gender;
- using sexual or gender-related comment or conduct to bully someone;
- spreading sexual rumours (including online);
- making suggestive or offensive comments or hints about members of a specific gender;
- making sexual propositions;
- verbally abusing, threatening, or taunting someone based on gender;
- bragging about sexual prowess;
- demanding dates or sexual favours;
- asking questions or talking about sexual activities;
- making an employee dress in a sexualized or gender-specific way;
- acting in a paternalistic way that someone thinks undermines their status or position of responsibility;
- making threats to penalize or otherwise punish a person who refuses to comply with sexual advances (known as reprisal).

In *Janzen v. Platy Enterprises Ltd.*, Chief Justice Brian Dickson addressed the deleterious effects of sexual harassment in the workplace (at paragraph 56):

> Without seeking to provide an exhaustive definition of the term, I am of the view that sexual harassment in the workplace may be broadly defined as unwelcome conduct of a sexual nature that detrimentally affects the work environment or leads to adverse job-related consequences for the victims of the harassment. It is … an abuse of power. When sexual harassment occurs in the workplace, it is an abuse of both economic and sexual power. Sexual harassment is a demeaning practice, one that constitutes a profound affront to the dignity of the employees forced to endure it. By requiring an employee to contend with unwelcome sexual actions or explicit sexual demands, sexual harassment in the workplace attacks the dignity and self-respect of the victim both as an employee and as a human being.

BOX 2.5 Is It Harassment?

Fact Situation

Doug owns a busy paralegal practice. Recently he hired a young female associate, Anne, to help out with Small Claims and residential tenancies matters. One day Anne is talking to Doug about a trial she has coming up in a couple of days. It is Anne's first trial. "I'm really nervous," she tells Doug. "I'm well prepared, everything is ready to go, but I keep thinking, what if I blow it and my client loses big time?"

"Don't worry about it," Doug says, grinning at her. "Dress for success. Wear high heels, a short skirt, and a low-cut blouse. If the judge is a guy, you'll win."

As it turns out, Anne gets a very good result for her client. When she tells Doug about it, he says, "See? I told you it would work." When Anne tells him that she wore a business suit and that the judge was a woman, Doug says, "You girls. You always stick together." Anne is upset and offended, but she doesn't say anything because she does not want to put her job at risk.

Question for Discussion

Is Doug's conduct sexual harassment?

OTHER HARASSMENT

The definition of harassment in s. 10(1) of the Code is not limited to sexual harassment. Any form of harassment in the workplace is forbidden by s. 5(2) of the Code. Guideline 4 gives the following examples of non-sexual harassment (refer to the Code and the case law, as the list is not exhaustive):

- the display of offensive material, such as racial graffiti;
- repeated racial slurs directed at the language or accent of a particular group; and/or
- verbal abuse or threats.

Policies and Procedures

A paralegal shall ensure that no one is discriminated against on a prohibited ground with respect to the provision of services (Rule 2.03(6)). A paralegal shall also ensure that her employment practices do not offend Rule 2.03 (Rule 2.03(7)). The Law Society has developed a series of best practices and model policies to assist paralegals and lawyers in promoting equity and diversity in all areas of their practice, including employment and provision of services. Guideline 4 recommends that paralegals implement these policies and procedures in their practice. They include:

- preventing and responding to workplace harassment and discrimination;
- promoting workplace equity in their firms;
- providing pregnancy/parental leaves and benefits;
- providing accommodations with regard to flexible work arrangements (subject to undue hardship); and

- providing accommodations with regard to religious beliefs, gender or sexual orientation, and disabilities (subject to undue hardship).

The equity model policies, publications, and reports can be found at the Law Society website. The Law Society also provides education and training to legal service providers regarding equity and diversity issues.

All members of your paralegal firm, including support staff and field placement students, should be familiar with your workplace policies and procedures. Copies should be included in your office procedures manual, and should be readily available to everyone in the workplace.

Paralegals should encourage all members of their firm—including other paralegals, support staff, and students—to participate in the education and training regarding equity and diversity issues that are provided by the Law Society.

Discrimination and Harassment Counsel

The Law Society Discrimination and Harassment Counsel provides its service free of charge to lawyers, paralegals, articling and field placement students, and the Ontario public. The Counsel confidentially assists anyone who may have experienced discrimination or harassment by a lawyer or paralegal, or within a law or paralegal firm. Although funded by the Law Society, the Counsel is completely independent of the Society. Contact information is posted at the Law Society website.

The Counsel provides advice and support, and reviews options with complainants. These may include:

- filing a complaint with the Law Society,
- filing a complaint with the Ontario Human Rights Tribunal, and
- allowing the Counsel to mediate a solution in cases where all parties agree.

CHAPTER SUMMARY

The *Paralegal Rules of Conduct* establish standards of professional conduct for paralegals in Ontario. As a paralegal, in order to avoid disciplinary action by the Law Society and to avoid bringing the reputation of the paralegal profession in Ontario into disrepute, you must know the Rules and comply with their standards for professional conduct.

The *Paralegal Professional Conduct Guidelines*, the By-Laws, and relevant case law or legislation will provide additional guidance as you read and interpret the Rules.

A paralegal has a duty to provide legal services and discharge all responsibilities to clients, tribunals, the public, and other members of the legal professions honourably and with integrity. A paralegal has a duty to uphold the standards and reputation of the paralegal profession and to assist in the advancement of its goals, organizations, and institutions. Paralegals who do not conduct themselves with integrity may harm their clients, and will damage their reputations within the paralegal profession as well as the reputation of the profession within the community.

A paralegal shall be courteous and civil, and shall act in good faith toward all persons with whom he has dealings in the course of his practice. Acting with civility means that a paralegal shall communicate politely and respectfully and act in a manner that does not cause unnecessary difficulty or harm to another. The obligation to be polite, respectful, and considerate of others extends to clients, opposing parties, other paralegals and lawyers, support staff, court and tribunal officers, court and tribunal staff, and Law Society representatives. The obligation applies regardless of the formality or informality of the venue, or the stage you are at in a matter.

Paralegals who engage in another profession, business, occupation, or other outside interest, or who hold public office at the same time as they provide legal services, shall not allow the outside interest or public office to jeopardize their integrity, independence, or competence.

A paralegal who acts as a mediator shall ensure that the parties to the mediation understand that she is not acting as a representative for either party, but as an impartial third party whose role is to help the parties resolve their dispute. She should also advise the parties that she cannot represent either of them in any subsequent legal matter related to the issues mediated.

Undertakings given by licensees are matters of the utmost good faith and must receive scrupulous attention. Except in exceptional circumstances, they should be made in writing at the time they are given, or confirmed in writing as soon as possible thereafter. Unless the language of an undertaking clearly states otherwise, a paralegal's undertaking is a personal promise and it is his responsibility to fulfill it.

A paralegal may be required to hold documents and property in trust until certain conditions have been performed. The conditions pursuant to which the documents and property are held are called trust conditions. Once a trust condition is accepted, it is binding upon a paralegal, whether it is imposed by another legal practitioner or by a layperson.

Paralegals shall respect the requirements of Ontario human rights laws. The principles of the Ontario *Human Rights Code* and related case law must be applied when interpreting Rule 2.03.

Paralegals shall not discriminate with respect to employment of others, or in dealings with other licensees or any other person on the prohibited grounds stated in the Code. They shall not engage in sexual or other forms of harassment of colleagues, staff members, clients, or any other person on any of the prohibited grounds. They shall ensure that no one is discriminated against on a prohibited ground with respect to the provision of services.

Paralegals are encouraged to implement the best practices and model policies developed by the Law Society to assist them in promoting equity and diversity in all areas of their practice.

The Discrimination and Harassment Counsel provides confidential assistance to anyone who may have experienced discrimination or harassment by a lawyer or paralegal, or within a law or paralegal firm.

KEY TERMS

accommodation, 39
acting in good faith, 33
acting with civility, 33
adverse impact discrimination, 41
ancestry, 39
best efforts, 37
breach of undertaking, 37
conflict of interest, 34
constructive discrimination, 41
creed, 39
diarize, 36
discrimination, 40
ethnic origin, 39
family status, 40
fulfill (or answer) an undertaking, 36
harassment, 41
legal practitioner, 38
marital status, 40
mediation, 35
mediator, 35
nepotism, 41
outside interest, 34
place of origin, 39
prohibited grounds, 39
record of offence, 40
tickler system, 36
trust condition, 38
undertaking, 36

REFERENCES

Advocates Society, *Principles of Civility for Advocates* (2006), reprinted with permission in Canadian Bar Association, *Code of Professional Conduct* (Ottawa: Canadian Bar Association, 2009), http://www.cba.org/cba/activities/pdf/codeofconduct.pdf.

Criminal Code, RSC 1985, c. C-46.

Gheslaghi v. Kassis, 2003 CanLII 7532, [2003] OJ no. 5196 (SCJ).

Human Rights Code, RSO 1990, c. H.19, as amended.

Janzen v. Platy Enterprises Ltd., [1989] 1 SCR 1252.

Law Society of Upper Canada, Equity Model Policies, Publications & Reports, http://rc.lsuc.on.ca/jsp/equity/policies-publications-reports.jsp.

Law Society of Upper Canada, *Paralegal Professional Conduct Guidelines* (October 2014) ("the Guidelines"), http://www.lsuc.on.ca/paralegal-conduct-guidelines.

Law Society of Upper Canada, *Paralegal Rules of Conduct* (October 2014) ("the Rules"), http://www.lsuc.on.ca/paralegal-conduct-rules.

Law Society of Upper Canada, *Rules of Professional Conduct* (October 2014), http://www.lsuc.on.ca/lawyer-conduct-rules.

O. Reg. 290/98, Business Practices Permissible to Landlords in Selecting Prospective Tenants for Residential Accommodation, http://www.e-laws.gov.on.ca/html/regs/english/elaws_regs_980290_e.htm.

Ontario Human Rights Commission (OHRC), "Policy on preventing sexual and gender-based harassment" (approved January 2011, updated May 2013), http://www.ohrc.on.ca/en/policy-preventing-sexual-and-gender-based-harassment-0.

Towne v. Miller, 2001 CanLII 28006, [2001] OJ no. 4241 (SCJ).

Workplace Safety and Insurance Act, 1997, SO 1997, c. 16, Sched. A.

REVIEW QUESTIONS

1. Define the following words and phrases. For review and study purposes, it is a good idea to note the source of your definition, and the section or rule number.
   - **a.** accommodation
   - **b.** acting in good faith
   - **c.** acting with civility
   - **d.** best efforts
   - **e.** breach of undertaking
   - **f.** conflict of interest
   - **g.** discrimination
   - **h.** fulfill an undertaking
   - **i.** harassment
   - **j.** mediation
   - **k.** mediator
   - **l.** outside interest
   - **m.** prohibited grounds
   - **n.** sexual harassment
   - **o.** trust condition
   - **p.** undertaking
2. **a.** You are asked for an undertaking to produce a document to an opposing party in a proceeding. It is a reasonable request. The document is relevant to issues in the proceeding. The obligation of full disclosure has been explained to your client. You have the original in your client matter file at your office. May you give the undertaking?

   b. You are asked for an undertaking to produce a document to an opposing party in a proceeding. The document is relevant to issues in the proceeding. The obligation of full disclosure has been explained to your client. You do not have the document in your possession. Your client says she may be able to obtain a copy from another person. May you give the undertaking?
3. One of your paralegal colleagues has a calendar on the wall in her office. It is in a corner behind a bookshelf. It cannot be seen from the door of her office, but it can be seen easily by anyone who approaches her desk, including other paralegals, staff, students, and clients. The calendar shows pictures of male firefighters posing in various states of undress, from shirtless to completely naked except for a very skimpy swimsuit. The calendar is sold to the public to raise money for a children's charity.

   You think the calendar is unprofessional and in very poor taste. When you tell your colleague that you find the calendar offensive, she laughs and says, "It's for a very good cause. Why don't you get a life?"

   Does the calendar constitute harassment?
4. As a paralegal, what tools should you use to promote equity and diversity in your workplace?

The Client

3

LEARNING OBJECTIVES

After reading this chapter, you will understand:

- A paralegal's duty to a client.
- The paralegal–client relationship.
- Who is a client?
- Prospective clients.
- The retainer agreement.
- The non-engagement letter.
- The limited scope retainer.
- Joint retainer clients.
- Clients with diminished capacity.
- Clients who are organizations.
- Phantom clients.
- Client identification and verification.

The Duty to the Client

duty of service
the paralegal's duty to be competent, maintain confidentiality, avoid conflicts of interest, and continue to represent the client unless the paralegal has good reason to withdraw; also known as the duty of loyalty

duty of loyalty
see duty of service

Guideline 5 states that one of the most important duties of a paralegal is the **duty of service** to the client:

> This duty includes obligations to be competent, maintain confidentiality, avoid conflicts of interest and continue to represent the client unless the paralegal has good reason for withdrawing. *As a result, it is important for the paralegal to know exactly who is a client because it is to the client that most of the duties outlined in the* Rules *are owed.* [emphasis added]

In the jurisprudence, this duty is referred to as the **duty of loyalty**. As the Ontario Court of Appeal noted in *Amato v. Welsh*:

> [58] The jurisprudence of the Supreme Court of Canada has repeatedly endorsed the importance to the administration of justice of the lawyer's duty of loyalty to his or her client. In particular, the Supreme Court has emphasized the lawyer's obligation to avoid conflicts of interest.
>
> [59] In *R v. Neil*, 2002 SCC 70, [2002] 3 SCR 631, at paras. 12 and 16, Binnie J, writing for the Supreme Court, described a lawyer's duty of loyalty to a client as a "defining principle" that is intertwined with the fiduciary nature of the lawyer–client relationship. As he observed, at para. 16, loyalty is frequently cited as one of the defining characteristics of a fiduciary. Justice Binnie explained, at para. 12, that the duty of loyalty has endured for almost two centuries precisely "because it is essential to the integrity of the administration of justice and it is of high public importance that public confidence in that integrity be maintained." He elaborated:
>
>> Unless a litigant is assured of the undivided loyalty of the lawyer, neither the public nor the litigant will have confidence that the legal system, which may appear to them to be a hostile and hideously complicated environment, is a reliable and trustworthy means of resolving their disputes and controversies. [Citations omitted.]
>
> [60] The content of the duty of loyalty is broad. *Neil* holds, at para. 19, that in addition to protecting confidential information, the duty of loyalty has "three other dimensions":
>
> (i) *the duty to avoid conflicting interests* ... including the lawyer's personal interest;
>
> (ii) *a duty of commitment to the client's cause* (sometimes referred to as "zealous representation") from the time counsel is retained, not just at trial, *i.e.* ensuring that a divided loyalty does not cause the lawyer to "soft peddle" his or her defence of a client out of concern for another client; and
>
> (iii) *a duty of candour* with the client on matters relevant to the retainer. ... If a conflict emerges, the client should be among the first to hear about it. [Citations omitted. Emphasis in original.]

paralegal–client relationship
the professional relationship between a paralegal and a client that gives rise to a range of duties that include the duties of competence, confidentiality, and avoidance of conflicts of interest, and the duty to continue to represent the client unless the paralegal has good reason for withdrawing

The principles stated in the passage above may also be applied to paralegal licensees.

The Paralegal–Client Relationship

Guideline 5 notes that the courts have made a distinction between a solicitor–client relationship and a solicitor–client retainer, and that the jurisprudence may be applied to define the paralegal–client relationship and the paralegal–client retainer.

The Paralegal–Client Relationship

The **paralegal–client relationship** encompasses all aspects of a paralegal's duty as a fiduciary to the client. It includes the duties of integrity, competence, honesty and candour, confidentiality, and avoidance of conflicts of interest. The duty of loyalty, discussed above, encompasses all of these duties.

A paralegal–client relationship may arise informally. If a paralegal has been asked for assistance and has provided assistance, a paralegal–client relationship arises.

The Paralegal-Client Retainer

The **paralegal–client retainer** (also called the **retainer**) is established when the client offers to hire the paralegal and the paralegal agrees to provide legal services to the client in a particular client matter. It is the contractual relationship between the client and the paralegal in that client matter. The terms of the paralegal–client retainer should be established in writing. Among other things, the written confirmation of the retainer should contain terms that identify who the client is and the person(s) who will provide instructions to the paralegal in the client matter.

When you have completed the services contracted for, the paralegal–client retainer ends for that particular client matter. However, the duties arising out of the paralegal–client relationship continue indefinitely.

paralegal–client retainer
the contractual relationship between the client and the paralegal, which establishes the scope of the retainer, what the client will be charged for the legal services provided, and other terms of the agreement; also called retainer

retainer
see paralegal–client retainer

retained
hired to represent a person in a legal matter

money retainer
payment for future legal services, which must be held in trust for the benefit of the client until part or all of those services have been provided and invoiced to the client

BOX 3.1 What Is a Retainer?

In a legal services context, the word "retainer" is used to mean several different things.

- To be **retained** means to be hired or engaged to represent a person in a client matter.
- A paralegal–client retainer (also called a retainer) is the agreement between a client and a paralegal that the paralegal shall provide legal services to the client in a particular matter. A retainer is the contractual relationship between a client and a paralegal in a particular client matter.
- A retainer agreement is a written contract between the paralegal and the client that sets out the terms of the contractual relationship, including the scope of the legal services to be provided in the client matter and the likely cost of those services, along with disbursements and Harmonized Sales Tax, to the client. The terms of the paralegal–client retainer may also be confirmed by a retainer (or engagement) letter, because they confirm the terms upon which the paralegal is engaged—that is, hired—by the client.
- A **money retainer** is money paid by the client to the paralegal for future legal services and reasonable disbursements and expenses in a client matter. A money retainer belongs to the client, and must be held in your mixed trust bank account for the benefit of the client until legal services have been provided and reasonable disbursements and expenses incurred, and the client has received an invoice for them.

Who Is a Client?

client
a person who consults a paralegal and on whose behalf the paralegal provides or agrees to provide legal services; or, having consulted the paralegal, reasonably concludes that the paralegal has agreed to provide legal services on his or her behalf; includes a client of the firm of which the paralegal is a partner or associate, whether or not the paralegal handles the client's work

Rule 1.02 defines a **client** as a person who:

> (a) consults a paralegal and on whose behalf the paralegal provides or agrees to provide legal services; or
> (b) having consulted the paralegal, reasonably concludes that the paralegal has agreed to provide legal services on his or her behalf
>
> and includes a client of the firm of which the paralegal is a partner or associate, whether or not the paralegal handles the client's work.

A person who has not consulted with a paralegal is not a client. A person who has consulted with a paralegal, but on whose behalf the paralegal has not rendered legal services or agreed to provide legal services, is not a client.

Under Rule 1.02(b), a person who has consulted with a paralegal and has formed a reasonable belief that the paralegal has agreed to render legal services on his or her behalf is a client. The person's belief that there is an agreement to render legal services must be reasonable.

Any person who is a client of the paralegal firm of which you are a partner or an associate is your client, regardless of whether you actually handle that person's work (Rule 1.02). A paralegal–client relationship exists between you and that client, and you owe the client certain duties, including the duty of confidentiality and the duty to avoid conflicts of interest. A firm-wide **conflicts checking system**, containing the names of all prospective and new clients, along with related and instructing parties, should be maintained to ensure that firm members do not breach a duty owed to a client.

conflicts checking system
a list of all clients (including prospective clients), opposing parties, and related parties, if any, that is checked to ensure that there are no conflicts of interest on any client files

How Does a Person Become a Client?

The usual stages in the process by which a person may become a client or near-client are:

1. Initial contact.
2. Initial consultation.
3. Paralegal–client retainer.

Initial Contact

In certain situations, a paralegal may owe certain duties to a person who does not fall within the definition of client at Rule 1.02.

In many cases, a person's initial contact with your firm may consist of nothing more than a voice message or brief telephone conversation with your legal assistant. The initial contact may or may not result in a formal consultation with you about the person's legal problem and her objectives. Regardless of the brevity or casual nature of the person's initial contact with your firm, depending upon how it is managed, at least two important duties may arise from it: the duty of confidentiality and the duty to avoid conflicts of interest.

If, at initial contact, the person shares any **confidential information** about the matter with your firm, your possession of that confidential information may give rise to the duty to hold the information in strict confidence and the duty to avoid conflicts of interest. Both duties continue indefinitely. Possession of the confidential information itself may give rise to a conflict of interest. If the information is relevant to another or related matter in which you have been retained, your duty to disclose the information for the benefit of your client in the other or related matter will conflict with your duty to the person from whom the information was obtained to hold the information in strict confidence, with the result that you may have to withdraw your services in the other or related matter.

confidential information any information touching on the business and affairs of a client acquired in the course of the paralegal–client relationship; a paralegal has a duty to hold all such information in strictest confidence and not to disclose it to any other person, unless authorized to do so by the client or required to do so by law (Rule 3.03(1))

Guideline 8 recommends that a paralegal should be cautious in accepting confidential information on an informal or preliminary basis from anyone, since possession of the information may prevent the paralegal from subsequently acting for another party in the same or a related matter.

If a person's initial contact with your firm will be with non-licensee staff, you may wish to consider implementing a firm protocol that limits information collected at initial contact to the correct spelling of the person's name, and a telephone number at which the person can be reached.

Initial Consultation

The initial consultation is the stage at which a person meets with you to discuss her legal matter, goals and expectations, and so on. At this stage, the person will be expected to share confidential information with you. For that reason, you should always perform a conflicts check before the initial consultation.

If, after reviewing the search results, you are satisfied that your representation would create a substantial risk of a conflict of interest, you may comply with your general duty to avoid actual or potential conflicts of interest by advising the person of the conflict and referring her to another licensee. If there are no conflicts, the initial consultation will go forward.

A person who has consulted with you about a legal matter but with whom a paralegal–client retainer has not yet been entered into may be called a **prospective client** (Guideline 9).

prospective client a person who consults a paralegal regarding a legal issue but has not yet retained the paralegal and for whom the paralegal has not yet agreed to provide legal representation

A conflict of interest can arise at any time. Regardless of whether you have been retained, you should conduct a conflicts search again after the initial consultation, when you have more information about the client matter and other parties. If a paralegal–client retainer is entered into, you should conduct a conflicts search when a new party is added in a client matter, or at any other critical point. The duty to avoid conflicts of interest continues indefinitely.

The prospective client may decline to retain you, or you may decline the retainer because of a conflict of interest, or for some other reason, such as a lack of competence. Nonetheless, because the prospective client has shared confidential information with you, you owe that person certain duties, those being, at a minimum, the duty of confidentiality and the duty to avoid conflicts of interest, both of which continue indefinitely.

BOX 3.2 Difficult Clients

Dealing with difficult clients can be very challenging. Difficult clients are often extremely demanding and very hard to satisfy. They may ignore or misinterpret your advice. They will require much more time, effort, and attention than your other clients.

You should consider avoiding difficult clients altogether, if possible. If it is not possible, then you must implement strategies for managing the paralegal–client relationship.

The first step in managing a difficult client is to recognize one when you see one. To determine whether a particular client is or may be difficult, consider whether the client:

- has come to you at the last minute, when a major deadline requiring a lot of work (such as a procedural deadline or a limitation period) is approaching;
- has already terminated relationships with other paralegals;
- has unrealistic expectations about the progress of the matter and its outcomes;
- makes constant demands on you and your staff;
- is clearly motivated by malice and has instituted proceedings solely for the purpose of injuring the other party; and/or
- questions and/or disregards your legal advice.

With a difficult client, you should consider taking careful notes of all discussions with the client, and confirming your advice and the client's instructions in writing at every stage of the client matter. If the client continues to be uncooperative or to give you inappropriate instructions, you may consider taking steps to withdraw from representation, subject to Rule 3.08.

Keep in mind that, when withdrawing from representation, you must try to minimize expense and avoid prejudice to the client, and do all that can reasonably be done to facilitate the orderly transfer of the matter to another licensee (Rules 3.08(10), (11)).

For more information on difficult clients, search for "Dealing with the Difficult Client" at the Law Society website, where you will find a very useful article on this topic by Carole Curtis.

scope of the retainer
the nature and extent of the legal services to be provided by the paralegal pursuant to the paralegal–client retainer

fees
the amount charged to a client by a paralegal for legal services provided by the paralegal to the client, including advice, correspondence, drafting pleadings and other documents, and time spent in court

disbursements
expenses related to the client matter that are paid by the paralegal on behalf of the client and for which the paralegal is entitled to be reimbursed

Written Confirmation of the Paralegal–Client Retainer

If, at the initial consultation, the prospective client decides to retain you and you agree to represent the prospective client, you should discuss with the client all the essential terms of the paralegal–client retainer, including the **scope of the retainer**—that is, the nature and extent of the legal services to be provided, the likely cost of those services, including legal fees, reasonable disbursements, harmonized sales tax (HST), and so on.

Fees are what you charge the client for the legal services you have provided to the client. Legal services may include legal advice, correspondence, research, drafting pleadings and other documents, and time spent in court. **Disbursements** are out-of-pocket expenses related to the client matter, such as court filing fees, photocopies, mileage, and so on, which are paid or incurred by you on behalf of the client and for which you are entitled to be reimbursed.

You must ensure that the client understands the scope of the legal services to be provided; how fees, disbursements, and HST will be charged; your billing practices; and any other terms of the paralegal–client retainer.

You should consider preparing a written confirmation of the terms of the paralegal–client retainer in every new client matter that is accepted by your firm. The written confirmation should be prepared at the outset of the paralegal–client retainer. A written confirmation of some kind should be prepared whether the client matter involves a $60 parking ticket, an unpaid debt of $7,500, or a possible fine of $50,000 upon conviction.

Depending on the nature of the client matter, written confirmation of the retainer may be done by:

- a retainer agreement signed by the paralegal and the client;
- an engagement letter delivered by the paralegal to the client; or
- a confirming memorandum delivered to the client by mail or fax.

Whatever the nature of the confirmation of retainer, it should be in writing, and a copy should be put in the file for that client matter.

The Retainer Agreement

The retainer agreement is a contract that sets out the terms upon which the client hires the paralegal and agrees to pay for the paralegal's services, and the terms upon which the paralegal agrees to provide those services to the client. It is signed by the paralegal and the client. The purpose of the retainer agreement is to promote certainty in paralegal–client relations.

The contents of the retainer agreement will vary, depending on the preferences of individual paralegals and the nature of the client matter. At a minimum, the retainer agreement should include the following:

- the name and address of the paralegal firm;
- the name and address of the client;
- if the client is an organization, the name(s) of the individual(s) in the organization who are authorized to give you instructions on the organization's behalf;
- the nature and scope of the work to be performed, including key steps in the process;
- if the retainer is a limited scope retainer, confirmation of the nature, extent, and scope of the services to be provided;
- confirmation that you are a firm of paralegal licensees;
- confirmation of permitted areas of practice for paralegal licensees;
- confirmation that the client's matter falls within the permitted areas of practice for paralegal licensees;
- an estimate of the time it will take to complete key steps, if appropriate;
- the name and hourly rate of the paralegal(s) responsible for the file;
- the names and hourly rates of other paralegals and staff who may assist with the file;
- if you are charging a fixed fee for the service, the agreed-upon amount;

- an estimate of the approximate cost of the legal services to be provided, with a statement of any assumptions upon which that estimate is based;
- the amount of the money retainer, with confirmation that the money will be placed in trust;
- the circumstances in which further money retainers may be required;
- the firm's billing policies, and the consequences of late payment;
- a request for any additional information or documents that you require from the client;
- a term that any settlement funds payable to the client or by the client to another person be made payable to your firm in trust;
- a term that upon receiving settlement funds payable to the client in your trust account and full and final releases being signed, you may create a final invoice for outstanding fees and disbursements in the matter, pay the invoice out of the settlement funds held in trust, and dispose of any balance remaining in trust as instructed by the client;
- events that will terminate the retainer; and
- a stipulation that any changes to the agreement shall be in writing.

All of the above terms should be discussed with the client at the initial consultation. If a money retainer was received at the initial consultation, the retainer agreement should acknowledge receipt, and confirm that the retainer has been deposited to your mixed trust bank account. The **mixed trust bank account** is a bank account in which client money is held.

mixed trust bank account
a trust account that holds money for more than one client matter; also referred to as "mixed trust account" and "trust account"

An engagement letter and a memorandum of confirmation may contain many of the same terms, as appropriate. However, they are not signed back by the client.

You will find a draft retainer agreement at Appendix 3.1, and a precedent engagement letter at Appendix 3.2.

The Non-Engagement Letter

A prospective client is not obliged to retain you, and you are not obliged to accept every retainer. In some circumstances (for example, a conflict of interest), you *shall* decline the retainer. When no retainer is entered into, you should confirm the **non-engagement** (that is, the failure to enter into an agreement for the provision of legal services) in writing to the person with a **non-engagement letter**.

non-engagement
failure to enter into a contract or agreement for legal services

non-engagement letter
a letter written by a paralegal to a client confirming that, in a particular matter, the paralegal has declined to provide legal services to the client, or that the client has declined to retain the paralegal

The non-engagement letter should contain the following:

- the date of the initial consultation;
- unequivocal confirmation that you have not been retained and will not be providing legal services for the matter discussed in the consultation;
- the reason(s) why you will not be providing legal services in the matter (for example, unauthorized area of law, conflict of interest, unavailability, lack of competence in the subject area, the person's inability to pay a retainer, the person has decided not to retain you);

- any upcoming limitation periods or procedural deadlines of which you are aware (in the case of a limitation period that is about to expire, you should urge the person to take immediate action);
- a recommendation that the person seek other legal representation; and
- a list of any documents or other property that has been returned to the person, or a confirmation that you do not have any documents or other property in your possession.

You must ensure that the person receives the non-engagement letter. If it will be sent by registered mail, a current mailing address for the person should be obtained at the initial consultation.

You should keep a copy of the non-engagement letter for your records. The person's information should be entered in your conflicts checking system. Your duties of confidentiality and avoidance of conflicts of interest continue indefinitely.

For sample non-engagement letters, see Appendixes 3.3 and 3.4.

Limited Scope Retainers (Rules 3.02(15)–(17); Guideline 6)

Limited scope retainers, also called "unbundled" legal services, are retainers where the client hires you to provide part, but not all, of the legal services required in a client matter. Some examples of limited scope retainers would be:

limited scope retainer
a retainer where the client hires a paralegal to perform one specific task, such as drafting a demand letter

- *Consultation:* A short meeting or phone call with a paralegal to obtain advice or direction with respect to a legal issue.
- *Document preparation:* The paralegal assists the client with a contract, pleading, or other legal document (for example, preparing a defence with a proposal of terms of payment in a Small Claims Court proceeding).
- *Limited representation before a tribunal, at a mediation, and so on:* The paralegal makes a single appearance in court or at a hearing, or assists the client with one particular stage of a matter only.

Before entering into a limited scope retainer, you must carefully assess whether, in the circumstances, it is possible to provide competent representation. You should consider interviewing the client as thoroughly as you would for a full retainer, having regard to limitation periods or other deadlines, and the possibility that the client should be referred to another licensee. For more information, see Dan Pinnington's article "Unbundled Legal Services: Pitfalls to Avoid" in *LawPRO Magazine*.

You shall advise the client honestly and candidly about the nature, extent, and scope of the services that you are able to provide. You should ensure that the client is fully informed of the nature of the arrangement and understands the scope and limitation of the services. Where appropriate, you shall also advise the client whether the services can be provided within the client's financial means (Rule 3.02(15)).

You shall confirm the services to be provided under the limited scope retainer in writing and give a copy to the client when it is practicable to do so (Rule 3.02(16)). In a limited scope retainer, it is very important that there be no confusion about the services to be provided. In the written confirmation, you should consider identifying the services that will be provided and the services that will not be provided so that there is no confusion as to the extent of the retainer. Guideline 14 suggests that a retainer agreement is particularly helpful in the circumstances of a limited scope retainer.

If it is not practicable to give a copy of the limited scope retainer agreement to the client, keep a copy in the client file and provide a copy to the client when it is possible to do so.

When providing services in a limited scope retainer, you must take care in your communications and by your conduct not to give the client or others the impression that you are providing services under a full retainer.

Rule 3.02(16) with respect to limited scope retainers does not apply if the legal services provided are captured by the exemptions in Rule 3.02(17), which are:

> (a) legal services provided by a licensed paralegal in the course of his or her employment as an employee of Legal Aid Ontario;
> (b) summary advice provided in community legal clinics, student clinics or under the *Legal Aid Services Act, 1998*;
> (c) summary advice provided through a telephone-based service or telephone hotline operated by a community-based or government funded program.
> (d) summary advice provided by the paralegal to a client in the context of an introductory consultation, where the intention is that the consultation, if the client so chooses, would develop into a retainer for legal services for all aspects of the legal matter; or
> (e) *pro bono* summary legal services provided in a non-profit or court-annexed program.

As with any other client who has retained you, a client with a limited scope retainer is owed the duties of competence, confidentiality, and avoidance of conflicts of interest. The client and any related parties must be entered into your conflicts checking system.

Joint Retainer Clients (Rules 3.04(7)–(13); Guideline 5)

joint retainer
an arrangement whereby a paralegal is hired to represent more than one client in a matter or transaction

joint clients
the clients in a joint retainer

A **joint retainer** is an arrangement wherein a paralegal agrees to represent two or more clients in the same matter. The clients in a joint retainer are called **joint clients**.

Guideline 9 notes that representing two or more clients in the same matter may result in a conflict of interest.

> Acting in a joint retainer places the paralegal in a potential conflict of interest. A paralegal has an obligation to all clients and in a joint retainer, the paralegal must remain loyal and devoted to all clients equally—the paralegal cannot choose to serve one client more carefully or resolutely than any other. If the interests of one client change during the course of the retainer, the paralegal may be in a conflict of interest.

Before agreeing to a joint retainer, you must clearly identify the clients to whom you will be providing legal services in order to ensure that you can fulfill your duties to them (Guideline 5). You must carry out a conflicts search to ensure that there are no conflicts of interest. Although the Rules do not require this, Guideline 9 recommends that, if a joint client is less sophisticated or more vulnerable than other joint client(s), you should consider recommending that the client obtain **independent legal advice** before consenting to the joint retainer to ensure that the client's consent to the joint retainer is informed, genuine, and not obtained through coercion. Independent legal advice is impartial confidential advice obtained from a competent licensee with no personal interest in the matter.

independent legal advice
impartial, confidential advice obtained from a competent licensee with no personal interest in the matter; also called ILA

Before accepting a joint retainer, you should determine who will provide you with instructions in the matter. You should confirm the arrangement in the retainer agreement. **Instructions** are directions or authorizations from a client to a paralegal with respect to a particular course of action to be taken in a matter.

instructions
directions or authorizations from a client to a paralegal with respect to a particular course of action to be taken in a matter

Before accepting a joint retainer, you shall advise the clients that (Rule 3.04(7)):

1. you have been asked to act for both or all of them;
2. no information received in connection with the matter from one client can be treated as confidential as far as any of the other joint clients are concerned; and
3. if a conflict develops that cannot be resolved, you cannot continue to act for both or all of the joint clients, and may have to withdraw completely.

If one of the proposed joint clients is a client with whom you have a continuing relationship and for whom you act regularly, before agreeing to act for the continuing client and one or more other clients in a matter or transaction, you shall advise the other joint client(s) of the continuing relationship and recommend that the other client(s) obtain independent legal advice with respect to the joint retainer (Rule 3.04(8)).

If you have advised all joint retainer clients in accordance with Rules 3.04(7) and (8) and they are in agreement that you should act for them, you shall obtain their consent (Rule 3.04(9)). Consent to a joint retainer must be obtained from each client in writing, or recorded through a separate written communication to each client (Rule 3.04(10)).

BOX 3.3 Consent (Rule 1.02)

"Consent" means fully informed and voluntary consent after disclosure:

(a) in writing, provided that where more than one person consents, each signs the same or a separate document recording his or her consent, or
(b) orally, provided that each person consenting receives a separate written communication recording his or her consent as soon as practicable.

Contentious Issue (Rules 3.04(11)–(13))

Although all clients may consent to the joint retainer, you shall avoid acting for more than one client if it is likely that a contentious issue will arise between them or that their interests, rights, or obligations will diverge as the matter progresses (Rule 3.04(11)).

Except as provided in Rule 3.04(13), discussed below, if a contentious issue arises between two clients who have consented to a joint retainer, you must not advise either of them on the contentious issue, and the following rules apply (Rule 3.04(12)):

> (a) The paralegal shall
> (i) refer the clients to other licensees for that purpose; or
> (ii) if no legal advice is required and the clients are sophisticated, advise them of their option to settle the contentious issue by direct negotiation in which the paralegal does not participate.
> (b) If the contentious issue is not resolved, the paralegal shall withdraw from the joint representation.

If your clients consent to a joint retainer and also agree that if a contentious issue arises you may continue to advise one of them, and a contentious issue does arise, you may advise the one client about the contentious issue. You shall refer the other client(s) to another licensee for that purpose (Rule 3.04(13)).

Client with Diminished Capacity (Rules 3.02(13), (14); Guidelines 5, 7)

client with diminished capacity a client whose capacity to make decisions is impaired because of minority, mental disability, illiteracy, or for some other reason

A **client with diminished capacity** is a client whose capacity to make decisions is impaired because of minority, mental disability, illiteracy, or for some other reason. You shall, as far as reasonably possible, maintain a normal professional relationship with a client with diminished capacity (Rule 3.02(13)).

A paralegal must be particularly sensitive to the individual needs of a client with diminished capacity. You should maintain a good professional relationship with the client, even if the client's ability to make decisions is impaired. You should also be aware of your duty to accommodate a client with diminished capacity (Guideline 7).

If the disability is such that the client no longer has the capacity to manage his legal affairs, you shall take appropriate steps that are within permitted practice for paralegals to have a lawfully authorized representative appointed (Rule 3.02(14)), keeping in mind your duty of confidentiality to the client.

If a client representative has been appointed to manage the legal affairs of a client with diminished capacity, at the outset of the relationship you must identify who the client is and determine whose instructions should be followed. In the event that you are required to act for both the client with diminished capacity and the client representative, you must comply with Rules 3.04(7) to (13) regarding joint retainers (Guideline 5).

A paralegal who is asked to provide services under a limited scope retainer to a client with diminished capacity should carefully consider and assess how, in the circumstances, it is possible to render those services in a competent manner (Guideline 7).

Acting for an Organization

If your client is an organization, you should determine which officers, employees, or agents of the organization may properly give you instructions on the client organization's behalf. This should be done at the commencement of the paralegal–client relationship, and confirmed in the written confirmation of the retainer. You should also confirm in the written confirmation of the retainer that you are acting for the organization, and not for the individuals who have been designated to give you instructions on its behalf (Guideline 5).

If you are retained to act for both an organization and one or more of its officers, employees, or agents in the same matter, you must comply with Rules 3.04(7) to (13) regarding joint retainers.

Phantom Clients

Phantom clients are not specifically addressed in the Rules, but they are discussed in the Guidelines. A **phantom client** is a person who believes that you are representing him, even though you have not been formally retained and may be completely unaware that the phantom client considers you to be his legal representative (Guideline 5). Nonetheless, depending on what happened during your initial encounter with the phantom client, a paralegal–client relationship—with its attendant duties—may exist between you and the phantom client.

phantom client
a person who believes that a paralegal is representing him, even though the paralegal has not been formally retained and may be unaware of the person's belief

Guideline 5 notes that one of the common ways that a phantom client is created is when a person consults with a paralegal, but does not clearly indicate whether she intends to retain the paralegal or pursue the matter. If, based on the consultation, the person has reasonable grounds for concluding that the paralegal has agreed to provide legal services on his or her behalf, a paralegal–client relationship may exist, even though there is no formal retainer.

Phantom clients cannot be avoided, but they can be managed. Guideline 5 recommends the following. When meeting with prospective clients, clearly identify who is the client, what is the client's matter, and who is to provide instructions. Do not engage in discussion of legal matters outside the working environment or a working relationship. Avoid casual social conversation with others about their legal problems. After a consultation with a person, confirm in writing the status of the paralegal–client relationship, by way of a retainer agreement, engagement letter, or non-engagement letter.

Discourage your clients from discussing legal advice with third parties. If third-party members are present at a client consultation, consider informing them in writing that you represent the client only, not them. You will find a sample letter advising third parties that you are not acting for them at Appendix 3.5.

BOX 3.4 Is There a Paralegal–Client Relationship?

For discussion, there follow some situations that may create a paralegal–client relationship. When answering the questions, consider the Rule 1.02 definition of "client":

> "client" means a person who:
>
> (a) consults a paralegal and on whose behalf the paralegal provides or agrees to provide legal services; or
>
> (b) having consulted the paralegal, reasonably concludes that the paralegal has agreed to provide legal services on his or her behalf
>
> and includes a client of the firm of which the paralegal is a partner or associate, whether or not the paralegal handles the client's work.

Fact Situation 1

Ms. W calls your office and speaks to your legal assistant about a *Human Rights Code* complaint. Your legal assistant takes down Ms. W's name, telephone number, address, and some details about the matter.

Your firm has no record of Ms. W in its conflicts checking system.

You call Ms. W and leave a message on her voice mail, asking her to return your call. She does not return your call, and you never hear from her again.

Question for Discussion

Is Ms. W your client?

Fact Situation 2

Mr. X meets with you at your office to consult with you about a *Highway Traffic Act* ticket. Based on the information he provides, you recommend that he consider requesting a meeting with the prosecutor to negotiate a plea to a lesser charge with fewer demerit points. He becomes agitated, and insists that he wants to have a trial in order to "fight the ticket," as he puts it. You advise him of your fee if the matter goes to trial, and tell him that if you are to represent him you will require a money retainer by certified cheque or credit card within 48 hours, because the deadline for filing a notice of intention to appear and plead is 10 days away.

You do not hear from Mr. X for several weeks. Then, one day, he phones you. He is very angry. He tells you that he was convicted of the *Highway Traffic Act* charge in his absence and now faces a fine and demerit points. "You were supposed to stay on top of all this!" he yells. "Instead, you didn't even show up to set a date for the trial! I'm going to report you to the Law Society!"

Questions for Discussion

1. Is Mr. X your client?
2. How could you have avoided the misunderstanding about the terms of the retainer?

Fact Situation 3

One morning at a local supermarket, you run into a neighbour in the produce section, where you are selecting a head of lettuce. Although you do not know her well, Neighbour stops to chat with you. She tells you that she has commenced an action in Small Claims Court against a mutual acquaintance, to whom you have in the past provided legal services in an unrelated matter. She seems upset about it. She gives you a detailed account of her reasons for commencing the action, makes several disparaging comments about the defendant, and from time to time asks you for your opinion. You listen politely, but do not comment. Several times you try to change the subject. When you do so, Neighbour becomes defensive and makes remarks such as "You think I've done the wrong thing, don't you?" and "I can tell that you think I don't have a good case."

Question for Discussion

Is Neighbour your client?

Fact Situation 4

Mr. Brown arranges to meet with you about a legal issue. He is accompanied to the initial consultation by his neighbour, Mr. Pink. Throughout the consultation, Mr. Pink takes a very active role, interrupting Mr. Brown when he is talking, reminding Mr. Brown of details he has forgotten, asking you questions, and so on. Mr. Pink appears to have some legal issues in common with those of Mr. Brown.

Question for Discussion

What issues are raised by Mr. Pink's conduct?

Fact Situation 5

Mr. Yi and his daughter, Violet, come to your office to discuss a residential tenancies problem. Violet is the person who phoned to set up the appointment. At the outset of the consultation, Violet explains to you that her father speaks Cantonese, but is not fluent in English, and that she is there to assist him. You neither speak nor understand Cantonese.

Violet then explains the situation to you in English. From time to time, Mr. Yi interrupts. Sometimes he asks her a question in Cantonese, and sometimes he speaks directly to you, repeating or clarifying something in English. His English is imperfect, but you can understand what he says.

For the most part, however, it is Violet who speaks. She explains that Mr. Yi rents the legal basement apartment in his house to a tenant who has been there for two years. Mr. Yi is a widower and lives alone on the main floor of the house. There is no written tenancy agreement. Mr. Yi never had any problem collecting the rent until two months ago, when the tenant lost her job. Violet says that they want you to commence an application to evict the tenant.

Question for Discussion

What ethical and professional issues arise in this situation?

Client Identification and Verification (By-law 7.1)

By-law 7.1, Part III applies to retainers in matters for new or existing clients entered into on or after December 31, 2008 (ss. 21, 25).

Unless otherwise noted, all references to section numbers in the following discussion refer to By-law 7.1, Part III.

Compliance with the By-law 7.1 Client Identification and Verification Requirements

By-law 7.1, Part III applies only to matters in which a licensee is retained to provide professional services to a new client or an existing client with a new matter on or after December 31, 2008.

Part III does not apply to client matters that were in existence prior to December 31, 2008; however, if you were retained in a new or related matter for any of those clients on or after December 31, 2008, you must comply with the client identification and verification requirements in Part III.

What Is the Difference Between Client Identification and Client Verification?

Client identification refers to information you obtain from the client regarding who the client is and what the client does. **Client verification** refers to information you must obtain in order to confirm that the client is who he says he is.

client identification information that By-law 7.1 requires a licensee to obtain from a client about who the client is and what he does

client verification information that By-law 7.1 requires a licensee to obtain in order to confirm that the client is who he says he is

Licensees shall obtain and record client identification information in accordance with the criteria set out in s. 23(1) for the client in every new client matter opened on or after December 31, 2008. This includes existing clients who retain you in new or related matters on or after December 31, 2008.

If you engage in or give instructions for the receiving, paying, or transferring of non-exempt funds on behalf of a client, then you shall obtain the additional client identification information set out in s. 23(2) and you shall comply with the client verification requirements set out in s. 23(4) (s. 22(1)(b)).

funds
cash, currency, securities, negotiable instruments, and other financial instruments that indicate a person's title or interest in them

negotiable instrument
an unconditional order or promise to pay an amount of money, which can be transferred—for example, cheques or banknotes (paper money)

Funds means cash, currency, securities, negotiable instruments, and other financial instruments that indicate a person's title or interest in them (s. 20). A **negotiable instrument** is an unconditional order or promise to pay an amount of money, which can be transferred—for example, cheques or banknotes (paper money).

Exemptions for Certain Licensees (s. 22(2))

You are not required to comply with the s. 23 client identification and verification requirements if (s. 22(2)):

(a) you provide professional services to, or engage in or give instructions in respect of the receiving, paying, or transferring of funds on behalf of your employer;
(b) you provide professional services, or engage in or give instructions in respect of the receiving, paying, or transferring of funds as an agent for another licensee who has already complied with the client identification and verification requirements set out in s. 23;
(c) you provide professional services to, or engage in or give instructions in respect of the receiving, paying, or transferring of funds on behalf of a client who was referred to you by another licensee who has already complied with the client identification and verification requirements set out in s. 23; or
(d) you provide professional services in the course of acting as a duty counsel under the *Legal Aid Services Act, 1998* as a duty counsel providing professional services through a duty counsel program operated by a not-for-profit organization or as a provider of legal aid services through the provision of summary advice under the *Legal Aid Services Act, 1998.*

With respect to (b) and (c) above, you shall require the licensee for whom you are acting as agent or from whom you received the referral to confirm in writing that she has already complied with the s. 23 client identification and verification requirements. You shall obtain a copy of every document used to verify the identity of an individual or organization for purposes of s. 23(4), including a copy of every document used by an individual acting on behalf of the licensee under s. 23(11).

Exemptions for Certain Types of Funds (s. 22(3))

You do not have to comply with the s. 23(2) client identification requirements or the s. 23(4) client verification requirements in respect of funds (s. 22(3)):

(a) paid to or received from a financial institution, public body, or reporting issuer (see definitions below);
(b) received from the trust account of another licensee or a lawyer;

(c) received from a peace officer, law enforcement agency, or other public official acting in an official capacity;
(d) paid or received pursuant to a court order;
(e) paid for a fine or penalty;
(f) paid or received in settlement of legal or administrative proceedings;
(g) paid or received for professional fees, disbursements, expenses, or bail; or
(h) paid, received, or transferred by electronic funds transfer.

Note that in the above cases, you are still required to comply with the client identification requirements set out in s. 23(1).

Clients Who Are Exempt from Client Identification and Verification (s. 22(4))

You are not required to comply with the s. 23(2) client identification requirements and the s. 23(4) verification requirements if your client is (s. 22(4)):

1. a financial institution,
2. a public body, or
3. a reporting issuer.

Note that you are still required to comply with the client identification requirements set out in s. 23(1).

For purposes of ss. 22(3) and (4), "financial institution" means (s. 20):

> (a) a bank to which the *Bank Act* (Canada) applies,
> (b) an authorized foreign bank within the meaning of section 2 of the *Bank Act* (Canada) in respect of its business in Canada,
> (c) a cooperative credit society, savings and credit union, credit union or caisse populaire that is regulated by an Act of a province or territory of Canada,
> (d) an association that is regulated by the *Cooperative Credit Associations Act* (Canada),
> (e) a company to which the *Trust and Loan Companies Act* (Canada) applies,
> (f) a loan or trust corporation regulated by an Act of a province or territory of Canada,
> (g) a ministry, department or agent of the government of Canada or of a province or territory of Canada if the ministry, department or agent accepts deposit liabilities in the course of providing financial services to the public, or
> (h) a subsidiary of an entity mentioned in clauses (a) to (g) where the financial statements of the subsidiary are consolidated with the financial statements of the entity.

For the purposes of ss. 22(3) and (4), "public body" means (s. 20):

> (a) a ministry, department or agent of the government of Canada or of a province or territory of Canada,

(b) a municipality incorporated by or under an Act of a province or territory of Canada, including a city, town, village, metropolitan or regional municipality, township, district, county, rural municipality, any other incorporated municipal body and an agent of any of them,

(c) a local board of a municipality incorporated by or under an Act of a province or territory of Canada, including any local board as defined in the *Municipal Act* and any similar body incorporated under the law of another province or territory,

(d) an organization that operates a public hospital and that is designated by the Minister of National Revenue as a hospital authority under the *Excise Tax Act* (Canada) or an agent of the organization,

(e) a body incorporated by or under an Act of Canada or of a province or territory of Canada for a public purpose, or

(f) a subsidiary of an entity mentioned in clauses (a) to (e) where the financial statements of the subsidiary are consolidated with the financial statements of the entity.

For the purposes of ss. 22(3) and (4), "reporting issuer" means (s. 20):

(a) a reporting issuer within the meaning of an Act of a province or territory of Canada in respect of the securities law of the province or territory,

(b) a corporation whose shares are traded on a stock exchange designated under section 262 of the *Income Tax Act* (Canada) and that operates in a country that is a member of the Financial Action Task Force on Money Laundering, or

(c) a subsidiary of an entity mentioned in clause (a) or (b) where the financial statements of the subsidiary are consolidated with the financial statements of the entity.

BOX 3.5 Reminder: Public and Private Companies

A **public company** (referred to as a "reporting issuer" in By-law 7.1, Part III) is a corporation whose shares are for sale to the general public. Public companies are subject to rigorous disclosure requirements under securities legislation.

A **private company** (also called a closely held company) is a corporation whose shares are not publicly traded. Its incorporating documents (1) restrict the right to sell shares, (2) limit the number of its shareholders (excluding employees) to 50, and (3) prohibit public trading of its shares or securities.

public company
a corporation whose shares are for sale to the general public and that is subject to rigorous disclosure requirements under securities legislation

private company
a corporation whose shares are not publicly traded; also called a closely held company

The Criteria for Client Identification and Verification (s. 23)

The criteria for identifying and verifying clients are set out in Table 3.1. Verification of identity forms for individuals, organizations, third-party beneficiaries, and principals are available at the Law Society website. You will find samples, adapted for use in paralegal firms, at Appendixes 3.6 and 3.7.

Client Verification, Non-Face-to-Face (s. 23(8))

You may use this form of client verification if you engage in or give instructions for the receiving, paying, or transferring of non-exempt funds on behalf of an individual client who is elsewhere in Canada or elsewhere in the world, so that you are unable to receive instructions from the client face-to-face (s. 23(8)). To comply with the s. 23(4) verification requirements, you must obtain an attestation from a commissioner of oaths or a guarantor certifying that he has verified the client's identity by looking at the appropriate independent source documents (ss. 23(7), (8)).

Any of the following may be used as a guarantor (s. 23(9)):

A. a dentist,
B. a physician,
C. a chiropractor,
D. a judge,
E. a magistrate or a justice of the peace,
F. a lawyer,
G. a licensee (in Ontario)
H. a notary (in Quebec),
I. a notary public,
J. an optometrist,
K. a pharmacist,
L. an accountant,
M. a professional engineer,
N. a veterinarian,
O. a police officer,
P. a nurse,
Q. a school principal.

You must exercise due diligence in confirming that the guarantor making the attestation is a member of one of these professions. **Due diligence** means exercising the prudence and vigilance that a reasonable and prudent paralegal would exercise in similar circumstances. In the case of a guarantor making an attestation, you should consider obtaining some form of confirmation of their professional status.

due diligence
in a legal context, exercising prudence and vigilance in determining the facts

The attestation must be printed on a legible photocopy of the document. It must include the name, occupation, address, and signature of the attestor, and the type and number of the document seen by the attestor (s. 23(10)). A sample attestation form for use by paralegal firms is available at the Law Society website. You will find the text of a sample attestation in Appendix 3.8.

Client Verification, Use of Agent (s. 23(11))

You may use this form of client verification if you engage in or give instructions for the receiving, paying, or transferring of non-exempt funds on behalf of a client who is outside of Canada, or as an alternative to the s. 23(8) procedure for verifying the identity of an individual client who is elsewhere in Canada.

Table 3.1 By-law 7.1 Criteria for Client Identification and Verification

Client Identification Requirements

You shall obtain the following information about the client when you are retained to provide legal services to the client (ss. 22(1)(a), 23(1)).

Whether the client is an individual or an organization, if the client is acting for or representing a third party, you shall obtain the following information for the third party also (s. 23(1)8).

Individual	Organization*
Full name	Full name
Business address and business telephone number, if applicable	Business address and business telephone number
Home address and home telephone number	The organization's incorporation or business identification number, if applicable The place of issue of its incorporation or business identification number, if applicable
Occupation(s)—does not have to be employment If the client refuses to provide this information, you must inform the client that you will be in breach of By-law 7.1 if you do not obtain this information and will be obliged to decline the retainer	The general nature of the type of business or activity engaged in by the client The name, position, and contact information for the person(s) authorized to provide instructions in the matter

Additional Client Identification Requirements When Handling Non-Exempt Funds (s. 22(1)(b))

Individual	Organization* (s. 23(2))
None	The name and occupation(s) of each director of the organization (other than an organization that is a securities dealer) The name, address, and occupation(s) of each person who owns 25% or more of the organization or of the shares of the organization You must make reasonable efforts to obtain the information above. Asking your client may be sufficient, or you may consult the corporate minute books if available or an online corporate registry service

Client Verification Requirements When Handling Non-Exempt Funds

Individual	Organization*
Verification shall take place immediately after you first engage in or give instructions for the receiving, paying, or transferring of funds (s. 23(5))	Verification shall take place no later than 60 days after you first engage in or give instructions for the receiving, paying, or transferring of funds (s. 23(6))

You shall take reasonable steps to verify the identity of the client and any third party that the client is acting for or representing using what you reasonably consider to be reliable, independent source documents, data, or information (s. 23(4)).

You should take reasonable steps to comply with the verification requirement as early as possible in the retainer.

You shall verify the identity of an individual who is authorized to give instructions on behalf of a client who is an organization.

Whether the client is an individual or an organization, if the client is acting for or representing a third party, you shall verify the identity of the third party also.

You shall complete and sign a verification of identity form for each individual, organization, third-party beneficiary, or principal, with photocopies of the documentation relied upon attached.

Examples of Independent Source Documents (s. 23(7))

Individual	Organization*
An original, government-issued identification that is valid and has not expired, and that you reasonably believe to be independent and reliable, such as: • a driver's licence • a birth certificate • a passport • a provincial or territorial health card (if such use is not prohibited by law)	If the client is a private company or society created under legislative authority: • a certificate of corporate status • an annual filing • a similar record obtained from a public body confirming the organization's existence If the client is a trust, partnership, or other organization that is not registered in any government registry, a constating document confirming the organization's existence, such as: • a trust agreement • a partnership agreement • articles of association • other similar records confirming the organization's existence as an organization

You shall retain a record of the information that you obtain and copies of all documents used to verify client identification for the longer of:

- the duration of the paralegal–client relationship, and for as long as is necessary to complete the work for which you were retained; and
- six years following the completion of the work for which you were retained.

* For the purposes of By-law 7, any of the following is considered to be an organization: a private company, a partnership, a fund, a trust, a co-operative, or an unincorporated association.

If the agent acting on your behalf is not an employee of your firm or a paralegal who provides legal services through your firm, you shall enter into a written agreement with the agent specifying the steps that the agent will be taking on your behalf to comply with the verification requirements (s. 23(11)). The agent may provide the information to you in the form of an attestation. See Appendix 3.8 for a sample attestation.

Previous Client Verification (s. 23(12))

For an individual client, a licensee complies with the s. 23(4) verification requirement if she has already verified the individual client's identity and recognizes the individual (s. 23(12)(a)).

For a client that is an organization, a licensee complies with the s. 23(2) identification requirements and the s. 23(4) verification requirements if she has already complied with those requirements with respect to the organization (s. 23(12)(b)).

Documentation (ss. 23(13), (14))

You shall obtain copies of every document used to verify the identity of any individual or organization, including copies of documents used by an agent for client verification under s. 23(11) (s. 23(13)).

You shall keep records of all information obtained for purposes of client identification and verification, including copies of supporting documents, attestations, and so on, for the longer of (s. 23(14)):

(a) the duration of the paralegal–client relationship, and for as long as is necessary to provide service to the client; and
(b) at least six years following completion of the work for which you were retained.

Criminal Activity (ss. 24, 27)

If, in the course of complying with the client identification and verification requirements set out in s. 23, a licensee knows or ought to know that she is or would be assisting a client in fraud or other illegal conduct, the licensee shall (s. 24)

> (a) immediately cease to and not further engage in any activities that would assist the client in fraud or other illegal conduct; and
> (b) if the licensee is unable to comply with clause (a), withdraw from the provision of the licensee's professional services to the client.

CHAPTER SUMMARY

A client is a person who consults with you and on whose behalf you provide or agree to provide legal services, or a person who, having consulted you, reasonably concludes that you have agreed to provide legal services on his or her behalf. In some circumstances, certain duties, including the duty of avoidance of conflicts of interest, may arise between a paralegal and a non-client. A paralegal should be cautious when accepting information on an informal or preliminary basis from a person. If it is confidential information, your possession of that information may prevent you from representing another party in the same matter or a related matter.

The paralegal–client relationship is to be distinguished from the paralegal–client retainer. The paralegal–client relationship encompasses a broad range of duties owed to the client. The paralegal–client retainer is the contractual relationship between you and the client in a particular client matter. It is established when the client agrees to retain you and you agree to provide legal services to the client. The terms of the paralegal–client retainer should be discussed with the client at the initial consultation, and confirmed in writing by way of a retainer agreement or engagement letter.

At the initial consultation, you may decide not to provide legal services to a person, or the person may decide not to retain you. You must confirm the non-engagement in writing to the person with a non-engagement letter.

When you have completed the services provided for in the retainer agreement, the paralegal–client retainer ends for that client matter. However, your duties to the client pursuant to the paralegal–client relationship continue indefinitely.

In your practice, you shall maintain a conflicts checking system, and the names of all clients and prospective clients, along with any related parties, should be entered into it.

A joint retainer is an arrangement where a paralegal agrees to represent two or more clients in the same matter. Before agreeing to a joint retainer, you must clearly identify your prospective clients to ensure that you can fulfill your duties to them, including the duty to avoid conflicts of interest. The terms of a joint retainer should be confirmed in writing in a retainer agreement; this includes, but is not limited to, who will provide instructions and how a contentious issue that is not related to the provision of legal services will be dealt with.

Clients with diminished capacity are clients whose ability to make decisions is diminished because of minority, mental disability, or for some other reason. A party who has been identified as being of diminished capacity must have a client representative appointed to protect the party's interest in a legal matter. The client representative may be a litigation guardian, the Office of the Children's Lawyer, or the Office of the Public Guardian and Trustee. You must identify who the client is and determine who will provide instructions in the matter at the outset of the relationship. If you are representing both the client with diminished capacity and the client representative, you must comply with the rules for joint retainers.

If your client is an organization, you should determine, and confirm in the retainer agreement or engagement letter, which individuals within the organization may properly give you instructions on the client organization's behalf. You should also confirm that you are acting for the organization, and not for the individuals who have been designated to give you instructions on its behalf.

A phantom client is a person who believes that you are representing him, even though you have not been formally retained and may be completely unaware that he considers you his legal representative. Although no retainer has been entered into with the phantom client, if you discussed legal matters or acquired confidential information during your encounter with that person, your possession of that information may give rise to certain duties, those being, at a minimum, to the duty of confidentiality and avoidance of conflicts of interest, both of which continue indefinitely.

Effective December 31, 2008, licensees shall comply with the client identification and verification requirements set out in By-law 7.1, Part III. See Table 3.1 at pages 68–69.

KEY TERMS

client, 52
client identification, 63
client verification, 63
client with diminished capacity, 60
confidential information, 53
conflicts checking system, 52
disbursements, 54
due diligence, 67
duty of loyalty, 50
duty of service, 50
fees, 54
funds, 64
independent legal advice, 59
instructions, 59
joint clients, 58
joint retainer, 58
limited scope retainer, 57
mixed trust bank account, 56
money retainer, 51
negotiable instrument, 64
non-engagement, 56
non-engagement letter, 56
paralegal–client relationship, 50
paralegal–client retainer, 51
phantom client, 61
private company, 66
prospective client, 53
public company, 66
retained, 51
retainer, 51
scope of the retainer, 54

REFERENCES

Amato v. Welsh, 2013 ONCA 258, [2013] OJ no. 1857.

Curtis, Carole, Dealing with the Difficult Client (October 2003), http://www.practicepro.ca/practice/pdf/DealingDifficultClientCaroleCurtis.pdf.

Highway Traffic Act, RSO 1990, c. H.8, as amended.

Human Rights Code, RSO 1990, c. H.19, as amended.

Insurance Act, RSO 1990, c. I.8, as amended.

Law Society of Upper Canada, *By-Laws* (2007), as amended ("the By-Laws"), http://www.lsuc.on.ca/with.aspx?id=1070.

Law Society of Upper Canada, *Paralegal Professional Conduct Guidelines* (October 2014) ("the Guidelines"), http://www.lsuc.on.ca/paralegal-conduct-guidelines.

Law Society of Upper Canada, *Paralegal Rules of Conduct* (October 2014) ("the Rules"), http://www.lsuc.on.ca/paralegal-conduct-rules.

Legal Aid Services Act, 1998, SO 1998, c. 26.

O. Reg. 258/98, Rules of the Small Claims Court, http://www.e-laws.gov.on.ca/html/regs/english/elaws_regs_980258_e.htm.

Pinnington, Dan, Unbundled Legal Services: Pitfalls to Avoid, *LAWPRO Magazine* 11:1, January 2012, http://www.practicepro.ca/LAWPROMag/Unbundled_Legal_Services.pdf.

REVIEW QUESTIONS

1. Define the following words and phrases. Provide the source of your definition, including the section or rule number.

a. client

b. client identification

c. client with diminished capacity

d. client verification

e. confidential information

f. conflicts checking system

g. conflict of interest

h. engagement letter

i. funds

j. instructions

k. non-engagement

l. non-engagement letter

m. paralegal–client relationship

n. paralegal–client retainer

o. phantom client

p. private company

q. public company

r. retainer agreement

s. scope of the retainer

2. Mr. A calls your office and speaks to your legal assistant about a *Highway Traffic Act* matter. The trial is scheduled for the following Wednesday. Your assistant takes down Mr. A's name, telephone number, and some details about the matter, including the charge and the trial date. He tells Mr. A that you will call him, and that a money retainer will be required before you will accept the retainer.

Later the same day, you call the number that Mr. A gave your legal assistant . You get a message that the number you are calling is out of service.

On the morning of the trial date, you receive a phone call from Mr. A. He tells you that he is waiting for you at the court house. "Where are you?" he says. "Today's the trial. Your assistant said you'd be here."

a. Are you required to appear on Mr. A's behalf at the hearing?

b. Is Mr. A your client?

3. Your client is a small, private company, owned by a wife and husband, specializing in property management of multi-unit residential buildings. You handle their Landlord and Tenant Board matters. The original retainer agreement with the corporation does not designate a person from whom you are to obtain instructions. In the past, you have always taken instructions from the wife, but recently the husband has become more active in the business and has begun instructing you as well. His management style is very different from his wife's, and sometimes the instructions he gives you are different from those you have already received from his wife.

What should you do?

4. You work in a firm of four paralegal licensees. You are contacted by Mrs. Q. She was referred to you by another licensee in the firm, who represented her in a Workplace Safety and Insurance Board matter three years ago. She wants to meet with you to discuss representation of her 15-year-old son, D, who is the defendant in a Small Claims Court action for damages related to property damage. You personally have never acted for D or for Mrs. Q before.

a. What step should you take before the initial consultation with D and Mrs. Q?

b. What are your obligations under By-law 7.1, Part III?

c. What are some professional and procedural issues that arise because of D's age?

APPENDIX 3.1 Retainer Agreement

[firm letterhead]

Retainer Agreement

General

[date] Client matter no. [ ]

[client name and address]

Dear **[name of client]**:

Re: [description of client matter]

1. Description of Services

You have asked us, and we have agreed, to act for you in the matter described below. On **[date]**, we met to discuss the scope of our firm's intended representation. The purpose of this letter is to summarize and confirm the terms of your engagement of us.

You retain us to represent you in connection with **[brief description of matter]**.

We anticipate that our representation will involve taking the following steps on your behalf. **[Using paragraph format, describe the steps to be taken in the matter. Keep your language simple and your sentences short and to the point.]**

At this time we have not been retained to represent you generally or in connection with any other matter. We will not be acting for you in any other matters.

We will work with you toward your desired outcome. However, all legal actions are subject to many possible variables, such as the availability of substantiating documents and other evidence, and the evidence brought forward by the other side—all of which affect the decision of a judge. For us to work toward your desired outcome, it will be necessary for you to abide by the terms described in this letter.

We will try to return your phone calls and respond to your letters as quickly as possible. Our practice is to return phone calls within two business days. If a matter is urgent, please contact us immediately and we will make every effort to respond to you on an urgent basis.

We wish to caution you that email is not a secure form of communication. You should use it for routine inquiries only.

… / 2

APPENDIX 3.1 Retainer Agreement *continued*

Retainer Agreement
Page 2 of 4

2. Licensed Paralegals

This will confirm that we are a firm of paralegal licensees. We are not lawyers. At present, paralegals are permitted to provide legal services in the following areas: the Small Claims Court; *Provincial Offences Act* matters in the Ontario Court of Justice; matters before federal and provincial tribunals; in summary conviction court in matters where the maximum penalty is a fine of not more than $5,000.00 and/or imprisonment for a term of not more than six months; and in claims for statutory accident benefits within the meaning of the *Insurance Act*, excluding a claim of an individual who has or appears to have a catastrophic impairment within the meaning of the Statutory Accident Benefits Schedule.

We are satisfied that your matter falls within a permitted area of practice for paralegal licensees.

We expect that most of the work will be performed or supervised by myself. I may be assisted by [**name**], an associate paralegal. For routine tasks, we may be assisted by a field placement student. We reserve the right to assign other paralegals in our firm to perform legal services if in our judgment that becomes necessary or desirable.

3. Fees

Our fee will be based principally on the time spent by us on your behalf. Records of all time will be kept and accounts will then be prepared and sent to you periodically.

Our hourly rates range from $75.00 to $90.00 for my associate to $100.00 for me.

While we expect that our fee will be calculated on the basis of our regular hourly rates, we reserve the right to charge more in appropriate cases, such as pressing circumstances, the requirement for work outside normal business hours, exceptionally successful or efficient representation, or special demands on us.

Based on the information provided by you at our initial consultation, we estimate that our total fees (not including disbursements and expenses) will be $[**amount**]. [**Describe the facts and circumstances that form the basis for the estimate.**] Our estimated fees may change should facts or circumstances arise which are unknown to us at this time. We will advise you promptly if there is any likelihood of an increase or decrease in our fees.

You will be charged HST on fees and HST on some disbursements.

APPENDIX 3.1 Retainer Agreement *continued*

4. Expenses and Allocated Charges (also called disbursements)

You will also be responsible for reimbursing us for expenses (also called disbursements) we incur on your behalf and office charges allocated to your file. These include long distance calls, faxes, postage, deliveries, travel expenses, photocopying, and filing and search charges, and all other reasonable out-of-pocket expenses and office charges. We do not charge for staff overtime on evenings or weekends in order to meet time deadlines.

5. Billing

We will invoice you from time to time as the matter proceeds. You will receive a final invoice upon completion of all services described in this agreement.

Payment is due on all of our accounts when rendered. If any account is not paid within 30 days, interest will be charged on the outstanding balance at a rate of 3.0% per annum from the date of the account, until paid.

6. Settlement Funds

During our initial consultation we discussed and you agreed that, in the event the matter settles, any settlement funds payable to you or by you to another party shall be paid to us in trust. If the settlement funds are payable to you, any outstanding fees and disbursements in the matter may be invoiced and paid in full out of the funds in trust. Any balance will then be disbursed to you unless you direct us otherwise in writing.

7. Money Retainer

Before we begin work on your behalf, we require a money retainer for future legal fees and proper disbursements and expenses in the amount of $[**amount**]. This will confirm that at the conclusion of our consultation you paid us a money retainer in this amount by credit card. The retainer will be placed in our trust account and will serve as a source of payment for all or part of our account or accounts when rendered. You will be asked to replenish the retainer from time to time. Any unused portion will be returned to you upon the completion or termination of our services.

APPENDIX 3.1 Retainer Agreement *concluded*

8. Termination of Legal Services

You have the right to terminate our services to you upon written notice to us.

Subject to our obligations to you to maintain proper standards of professional conduct, we reserve the right to terminate our services to you for good reasons that include, but are not limited to:

(a) if you fail to cooperate with us in any reasonable request;

(b) if our continuing to act for you would be unethical or impractical;

(c) if our retainer has not been paid; or

(d) if you fail to pay our accounts when rendered.

If you terminate our services or we withdraw, you would only have to pay our fees and expenses up until the time we stopped acting for you.

9. Agreement

Any changes to this agreement must be made in writing.

If you want us to proceed on the basis described above, please sign the enclosed copy of this letter in the space provided and return it to us in the enclosed self-addressed envelope. If you decide that you do not want us to proceed on your behalf in this matter, please inform us promptly in writing.

Yours truly,

[paralegal firm name]

[signature]

[signatory name]

Licensed Paralegal

I have read and understood the retainer agreement, and agree to its terms.

____________________	______________
Signatory	Date

Adapted from the precedent retainer agreement at http://www.lawpro.ca.

APPENDIX 3.2 Engagement Letter

[firm letterhead]

June 14, 20— Client matter no. 632

Mrs. Maxine Chong
67 Harmony Avenue
Toronto, ON M4J 1J3

Dear Mrs. Chong:

Re: LeeAnn Kingman

Small Claims Court action

Further to our meeting on June 12, 20—, this will confirm that you have retained us to act in the above matter. By a tenancy agreement dated January 13, 20—, Ms. Kingman rented your basement apartment from February 1, 20— until April 17, 20—. The monthly rent was $775.00 including water, heat, and hydro. Ms. Kingman did not pay a last month's rent deposit, and during her tenancy Ms. Kingman paid no rent. As well, she harassed you and interfered with your reasonable enjoyment of the premises, causing damage to your health. Ms. Kingman vacated the premises on April 17, 20—.

You have instructed us to commence an action immediately in Small Claims Court for $25,000.00 for unpaid rent, damage to property, and pain and suffering, plus interest and costs. You have agreed to waive any amounts you might recover over and above $25,000.00 in order to bring the matter within Small Claims Court jurisdiction.

We anticipate that our representation will involve taking the following steps on your behalf. We will file a plaintiff's claim and serve the claim on the defendant. If Ms. Kingman does not file a defence within the time prescribed by the *Rules of the Small Claims Court*, we will request that the clerk note her in default. We may then obtain default judgment by a motion in writing for an assessment of damages or at an assessment hearing. If Ms. Kingman files a defence, we will make every effort to settle the matter, subject to your instructions. A settlement conference will be scheduled for no later than 90 days after Ms. Kingman's defence is filed. If the matter does not settle, we will prepare for and represent you at trial.

. . . / 2

APPENDIX 3.2 Engagement Letter *continued*

We also wish to confirm our agreement as to fees and payment. We charge $100.00 per hour for legal services. You will also be billed for any out-of-pocket expenses (also known as disbursements) that may be incurred, such as court filing fees and so on. We will advise you before incurring any extraordinary disbursements. At the moment, the only extraordinary disbursement we anticipate is the fee for your treating physician's report.

We will bill you approximately monthly, depending on the amount of work that is completed on your file during that period of time. The amount of time and expenses that will be required to represent you in this matter cannot be predicted at this time. However, as we discussed, if Ms. Kingman fails to file a defence and we obtain default judgment, we estimate that our total fees will not exceed $1,500.00 exclusive of disbursements. If Ms. Kingman files a defence and the matter goes to trial, we estimate that our total fees will not exceed $3,500.00 exclusive of disbursements. We are not guaranteeing that we can accomplish the work for this sum, but are representing to you that the amount appears reasonable in the circumstances. We will advise you before undertaking any procedures that will substantially increase the amount of your fees, and will obtain your instructions to proceed.

This will confirm that you have provided us with a money retainer of $1,000.00. This money has been placed in our trust account and will be applied to payment of invoices when delivered. You may be asked to provide further money retainers from time to time as the matter goes forward.

As we discussed at our meeting, will you please forward copies of the tenancy agreement and the Notice of Early Termination to us as soon as possible. We will also require copies of your medical records and bills for the period of Ms. Kingman's tenancy and afterward. These documents will be returned to you when the matter is concluded.

We will make every effort to reach a settlement with Ms. Kingman in accordance with your instructions. However, we cannot guarantee success or that we will be able to reach a negotiated settlement. This will confirm that you have agreed that, if the matter does settle in your favour, the settlement funds are to be paid to us in trust and any outstanding fees or disbursements may be paid from those funds upon delivery of a final invoice. We will then pay any unused portion to you.

As I advised you, we are a paralegal firm. We are not lawyers. Paralegals are restricted to providing legal services in areas of permitted practice for licensed paralegals. You have

APPENDIX 3.2 Engagement Letter *concluded*

indicated that you wish to proceed in Small Claims Court. Small Claims Court is a permitted area of practice for paralegals.

You have the right to terminate our services to you upon written notice to us. Subject to our obligations to you to maintain proper standards of professional conduct, we reserve the right to terminate our services to you for good reasons that include, but are not limited to:

(a) if you fail to cooperate with us in any reasonable request;

(b) if our continuing to act for you would be unethical or impractical;

(c) if our retainer has not been paid; or

(d) if you fail to pay our accounts when rendered.

If you terminate our services or we withdraw, you would only have to pay our fees and expenses up until the time we stopped acting for you.

I trust that the foregoing is satisfactory. If you have any questions or concerns, please contact me.

I will try to respond to your phone calls and emails as quickly as possible. If a matter is urgent, I will make every effort to respond to you on an urgent basis.

Yours very truly,

Prior Mustafa LLP

Joseph Mustafa

Joseph Mustafa
Licensed Paralegal

APPENDIX 3.3 Non-Engagement Letter (Conflict of Interest—Client Declines Retainer)

[firm letterhead]

[date] **[file number]**

[client name and address]

Dear **[client name]**:

Re: [client matter]

As we discussed during our **[telephone conversation/meeting/initial consultation]** on **[date]**, a preliminary search revealed that **[paralegal firm name]** has a conflict of interest in this matter. We provided you with details of the conflict and asked you to decide whether you wished to consent to the retainer based on this disclosure. You have now advised that you do not wish to retain us.

Please be aware that whatever claim you have may be barred by the passage of time. Since time limitations may be critical to your case, we recommend that you immediately contact another paralegal or a lawyer for assistance regarding your matter. If you do not have another paralegal or lawyer in mind to represent you, the Law Society maintains on its website (http://www.lsuc.on.ca) a directory of paralegals and lawyers who may be available to assist you, or you may wish to contact the Law Society Referral Service at **[current contact numbers at http://www.lsuc.on.ca]**.

We confirm that we do not have any documents belonging to you. All documents were returned to you at the conclusion of the initial consultation.

Although we were not able to assist you in this matter, we hope that you will consider **[paralegal firm name]** in the event that you require legal services in the future.

Thank you again for your interest in this firm.

Yours truly,

[paralegal firm name]

[signature]

[signatory name]

Licensed Paralegal

Adapted from the Law Society of British Columbia website (http://www.lawsociety.bc.ca) and the Law Society of Upper Canada website (http://www.lsuc.on.ca).

APPENDIX 3.4 Non-Engagement Letter (Conflict of Interest—Paralegal Firm Declines Retainer)

[firm letterhead]

[date] **[file number]**

[client name and address]

Dear [**client name**]:

Re: [client matter]

As we discussed during our [**telephone conversation/meeting/initial consultation**] on [**date**], before [**paralegal firm name**] could agree to represent you in this matter, we had to investigate whether this representation could adversely affect existing or former clients' interests or whether there might be some other reason that we would be unable to adequately represent your interests.

On [**date**], we performed a conflict of interest check and found that our firm does indeed have a conflict of interest in this case. Unfortunately, we therefore cannot represent you and we must decline to do so in this matter.

Please be aware that whatever claim you have may be barred by the passage of time. Since time limitations may be critical to your case, we recommend that you immediately contact another paralegal or a lawyer for assistance regarding your matter. If you do not have another paralegal or lawyer in mind to represent you, the Law Society maintains on its website (http://www.lsuc.on.ca) a directory of paralegals and lawyers who may be available to assist you, or you may wish to call the Law Society Referral Service at [**current contact numbers at http://www.lsuc.on.ca**].

We confirm that we do not have any documents belonging to you. All documents were returned to you at the conclusion of the initial consultation.

Although we were not able to assist you in this matter, we hope that you will consider [**paralegal firm name**] in the event that you require legal services in the future.

Thank you again for your interest in this firm.

Yours truly,

[paralegal firm name]

[signature]

[signatory name]

Licensed Paralegal

Adapted from the Law Society of British Columbia website (http://www.lawsociety.bc.ca) and the Law Society of Upper Canada website (http://www.lsuc.on.ca).

APPENDIX 3.5 Model "I am not your legal representative" Letter

[firm letterhead]

[delivery method]

[date]

[non-client address]

Dear [**name of recipient**]:

Re: [description of matter]

This letter is further to our meeting on [**date**]. This will confirm that we will be representing [**name the party or parties the firm will represent**] in connection with [**provide details regarding the nature of the firm's mandate or the transaction**].

Although we understand that you have a personal involvement in this matter and we anticipate that we may have further contact with you, this letter will confirm that you, personally, are not our client. For this reason, we recommend that you consult with your own legal representative regarding issues that may affect your personal interests in this matter.

We further confirm that we have not received any confidential information regarding your interests in the matter. [**where communications with the non-client involved document or property exchange:** We are returning with this letter those documents we reviewed regarding this matter and confirm that we are not in possession of any documents or property belonging to [**non-client**]].

Please confirm your receipt of this letter by signing and returning a copy to my attention.

Thank you for your prompt response.

Yours truly,

[paralegal firm name]

[signature]

[signatory name]

Licensed Paralegal

I, [**non-client name**], acknowledge receipt of the above letter and my agreement with its contents.

______________________________ ______________________

Signature Date

Adapted by the Task Force from portions of a precedent letter by William Freivogel, an American expert on conflicts matters and precedent from the Law Society of British Columbia website.

APPENDIX 3.6 Verification of Identity (Individual)

[paralegal firm name]

Licensed Paralegals

VERIFICATION OF IDENTITY

(For use where the client or third party is an individual)

Name: ______________________________

Address (home): ______________________________

Telephone number (home): ______________________________

Address (business): ______________________________

Telephone number (business): ______________________________

Occupation(s): ______________________________

Original Document Reviewed—Copy Attached

___ Driver's licence

___ Birth certificate

___ Passport

___ Other (specify type): ______________________________

Meeting date identity verified: ______________________________

Identity verified by: ______________________________

Date file reviewed by paralegal: ______________________________

Name of paralegal: ______________________________

APPENDIX 3.7 Verification of Identity (Organization)

[paralegal firm name]

Licensed Paralegals

VERIFICATION OF IDENTITY

(For use where the client or third party is an organization)

Name: ______________________________

Address (business): ______________________________

Telephone number (business): ______________________________

Incorporation or Business Identification Number: ______________________________

Place of issue of number: ______________________________

Type of business or activity: ______________________________

Person Authorized to Instruct

Name: ______________________________

Position: ______________________________

Telephone number: ______________________________

Original Document Reviewed—Copy Attached

___ Driver's licence

___ Birth certificate

___ Passport

___ Other (specify type): ______________________________

. . . / 2

APPENDIX 3.7 Verification of Identity (Organization) *concluded*

Names and occupation(s) of directors:

[list]

Names, addresses, and occupation(s) of owners or shareholders owning a 25% interest or more of the organization or shares in the organization:

[list]

Original Document Reviewed—Copy Attached

___ Certificate of corporate status

___ Annual filings of the organization (specify type): ______________________

___ Partnership agreement

___ Trust agreement

___ Articles of association

___ Other (specify type): ______________________

Meeting date identity verified: ______________________

Identity verified by: ______________________

Date file reviewed by paralegal: ______________________

Name of paralegal: ______________________

APPENDIX 3.8 Attestation for Verification of Identity When the Client or Third Party Is Present in Canada and Is Not Instructing the Paralegal Face-to-Face

INSTRUCTIONS

The Attestor should photocopy the identity document being used to verify identity and ensure that it is legible, unexpired, and shows the name of the person whose identity is being verified, the number of the document, the name of the issuing authority, the date of issue, and a photograph of the person.

The Attestor will *print* the following attestation on the photocopy and date and sign the attestation.

> I, the Attestor named below, hereby certify to [**name of paralegal receiving the attestation**] that I met with [**name of person**] on [**date**] and verified this person's identity by examining the original of this person's identity document, of which a photocopy is contained on this page. The photograph in the identity document is a true likeness of the said person, and to the best of my knowledge and belief the identity document that I examined is valid and unexpired.
>
> Attested to by me at ____________________, on ____________ _____, 20_____ .

Signature of attestor: ______________________________

Printed name of attestor: ______________________________

Title or profession of attestor: ______________________________

Address of attestor for service: ______________________________

____

Telephone number of attestor: ______________________________

4 Duty to Clients

LEARNING OBJECTIVES

After reading this chapter, you will understand:

- The role of the paralegal as fiduciary.
- Competence and quality of service.
- Advising clients.
- Client service and communication.
- Honesty and candour.
- The duty of confidentiality.
- Justified or permitted disclosure.
- Avoidance of conflicts of interest.
- Preservation of client property.
- Withdrawal from representation.

The Paralegal as Fiduciary

fiduciary relationship a relationship of trust and confidence between two persons in which one person (the fiduciary) is required to act with scrupulous good faith, honesty, and candour for the benefit of the other person

fiduciary a person who must act with scrupulous good faith, honesty, and candour for the benefit of another person, who places absolute trust and confidence in the fiduciary

beneficiary a person who benefits from the efforts of another

The paralegal–client relationship is governed by a set of overlapping obligations and responsibilities.

Many of a paralegal's duties and obligations to a client arise out of the fiduciary relationship between the paralegal and the client. A **fiduciary relationship** is a relationship of absolute trust and confidence between two persons, in which one person (the **fiduciary**) is required to act with scrupulous good faith, honesty, and candour for the benefit of the other person (the **beneficiary**). In the paralegal–client relationship, the paralegal is the fiduciary and the client is the beneficiary. The paralegal must put the client's interests ahead of her own in all dealings with the client. The client is entitled to place absolute confidence, reliance, and trust in the paralegal.

The fiduciary relationship between the paralegal and the client gives rise to a special standard of care, or ethical duty, based in the law of trusts. The paralegal must comply with this special standard of care for the benefit of the client. The standard of care imposes the duties of honesty and candour, confidentiality, avoidance of conflicts of interest, and accounting for client property. These duties characterize the paralegal–client relationship and are codified in the *Paralegal Rules of Conduct*.

Competence and Quality of Service (Rule 3.01; Guideline 6)

General

Section 41 of the *Law Society Act* sets the general standard for professional competence on the part of licensees:

> **Interpretation—standards of professional competence**
>
> 41. A licensee fails to meet standards of professional competence for the purposes of this Act if,
>
> (a) there are deficiencies in,
>
> (i) the licensee's knowledge, skill or judgment,
>
> (ii) the licensee's attention to the interests of clients,
>
> (iii) the records, systems or procedures of the licensee's professional business, or
>
> (iv) other aspects of the licensee's professional business; and
>
> (b) the deficiencies give rise to a reasonable apprehension that the quality of service to clients may be adversely affected.

The public has certain reasonable expectations of paralegal licensees.

1. A licensed paralegal is held out to be knowledgeable, skilled and capable in his or her permissible area of practice. A client hires a legal service provider because the client does not have the knowledge and skill to deal with the legal system on his or her own. When a client hires a paralegal, the client expects that the paralegal is competent and has the ability to properly deal with the client's case.

2. A paralegal should not undertake a matter without honestly feeling competent to handle it, or being able to become competent without undue delay, risk, or expense to the client. *This is an ethical consideration and is distinct from the standard of care that a tribunal would invoke for purposes of determining negligence.*

• • •

4. Competence is founded upon both ethical and legal principles. Competence involves more than an understanding of legal principles; it involves an adequate knowledge of the practice and procedures by which such principles can be effectively applied. To accomplish this, the paralegal should keep abreast of developments in all areas of law in which the paralegal provides legal services. [Guideline 6; emphasis added]

In addition to any remedies sought by a client who has suffered damage or harm as a result of a paralegal's lack of competence, an incompetent paralegal may also be subject to disciplinary action by the Law Society.

Paralegals who fail to meet standards of professional competence when providing legal services to the public may cause harm to their clients, and to their business partners and associates. They may also bring the paralegal profession and the justice system into disrepute.

The Competent Paralegal (Rules 3.01(1)–(3))

The duty of competence is mandatory. A paralegal shall perform any services undertaken on a client's behalf to the standard of a competent paralegal (Rule 3.01(1)). You are required to recognize a task for which you lack competence and the disservice that would be done to the client by undertaking that task. You shall not undertake a matter without being competent to handle it or being able to become competent without undue delay or expense to the client (Rule 3.01(2)). You shall not undertake to represent a client in a matter unless you are familiar with the legal principles and procedures governing the applicable area of law, or are confident that you can become familiar with those legal principles and procedures in a timely and cost-effective manner.

In some cases you may be competent to represent the client at the commencement of the retainer, but because of circumstances or developments as the client matter goes forward that could not have been foreseen at its outset, your knowledge, skills, and attributes are no longer adequate. Rule 3.01(3) states:

> (3) If a paralegal discovers that he or she lacks the competence to complete the task for which he or she has been retained, the paralegal shall:
>
> (a) decline to act;
>
> (b) obtain the client's consent to retain, consult or collaborate with another licensee who is competent and licensed to perform that task; or
>
> (c) obtain the client's consent for the paralegal to become competent without undue delay, risk or expense to the client.

The client's consent shall be fully informed and voluntary after disclosure. It shall be given in writing or confirmed in writing.

When assessing your own competence, keep in mind that a lack of competence on your part may do the client a disservice, bring discredit to the paralegal profession, and bring the administration of justice into disrepute. The best time to turn your mind to this is before accepting the retainer, at which time you may decline to act if you are not satisfied that you possess the knowledge and skills required by the client matter. If you decline to act, you should consider recommending that the client seek other legal representation. You should also consider sending a non-engagement letter to the client confirming that you have not accepted the retainer and stating your reasons.

Sometimes a matter takes a direction that could not have been anticipated when you accepted the retainer. If you are no longer competent to act for a client because of unforeseen developments in an ongoing matter, and if the options stated in paragraphs (b) and (c) of Rule 3.01(3) are not workable in the circumstances, you shall withdraw from representation. Subject to restrictions upon withdrawal in criminal and quasi-criminal cases or the direction of a tribunal, lack of competence is a ground for mandatory withdrawal of legal representation (Rule 3.08(5)(c)).

Regardless of expertise, a paralegal licensee shall not provide legal services to a client in an unauthorized area of law. Clients with such matters should be directed to the Lawyer Referral Service or referred to a lawyer.

Limited Scope Retainers (Rules 3.02(15)–(17); Guideline 6)

Limited scope retainers are discussed in Chapter 3. A limited scope retainer is a retainer where the client hires you to provide part, but not all, of the legal services required in a client matter. The duty to provide competent representation applies to limited scope retainers.

> A paralegal may provide legal services under a limited scope retainer, but must carefully assess in each case whether, under the circumstances, it is possible to render those services in a competent manner. Although an agreement for such services does not exempt a paralegal from the duty to provide competent representation, the limitation is a factor to be considered when determining the legal knowledge, skill, thoroughness and preparation reasonably necessary for the representation. The paralegal should ensure that the client is fully informed of the nature of the arrangement and clearly understands the scope and limitation of the services (Guideline 6).

Who Is Competent? (Rule 3.01(4))

competent paralegal a paralegal who has and applies the relevant skills, attributes, and values appropriate to each matter undertaken on behalf of a client

A **competent paralegal** is a paralegal who has and applies the relevant knowledge, skills, and attributes appropriate to each matter undertaken on behalf of a client. Competence includes (Rule 3.01(4)):

> (a) knowing general legal principles and procedures and the substantive law and procedures for the legal services that the paralegal provides;
>
> (b) investigating facts, identifying issues, ascertaining client objectives, considering possible options, and developing and advising clients on appropriate courses of action;

(c) implementing, as each matter requires, the chosen course of action through the application of appropriate skills, including,

(i) legal research,
(ii) analysis,
(iii) application of the law to the relevant facts,
(iv) writing and drafting,
(v) negotiation,
(vi) alternative dispute resolution,
(vii) advocacy, and
(viii) problem-solving;

(d) representing the client in a conscientious, diligent, and cost-effective manner;

(e) communicating with the client at all relevant stages of a matter in a timely and effective manner;

(f) answering reasonable client requests in a timely and effective manner;

(g) ensuring that all applicable deadlines are met;

(h) managing one's practice effectively;

(i) applying intellectual capacity, judgment, and deliberation to all functions;

(j) pursuing appropriate training and development to maintain and enhance knowledge and skills;

(k) adapting to changing requirements, standards, techniques and practices; and

(l) complying in letter and in spirit with all requirements pursuant to the *Law Society Act*.

BOX 4.1 Should You Accept the Retainer?

Fact Situation

You are a licensed paralegal specializing in *Highway Traffic Act* matters. You also do some residential tenancies work.

You have been consulted by a residential tenant who has applied to the Landlord and Tenant Board for an abatement (reduction) of rent on grounds of non-repair of the premises by the landlord. The matter went to voluntary mediation, but did not settle. A hearing date has been set for two weeks' time. The tenant has come to you because she does not feel comfortable about attending at a hearing without representation.

The residential tenancies matters that you have handled have all been landlord applications for termination of the tenancy for non-payment of rent. You have several other matters that require your attention in the next few weeks, including a settlement conference, a Small Claims Court trial, and appearances in the Ontario Court of Justice.

Question for Discussion

Should you accept the retainer?

Knowledge and Investigation (Rules 3.01(4)(a), (b))

A competent paralegal is required to know general legal principles and procedures, and the substantive law and procedures for the legal services the paralegal provides (Rule 3.01(4)(a)). **Substantive law** is the statutory law and jurisprudence that creates, defines, and interprets the rights and obligations of those who are subject to it.

substantive law
the statutory law and jurisprudence that creates, defines, and interprets the rights and obligations of those who are subject to it

procedural law
the rules for judicial enforcement of a person's legal rights and obligations as set out in substantive law

Procedural law sets out the methods or procedures for enforcement of those rights or seeking redress for a wrong or harm.

In addition to knowing the law, the competent paralegal shall investigate facts, identify issues, ascertain client objectives, consider possible options, and advise the client on appropriate courses of action. You will gather, review, and consider all necessary information before advising the client as to a course or courses of action that will meet the client's goals. You will also ensure that you advise the client of any foreseeable risks and/or costs associated with the course of action.

Unless the client instructs otherwise, you should investigate the client matter in sufficient detail to be able to provide an opinion, even where you have been retained to provide services under a limited scope retainer. If the circumstances do not justify a detailed investigation with consequent expense to the client, you should state that in the opinion to the client.

If some or all of the client's objectives are not achievable, the client should be advised.

This process of evaluating facts and issues with reference to client goals and expectations should happen at every stage of the proceeding, as your knowledge of the facts, issues, and possible outcomes evolves.

Applying Skills and Judgment (Rules 3.01(4)(c), (i), (l))

A competent paralegal applies intellectual capacity, judgment, and deliberation to all functions. In every new client matter, a competent paralegal gathers, reviews, and considers all necessary and available information; uses her knowledge and judgment to form an opinion; and advises the client of courses of action appropriate to the client's goals and circumstances, as well as foreseeable risks and costs.

Having obtained the client's instructions, a competent paralegal then uses her judgment and the appropriate skills to implement the chosen course(s) of action. Appropriate skills include legal research, analysis, application of legal principles to the relevant facts, writing and drafting, negotiation, alternative dispute resolution, advocacy, and problem-solving. In this context, judgment means the capacity to assess situations or circumstances carefully, and make decisions that are reasonable and sensible in view of the client's circumstances.

professional judgment
the competent paralegal's capacity to assess situations or circumstances carefully and to make sensible decisions about client matters and her own conduct

The competent paralegal must also apply her **professional judgment** to client matters, as well as to her other activities as a paralegal. A competent paralegal knows the Rules and understands why each rule is important. The paralegal uses this knowledge and understanding to guide her own conduct.

The Introduction to the Guidelines states:

> Neither the *Rules* nor the Guidelines can cover every situation; they should be interpreted and applied with common sense and in a manner consistent with the public interest and the integrity of the profession. It is expected that a paralegal will exercise his or her professional judgment in interpreting the Guidelines, keeping in mind the paralegal's obligations to the client, the court or tribunal and the Law Society.

Client Service and Communication (Rules 3.01(4)(d), (e), (f), (g))

A competent paralegal represents the client in a conscientious, diligent, and cost-effective manner; ensures that all applicable deadlines are met; and communicates effectively with the client. Effective communication includes communicating with the client at all relevant stages of a matter in a timely and effective manner, and answering reasonable client requests in a timely and effective manner.

Guideline 6 notes that client service is an important part of competence:

> Most of the complaints received by the Law Society relate to client service, such as not communicating with a client, delay, not following client instructions, and not doing what the paralegal or lawyer was retained to do.
>
> Rule 3.01(4) contains important requirements for paralegal–client communication and service. In addition to those requirements, a paralegal can provide more effective client service by
>
> - keeping the client informed regarding his or her matter, through all relevant stages of the matter and concerning all aspects of the matter,
> - managing client expectations by clearly establishing with the client what the paralegal will do or accomplish and at what cost, and
> - being clear about what the client expects, both at the beginning of the retainer and throughout the retainer.
>
> A paralegal should meet deadlines, unless the paralegal is able to offer a reasonable explanation and ensure that no prejudice to the client will result. Whether or not a specific deadline applies, a paralegal should be prompt in prosecuting a matter, responding to communications and reporting developments to the client. In the absence of developments, contact with the client should be maintained to the extent the client reasonably expects.

A written confirmation of the terms of the paralegal–client retainer at the outset of the paralegal–client retainer by way of a retainer agreement or engagement letter is an excellent communication tool for managing client expectations about the legal services to be provided by the paralegal and the cost of those services, along with the other terms of the contractual relationship, including billing practices, the money retainer, events that would lead to termination of the retainer, and so on. Retainer agreements and engagement letters are discussed in Chapter 3. You will find samples at Appendixes 3.1 and 3.2.

When providing services under a limited scope retainer, it is very important to identify clearly the services that will be provided and those that will not be provided to the client under the limited scope retainer. A written retainer agreement, signed back to you by the client, is recommended in these circumstances.

You should be cautious about giving unqualified assurances at the commencement of the paralegal–client relationship, when you may not have complete information about the client matter. Any opinions about outcomes that you provide at the commencement of the retainer should clearly state the facts, law, circumstances, and assumptions upon which you are relying, and should be confirmed in writing by way of a retainer agreement or engagement letter.

During the course of the retainer, as your knowledge of the facts and issues evolves, you may find that the outcomes you predicted at the outset of the retainer are no longer achievable. Or your client's expectations may change over time, so that the retainer agreement or engagement letter no longer addresses the client's goals. In either of these cases, you must advise the client of the situation immediately and obtain the client's instructions. You should confirm the client's instructions and the particulars of any new agreement in writing.

The economics of a small paralegal practice may not always be conducive to effective client communication. If you operate a busy legal services practice that depends on competitive fees and high volume to generate profit, you may be disinclined to confirm every client retainer in writing, or keep the client informed of steps being taken in the matter. It may not seem cost-effective to report the outcome to the client in writing. However, it is sound practice management to do these things. Not doing them may adversely affect the quality of your service to clients, cause damage to the paralegal–client relationship, and bring the paralegal profession into disrepute.

BOX 4.2 Reminder: Write It Down!

Keep a Record and File It

In Tim Lemieux's online article "Is anyone listening?" (published by the Lawyers' Professional Indemnity Company in *LawPro Magazine*) he notes that one of the biggest issues that arises when a client complains about a lawyer's failure to follow instructions is the lawyer's failure to document those instructions.

One of the most important things to remember when consulting with a client is: *always keep a record of the client's instructions*. When the consultation is concluded, *put the record of the client's instructions in the client file*. A written record of client instructions gives a licensee something to refer to and follow when implementing client instructions, and protects the licensee in the event that a dispute arises with the client as to what the client's instructions were.

During the initial consultation, and subsequently as the client matter goes forward, you should take notes of all conversations with and advice to the client, and the client's instructions to you. You should keep a written record of every telephone conversation.

Copies of all notes and correspondence should be kept in an appropriate subfile in the client file. This will assist you in the event of an action in negligence and/or disciplinary action by the Law Society.

Paralegal Practice Tip: Initial Client Consultation

During the initial consultation, you should take detailed notes of what the client says and of what you say to the client. You may wish to use a standard checklist that covers topics such as:

- how the client heard about you (for marketing purposes);
- confirmation or verification of the client's identity;
- confidentiality;
- conflicts of interest;
- the nature of the client's problem;
- approaching procedural deadlines or limitation periods;
- whether the client's matter falls within authorized areas of paralegal practice;
- whether the client's matter falls within your areas of professional competence;
- the client's goals expectations;
- if you feel competent to give an opinion at the initial consultation, the client's options;
- the legal services you can provide, and their cost.

If the client indicates that she wishes to retain you, you should go over the terms of the paralegal–client retainer with the client at the initial consultation, and confirm those terms in writing by way of a retainer agreement or engagement letter.

Practice Management (Rule 3.01(4)(h))

A competent paralegal is required to manage his practice effectively. Effective practice management means having staff, systems, policies, and procedures in place to ensure that you can meet your professional obligations.

> In a busy office, practice management includes ensuring that there is sufficient staff to assist the paralegal in fulfilling his or her professional responsibilities, for example, ensuring that communications from clients, other paralegals or lawyers are responded to and that financial records are kept in accordance with the requirements of By-law 9.
>
> Competent practice management requires that the paralegal effectively manage his or her staff, time, finances and client information. A paralegal should consider the following practice management tools:
>
> - workplace policies and business procedures for staff,
> - planning and reminder systems, and time docketing systems for time management, and
> - filing, organizational and storage systems for management of client information and a system for effectively identifying and avoiding conflicts (Guideline 6).

Appropriate technology can be very helpful in managing a busy legal services practice efficiently and cost-effectively.

Practice management is discussed in more detail in Chapter 7.

Continuing Professional Development (Rules 3.01(4)(j), (k); By-law 6.1)

A competent paralegal pursues appropriate training and development to maintain knowledge and skills, in order to adapt to changing requirements, standards, techniques, and practices.

> A paralegal is responsible for remaining competent throughout his or her career. A competent paralegal understands that maintaining competence is an ongoing professional commitment that requires the paralegal to constantly assess his or her knowledge and skills (Guideline 6).

As of this writing, the Law Society requires licensees who are practising law or providing legal services to complete at least 12 hours of continuing professional development (CPD) in each calendar year (By-law 6.1). The 12-hour minimum consists of a minimum of three "professionalism hours" and a minimum of nine "substantive hours." Professionalism hours are time spent on topics related to ethics, professionalism, and/or practice management. Professionalism hours must be accredited by the Law Society of Upper Canada. Substantive hours are time spent on substantive or procedural law topics and related skills. Some non-legal subjects may be eligible for use as substantive hours if they are relevant to the licensee's practice and professional development.

Lawyers and paralegals in the 100 percent fee-paying category are subject to the mandatory CPD requirement. Lawyers and paralegals in other fee categories who are providing legal services to clients, including as a life member or on a *pro bono* basis in a program or Legal Aid clinic approved by Pro Bono Law Ontario, are also subject to the mandatory CPD requirement (By-law 6.1, s. 2(1)).

A licensee to whom the CPD requirement applies is required to report annually to the Law Society with respect to eligible CPD activities completed in that year. A licensee to whom the CPD requirement applies shall keep all documents substantiating the licensee's completion of the eligible activities reported by her or him in a particular year until December 31 of the year following the year in which the activities were reported.

For current information on CPD, refer to By-law 6.1 and to the Continuing Professional Development Requirement materials at the Law Society website.

Failing to Be Competent

A paralegal should not undertake a matter without honestly feeling competent to handle it, or being able to become competent without undue delay, risk, or expense to the client. This is an ethical consideration. It is distinct from the standard of care that a tribunal would invoke for purposes of determining negligence.

Guideline 6 states:

> The *Rules* do not require a standard of perfection. An error or omission, even though it might be actionable for damages in negligence or contract, will not necessarily constitute a breach of Rule 3.01. Conversely, incompetent professional practice may constitute professional misconduct whether or not the error or omission is actionable through the courts for professional negligence. While damages may be awarded for negligence, incompetence can give rise to the additional sanction of disciplinary action.

Advising Clients (Rule 3.02; Guideline 7)

Quality of Service (Rules 3.02(1)–(3))

Rule 3.02 sets out at subrules (1) to (3) a paralegal's obligations when advising clients.

> (1) A paralegal has a duty to provide courteous, thorough and prompt service to clients. The quality of service required of a paralegal is service that is competent, timely, conscientious, diligent, efficient and civil.
>
> (2) A paralegal shall be honest and candid when advising clients.
>
> (3) A paralegal shall not undertake or provide advice with respect to a matter that is outside his or her permissible scope of practice.

Honesty and Candour

honest and candid being truthful, forthright, and sincere, and looking at both sides of each issue without bias

Being **honest and candid** means being truthful, forthright, and sincere, and looking at both sides of each issue without bias.

> A paralegal has a duty of candour with the client on matters relevant to the retainer. A paralegal is required to inform the client of information known to the paralegal that may affect the interests of the client in the matter.

A paralegal must honestly and candidly advise the client regarding the law and the client's options, possible outcomes and risks of his or her matter, so that the client is able to make informed decisions and give the paralegal appropriate instructions regarding the case. Fulfillment of this professional responsibility may require a difficult but necessary conversation with a client and/or delivery of bad news. It can be helpful for advice that is not well-received by the client to be given or confirmed by the paralegal in writing.

When advising a client, a paralegal

- should explain to and obtain agreement from the client about what legal services the paralegal will provide and at what cost. Subject to any specific instructions or agreement, the client does not direct every step taken in a matter. Many decisions made in carrying out the delivery of legal services are the responsibility of the paralegal, not the client, as they require the exercise of professional judgment. However, the paralegal and the client should agree on the specific client goals to be met as a result of the retainer. This conversation is particularly important in the circumstances of a limited scope retainer.
- should explain to the client under what circumstances he or she may not be able to follow the client's instructions (for example, where the instructions would cause the paralegal to violate the *Rules*).
- should ensure that clients understand that the paralegal is not a lawyer and should take steps to correct any misapprehension on the part of a client, or prospective client (Guideline 7).

You shall never undertake or provide advice regarding a matter that is outside the scope of permitted practice for paralegals.

Bad News

Clients like to hear good news. If they intend to commence an action for damages in Small Claims Court, they want to hear that they have a good case and will get the result they are seeking. If they are trying to terminate a residential tenancy, they want to hear that they will get an eviction order. If they are disputing a speeding ticket, they want to hear that the proceeding will be quashed due to irregularities on the face of the charging document.

Your duty to be honest and candid applies when the news is good and when it is bad. The downside of being honest and candid about bad news is that, if the client is not happy with what he hears, he may seek legal assistance elsewhere. In a competitive market, it can be difficult to let any client walk out the door, however unreasonable his expectations. Nonetheless, your professional duty requires you to give honest, candid advice as to the merits of the matter and whether the client's objectives are achievable.

Guideline 7 recommends that advice that is not well received by the client be given in writing, or confirmed in writing.

The Retainer

At the outset of the retainer you must honestly and candidly advise the client regarding the law and the client's options, as well as possible outcomes and risks, so that the client is able to make informed decisions and give you appropriate instructions in the matter. You should discuss with the client the scope of the retainer—that is, what legal services you will provide, and at what cost—and obtain agreement from the client. The terms of the retainer should be confirmed in writing by way of a retainer agreement or engagement letter.

In the case of a limited scope retainer, you shall confirm the services to be provided in writing and give the client a copy when it is practicable to do so (Rule 3.02(16)). It is recommended that you use a retainer agreement to confirm a limited scope retainer (Guideline 14). The retainer agreement should state both the legal services that will be provided under the terms of the retainer, and the legal services that will not be provided, so that there is no confusion or misapprehension on the part of the client as to the scope of the retainer.

Generally, you do not have to seek client instructions for decisions that require the exercise of your professional judgment as to how the matter should proceed. However, you should explain the circumstances in which you may not be able to accept or act on the client's instructions—if, for instance, following the client's instructions would cause you to violate the Rules.

BOX 4.3 When Should I Ask My Client for Instructions?

Clients hire you because you have professional knowledge and competence that they do not, and they pay you for that knowledge and competence.

If you are representing a plaintiff in a Small Claims Court proceeding, you are expected to apply your knowledge and skills to advancing the matter through the various procedural stages without seeking the client's instructions at every stage. Doing otherwise would be a waste of your time and the client's money. However, you should keep the client informed of the progress of the matter.

What if the defendant makes a proposal of terms of payment? You should inform your client of the proposal. Keeping in mind your duty to promote compromise and settlement, you should advise him whether you think the proposal is reasonable or unreasonable, and why. Depending on the circumstances, you may wish to advise your client to dispute the proposal of terms of payment by requesting a terms of payment hearing.

The final decision must be the client's, unless you have a written agreement or written instructions to the contrary.

In a provincial offences or criminal matter, you should never enter into an agreement with a prosecutor about a guilty plea without first advising your client about the prospects for an acquittal and the consequences of the guilty plea, ensuring that the client understands the elements of the offence, and obtaining the client's voluntary instructions to agree to the guilty plea.

Dishonesty, Fraud, or Crime by a Client or Others (Rules 3.02(4)–(8))

A paralegal shall not knowingly assist in or encourage any dishonesty, fraud, crime, or illegal conduct. A paralegal shall not advise a client or any other person on how to violate the law and avoid punishment (Rule 3.02(4)).

When you are retained by a client, you shall make reasonable efforts to ascertain the purpose and objectives of the retainer, and to obtain information about the client that is necessary to fulfill your obligation under Rule 3.02(4) (Rule 3.02(5)).

> A paralegal must be alert to the warning signs that may indicate dishonesty or illegal conduct by a client or any other person. The paralegal may need to, or be forced to, withdraw from representing a client where the client takes part in this type of dishonourable conduct.
>
> The requirement in subrule (5) is especially important where a paralegal has suspicions or doubts about whether he or she might be assisting a client in crime or fraud. For example, if a paralegal is consulted by a prospective client who requests the paralegal to deposit an amount of cash into the paralegal's trust account but is vague about the purpose of the retainer, the paralegal has an obligation to make further inquiries about the retainer. The paralegal should also have regard to the provisions of By-law 9 regarding cash transactions. The paralegal should make a record of the results of these inquiries (Guideline 7).

You shall not use your trust account for purposes not related to the provision of legal services (Rule 3.02(6)).

You shall not act or do anything or omit to do anything in circumstances where you ought to know that, by acting, doing the thing, or omitting to do the thing, you are being used by a client, by a person associated with a client, or by any other person to facilitate dishonesty, fraud, crime, or illegal conduct (Rule 3.02(7)).

> A client or another person may attempt to use a paralegal's trust account for improper purposes, such as hiding funds, money laundering, or tax sheltering. These situations highlight the fact that when handling trust funds, it is important for a paralegal to be aware of his or her obligations under the Rules and the Law Society's By-Laws regulating the handling of trust funds (Guideline 7).

When accepting cash, you should keep in mind the provisions regarding cash transactions in By-law 9, Part III. You shall not receive or accept from a person, in respect of any one client file, cash in an aggregate amount of Canadian $7,500 or more, or its equivalent in foreign currency (By-law 9, s. 4(1)). Section 4(1) applies to any transaction involving funds, if you receive or pay them, or transfer them by any means (s. 5), unless the transaction falls within one of the exemptions in s. 6. "Funds" means cash, currency, securities and negotiable instruments, or other financial instruments that indicate the person's title or interest in them.

Cash transactions are problematic. You should be wary of a person who insists on paying with cash. You should consider implementing a policy of not accepting cash payments, or accepting cash payments in a limited amount. Clients should be advised of this policy at the initial consultation and in the written retainer agreement or engagement letter.

Dishonest or Fraudulent Activity by an Organization (Rule 3.02(8))

If you are employed or retained by an organization to act in a matter in which you know that the organization has acted, is acting, or intends to act dishonestly, fraudulently, criminally, or illegally, then you shall do the following in addition to your obligations under Rule 3.02(4) (Rule 3.02(8)):

> (a) advise the person from whom the paralegal takes instructions and the chief legal officer, or both the chief legal officer and the chief executive officer, that the conduct is, was or would be dishonest, fraudulent, criminal, or illegal and should be stopped,
>
> (b) if necessary because the person from whom the paralegal takes instructions, the chief legal officer, or the chief executive officer refuses to cause the conduct to be stopped, advise progressively the next highest persons or groups, including ultimately, the board of directors, the board of trustees, or the appropriate committee of the board, that the conduct was, is or would be dishonest, fraudulent, criminal, or illegal and should be stopped, and
>
> (c) if the organization, despite the paralegal's advice, continues with or intends to pursue the wrongful conduct, withdraw from acting in the matter in accordance with rule 3.08.

Rule 3.02(8) speaks of conduct that is dishonest, fraudulent, criminal, or illegal, and this conduct would include acts of omission as well as acts of commission. Conduct likely to result in substantial harm to the organization, as opposed to genuinely trivial misconduct by an organization, would invoke these rules (Guideline 7).

Withdrawal from representation (Rule 3.08) is discussed under the heading "Withdrawal from Representation" in this chapter.

Threatening Criminal Proceedings (Rules 3.02(9), (10), 3.08(5), 4.01(5))

A paralegal's duty of integrity and civility requires that a paralegal should not threaten others. Rule 3.02(9) prohibits the following conduct:

> (9) A paralegal shall not, in an attempt to gain a benefit for a client, threaten, or advise a client to threaten:
>
> (a) to initiate or proceed with a criminal or quasi-criminal charge; or
>
> (b) to make a complaint to regulatory authority.

Rule 3.02(9)(b) does not apply to an application made in good faith to a regulatory authority for a benefit to which a client may be legally entitled (Rule 3.02(10)).

When representing a complainant or potential complainant, a paralegal advocate shall not attempt to gain a benefit for a complainant by threatening the laying of a criminal charge or by offering to seek or to procure the withdrawal of a criminal charge (Rule 4.01(5)(n)).

Subject to the direction of a tribunal, you shall withdraw from representation if your client in a litigation matter instructs you to advise another party that you will have criminal charges laid against them if they do not accede to your client's demands (Rule 3.08(5)(b)).

It is an abuse of a tribunal's process to threaten to make or to make a complaint in order to gain an advantage in a civil action, even if the client in the civil action has a legitimate claim for damages.

Settlement and Dispute Resolution (Rules 3.02(11), (12))

A paralegal shall advise and encourage a client to compromise or settle a dispute whenever it is possible to do so on a reasonable basis, and shall discourage the client from commencing or continuing useless legal proceedings (Rule 3.02(11)).

The paralegal shall consider the use of alternative dispute resolution (ADR) when appropriate, inform the client of ADR options, and, if so instructed, take steps to pursue those options (Rule 3.02(12)). **Alternative dispute resolution** is resolution of a dispute through negotiation, mediation, arbitration, or similar means, instead of litigation.

alternative dispute resolution
resolution of a dispute through negotiation, mediation, arbitration, or similar means, instead of litigation

Some tribunals have early resolution processes built into their procedure. The Landlord and Tenant Board offers voluntary mediation services to landlords and tenants in applications filed under the *Residential Tenancies Act*. Mediation is a mandatory first step in dispute resolution in Statutory Accident Benefits Schedule claims under the *Insurance Act*. In *Provincial Offences Act* prosecutions in the Ontario Court of Justice, defendants charged in designated jurisdictions have the option of requesting a meeting with the prosecutor to discuss resolution of the offence instead of going directly to trial (*Provincial Offences Act*, s. 5.1). In a proceeding in the Small Claims Court, early resolution is encouraged by the obligation of mandatory full disclosure by all parties at every stage of the proceeding (Rules of the Small Claims Court, Rules 7.01(2)2, 9.02(1)2, 10.01(4)2); the proposal of terms of payment option on the Form 9A Defence (Rules of the Small Claims Court, Rule 9.03); and mandatory attendance by all parties at a settlement conference which must take place by no later than 90 days after the first defence has been filed (Rules of the Small Claims Court, Rule 13).

Useless Legal Proceedings

Ultimately, it is the client's decision whether or not to commence a legal proceeding. Your role is to gather information about a client matter; ascertain the client's goals; and give the client honest, candid advice about the merits and weaknesses of the matter, its potential outcomes and potential risks, its cost, and so on.

The best possible outcome for a prospective client is not always achieved by a legal proceeding. In some cases, it may be advisable to take no legal action at all. Some clients believe that a sense of grievance—of having been wronged by others—automatically entitles them to some sort of remedy at law. If you are satisfied—based on the information provided by the client at the initial consultation, your knowledge of the applicable law, and your review of any additional information or resources that you consider necessary—that there is no legal basis for commencing a proceeding, you must advise the client of this at or soon after the initial consultation. If you have advised a prospective client that you believe his claim to be wholly without merit, and the client instructs you to commence a proceeding, you should consider declining the retainer. You should advise the client of your decision, and confirm it in writing in a non-engagement letter.

Client with Diminished Capacity (Rules 3.02(13), (14))

A client with diminished capacity is a client whose capacity to make decisions is impaired because of minority, mental disability, illiteracy, or for some other reason. You shall, as far as reasonably possible, maintain a normal professional relationship with a client with diminished capacity (Rule 3.02(13)).

A paralegal must be particularly sensitive to the individual needs of a client with diminished capacity. You should maintain a good professional relationship with the client, even if the client's ability to make decisions is impaired. You should also be aware of your duty to accommodate a client with diminished capacity (Guideline 7).

If the disability is such that the client no longer has the capacity to manage his legal affairs, you shall take appropriate steps that are within the scope of permitted practice for paralegals to have a lawfully authorized representative appointed (Rule 3.02(14)), keeping in mind your duty of confidentiality to the client. If the procedures for appointment of a lawfully authorized representative are outside the scope of permitted practice for paralegals, the matter must be referred to a lawyer.

Medical–Legal Reports (Rules 3.02(18)–(20))

In the course of providing legal services to a client, you may be required to obtain a medical–legal report from a physician or other health professional containing that person's opinion or findings on the client's mental and/or physical health or other matters. In these circumstances, you will need to consider whether the findings in the report advance or harm the client's cause, and also whether the findings in the report may cause injury or harm to the client.

Where the findings in the report do not advance the client's cause, Guideline 7 recommends the following:

> On occasion, in the course of representing and advising a client, a paralegal may need to obtain a report from an expert to help the client's case. Since a medical–legal report may contain information sensitive to the client, a paralegal has special responsibilities where such reports are concerned.
>
> After an expert has been hired, but before the report has been prepared, the paralegal should speak to the expert to see if the findings in the report will advance the client's cause. If the findings do not, and subject to any legal requirements, the paralegal may decide not to obtain a *written* report.

Rules 3.02(18), (19), and (20) speak to situations where the findings in the report may cause injury or harm to the client.

A paralegal who receives a medical–legal report from a physician or health professional that is accompanied by a proviso that it not be shown to the client shall return the report immediately to the physician or health professional, without making a copy, unless the paralegal has received specific instructions to accept the report on that basis (Rule 3.02(18)). The client's consent to this arrangement shall be fully informed and voluntary, and confirmed in writing.

A paralegal who receives a medical–legal report from a physician or health professional containing opinions or findings that, if disclosed, might cause harm or injury to the client, shall attempt to dissuade the client from seeing the report but, if the client insists, the paralegal shall produce the report (Rule 3.02(19)).

If a client insists on seeing a medical–legal report about which the paralegal has reservations for the reasons noted in subrule (19), the paralegal shall recommend that the client attend at the office of the physician or health professional to see the report, in order that the client will have the benefit of the expertise of the physician or health professional in understanding the significance of the conclusions contained in the medical–legal report (Rule 3.02(20)).

Errors (Rule 3.02(21))

You have specific duties to fulfill if you discover an error or omission. An **error** is an action by a legal representative that may result in harm to a client. An **omission** is a failure to act by a legal representative that may result in harm to a client.

error
an action by a legal representative that may cause harm to a client

omission
a failure to act by a legal representative that may cause harm to a client

You are accountable for your own errors and omissions in matters for which you are responsible, and for those of any persons acting under your supervision in matters for which you are responsible. Rule 3.02(21) states:

> (21) If, in connection with a matter for which a paralegal is responsible, the paralegal discovers an error or omission that is or may be damaging to the client and that cannot be rectified readily, the paralegal shall
>
> (a) promptly inform the client of the error or omission, being careful not to prejudice any rights of indemnity that either of them may have under an insurance, client's protection or indemnity plan, or otherwise;
>
> (b) recommend that the client obtain legal advice elsewhere concerning any rights the client may have arising from the error or omission; and
>
> (c) advise the client that, in the circumstances, the paralegal may no longer be able to act for the client.

As well, you must give prompt notice to your errors and omissions insurer of the circumstances giving rise to a possible claim, so that the client's protection from that source will not be prejudiced. When giving notice to the insurer, you must be careful to observe your duty of confidentiality to the client.

Official Language Rights (Rule 3.02(22))

French and English are the two official languages of Canada. When advising French-speaking clients, you shall, where appropriate, inform them of their language rights, including their right to be represented by a paralegal who is competent to provide legal services in the French language.

Guideline 7 recommends that you refer to the following, where appropriate, when advising the client:

- Subsection 19(1) of the *Constitution Act, 1982* on the use of French or English in any court established by Parliament,
- Section 530 of the *Criminal Code* (Canada) on an accused's right to a trial before a court that speaks the official language of Canada that is the language of the accused,
- Section 126 of the *Courts of Justice Act* that requires that a proceeding in which the client is a party be conducted as a bilingual (English and French) proceeding, and
- Subsection 5(1) of the *French Language Services Act* for services available in French from Ontario government agencies and legislative institutions.

Confidentiality (Rule 3.03; Guideline 8)

Confidential Information (Rules 3.03(1)–(3))

The Duty

Rule 3.03(1) states:

> (1) A paralegal shall, at all times, hold in strict confidence all information concerning the business and affairs of a client acquired in the course of their professional relationship and shall not disclose any such information unless:
> (a) expressly or impliedly authorized by the client;
> (b) required by law or by order of a tribunal of competent jurisdiction to do so;
> (c) required to provide the information to the Law Society; or
> (d) otherwise permitted by this rule.

The duty of confidentiality begins at the commencement of the paralegal–client relationship. It continues indefinitely after the paralegal has ceased to act for the client, whether or not differences have arisen between them (Rule 3.03(2)).

The paralegal shall keep the client's papers and other property out of sight and out of reach of those not entitled to see them (Rule 3.03(3)).

Guideline 8 provides the following context for the duty of confidentiality:

1. A paralegal cannot render effective professional service to a client, unless there is full and unreserved communication between them. The client must feel completely secure that all matters discussed with the paralegal will be held in strict confidence. The client is entitled to proceed on this basis, without any express request or stipulation.
2. A paralegal's duty of loyalty to a client prohibits the paralegal from using any client information for a purpose other than serving the client in accordance with the terms of the retainer. A paralegal cannot disclose client information to serve another client or for his or her own benefit.

The duty of confidentiality arises out of the fiduciary relationship between the paralegal and the client. As a fiduciary, the paralegal is required to act with scrupulous good faith, honesty, and candour for the benefit of the client. The paralegal must put the client's interests ahead of her own in all dealings with the client. The client is entitled to place absolute confidence, reliance, and trust in the paralegal. For that relationship of absolute trust to exist, the client must have complete confidence that information shared with the paralegal will not be passed on to others, except with the client's authorization or as required by law or the Rules. The client must also have complete confidence that information shared with the paralegal will not be used for a purpose other than serving the client.

The Scope of the Duty (Rules 3.03(1), (3))

The duty of confidentiality applies to all information of any kind that you acquire from or on behalf of a client during the paralegal–client relationship, including the client's identity and the fact that the client has consulted or retained you. It also applies to information that is not relevant to the specific matter for which you have been retained, and to information about the client that others may already have. Guideline 8 explains that:

> The obligation to protect client information extends to information whether or not it is relevant or irrelevant to the matter for which the paralegal is retained. The source of the information does not matter. The information could be received from the client or from others. The information may come in any form—the spoken word, paper, computer documents, e-mails, audio or video recordings. The obligation also extends to the client's papers and property, the client's identity and the fact that the client has consulted or retained the paralegal.
>
> A paralegal should be cautious in accepting confidential information on an informal or preliminary basis from anyone, since possession of the information may prevent the paralegal from subsequently acting for another party in the same or a related matter.
>
> Generally, unless the nature of the matter requires such disclosure, a paralegal should not disclose having been retained by a person about a particular matter, or consulted by a person about a particular matter, whether or not a paralegal–client relationship has been established between them.

The duty of confidentiality is owed to all clients of your paralegal firm by all licensees in the firm, including associates, as well as anyone in your employment or under your supervision, including students.

Any time you hire new staff or accept a new field placement student, you should consider requiring them to review Rule 3.03, the applicable Guidelines, and your firm confidentiality policy, and to sign a confidentiality agreement. A copy of the signed agreement should be placed in their personnel file. Your firm confidentiality policy should state the possible sanctions for breach of the duty by staff or students.

Duration of the Duty (Rule 3.03(2))

The duty of confidentiality arises when the paralegal–client relationship begins. It may apply to persons with whom there is no paralegal–client retainer, if confidential information is received from the person at the initial contact. It applies to prospective clients who consult with you, whether or not a paralegal–client retainer is entered

continuing client
a client for whom a paralegal acts in several different matters or transactions over a period of time

into. It applies to clients who have retained you in a single client matter, and to **continuing clients**. Continuing clients are clients who retain you in multiple client matters over a period of time.

Guideline 8 recommends that a paralegal should be cautious in accepting confidential information on an informal or preliminary basis from anyone, and notes that problems can arise when information is provided to a paralegal or a paralegal firm by a prospective client.

The duty of confidentiality continues indefinitely. This means that it continues:

- regardless of the nature or brevity of the initial contact, if confidential information about a person's matter was provided to the paralegal;
- regardless of whether or not a paralegal–client retainer was entered into;
- after the professional relationship has ended, and regardless of the circumstances in which it ended;
- after the paralegal–client retainer has ended; and
- after the death of the client or other person to whom you owe the duty.

Who Owes the Duty? (Rules 3.01(1), (3), 8.01(1))

The paralegal, and all other employees of the paralegal firm, owe the duty of confidentiality to every client. A paralegal must ensure that his or her employees, and anyone involved with the client's matter, understand the duty of confidentiality as set out in the Rules. The paralegal is ultimately responsible if someone employed by the paralegal discloses confidential information without client authorization or as permitted by the Rules (Guideline 8).

BOX 4.4 Confidentiality: Use of Precedent Documents

Fact Situation

You are a student in a Paralegal program at an Ontario college. You are completing your field placement requirement in the collections department at a law firm. You have been given a lot of interesting work to do in collections, and you have kept copies of many of the documents you worked on to use as precedents.

You are chatting about field placements with some classmates who are also on field placement one weekend. They are impressed by your enthusiasm and the quality of work that you are being given, and ask if they can take a look at your precedent binder. The four of you agree to meet for lunch on the following weekend.

The binder contains demand letters, reporting letters, Small Claims Court pleadings, and enforcement documents. At the lunch meeting, your classmates look through these documents with interest. They are particularly impressed by some of the corporate clients you have done work for.

Question for Discussion

Have you breached the duty of confidentiality?

Inadvertent Disclosure

Guideline 8 suggests that the following steps may assist a paralegal in meeting his or her obligation to protect confidential client information:

- not disclosing having been consulted or retained by a particular person unless the nature of the matter requires disclosure,
- taking care not to disclose to one client confidential information about another client and declining any retainer that might require such disclosure,
- being mindful of the risk of disclosure of confidential information when the paralegal provides legal services in association with other licensees in cost-sharing, space-sharing or other arrangements, and taking steps to minimize the risk,
- avoiding indiscreet conversations about a client's affairs, even with the paralegal's spouse or family,
- shunning any gossip about a client's affairs, even though the client is not named or otherwise identified,
- not repeating any gossip or information about a client's business or affairs that is overheard or recounted to the paralegal, and
- avoiding indiscreet shop-talk between colleagues that may be overheard by third parties.

You should never discuss a client or anything connected with a client matter with anyone not entitled to the information. Persons who are not entitled to client information include friends, spouses, partners, members of your family, and other licensees unless the nature of the client matter requires disclosure to a licensee. You should not share client information with any of the foregoing in any circumstances, even if the client is not named or otherwise identified and the discussion is couched in general terms.

You should never discuss client matters in public areas of the paralegal firm, where you may be overheard by non-members of the firm.

BOX 4.5 Confidentiality: Conversation with Friends

Fact Situation

You are a paralegal student completing your field placement requirement in a paralegal firm. At the end of the last week of your placement, you arrange to meet with some other students from your program at a local restaurant for drinks and dinner, to celebrate the end of placement. Over the course of the evening, you discuss a couple of your client files in general terms, without mentioning client names. People at adjoining tables can hear some of your remarks, but you think it is okay to talk about the files because the placement is over and no one will be able to figure out who you are talking about anyway.

Question for Discussion

Have you breached the duty of confidentiality?

Literary Works

You are not permitted to use confidential information about a client for your own benefit, for the benefit of third parties, or to the disadvantage of the client. This duty continues indefinitely. It applies whether you are writing a murder mystery, appearing on a television show to discuss your famous cases, or blogging.

If you intend to use confidential information about a living client in a publication of any kind, you must first obtain the client's fully informed, voluntary consent in writing. If the client is deceased, you should seek authorization from the client's estate.

Office Procedures

A paralegal shall assume complete professional responsibility for all business entrusted to him or her (Rule 8.01(1)). Among other things, this means that you are ultimately responsible for ensuring compliance with the duty of confidentiality in your firm. To ensure that the confidentiality of client information is protected, Guideline 8 recommends that a paralegal establish office procedures, such as:

- recording the identity and particulars of every client or potential client,
- screening for conflicts of interest when a potential client first contacts the firm, and prior to his or her disclosure of confidential information to the paralegal,
- establishing a communication policy with each client outlining how communications between the client and firm will be conducted,
- keeping file cabinets away from the reception area,
- placing computer screens so they cannot be viewed by people not in the firm,
- keeping client files out of sight,
- locking file cabinets when no one is in the office,
- limiting access to client files only to staff who work on the matter,
- shredding confidential information before discarding,
- ensuring appropriate security for off-site storage of files,
- taking steps to protect confidential information obtained and sent in an electronic form,
- ensuring that all staff understand their obligations with respect to confidentiality, and
- limiting access to confidential information by outside service providers.

An office policies and procedures manual is a useful management tool for improving staff efficiency and ensuring that staff, including field placement students, understand their obligations under the Rules and By-Laws. Practice management issues are discussed in Chapter 7.

Justified or Permitted Disclosure (Rules 3.03(1), (4)–(9))

In addition to stating the general duty of confidentiality, Rule 3.03(1) also provides four exceptions to the duty:

> (1) A paralegal shall, at all times, hold in strict confidence all information concerning the business and affairs of a client acquired in the course of their professional relationship and shall not disclose any such information unless:
>
> (a) expressly or impliedly authorized by the client;

(b) required by law or by order of a tribunal of competent jurisdiction to do so;
(c) required to provide the information to the Law Society; or
(d) otherwise permitted by this rule.

Disclosure with Client Authority (Rule 3.03(1)(a))

You may disclose confidential client information if the client authorizes the disclosure. Client authorization may be express or implied.

Implied Authorization

Implied authorization is not spoken or written down, but is implied by the paralegal–client relationship and the nature of the client matter. For example, where a paralegal is retained to represent a client in a Small Claims Court matter, the paralegal has the client's implied authority to disclose enough information to complete the necessary forms (Guideline 8). A paralegal also has implied authorization to disclose particulars of the client matter to partners, associates, and, to the extent necessary, non-licensee employees of the firm, unless the client directs otherwise. You must ensure that anyone to whom confidential client information is disclosed understands his or her duty to hold that information in strict confidence, both during employment with the firm and indefinitely afterward.

implied authorization
client authorization to reveal confidential information that is not spoken or written down, but is implied by the paralegal–client relationship and the nature of the client matter

Express Authorization

Express (or explicit) authorization means that the client provides you with fully informed and voluntary spoken or written authorization to disclose particular information to specified third parties. If the authorization is spoken, it shall be confirmed in writing as soon as is practicable. Guideline 8 recommends that you consider the following issues when considering disclosing confidential information with the express authorization of the client:

express (or explicit) authorization
fully informed and voluntary written or spoken authorization given by the client to the paralegal permitting disclosure of confidential information to specified third parties; if spoken, then the client shall receive a written confirmation of the consent as soon as is practicable

- whether the client understands his or her right to confidentiality,
- whether the client understands the potential implications of disclosure,
- whether the client has shown a clear, informed and voluntary intention to forego the right to confidentiality, and
- whether, in the particular circumstances, it would be prudent to obtain the client's written authorization to disclose.

If you decide that a written authorization is advisable, the written authorization should state, at a minimum:

- the extent of the disclosure,
- any restrictions on disclosure,
- the persons to whom disclosure will be provided, and
- the period of time for disclosure, if appropriate.

You should go over the terms of the disclosure with the client and ensure that the client understands those terms before the client signs the authorization.

BOX 4.6 Office Procedures

Fact Situation

You are a paralegal licensee. You run a small but profitable practice and have one employee, an office assistant named Dana.

Dana's workspace is set up in the reception area. A counter separates her workspace from the public area. Because your practice is a busy one, Dana's workspace is often covered with client files. Anyone standing at the counter can see the labels on the files, and the contents of any files that are open. Her computer monitor is visible from some parts of the public area. People waiting in the public area can overhear Dana's telephone conversations with clients.

For ready access, Dana keeps active files that she is not working on in a small, locked filing cabinet in her workspace in the reception area. Before she leaves at the end of the day, she is careful to refile any loose documents in the correct client files. She leaves the files she is working on in a neat pile by her computer monitor.

Questions for Discussion

1. Do your office procedures preserve client confidentiality?
2. If not, who is responsible for the breach of confidentiality? What can be done to remedy this?

Disclosure Without Client Authority: Justified or Permitted Disclosure (Rules 3.03(4)–(9))

Where the law or an order of a tribunal of competent jurisdiction requires that a paralegal shall disclose confidential information without the client's authorization to do so, the disclosure is said to be justified. **Justified disclosure** is mandatory.

justified disclosure mandatory disclosure of confidential information without the client's authority

permitted disclosure discretionary disclosure of confidential information by a paralegal without the client's authority

Where the rules state that a paralegal may reveal confidential information without the client's authorization to do so, the disclosure is said to be permitted. **Permitted disclosure** is discretionary on the part of the paralegal.

A paralegal shall not disclose more information than is necessary when he or she discloses confidential information as required or permitted by Rules 3.03(4) to (7) (Rule 3.03(9)).

Guideline 8 points out that Rule 3.03 does not permit a paralegal to reveal confidential information about past criminal conduct, or to prevent future illegal criminal conduct that does not involve death or serious bodily harm.

Justified Disclosure (Rules 3.03(4), (9))

A paralegal shall disclose confidential information when required by law or by order of a tribunal of competent jurisdiction.

If you are ordered by a court or tribunal to disclose confidential information, before complying with the order, you should first satisfy yourself that the court or tribunal has jurisdiction (that is, legal authority) to make the order. If you are not competent to determine this issue yourself, you should seek legal assistance.

If you are satisfied that the order is valid, you should advise your client of the terms of the order and of the obligation to comply with its terms.

You shall not disclose more information than is required by the court or tribunal order (Rule 3.03(9)).

Permitted Disclosure (Rules 3.03(5)–(9))

Permitted disclosure is at the discretion of the paralegal. Disclosure of confidential information without client authority is permitted in the following circumstances:

- if you believe upon reasonable grounds that there is an imminent risk of death or serious bodily harm, and disclosure is necessary to prevent the death or harm (Rule 3.03(5));
- to defend against allegations that you or your employees have committed a criminal offence involving a client's affairs (Rule 3.03(6)(a));
- to defend against allegations that you or your employees are civilly liable with respect to a matter involving a client's affairs (Rule 3.03(6)(b));
- to defend against allegations that you or your employees have committed acts of professional negligence (Rule 3.03(6)(c)); or
- to defend against allegations that you or your employees have engaged in acts of professional misconduct or conduct unbecoming a paralegal (Rule 3.03(6)(d));
- to establish or collect your fees (Rule 3.03(7)).

You may disclose confidential information to a lawyer or another paralegal to secure legal advice about your proposed conduct (Rule 3.03(8)).

You shall not disclose more confidential information than is necessary when disclosing confidential information as required or permitted by subrules (4), (5), (6), and (7) (Rule 3.03(9)).

IMMINENT RISK OF DEATH OR SERIOUS BODILY HARM (RULES 3.03(5), (8), (9))

You may reveal confidential information without client authority pursuant to Rule 3.03(5) if you believe on reasonable grounds that there is an imminent risk of death or serious bodily harm, and disclosure is necessary to prevent the harm.

> Serious psychological harm may constitute serious bodily harm if it substantially interferes with the health or well-being of an individual.
>
> A paralegal who believes that disclosure may be warranted may wish to seek legal advice. In assessing whether disclosure of confidential information is justified to prevent death or serious bodily harm, the paralegal should consider a number of factors, including:
>
> a) the likelihood that the potential injury will occur and its imminence;
> b) the apparent absence of any other feasible way to prevent the potential injury; and
> c) the circumstances under which the paralegal acquired the information of the client's intent or prospective course of action.
>
> If confidential information is disclosed, the paralegal should record the circumstances of the disclosure as soon as possible (Guideline 8).

Rule 3.03(5) does not permit you to reveal confidential information about past criminal conduct, or in order to prevent future illegal or criminal conduct that does not involve death or serious bodily harm (Guideline 8).

FUTURE HARM AND IMMINENT RISK

The harm must be something that will occur in the future. If a client confesses to a harm committed in the past, you shall keep the disclosure confidential.

"Imminent" means something that is pending—that is about to happen very soon. Generally, the client must threaten to commit the harm in the immediate future. On the subject of what constitutes imminence, the Supreme Court of Canada in *Smith v. Jones*, at para. 84, had this to say:

> The risk of serious bodily harm or death must be imminent if ... [confidential] communications are to be disclosed. That is, the risk itself must be serious: a serious risk of serious bodily harm. The nature of the threat must be such that it creates a sense of urgency. This sense of urgency may be applicable to some time in the future. Depending on the seriousness and clarity of the threat, it will not always be necessary to impose a particular time limit on the risk. It is sufficient if there is a clear and imminent threat of serious bodily harm ... , and if this threat is made in such a manner that a sense of urgency is created. A statement made in a fleeting fit of anger will usually be insufficient .... On the other hand, imminence as a factor may be satisfied if a person makes a clear threat to kill someone that he vows to carry out three years hence when he is released from prison. If that threat is made with such chilling intensity and graphic detail that a reasonable bystander would be convinced that the killing would be carried out, the threat could be considered to be imminent.

The threat must be unconditional. There must be no mention of intervening events or preconditions to causing the harm.

DEATH OR SERIOUS BODILY HARM

The imminent risk to the victim or victims must be death or serious bodily harm. Serious bodily harm includes serious psychological harm that substantially interferes with health or well-being—in other words, psychological damage that seriously undermines physical health.

REASONABLE GROUNDS

The test for reasonable grounds is both objective and subjective. Having heard the unconditional threat to cause death or serious bodily harm, you must decide whether a reasonable person would, in all of the circumstances, be convinced that the threat will be carried out by the person uttering it. This is the objective standard.

You must also personally believe, based on what you know of the client, her means and capacity for committing the harm threatened, and any other relevant circumstances, that she will carry out the threat. This is the subjective standard.

NECESSARY TO PREVENT DEATH OR HARM

Disclosure of confidential information without the client's authority is permitted only if all of the above conditions are satisfied and you are convinced that the disclosure is necessary to prevent the death or harm threatened by the client—in other words, the information necessary to prevent the harm is not available from any other source.

If it is practicable, you may consider applying to a court for an order permitting necessary disclosure.

You may wish to consider consulting with a lawyer or another paralegal to secure legal advice about your proposed conduct. This is a ground of permitted disclosure under Rule 3.03(8).

DEFENDING CIVIL LIABILITY OR ALLEGATIONS OF PROFESSIONAL NEGLIGENCE, MISCONDUCT, OR CONDUCT UNBECOMING A PARALEGAL (RULES 3.03(6), (8), (9))

You may, without client authority, reveal confidential information to defend against allegations that you or your employees:

- have committed a criminal offence involving a client's affairs;
- are civilly liable with respect to a matter involving a client's affairs;
- have committed acts of professional negligence; or
- have engaged in acts of professional misconduct or conduct unbecoming a paralegal (Rule 3.03(6)).

When responding to allegations of criminal wrongdoing or civil liability, you are permitted to disclose only as much confidential information as is necessary to defend yourself against the allegations (Rule 3.03(9)).

You may wish to consider consulting with a lawyer or another paralegal to secure legal advice about your proposed conduct. This is a ground of permitted disclosure under Rule 3.03(8).

BOX 4.7 Reminder: Keep a Written Record

If you find yourself in a situation to which Rule 3.03(5) may apply, you should consider taking several steps. First, if it is feasible in the circumstances, you should discuss your concerns with your client, and try to suggest solutions. If your client is unreceptive, you should carefully consider what you know of your client, and the likelihood that he will cause serious harm or death to himself or to others. If you are satisfied that your belief that serious harm or death will occur is reasonable, and that the serious harm or death is imminent, you should reveal only enough information to prevent it from occurring.

You should keep detailed notes of the circumstances that gave rise to your concerns, of any conversations with your client about your concerns, and of subsequent steps taken by you and your reasons for taking those steps. Your notes will be of assistance in the event of any future complaints or actions against you.

You may wish to consider consulting with a lawyer or another paralegal to secure legal advice about your proposed conduct. This is a ground of permitted disclosure under Rule 3.03(8).

ESTABLISHING OR COLLECTING FEES (RULES 3.03(7), (9))

A paralegal may disclose confidential information in order to establish or collect her fees.

You shall not disclose more confidential information than is necessary to establish a fee or collect an unpaid fee.

> If a paralegal wishes to use a collection agency for an outstanding account, the information provided to the collection agency should be limited to that necessary to collect the fees. Information contained in documents that is not necessary to enforce payment should either be deleted or blocked out (Guideline 8).

Other Obligations Relating to Confidential Disclosure

Security of Court Facilities (Rules 3.03, 6.01(3))

A paralegal who has reasonable grounds for believing that a dangerous situation is likely to develop at a court facility shall inform the persons having responsibility for security at the facility and give particulars. This professional obligation is mandatory.

If the paralegal's reasonable belief is based on confidential information, the paralegal shall consider her obligations under Rule 3.03. Guideline 8 recommends that a paralegal who discloses confidential information to prevent a dangerous situation from developing at a court facility should consider providing this information to the persons having responsibility for security at the facility anonymously, or through another paralegal or a lawyer.

Duty to Report Misconduct (Rules 3.03, 9.01(2))

A paralegal shall report professional misconduct to the Law Society unless to do so would be unlawful or would involve a breach of confidentiality between the paralegal and the paralegal's client. The obligation to report misconduct applies to the paralegal's own conduct, as well as that of other licensees.

If the paralegal learns of the misconduct of another licensee from a client, the paralegal must obtain the client's consent to disclose information about the client to the Law Society. The consent should be written or confirmed in writing.

If the client will not consent to disclosure of any information about herself to the Law Society, the paralegal must report the misconduct to the Law Society in a way that does not disclose any client information.

Rules 6.01(3) and 9.01(2) are discussed in more detail in Chapter 6.

Personal Information Protection and Electronic Documents Act (PIPEDA)

The *Personal Information Protection and Electronic Documents Act* (PIPEDA) applies to the collection, use, or disclosure of personal information by organizations in the course of any commercial activity within a province (s. 4(1)). Organizations and/or activities in provinces that have adopted substantially similar privacy legislation may be exempted from PIPEDA by the federal government. Because there is no substantially similar privacy legislation that applies to commercial activity in the province, PIPEDA applies to commercial activity in Ontario.

PIPEDA sets up procedures for the collection, use, and disclosure of personal information. These procedures are intended to give individuals control over how their personal information is handled in the private sector. An organization is responsible for the protection of personal information and the fair handling of it at all times, both within the organization and in dealings with third parties.

In the course of providing legal services to the public, a paralegal collects, uses, and discloses personal information about clients. That information is already protected by your professional and ethical duty to hold client information in strict confidence, and not to disclose it except with the client's authorization or as required by law. However, because paralegal firms are engaged in commercial activity in Ontario, PIPEDA applies to the provision of legal services. You must implement a privacy policy and procedures in compliance with PIPEDA requirements.

"Complying with the *Personal Information Protection and Electronic Documents Act*," a fact sheet prepared by the Office of the Privacy Commissioner of Canada, outlines the Act's requirements. The fact sheet sets out the private sector's responsibilities under PIPEDA as follows:

1. **Accountability:** Appoint an individual (or individuals) to be responsible for your organization's compliance; protect all personal information held by your organization or transferred to a third party for processing; and develop and implement personal information policies and practices.
2. **Identifying purposes:** Your organization must identify the reasons for collecting personal information before or at the time of collection. Before or when any personal information is collected, identify why it is needed and how it will be used; document why the information is collected; inform the individual from whom the information is collected why it is needed; identify any new purpose for the information and obtain the individual's consent before using it.
3. **Consent:** Inform the individual in a meaningful way of the purposes for the collection, use or disclosure of personal data; obtain the individual's consent before or at the time of collection, as well as when a new use is identified.
4. **Limiting collection:** Do not collect personal information indiscriminately; do not deceive or mislead individuals about the reasons for collecting personal information.
5. **Limiting use, disclosure, and retention:** Use or disclose personal information only for the purpose for which it was collected, unless the individual consents, or the use or disclosure is authorized by the Act; keep personal information only as long as necessary to satisfy the purposes; put guidelines and procedures in place for retaining and destroying personal information; keep personal information used to make a decision about a person for a reasonable time period. This should allow the person to obtain the information after the decision and pursue redress; destroy, erase or render anonymous information that is no longer required for an identified purpose or a legal requirement.
6. **Accuracy:** Minimize the possibility of using incorrect information when making a decision about the individual or when disclosing information to third parties.
7. **Safeguards:** Protect personal information against loss or theft; safeguard the information from unauthorized access, disclosure, copying, use or modification; protect personal information regardless of the format in which it is held.

8. **Openness:** Inform your customers, clients and employees that you have policies and practices for the management of personal information; make these policies and practices understandable and easily available.
9. **Individual access:** When requested, inform individuals if you have any personal information about them; explain how it is or has been used and provide a list of any organizations to which it has been disclosed; give individuals access to their information; correct or amend any personal information if its accuracy and completeness is challenged and found to be deficient; provide a copy of the information requested, or reasons for not providing access, subject to exception set out in Section 9 of the Act; an organization should note any disagreement on the file and advise third parties where appropriate.
10. **Provide recourse:** Develop simple and easily accessible complaint procedures; inform complainants of avenues or recourse. These include your organization's own complaint procedures, those of industry associations, regulatory bodies and the Privacy Commissioner of Canada; investigate all complaints received; take appropriate measures to correct information handling practices and policies.

PIPEDA does not apply to an employee's name, title, business address, or telephone number, or other employee information gathered by organizations engaged in commercial activity in the private sector. However, you may wish to review your employment privacy practices, and consider including employees in your privacy policy.

Conflicts of Interest (Rule 3.04; Guideline 9)

General

Rule 1.02 defines "conflict of interest" as the existence of a substantial risk that a paralegal's loyalty to or representation of a client would be materially and adversely affected by the paralegal's own interest or the paralegal's duties to another client, a former client, or a third person. The risk must be more than a mere possibility; there must be a genuine, serious risk to the duty of loyalty or to client representation arising from the retainer.

Guideline 9 notes that conflicts of interest can arise in many different circumstances.

> The following are examples of situations in which conflicts of interest commonly arise requiring a paralegal to take particular care to determine whether a conflict of interest exists:
>
> (a) A paralegal acts as an advocate in one matter against a person when the paralegal represents that person on some other matter.
> (b) A paralegal, an associate, a partner or a family member has a personal financial interest in a client's affairs or in a matter in which the paralegal is requested to act for a client.
> (c) A paralegal has a sexual or close personal relationship with a client.
> (d) A paralegal or the paralegal's firm acts for a public or private corporation and the paralegal serves as a director of the corporation. These two roles may result in a conflict of interest or other problems.

A paralegal shall not act or continue to act for a client where there is a conflict of interest, except as permitted by Rule 3.04 (Rule 3.04(1)).

A paralegal shall not advise or represent opposing parties in a dispute (Rule 3.04(2)). A **dispute** is an argument or disagreement between two or more persons in which the interest of one side is adverse to the interest of the other side. A paralegal cannot act for opposing parties in a dispute, because to do so would adversely influence the paralegal's judgment on behalf of and loyalty to one or both parties.

dispute
an argument or disagreement between two or more parties in which the interest of one side is adverse to that of the other side

To Whom Is the Duty Owed?

You owe the duty of avoiding conflicts of interest to all clients, including former clients and prospective clients. You should identify potential conflicts of interest at the first contact with a prospective client (Guideline 9).

The Rule 1.02 definition of "client" includes a client of the firm of which the paralegal is a partner or associate, whether or not the paralegal handles the client's work.

> Since every client of a paralegal firm is also the client of every other paralegal employed at the firm, if one paralegal in the firm has a conflict of interest in a matter, then all paralegals in the firm have a conflict in that matter. As a result, when checking for conflicts, the paralegal should review the names of all current and former clients of the firm and not just the clients personally served by the individual paralegal (Guideline 9).

Managing Conflicts of Interest

How do you find out whether a conflict of interest may exist in a particular client matter? Guideline 9 recommends that a paralegal should use a conflicts checking system to assist in managing conflicts.

A conflicts checking system is a searchable database of information about prospective, current, and former clients, as well as information about related persons and opposing or adverse parties. The database should include fields for the following information (the list is not exhaustive):

- client's name, and aliases and former names, if applicable;
- client contact information;
- date the file was opened;
- client file name and active file code;
- subject matter of the file;
- date the file was closed, and closed file code; and
- names and contact information of related persons, and of conflicting or adverse parties (if available), cross-referenced to the client file.

The database may be maintained in a paper or electronic format. Some legal software applications automatically enter client and other data into a conflicts database as new client matters are opened.

Guideline 9 notes that conflicts of interest may arise at any time in a client matter. A paralegal should examine whether a conflict of interest exists not only at the outset, but throughout the duration of a retainer, because new circumstances or information may establish or reveal a conflict of interest.

As part of your conflicts checking system, you should have standard office procedures in place for conducting a conflicts search at critical points in the paralegal–client relationship. Your first search should take place after the initial contact with a prospective client. You should search for conflicts again when you have more information about the client, and related or adverse parties. If a retainer is entered into, you should consider conducting a conflicts search any time a new party is added in a proceeding. If a conflict arises after you are retained, you may be required to withdraw from representing the client.

Conflict of Interest: Client Consent (Rules 3.04(3)–(6))

Rule 3.04(1) states that "a paralegal shall not act or continue to act for a client where there is a conflict of interest, except as permitted under this rule." Rules 3.04(3) and (4) permit you to act or continue to act for a client where there is a conflict of interest if you obtain the client's consent to do so.

> (3) A paralegal shall not represent a client in a matter when there is a conflict of interest unless
>
> (a) there is express or implied consent from all clients; and
>
> (b) it is reasonable for the paralegal to conclude that he or she is able to represent each client without having a material adverse effect upon the representation of or loyalty to the other client.
>
> (4) For the purpose of this rule:
>
> (a) Express consent must be fully informed and voluntary after disclosure.
>
> (b) Consent may be implied and need not be in writing where all of the following apply:
>
> (i) the client is a government, financial institution, publicly traded or similarly substantial entity, or an entity with in-house counsel,
>
> (ii) the matters are unrelated,
>
> (iii) the paralegal has no relevant confidential information from one client that might reasonably affect the representation of the other client, and
>
> (iv) the client has commonly consented to lawyers acting for and against it in unrelated matters.

Consent—Prospective Client

If practicable, whenever a prospective client contacts your firm, certain information (such as the client's name, including any aliases, and contact information) should be obtained from the client and entered immediately into your conflicts checking system. A conflicts search should be carried out before there is any further contact with the prospective client. The results of the search should be reviewed by the paralegal.

If the search reveals a conflict or potential conflict, you must consider whether you should accept the retainer or decline to represent the prospective client. To comply with Rule 3.04(3), you must obtain express or implied consent from all clients affected by the conflict, *and* it must be reasonable for you to conclude that you are able to represent each client without that representation having a material adverse effect upon the representation of or loyalty to the other client.

> At the time that a paralegal becomes aware of a conflict, or potential conflict, the paralegal should consider whether to accept the retainer, or to continue to act. This applies even where the client consents or where the retainer would not, in the paralegal's opinion, breach the *Rules*. The paralegal should consider the delay, expense and inconvenience that would arise for the client and/or the paralegal, should the paralegal be required to withdraw from the matter at a later stage in the proceedings (Guideline 9).

If you have considered the nature of the conflict and have reasonably concluded that you are able to represent each client without such representation having a material adverse effect upon the representation of or loyalty to the other client or clients, you may accept the retainer if all clients consent (Rule 3.04(3)(a)). Where the conditions of Rule 3.04(4)(b) are met, the consent may be implied and need not be in writing. Where express consent is required, to comply with Rule 3.04(4)(a) you must first disclose the conflict or potential conflict to the prospective client and the other client(s). Your disclosure must provide sufficient detail about the conflict to enable the clients to make an informed decision about whether retaining you is in their best interest in the circumstances.

> Disclosure is an essential element to obtaining a client's consent. The client needs to know of anything that may influence the paralegal's judgment or loyalty. Once the paralegal has provided the client with all the details, the paralegal must allow the client time to consider them or to ask for further clarification (Guideline 9).

If, having reviewed the information provided, the prospective client and the other client(s) consent to your representation, you may accept the client retainer. The consent of the prospective client, and other client(s) must be express consent—that is, it must be clearly stated and unequivocal. It should be obtained or confirmed in writing. If the consent is in writing, each client must sign the same or a separate document recording the consent. If the consent is oral (spoken), each consenting client must receive a separate written communication confirming their consent as soon as practicable.

BOX 4.8 Conflicts of Interest: Who Is the Client?

Any person who is a client of the paralegal firm of which you are a partner or an associate is a client, regardless of whether you actually handle that person's work (Rule 1.02). In a busy firm with many clients and/or a high client turnover, you may have no knowledge of a client's existence or that your firm ever represented him. Nevertheless, a paralegal–client relationship exists between you and that client and entails various duties, including the duty of confidentiality and the duty to avoid conflicts of interest.

Since every client of a paralegal firm is also the client of every other paralegal in the firm, if one paralegal has a conflict of interest in a matter, then all paralegals in the firm have a conflict of interest in that matter (Guideline 9).

This means that when you check for conflicts, you must search the names of all current and former clients of the firm, not just the clients you personally represented or represent.

Conflict of Interest—Prospective Client Does Not Retain Paralegal

If, having reviewed the disclosure provided, the prospective client declines to retain you, the client's decision should be confirmed in a non-engagement letter. The non-engagement letter must recommend that the client obtain independent legal representation from a competent paralegal or lawyer with no personal interest in the matter. **Independent legal representation** is legal advice and assistance from a competent paralegal or lawyer with no personal interest in the matter. See Appendix 3.3 for a sample non-engagement letter to a prospective client who has declined to retain you based on a conflict of interest.

independent legal representation
legal advice and assistance from a competent paralegal or lawyer with no personal interest in the matter

Conflict of Interest—Paralegal Declines Retainer

Guideline 9 notes that there may be situations where the only way to deal with a conflict is to refuse to act. This may occur when the nature of the conflict makes it impossible for you to provide full disclosure to a prospective client, or where it is not reasonable for you to conclude that you are able to represent each client without that representation having a material adverse effect upon your representation of or loyalty to the other client.

> There may be situations where it is impossible for a paralegal to give a client or prospective client all necessary information. This may happen when the details about the conflict involve another client or a former client. Since a paralegal cannot reveal confidential information regarding another client, the paralegal may only say that there is a conflict and that he or she cannot continue with or accept the retainer.
>
> . . .
>
> In some cases, the only way to deal with the conflict is to refuse to act. The paralegal may have to decline the retainer at the outset or may have to terminate the retainer and withdraw from representing the client at a later time. A paralegal may need to take this step even where the client wants the paralegal to accept the retainer, or to continue to act (Guideline 9).

You should confirm your decision to decline the retainer in writing in a non-engagement letter. The non-engagement letter must recommend that the client obtain independent legal representation.

> In circumstances where the paralegal is prohibited from acting for a client or prospective client, the paralegal must suggest that the individual obtain his or her own independent legal representation. *Independent legal representation* means that the individual has retained a legal representative, either a paralegal or lawyer, to act as his or her own representative in the matter. This retained representative is objective and does not have any conflicting interest with regards to the matter (Guideline 9).

See Appendix 3.4 for a sample non-engagement letter to a prospective client based on a conflict of interest.

Consent—Existing Client

Existing client matters should be checked for conflicts at critical points throughout the paralegal–client retainer. You should conduct a conflict search any time a new party is added or new information about the client matter comes to light. If a conflict arises after you are retained, you may be required to withdraw from representing the client.

If a conflict search reveals a conflict or potential conflict in an existing client matter, you must consider whether or not to continue to act in the matter, having regard to Rules 3.04(1), (2), and (3)(b), and Guideline 9.

Conflict of Interest—Client Terminates Retainer

If, having reviewed the disclosure provided, the client decides to terminate the retainer, you should confirm the termination of the retainer in writing. If the client requests that the matter be transferred to another paralegal or a lawyer, you should obtain a direction, in writing and signed by the client, for release of the client's file to the successor licensee. If the client collects the file herself, you should obtain an acknowledgment in writing and signed by the client confirming that she has received the file.

Conflict of Interest—Paralegal Withdraws From Representation

If, having considered the nature of the conflict, Rule 3.04, and Guideline 9, you conclude that you must terminate the retainer and withdraw from representing the client, you must advise the client that there is a conflict of interest and that you must withdraw from representation. You should confirm your decision in writing to the client.

When withdrawing your services, you shall comply with Rule 3.08. You must give the client notice that is appropriate to the circumstances, try to minimize expense and avoid prejudice to the client, and do all that reasonably can be done to facilitate the orderly transfer of the client matter to a successor licensee.

Consent—Future Conflicts

Guideline 9 suggests that a paralegal may be able to request that a client consent in advance to conflicts that might arise in future:

> The effectiveness of such consent is generally determined by the extent to which the client understands the material risks involved. A paralegal may wish to recommend that the client obtain independent legal advice before deciding whether to provide consent. Advance consent should be recorded in writing.

The commentary to Rule 3.4-2 of the *Rules of Professional Conduct* elaborates as follows:

> As the effectiveness of such consent is generally determined by the extent to which the client reasonably understands the material risks that the consent entails, the more comprehensive the explanation of the types of future representations that might arise and the actual and reasonably foreseeable adverse consequences of those representations, the greater the likelihood that the client will have the

> requisite understanding. A general, open-ended consent will ordinarily be ineffective because it is not reasonably likely that the client will have understood the material risks involved. If the client is an experienced user of the legal services involved and is reasonably informed regarding the risk that a conflict may arise, such consent is more likely to be effective, particularly if, for example, the client is independently represented by other counsel in giving consent and the consent is limited to future conflicts unrelated to the subject of the representation.

Independent legal advice is discussed below.

Implied Consent (Rule 3.04(4)(b))

Consent may be implied and need not be in writing where all of the following apply (Rule 3.04(4)(b)):

> (i) the client is a government, financial institution, publicly traded or similarly substantial entity, or an entity with in-house counsel,
> (ii) the matters are unrelated,
> (iii) the paralegal has no relevant confidential information from one client that might reasonably affect the representation of the other client, and
> (iv) the client has commonly consented to lawyers acting for and against it in unrelated matters.

Independent Legal Advice

In certain situations, the client's informed and written consent is not enough to allow you to accept or continue with a matter. This may happen when the conflict is such that the client cannot possibly assess all of its possible implications without impartial, confidential, professional assistance. It may also happen where the client is unsophisticated or vulnerable.

independent legal advice impartial, confidential advice obtained from competent counsel with no personal interest in the matter; also called ILA

Guideline 9 recommends that, in such circumstances, the client receive **independent legal advice** with regard to the matter or transaction before you take any further steps in the client matter:

> An independent legal advisor is another paralegal or a lawyer who can provide the client with *independent legal advice*. This advisor is unrelated to the client's matter, associated parties or the paralegal. He or she is unbiased and objective and does not have a conflict of interest. [Emphasis in original.]

Conflicts of Interest Arising from Personal Relationships (Rule 3.04(1))

There is nothing in the Rules that prohibits a paralegal from providing legal services to family members or friends. However, you have the same duty to avoid existing or potential conflicts of interest when representing friends and family members as you do when representing other clients. If there is anything in your personal relationship with a friend or a family member who is a prospective client that may adversely affect your judgment on behalf of or loyalty to that person, you should consider declining the retainer.

> A conflict of interest may arise when a paralegal provides legal services to a friend or family member, or when the client and the paralegal have a sexual or intimate personal relationship. In these circumstances, the paralegal's personal feelings for the client may impede the paralegal's ability to provide objective, disinterested professional advice to the client. Before accepting a retainer from or continuing a retainer with a person with whom the paralegal has a sexual or intimate personal relationship, a paralegal should consider the following factors:
>
> - The vulnerability of the client, both emotional and economic;
> - The fact that the paralegal and client relationship may create a power imbalance in favour of the paralegal or, in some circumstances, in favour of the client;
> - Whether the sexual or intimate personal relationship may jeopardize the client's right to have all information concerning the client's business and affairs held in strict confidence. For example, the existence of the personal relationship may obscure whether certain information was acquired by the paralegal in the course of the paralegal and client relationship;
> - Whether such a relationship may require the paralegal to act as a witness in the proceedings;
> - Whether such a relationship may interfere with the paralegal's fiduciary obligations to the client, including his or her ability to exercise independent professional judgment and his or her ability to fulfill obligations owed as an officer of the court and to the administration of justice (Guideline 9).

Generally, there is no conflict of interest if another paralegal at the firm who does not have a personal or intimate relationship with the client handles the client's matter.

BOX 4.9 Personal Relationships

Fact Situation

A year ago, you broke off a relationship with a man with whom you were sexually involved for over two years. You were never really committed to the relationship, and toward the end you became very impatient with his inability to make decisions and what you perceived as his manipulative behaviour and emotional dependency on you. When he began to pressure you to marry him, you ended the relationship.

After you stopped seeing him, he phoned and emailed you frequently, promising to change whatever was wrong and asking to see you. You did not respond to his calls or emails, and after five or six months, they tapered off and finally ceased.

Two days ago, your former partner contacted you at your firm. He assured you that his reasons for wanting to see you were purely professional—to consult with you about some problems he was having with his landlord.

You suspect that this is just another ploy for getting back into your life. You would prefer to have nothing more to do with him.

Question for Discussion

Are you obliged to represent this client?

Conflicts of Interest Arising from Outside Interests (Rules 2.01(4), (5), 3.04; Guidelines 2, 9)

A paralegal who engages in another profession, business, occupation, or other outside interest, or who holds public office at the same time that she is providing legal services, shall not allow the outside interest or public office to jeopardize the paralegal's integrity, independence, or competence (Rule 2.01(4)). A paralegal shall not allow involvement in an outside interest or public office to impair the exercise of her independent judgment as a paralegal on behalf of a client (Rule 2.01(5)). The question of whether and to what extent it is proper for the paralegal to engage in the outside interest will be subject to any applicable by-law or rule of the Law Society.

> The term "outside interest" covers the widest range of activities. It includes activities that may overlap or be connected with provision of legal services, for example, acting as a director of a corporation or writing on legal subjects, as well as activities less connected such as, for example, a career in business, politics, broadcasting or the performing arts.
>
> When participating in community activities, a paralegal should be mindful of the possible perception that the paralegal is providing legal services and a paralegal–client relationship has been established. A paralegal should not carry on, manage or be involved in any outside interest in such a way that makes it difficult to distinguish in which capacity the paralegal is acting, or that would give rise to a conflict of interest or duty to a client.
>
> It is the paralegal's responsibility to consider whether the outside interest may impair his or her ability to act in the best interest of his or her client(s). If so, the paralegal must withdraw, either from representation of the client or from the outside interest (Guideline 2).

Guideline 9 notes that a conflict of interest may arise from the paralegal's outside interests:

> If a paralegal has other businesses or interests separate from his or her paralegal firm, those interests may influence the way the paralegal serves clients. Whatever the outside interest, a paralegal must guard against allowing those outside interests to interfere or conflict with his or her duties to clients.
>
> If a paralegal is in public office while still providing legal services to clients, the paralegal must not allow his or her duties as a public official to conflict with his or her duties as a paralegal. If there is a possibility of a conflict of interest, the paralegal should avoid it either by removing himself or herself from the discussion and voting in the public capacity or by withdrawing from representation of the client.

BOX 4.10 Outside Interests

You are a partner, along with two other paralegals, in a paralegal firm. You serve on the board of directors of a publicly funded community legal clinic that provides legal advice and services to people in the community who meet income and other criteria set by the funding agency. Many of the clinic's clients are residential tenants. The services provided by the clinic include summary advice and, in some cases, representation before the Landlord and Tenant Board. As a director, your role is to review budgetary and administrative issues, as well as clinic outreach and other initiatives within the clinic mandate. You do not provide legal advice to the clinic. You are not privy to confidential information about individual client matters.

One of your partners has several clients who are residential landlords. During a conversation with you, she mentions that she is going to be busy for the next few months dealing with multiple applications by tenants in a residential complex owned by one of her landlord clients, XYZ Properties Inc. The paralegal representing the tenants is an employee of the legal clinic upon whose board you serve. "They're asking for thousands of dollars in rent abatements for non-repair, breaches of the Fire Code, you name it," your partner says. "My guy won't be happy when he finds out you're a director on their board. He'll think it's a conflict of interest."

"He's your client, not mine," you reply. "I don't owe him anything. And I haven't done anything wrong."

Questions for Discussion

Is XYZ Properties Inc. your client? If yes, is there a conflict of interest?

Acting Against Former Clients (Rules 3.04(2), (5)(a), (b))

A paralegal shall not advise or represent opposing parties in a dispute (Rule 3.04(2)).

Acting Against Former Clients in the Same or Related Matters (Rules 3.04(2), (5)(a), (b))

Unless the former client consents, a paralegal shall not act against a former client in the same matter or a related matter (Rules 3.04(5)(a), (b)). The client consent must be fully informed and voluntary after disclosure. It should be in writing or confirmed in writing.

You are prohibited from acting against a former client in the same matter because you possess confidential information about the client that is relevant to issues in the matter. Your duty to the former client requires you to hold that information in strict confidence. Your duty as legal representative to an adverse party in the same proceeding requires you to disclose that information for the adverse party's benefit, to the possible detriment of your former client. The two duties conflict.

A related matter is a matter involving issues that are similar or related to the issues in the original client matter. If you have acted for a client in a matter, you shall not, after that, act against the former client in a matter related to the client matter.

You are prohibited from doing so because you possess confidential information about the former client from the original client matter that is relevant to issues in the related matter. Your duty to the former client requires you to hold that information in strict confidence. Your duty as legal representative to an adverse party in the related matter may require you to disclose that information for the benefit of the adverse party, to the possible detriment of the former client. The two duties conflict.

Acting against a former client in the same or a related matter also raises issues about your loyalty to your clients.

Acting Against Former Clients in New Matters (Rules 3.04(5)(c), (6))

Unless the former client consents, a paralegal shall not act against a former client in any new matter except as provided in subrule (6), if the paralegal has relevant confidential information arising from the representation of the former client that may prejudice the client (Rule 3.04(5)(c)).

Rule 3.04(6) states:

> (6) If a paralegal has acted for a client and obtained confidential information relevant to a matter, the paralegal's partner or employee may act in a subsequent matter against that client, provided that:
>
> (a) the former client consents to the paralegal's partner or employee acting; or
>
> (b) the paralegal's firm establishes that it has taken adequate measures on a timely basis to ensure that there will be no risk of disclosure of the former client's confidential information to the other licensee having carriage of the new matter.

With respect to "adequate measures," the guidelines in the commentary to Rule 3.4-26 of the *Rules of Professional Conduct* may be of some assistance to a paralegal firm that is contemplating acting against a former client whose confidential information from the former matter is relevant in the subsequent matter. The following suggestions have been adapted from the guidelines in the commentary to Rule 3.4-26, and are for information only.

- The former licensee who possesses relevant confidential information from the former matter (the "former licensee") should have no involvement in the subsequent matter.
- The former licensee and the subsequent licensee who is acting against the client in the current matter (the "subsequent licensee") should have no discussions about the former matter or the subsequent matter.
- No persons who worked on the former matter should work on the subsequent matter.
- The subsequent matter should be discussed only by persons designated to work on the subsequent matter.
- The files in the former matter (including computer files) should be segregated from and inaccessible to persons working on the subsequent matter.
- The former licensee's office or work station and those of any other persons who worked on the former matter should be located away from the offices or work stations of persons working on the subsequent matter.
- In the case of a paralegal firm with multiple offices, consideration should be given to referring the matter to a licensee at another office.
- The former client or the former client's representative should be advised of the measures adopted by the paralegal firm to ensure that there is no

disclosure of confidential information from the former matter to persons working on the subsequent matter.

Paralegal Guideline 9 recommends that:

> Even where the *Rules* do not prohibit a paralegal from acting against a … former client, the paralegal should consider whether to accept the retainer (or continue acting). To act against a … former client may damage the paralegal–client relationship, [and] may result in court proceedings or a complaint to the Law Society.

Joint Retainers (Rules 3.04(7)–(13); Guidelines 5, 9)

A joint retainer is an arrangement where a paralegal agrees to represent two or more clients in the same matter. The clients in a joint retainer are called joint clients.

> Acting in a joint retainer places the paralegal in a potential conflict of interest. A paralegal has an obligation to all clients and in a joint retainer, the paralegal must remain loyal and devoted to all clients equally—the paralegal cannot choose to serve one client more carefully or resolutely than any other. If the interests of one client change during the course of the retainer, the paralegal may be in a conflict of interest (Guideline 9).

Before agreeing to a joint retainer, you must clearly identify the clients to whom you will be providing legal services, to ensure that you can fulfill your duties to them (Guideline 5). You must carry out a conflicts search to ensure that there are no conflicts of interest.

Although the Rules do not require this, Guideline 9 recommends that:

> In cases where one of the joint clients is not sophisticated or is vulnerable, the paralegal should consider the provisions of Rule 3.02(13) and (14) regarding clients [with diminished capacity]. The paralegal may want to recommend that the client obtain independent legal advice prior to agreeing to the joint retainer. This will ensure that the client's consent to the joint retainer is informed, genuine [and] not obtained through coercion.

Before accepting a joint retainer, you should determine who will provide you with instructions in the matter. You should confirm the arrangement in the retainer agreement.

Rule 3.04(7) states that:

> (7) Before agreeing to act for more than one client in a matter or transaction, a paralegal shall advise the clients that
>
> (a) the paralegal has been asked to act for both or all of them;
>
> (b) no information received in connection with the matter from one client can be treated as confidential so far as any of the others are concerned; and
>
> (c) if a conflict develops that cannot be resolved, the paralegal cannot continue to act for both or all of them and may have to withdraw completely.

If a paralegal has a continuing relationship with a client for whom he or she acts regularly, before agreeing to act for that client and another client in a matter or transaction, the paralegal shall advise the other client of the continuing relationship and recommend that the client obtain independent legal advice about the joint retainer (Rule 3.04(8)). A **continuing relationship** is a paralegal–client relationship where you act for the same client in several different matters or transactions over a period of time. A continuing client is a client for whom you act in several different matters or transactions over a period of time.

continuing relationship a paralegal–client relationship where a paralegal acts for the same client in several different matters or transactions over a period of time

If you have advised all joint retainer clients in accordance with Rules 3.04(7) and (8) and they are in agreement that you should act for them, you shall obtain their consent (Rule 3.04(9)). Consent to a joint retainer must be obtained from each client in writing, or recorded through a separate written communication to each client (Rule 3.04(10)).

Contentious Issue (Rules 3.04(11)–(13))

Although all clients may consent to the joint retainer, you shall avoid acting for more than one client if it is likely that a contentious issue will arise between them or that their interests, rights, or obligations will diverge as the matter progresses (Rule 3.04(11)).

Rule 3.04(12) states that:

> (12) Except as provided by subrule (13) if a contentious issue arises between two clients who have consented to a joint retainer, the paralegal must not advise either of them on the contentious issue and the following rules apply:
>
> (a) The paralegal shall
>
> (i) refer the clients to other licensees for that purpose; or
>
> (ii) if no legal advice is required and the clients are sophisticated, advise them of their option to settle the contentious issue by direct negotiation in which the paralegal does not participate.
>
> (b) If the contentious issue is not resolved, the paralegal shall withdraw from the joint representation.

If your clients consent to a joint retainer and also agree that, if a contentious issue arises, you may continue to advise one of them, and a contentious issue does arise, you may advise the designated client about the contentious issue. You shall refer the other client(s) to another licensee for that purpose (Rule 3.04(13)).

Unrepresented Parties (Rules 3.04(7)–(13), 4.05)

When providing legal services, you may find yourself dealing with opposing parties or other individuals with an interest in the matter who are not represented by a paralegal or a lawyer. A conflict of interest may arise if the unrepresented person comes to believe that you are protecting his or her interests.

Rule 4.05 states that:

> When a paralegal deals on a client's behalf with an unrepresented person, the paralegal shall:
>
> (a) take care to see that the unrepresented person is not proceeding under the impression that his or her interests will be protected by the paralegal; and

> (b) make clear to the unrepresented person that the paralegal is acting exclusively in the interests of the client and accordingly his or her comments may be partisan.

Making it clear to the unrepresented person that you are acting exclusively in the interests of your own client may require more than simply saying this to the unrepresented person. In some circumstances, it may be prudent to send the unrepresented person confirmation in writing. You will find an example of an "I am not your legal representative" letter in Appendix 3.5 at page 83.

If an unrepresented person who is an opposing party requests that you advise or act on the unrepresented person's behalf in the matter, you are not permitted to accept the retainer. If the unrepresented person has some other kind of interest in the matter (for example, is a co-accused), you may be permitted to act, but you must comply with Rules 3.04(7) to (13) about joint retainers (Guideline 9).

Multi-Discipline Practice (By-law 7, Part III; Rules 3.04(14), 8.01)

A **multi-discipline practice** is a business arrangement that permits paralegal licensees to enter into a partnership or association that is not a corporation with non-licensees to provide to clients the services of a non-licensee who practises a profession, trade, or occupation that supports or supplements the provision of legal services (By-law 7, s. 18(1)). The paralegal licensee must have effective control over the provision of services by non-licensees to clients of the multi-discipline practice (By-law 7, s. 18(2)2).

multi-discipline practice a business arrangement that permits paralegal licensees to provide to clients the services of a non-licensee who practises a profession, trade, or occupation that supports or supplements the provision of legal services; also called MDP

In a multi-discipline practice, a paralegal should be careful to ensure that the client understands that he or she is receiving legal services from the paralegal only.

> If advice or service is sought from non-licensed members of the firm, it should be sought and provided independently of and outside the scope of the retainer for the provision of legal services. A paralegal should also be aware that advice or services provided by a non-licensed member of the firm will be subject to the constraints outlined in the relevant by-laws and rules governing multi-discipline practices. One way to distinguish the advice or services of non-licensed members of the firm is to ensure that such advice or services is provided from a location separate from the premises of the multi-discipline practice (Guideline 7).

A paralegal in a multi-discipline practice is required to assume complete professional responsibility for all business entrusted to him or her (Rule 8.01(1)). In accordance with By-law 7.1 and Rule 8.01(5), a paralegal in a multi-discipline practice shall ensure that non-licensee partners and associates comply with the Rules and all ethical principles that govern paralegals in the discharge of their professional obligations. These professional and ethical duties include the duty to hold all client information in strict confidence and the duty to avoid conflicts of interest.

A paralegal in a multi-discipline practice must ensure that the client understands that legal services are provided by the paralegal, and supplemented by the professional services of non-licensee partners and associates. A paralegal in a multi-discipline practice must also ensure that non-licensee partners and associates comply with the rules regarding the avoidance of conflicts of interest when providing professional services within the paralegal practice, and when carrying on business or fulfilling professional undertakings outside of the paralegal practice.

Affiliations (By-law 7, Part IV; Rules 1.02, 3.04(15)–(17))

A paralegal firm may form an affiliation with a non-legal entity whose members practise a profession, trade, or occupation that supports or supplements the paralegal's provision of legal services ("affiliated entity"). An **affiliation** is considered to have formed when the paralegal on a regular basis joins with the **affiliated entity** in the delivery and promotion of their services to the public (By-law 7, s. 31(2)).

affiliation
an arrangement whereby a paralegal services firm provides legal services to the public jointly with a non-legal entity whose members practise a profession, trade, or occupation that supports or supplements the paralegal's provision of legal services

affiliated entity
any person or group of persons other than a person or group authorized to provide legal services in Ontario; a non-licensee or group of non-licensees

> A conflict of interest may arise from a paralegal's, or his or her associate's, interest in an affiliated firm of non-licensees where that interest conflicts with the paralegal's duties to a client. Rule 3.04(15) and (16) impose disclosure and consent requirements on a paralegal in an affiliation.
>
> Conflicts of interest arising out of a proposed retainer by a client should be addressed as if the paralegal's practice and the practice of the affiliated entity were one where the paralegal accepts a retainer to provide legal services to that client jointly with non-legal services of the affiliated entity.
>
> The affiliation is subject to the same conflict of interest rules as apply to paralegals (Guideline 9).

Rule 3.04(15) states that:

> (15) Where there is an affiliation, before accepting a retainer to provide legal services to a client jointly with non-legal services of an affiliated entity, a paralegal shall disclose to the client
>
> (a) any possible loss of confidentiality because of the involvement of the affiliated entity, including circumstances where a non-licensee or staff of the affiliated entity provide services, including support services, in the paralegal's office,
>
> (b) the paralegal's role in providing legal services and in providing non-legal services or in providing both legal and non-legal services, as the case may be,
>
> (c) any financial, economic or other arrangements between the paralegal and the affiliated entity that may affect the independence of the paralegal's representation of the client, including whether the paralegal shares in the revenues, profits or cash flows of the affiliated entity; and
>
> (d) agreements between the paralegal and the affiliated entity, such as agreements with respect to referral of clients between the paralegal and the affiliated entity, that may affect the independence of the paralegal's representation of the client.

After making the disclosure required by Rule 3.04(15), a paralegal shall obtain the client's consent before accepting a retainer under that subrule (Rule 3.04(16)). The consent shall be in writing or confirmed in writing.

Transfers Between Paralegal Firms (Rule 3.05)

Problems concerning confidential information may arise when a paralegal changes firms and the former paralegal firm and the new paralegal firm act for opposing clients in the same or a related matter. The potential risk is that confidential information about the client from the paralegal's former office may be revealed to the members of the new firm and used against that client. A paralegal should carefully review the Rules when transferring to a new office or when a new paralegal is about to join the paralegal firm (Guideline 9).

BOX 4.11 What Is "Confidential Information" for Purposes of Rule 3.05?

The duty of confidentiality requires a paralegal to hold in strict confidence all information concerning the business and affairs of the client acquired in the course of the professional relationship, without regard to the nature or source of the information or the fact that others may share the knowledge.

Rules 3.4-17 to 3.4-26 of the *Rules of Professional Conduct* deal with transfers between firms by lawyers. They are the equivalent of Rule 3.05 of the *Paralegal Rules of Conduct*.

For purposes of transfers between law firms by lawyers, the definition in Rule 3.4-17 restricts "confidential information" to information obtained from a client that is not generally known to the public.

The commentary to Rule 3.4-17 states that the duties imposed by the rule concerning confidential information should be distinguished from the general ethical duty to hold in strict confidence all information concerning the business and affairs of the client acquired in the course of the professional relationship.

Rule 3.05 of the Paralegal Rules distinguishes between "confidential information"—that is, client information that, if disclosed to a paralegal in the new paralegal firm, might prejudice the client (Rule 3.05(2))—and "relevant information"—that is, client information that, if disclosed, would not prejudice the client (Rule 3.05(4)). An example of relevant information might be the client's name, if it has already been disclosed on public documents such as pleadings.

Rule 3.05(1) states that:

> (1) This rule applies where a paralegal transfers from one paralegal firm ("former paralegal firm") to another ("new paralegal firm"), and either the transferring paralegal or the new paralegal firm is aware at the time of the transfer or later discovers that,
>
> (a) the new paralegal firm represents a client in a matter that is the same as or related to a matter in which the former paralegal firm represents its client ("former client");
>
> (b) the interests of those clients in that matter conflict; and
>
> (c) the transferring paralegal actually possesses relevant information respecting that matter.

If the transferring paralegal possesses confidential information respecting a former client that may prejudice the former client if disclosed to a paralegal in the new paralegal firm, the new paralegal firm shall cease representation of its client unless the former client consents to the new paralegal firm's continued representation or the new paralegal firm establishes that it is in the interests of justice that it continue to represent the client (Rule 3.05(2)). The former client's consent shall be fully informed and voluntary after disclosure, and shall be in writing or confirmed in writing.

In deciding whether or not it is appropriate to continue to act for a client, the new paralegal firm shall consider all of the circumstances, including:

(a) the adequacy and timing of the measures taken to ensure that no disclosure of the former client's confidential information to any paralegal of the new paralegal firm will occur;
(b) the availability of suitable alternative representation;
(c) the measures taken to ensure that no disclosure of the former client's confidential information to any paralegal in the new paralegal firm will occur;
(d) the extent of any prejudice to any party;
(e) the good faith of the parties; and
(f) issues affecting the public interest (Rule 3.05(3)).

If a transferring paralegal possesses relevant information respecting a former client but that information is not confidential information as defined in Rule 3.05(2), the paralegal shall execute an affidavit or solemn declaration to that effect, and the new paralegal firm shall:

(a) notify its client and the former client, or if the former client is represented in that matter by a licensee, notify that licensee, of the relevant circumstances and its intended action under this rule; and
(b) deliver to the persons referred to in clause (a) a copy of the paralegal's affidavit or solemn declaration executed under this subrule (Rule 3.05(4)).

A transferring paralegal who possesses confidential information about a former client under Rule 3.05(2), or relevant (but not confidential) information under Rule 3.05(4), shall not, unless the former client consents:

(a) participate in any manner in the new paralegal firm's representation of the client in that matter; or
(b) disclose any confidential information respecting the former client (Rule 3.05(5)).

The former client's consent shall be fully informed and voluntary after disclosure, and shall be in writing or confirmed in writing.

No paralegal in the new paralegal firm shall discuss the new paralegal firm's representation of its client or the former paralegal firm's representation of the former client with a transferring paralegal described in Rule 3.05(2) or 3.05(4), unless the former client consents (Rule 3.05(6)).

Anyone with an interest in a matter referred to in Rule 3.05, or who represents a party in a matter referred to in Rule 3.05, may apply to a tribunal of competent jurisdiction for a determination of any aspect of the rule.

Doing Business with a Client (Rule 3.06; Guideline 9)

General (Rule 3.06(1))

Guideline 9 cautions paralegals about entering with a client or clients into any business arrangement that is unrelated to the provision of paralegal services. This includes any transaction with a client, including lending or borrowing money, buying or selling property, accepting a gift, giving or acquiring ownership, security or other pecuniary interest in a company or other entity, recommending an investment, and entering into a common business venture.

Since the paralegal is or was the client's advisor, the paralegal may have a conflict of interest. The paralegal may unknowingly influence the client to agree to an arrangement that may be unfair or unreasonable to the client (Guideline 9).

Rule 3.06(1) states that a paralegal must not enter into a transaction with a client unless the transaction is fair and reasonable to the client, the client consents to the transaction, and the client has independent legal representation with respect to the transaction.

Rule 3.06 does not apply to a transfer of a non-material interest in a publicly traded enterprise (Rule 3.06(4)). A non-material interest is an interest that does not affect control or management of the publicly traded enterprise.

Transactions with Clients (Rules 3.06(1)–(3))

If a paralegal is representing a client, and the client intends to enter into a transaction with the paralegal representative, or with a privately held corporation or other business entity in which the paralegal has an interest, the paralegal, before accepting the retainer, must ensure compliance with Rule 3.06(1) and Rule 3.06(2), quoted below:

> (2) Subject to subrule (3), if a client intends to enter into a transaction with a paralegal who is representing the client, or with a corporation or other entity in which the paralegal has an interest other than a corporation or other entity whose securities are publicly traded, the paralegal, before accepting any retainer,
>
> (a) shall disclose and explain the nature of the conflicting interest to the client, or, in the case of a potential conflict, how and why it might develop later;
>
> (b) shall recommend independent legal representation and shall require that the client receive independent legal advice; and
>
> (c) if the client requests the paralegal to act, shall obtain the client's written consent.

Rule 3.06(3) states that if a client intends to pay for legal services by transferring to a paralegal a share, participation or other interest in property or in an enterprise, the paralegal shall recommend, but need not require, that the client receive independent legal advice before agreeing to act for the client.

Note that, for purposes of compliance with Rule 3.06(3), making the recommendation to obtain independent legal advice to the client before accepting the retainer is mandatory. However, the client may then make up her own mind about whether she wishes to seek independent legal advice or not. So long as you have made the recommendation, you have complied with the rule. You should consider making the recommendation to obtain independent legal advice in writing.

If you do not choose to make disclosure of the conflicting interest, or cannot do so without breaching a confidence, you shall decline the retainer (Rule 3.06(5)). You should consider sending the client a non-engagement letter confirming that you have declined the retainer and stating your reasons for doing so.

Borrowing from Clients (Rule 3.06(6))

Rule 3.06(6) states that:

> (6) A paralegal shall not borrow money from a client unless,
> (a) the client is a lending institution, financial institution, insurance company, trust corporation or any similar institution whose business includes lending money to members of the public; or
> (b) the client is a related person as defined in section 251 of the *Income Tax Act* (Canada) and the paralegal is able to discharge the onus of proving that the client's interests were fully protected by the nature of the case and by independent legal advice or independent legal representation.

BOX 4.12 Who Are Related Persons as Defined in Section 251 of the Income Tax Act (Canada)?

Rule 3.06(6)(b) refers to the definition of "related persons" in s. 251 of the *Income Tax Act*, which is defined there as follows:

Definition of "related persons"

251(2) For the purpose of this Act, "related persons," or persons related to each other, are

(a) individuals connected by blood relationship, marriage or common-law partnership or adoption;

(b) a corporation and

(i) a person who controls the corporation, if it is controlled by one person,

(ii) a person who is a member of a related group that controls the corporation, or

(iii) any person related to a person described in subparagraph 251(2)(b)(i) or 251(2)(b)(ii); and

(c) any two corporations

(i) if they are controlled by the same person or group of persons,

(ii) if each of the corporations is controlled by one person and the person who controls one of the corporations is related to the person who controls the other corporation,

(iii) if one of the corporations is controlled by one person and that person is related to any member of a related group that controls the other corporation,

(iv) if one of the corporations is controlled by one person and that person is related to each member of an unrelated group that controls the other corporation,

(v) if any member of a related group that controls one of the corporations is related to each member of an unrelated group that controls the other corporation, or

(vi) if each member of an unrelated group that controls one of the corporations is related to at least one member of an unrelated group that controls the other corporation.

Corporations related through a third corporation

251(3) Where two corporations are related to the same corporation within the meaning of subsection 251(2), they shall, for the purposes of subsections 251(1) and 251(2), be deemed to be related to each other.

Guarantees by Paralegal (Rules 3.06 (7), (8))

A **guarantee** is an agreement to make oneself liable or responsible to a lender for the payment of a debt if the debtor defaults in payment.

guarantee
an agreement to make oneself liable or responsible to a lender for the payment of a debt if the debtor defaults in payment

Rule 3.06(8) states that:

> (8) A paralegal may give a personal guarantee if,
> (a) the lender is a lending institution, financial institution, insurance company, trust company or any similar corporation whose business includes lending money to members of the public, and the lender is directly or indirectly providing funds solely for the paralegal, the paralegal's spouse, parent or child;
> (b) the transaction is for the benefit of a non-profit or charitable institution where the paralegal as a member or supporter of such institution is asked, either individually or together with other members or supporters of the institution to provide a guarantee; or
> (c) the paralegal has entered into a business venture with a client and the lender requires personal guarantees from all participants in the venture as a matter of course and,
> (i) the paralegal has complied with the requirements of these Rules regarding the avoidance of conflicts of interest, and
> (ii) the lender and the participants in the venture who are or were clients of the paralegal have received independent legal representation.

In any other circumstances, the paralegal shall not guarantee personally or otherwise provide security for any indebtedness in respect of which a client is a borrower or a lender (Rule 3.06(7)).

BOX 4.13 What Is a Guarantee?

A guarantee is an agreement to make oneself liable or responsible to a lender for the payment of a debt if the debtor defaults in payment. The lender is the person or institution lending the money to the debtor. The debtor is the person who owes the money. The person making the guarantee to pay the debt if the debtor fails to pay is called a guarantor.

In other words, the guarantor undertakes to pay the lender personally if the debtor fails to pay the debt.

It is in the guarantor's best interest that the debtor pay the debt, so that the guarantor does not have to pay it. If the debtor fails to pay the debt, the guarantor's interest and the debtor's interest may become adverse. The guarantor is bound by the promise to pay in the event of default by the debtor, but would prefer that the debtor pay the debt. The debtor, if unable to pay the debt for whatever reason, is relying upon the guarantor to honour the promise to pay. The lender does not care who pays the debt, so long as it is paid.

Judicial Interim Release (Rule 3.06(9), (10))

Rule 3.06(9) states that:

> (9) Subject to subrule (10), a paralegal shall not in respect of any accused person for whom the paralegal acts
> (a) act as a surety for the accused;
> (b) deposit with a court the paralegal's own money or that of any firm in which the paralegal is a partner to secure the accused's release;
> (c) deposit with any court other valuable security to secure the accused's release; or
> (d) act in a supervisory capacity to the accused.

surety
a person who is responsible for an accused, and exercises supervisory functions over the defendant; the surety must ensure that the accused attends court as required until the case is concluded and abides by any conditions of judicial interim release

A **surety** is a person who is responsible for an accused, and exercises supervisory functions over the defendant. The surety must ensure that the accused attends court as required until the case is concluded and abides by any conditions of judicial interim release.

A paralegal may do any of the things referred to in Rule 3.06(9) if the accused is in a family relationship with the paralegal and the accused is represented by the paralegal's partner or associate (Rule 3.06(10)).

Client Property (Rule 3.07; By-law 9; Guideline 10)

Paralegal as Fiduciary with Respect to Client Property (Rule 3.07(1))

A paralegal is a fiduciary with respect to any property of the client that comes into the paralegal's possession. As a fiduciary, the paralegal holds client property, including client money, in trust for the client.

Documents that are given to the paralegal at the outset of the paralegal–client retainer, as well as those that are prepared by or given to the paralegal in the course of the retainer, also belong to the client.

A paralegal shall care for a client's property as a careful and prudent owner would when dealing with similar property and shall observe all relevant rules and law about the preservation of property entrusted to a fiduciary (Rule 3.07(1)).

Dealing with Client Property (Rules 3.07(2)–(6); By-law 9, s. 18.9)

A paralegal shall promptly notify the client of the receipt of any money or other property of the client, unless satisfied that the client is aware they have come into the paralegal's custody (Rule 3.07(2)).

A paralegal shall clearly label and identify the client's property and place it in safekeeping, distinguishable from the paralegal's own property (Rule 3.07(3)). Money retainers and other client money (such as settlement funds payable to the client, where there is a client direction that such funds shall be paid to the paralegal in trust) shall be deposited to a trust bank account that is separate from a paralegal's personal account and the firm's operating account. Other personal property that is held in trust by the paralegal on behalf of the client shall be held in a place of safekeeping separate from the paralegal's own property. For example, you would not store client valuables in the same safe deposit box that you use for your own valuables.

A paralegal shall maintain such records as are necessary to identify a client's property that is in the paralegal's custody (Rule 3.07(4)). Minimum bookkeeping requirements for money that is held in trust by the paralegal for the benefit of the client are set out at By-law 9, Part V. For property that is not money, a paralegal shall maintain a **valuable property record** in accordance with By-law 9, s. 18.9.

valuable property record
a record of all property, other than money, held in trust for clients, as required by By-law 9, s. 18(9)

> **Requirement to maintain financial records**
>
> 18. Every licensee shall maintain financial records to record all money and other property received and disbursed in connection with the licensee's professional business, and, as a minimum requirement, every licensee shall maintain, in accordance with sections 21, 22 and 23, the following records:
>
> . . .
>
> 9. A record showing all property, other than money, held in trust for clients, and describing each property and identifying the date on which the licensee took possession of each property, the person who had possession of each property immediately before the licensee took possession of the property, the value of each property, the client for whom each property is held in trust, the date on which possession of each property is given away and the person to whom possession of each property is given.

Guideline 10 discusses what client property should or should not be recorded in the valuable property record:

> The valuable property record documents the paralegal's receipt, storage and delivery of client property. Client property may include, for example:
>
> - stocks, bonds or other securities in bearer form,
> - jewelry, paintings, furs, collector's items or any saleable valuables, and
> - any property that a paralegal can convert to cash on his or her own authority.
>
> The valuable property record should not include items that cannot be sold or negotiated by the paralegal, for example, wills, securities registered in the client's name, corporate records or seals. A paralegal should maintain a list of these items, but that list should be separate from the valuable property record.

A paralegal shall account promptly for a client's property that is in the paralegal's custody and, upon request, shall deliver it to the order of the client or, if appropriate, at the conclusion of the retainer (Rule 3.07(5)). If a paralegal is unsure of the proper person to receive a client's property, the paralegal shall apply to a tribunal of competent jurisdiction for direction (Rule 3.06(6)).

BOX 4.14 Valuable Property Record

Pending the outcome of a Small Claims Court action against him for delivery of personal property, your client, Felix Krull, is ordered by the court to deliver to you to hold in safekeeping a laptop computer and digital camera, ownership of which is in dispute in the proceeding. Mr. Krull places the laptop computer and digital camera in your safekeeping on January 5, 20—. On March 3, 20—, the matter settles on terms that the digital camera is to be delivered to the plaintiff, Andrew Ekpunobe, and your client is to keep the laptop. In accordance with the settlement agreement, and pursuant to a written direction from Mr. Krull, dated March 7, 20—, the digital camera is delivered to Andrew Ekpunobe and the laptop is delivered to Mr. Krull.

At the end of these transactions, the valuable property record would look like this:

Schwarz and Berryman Professional Corporation
Licensed Paralegals
Valuable Property Record

Client	Description of property	Date received	Received from	Value	Delivered to	Date of delivery
KRULL, Felix	Sony laptop	Jan 05, 20—	KRULL, Felix	$1,199.99	KRULL, Felix	Mar 07, 20—
KRULL, Felix	Canon digital camera	Jan 05, 20—	KRULL, Felix	$1,279.99	EKPUNOBE, Andrew	Mar 07, 20—

The Client File (Rule 3.07(1), (5))

Documents that are provided to the paralegal by the client or created during the paralegal–client retainer as part of the services provided are the property of the client. Accordingly, a paralegal must preserve the contents of the client file for the benefit of the client, in accordance with Rule 3.07(1), and deliver the client file to the order of the client, or, if appropriate, at the conclusion of the retainer (Rule 3.07(5)). Guideline 10 comments that:

> The duty to preserve client property also applies to the documents that a client may give to the paralegal at the beginning of the paralegal–client relationship and documents that are created or collected by the paralegal for the client's benefit during the relationship.
>
> The courts have developed law on the issue of the client file as between lawyers and clients. This jurisprudence may be applied to define the paralegal's client file in future. Generally, documents provided to a lawyer at the start of the retainer and those created during the retainer as part of the services provided, would belong to the client. These include
>
> - originals of all documents prepared for the client,
> - all copies of documents for which copies the client has paid,
> - a copy of letters from a lawyer to third parties or from a third party to a lawyer,
> - originals of letters from a lawyer to the client (presumably these would have already been sent to the client in the course of the retainer),

- copies of case law,
- briefs,
- memoranda of law, where the client paid for preparation of the memoranda,
- notes or memoranda of meetings with opposing parties or their representatives, court or tribunal conferences, interviews of witnesses, etc.,
- trial preparation documents, trial briefs, document briefs, trial books,
- copies of vouchers and receipts for disbursements a lawyer made on the client's behalf,
- experts' reports,
- photographs, and
- electronic media such as computer discs.

When the paralegal–client retainer is terminated before the client matter is concluded, you shall deliver the above documents to the client (subject to the paralegal's right to a lien for unpaid fees) (Rule 3.08(11)). If the client is collecting the documents personally, you should arrange for the client to sign an acknowledgment of receipt of the documents. If the client instructs you to release the documents to a successor licensee, you should obtain a written direction confirming those instructions, signed by the client. A **direction** is a written document, signed by the client, that instructs the paralegal to take a particular course of action in a client matter. In the context of early termination of the retainer, the direction would instruct the paralegal to release the client file to the successor licensee.

direction
a written document, signed by the client, that instructs a paralegal to take a particular course of action in a client matter

When you close the file in a client matter that is concluded, you shall return the above documents to the client (subject to the paralegal's right to a lien for unpaid fees) (Rule 3.08(11)). You should arrange for the client to sign an acknowledgment indicating receipt of the documents. The acknowledgment may be filed in the client's closed file.

Documents belonging to the paralegal, such as notes or memoranda of meetings or telephone conversations with the client, would not have to be provided to the client.

Guideline 10 recommends that you make, at your own cost, copies of all client documents, and keep them to defend against complaints or claims that may be made against you in future. The copies should be filed in the client's closed file.

Withdrawal from Representation (Rule 3.08; Guideline 11)

The client may terminate the paralegal–client relationship at any time, for any reason.

A paralegal shall not withdraw from representation of a client except for good cause and on reasonable notice to the client (Rule 3.08(1)).

Whether a paralegal has good cause for withdrawal will depend on many factors, including:

- the nature and stage of the matter,
- the relationship with the client,

- the paralegal's expertise and experience, and
- any harm or prejudice to the client that may result from the withdrawal (Guideline 11).

The factors above may also assist a paralegal to determine what is reasonable notice in the circumstances. In this context, notice comprises both determining what persons must be notified, and providing a reasonable amount of time for the client to seek other legal representation and for the successor licensee to review the file.

> [A]n essential element of reasonable notice is notification to the client, unless the client cannot be located after reasonable efforts. … Every effort should be made to ensure that withdrawal occurs at an appropriate time in the proceedings in keeping with the paralegal's obligations. The tribunal, opposing parties and others directly affected should also be notified of the withdrawal (Guideline 11).

The commentary to Rule 3.7-1 of the *Rules of Professional Conduct* notes that:

> No hard and fast rules can be laid down about what will constitute reasonable notice before withdrawal, and how quickly a lawyer may cease acting after notification will depend on all relevant circumstances. Where the matter is covered by statutory provisions or rules of court, these will govern. In other situations, the governing principle is that the lawyer should protect the client's interests to the best of the lawyer's ability and should not desert the client at a critical stage of a matter or at a time when withdrawal would put the client in a position of disadvantage or peril.

A paralegal may be guided by the same principles in a situation where withdrawal from representation is being contemplated. The withdrawal should be done in a manner that permits the client to retain other representation and go forward in the matter without suffering prejudice or harm by reason of the previous licensee's withdrawal. If you are at a critical procedural stage in a matter, such that prejudice or harm to the client would be unavoidable if you were to withdraw your services, you may be required to continue your representation of the client.

BOX 4.15 Withdrawal from Representation

Fact Situation

You are representing Jane Doe in an application by her residential landlord for early termination of her tenancy on grounds that she has substantially interfered with other tenants' reasonable enjoyment of the residential complex. According to the landlord's application, Jane's two sons, who are 11 and 13, are left unsupervised on a regular basis. They play loud music, slam doors, have violent fights, and make a lot of noise at all hours of the day and night, disturbing the tenants in the neighbouring apartments. Witnesses have seen the 11-year-old throwing things, including a glass bottle, off the balcony of their apartment, which is on the tenth floor. There is a pedestrian walkway and a playground below their balcony.

The matter went to voluntary mediation, but there was no settlement.

You have spoken to the paralegal for the landlord, and she has advised you that if the matter goes to a hearing, the landlord will call the building manager and four tenants as witnesses. She has given you copies of the complaint letters and the building manager's complaints log. Two of the tenants are threatening to leave the building if the matter is not resolved.

Jane has admitted to you that she is not home a lot. She has to work two jobs to support her sons and herself, so the boys are often left unsupervised.

The hearing date is set for May 15. It is now April 30. The landlord has just sent you a written offer to settle, stipulating that Jane will have 60 days to find another place to live, failing which the landlord may go forward with the application for her eviction.

You have carefully considered the matter, and you believe that, if the matter goes to a hearing, Jane may be unsuccessful and there will be an order for immediate eviction. You have advised Jane that you think it would be prudent to accept the landlord's offer. Jane thinks this is outrageous. She wants to have a hearing and assert her rights. She is convinced that the landlord cannot just kick her out, when she has lived in the building for five years and there were no complaints until six months ago. "Who are you working for?" she shouts at you. "Me or the landlord?"

At the outset of the matter, you did not request a money retainer. At the beginning of April, you sent Jane an interim invoice for $500.00. She has not paid it.

You do not think that Jane is making good decisions right now. You do not believe that going to a hearing is in her best interests. You would like to give Jane notice that you are withdrawing from representation. You think that it will be a wake-up call for her to start listening to your advice.

Questions for Discussion

1. Are you entitled to withdraw your services based on Jane's refusal to listen to your advice?
2. Can you withdraw without causing prejudice or harm to Jane?
3. Are there any other grounds for withdrawal from representation?
4. Can you give Jane notice that you are withdrawing from representation for the reason stated in the fact situation?

Types of Withdrawal

Rule 3.08 specifies a paralegal's obligations when withdrawing legal services. It sets out situations in which the paralegal

- may choose to withdraw (*optional withdrawal*),
- must withdraw (*mandatory withdrawal*), and
- must comply with special rules (*withdrawal from quasi-criminal and criminal cases*) (Guideline 11).

Optional Withdrawal: Serious Loss of Confidence (Rules 3.08(1)–(4))

In certain situations outlined in Rule 3.08, the paralegal may choose to withdraw from representation, but is not obligated to withdraw.

Subject to Rules 3.08(7), (8), and (9), and the direction of a tribunal, a paralegal may withdraw if there has been a serious loss of confidence between the paralegal and the client (Rule 3.08(2)). The rules of the tribunal may require that you apply to the tribunal for direction. For example, Rule 2.4 of the *Criminal Rules of the Ontario Court of Justice* requires a pretrial application where the relief sought is withdrawal as counsel of record or appointment or removal of counsel, and that the pretrial application be heard at least 60 days before trial unless the court orders otherwise. In criminal and quasi-criminal matters, withdrawal on grounds of serious loss of confidence is subject to the restrictions set out in Rules 3.08(7), (8), and (9).

serious loss of confidence
a situation in which the paralegal and the client no longer trust and rely on each other, making it impossible to have a normal paralegal–client relationship

A **serious loss of confidence** means that the paralegal and the client can no longer trust and rely on each other, making it impossible to have a normal paralegal–client relationship (Guideline 11). Rule 3.08(3) states that "[w]ithout limiting subrule (2), a paralegal may withdraw if the client deceives the paralegal or refuses to accept and act upon the paralegal's advice on a significant point."

Other types of client conduct that may constitute grounds for withdrawal due to a serious loss of confidence might be unreasonable behaviour or lack of cooperation on the part of the client where serious matters are at issue, refusal to communicate with the paralegal, and/or refusal to provide proper instructions.

Whatever the circumstances, a paralegal shall not threaten to withdraw as a device to force a hasty decision by the client on a difficult question (Rule 3.08(4)).

Mandatory Withdrawal (Rules 3.08(1), (5))

In certain situations, you shall withdraw from representation, even if you wish to continue with the retainer or the client wants you to continue as her legal representative. Rule 3.08(5) states:

> (5) Subject to subrules (7), (8) and (9) and the direction of the tribunal, a paralegal shall withdraw if,
> (a) discharged by the client;
> (b) the client's instructions require the paralegal to act contrary to the Rules or by-laws; or
> (c) the paralegal is not competent to continue to handle the matter.

Depending on the circumstances, failure to withdraw pursuant to Rule 3.08(5) may result in disciplinary action.

Non-payment of Fees (Rules 3.08(1), (6))

Subject to subrules (7), (8), and (9) and the direction of a tribunal, unless serious prejudice to the client would result, a paralegal may withdraw from a case if, after reasonable notice, the client fails to provide a retainer or funds on account of disbursements or fees (Rule 3.08(6)). You should consider including notice to the client of possible withdrawal of services on this ground in the retainer agreement or engagement letter.

The timing of the withdrawal is critical when withdrawing from representation for non-payment of fees. If the client would suffer serious prejudice or harm by reason of your withdrawal for non-payment of fees, you may be required to continue to represent the client, even if your fees remain unpaid. Rule 3.08(8) specifically states that, in a quasi-criminal or criminal case, a paralegal may not withdraw because of non-payment of fees if the date set for the trial of the case is not far enough removed for the client to obtain other representation or to give the successor licensee sufficient time to prepare adequately for trial, and if an adjournment of the trial date would prejudice the client's interests.

Withdrawal from Quasi-Criminal and Criminal Cases (Rules 3.08(1), (7)–(9))

When representing a client in a quasi-criminal or criminal matter, there are special rules for withdrawal from representation that apply whether withdrawal is optional or mandatory, or for non-payment of fees. As of this writing, these rules apply to summary conviction matters and to *Provincial Offences Act* prosecutions.

Guideline 11 notes that whether a paralegal may withdraw in these types of matters has to do with the amount of time between *the withdrawal* (the date and time the paralegal intends to stop representing the client) and *the trial* (the date and time the client's trial begins).

> Generally, the amount of time between the withdrawal and trial must be sufficient to allow the client to hire another representative and the new representative to prepare properly for trial.
>
> While the *Rules* do not require the paralegal to make an application to be removed as the client's representative, most tribunal rules do. Therefore, the paralegal should consult the rules of the tribunal to determine what process is to be followed. The paralegal must not tell the tribunal or the prosecutor the reasons for withdrawal, unless disclosure is justified in accordance with the *Rules*.
>
> The paralegal may seek to adjourn the trial to give the client or the new representative more time to prepare, as long as the adjournment does not prejudice the client (Guideline 11).

Permitted Withdrawal for Non-Payment of Fees or Other Adequate Cause (Rule 3.08(7))

Rule 3.08(7) permits withdrawal in quasi-criminal and criminal matters in the following circumstances:

> (7) A paralegal who has agreed to act in a quasi-criminal or criminal case may withdraw because the client has not paid the agreed fee or for other adequate cause if the interval between the withdrawal and the date set for trial of the case is sufficient to enable the client to obtain alternate representation and to allow such other licensee adequate time for preparation and if the paralegal,
>
> (a) advises the client, preferably in writing, that the paralegal is withdrawing and the reason for the withdrawal;
>
> (b) accounts to the client for any monies received on account of fees and disbursements;

(c) notifies the prosecution in writing that the paralegal is no longer acting;

(d) in a case where the paralegal's name appears in the records of the court as acting for the accused, notifies the clerk or registrar of the appropriate court in writing that the paralegal is no longer acting; and

(e) complies with the applicable rules of the tribunal or court.

Although the Rules do not require you to apply to the tribunal to be removed as the client's paralegal, the rules or practice directions of the court may require that you do so. When withdrawing from representation, you should ensure that you follow the correct procedures for the tribunal in which the matter is being heard.

With respect to Rule 3.08(7)(e), a reminder: Rule 2.4 of the *Criminal Rules of the Ontario Court of Justice* requires a pretrial application where the relief sought is withdrawal as counsel of record or appointment or removal of counsel, and that the pretrial application be heard at least 60 days before trial, unless the court orders otherwise.

Withdrawal Not Permitted for Non-Payment of Fees—Quasi-Criminal and Criminal Cases (Rule 3.08(8))

Rule 3.08(8) states that:

> (8) A paralegal who has agreed to act in a quasi-criminal or criminal case may not withdraw because of non-payment of fees if the date set for the trial of the case is not far enough removed to enable the client to obtain the services of another licensee or to enable the other licensee to prepare adequately for trial and if an adjournment of the trial date cannot be obtained without adversely affecting the client's interests.

Withdrawal from Representation for Reasons Other Than Non-Payment of Fees—Quasi-Criminal and Criminal Cases (Rule 3.08(9))

Rule 3.08(9) states that:

> (9) If,
>
> (a) a paralegal is justified in withdrawing from a quasi-criminal or criminal case for reasons other than non-payment of fees; and
>
> (b) there is not a sufficient interval between a notice to the client of the paralegal's intention to withdraw and the date when the case is to be tried to enable the client to obtain the services of another licensee and to enable the new licensee to prepare adequately for trial,
>
> the paralegal, unless instructed otherwise by the client, shall attempt to have the trial date adjourned and may withdraw from the case only with permission of the court before which the case is to be tried.

Manner of Withdrawal (Rules 3.08(10)–(13))

Guideline 11 recommends that a paralegal manage client expectations about what will happen if the relationship ends or the matter concludes from the outset of the client matter.

To avoid misunderstandings, it will be helpful for the paralegal to explain to the client, at the beginning of the relationship

- that all documents to which the client is entitled will be returned to the client when their relationship ends or the matter concludes, and
- which documents in the file will belong to the paralegal, so that they will be kept by the paralegal when their relationship ends or the matter is finished.

To ensure that the client understands these details, the paralegal should consider including them in his or her engagement letter or retainer agreement.

When a paralegal withdraws, he or she shall try to minimize expense and avoid prejudice to the client and shall do all that can reasonably be done to facilitate the orderly transfer of the matter to the successor licensee (Rule 3.08(10)).

Rules 3.08(11) to (13) state that:

> (11) Upon discharge or withdrawal, a paralegal shall,
> (a) deliver to the client or to the order of the client all papers and property to which the client is entitled (subject to the paralegal's right to a lien);
> (b) subject to any applicable trust conditions, give the client all information that may be required in connection with the case or matter;
> (c) account for all funds of the client then held or previously dealt with, including the refunding of any monies not earned during the representation;
> (d) promptly render an account for outstanding fees and disbursements;
> (e) cooperate with the successor licensee so as to minimize expense and avoid prejudice to the client; and
> (f) comply with the applicable rules of court.
> (12) In addition to the obligations set out in subrule (11), upon discharge or withdrawal, a paralegal shall notify the client in writing, stating:
> (a) the fact that the paralegal has withdrawn;
> (b) the reasons, if any, for the withdrawal; and
> (c) in the case of litigation, that the client should expect that the hearing or trial will proceed on the date scheduled and that the client should retain a new legal practitioner promptly.
> (13) If the paralegal who is discharged or withdraws is a member of a firm, the client shall be notified that the paralegal and the firm are no longer acting for the client.

Successor Licensee (Rule 3.08(14))

Guideline 11 comments that:

> When the paralegal withdraws, he or she is subject to restrictions relating to the disclosure of client information. [For example, the paralegal should not reveal] the reason for withdrawing to a *successor* (a paralegal or lawyer who accepts the client's matter after the original paralegal has withdrawn). Refer to Guideline 8: Confidentiality for further information on this subject.
>
> If a paralegal's services are terminated while the client's matter is ongoing and the client requests that the matter be transferred to a new paralegal or lawyer, the paralegal should confirm, in writing, the termination of the retainer. The

> paralegal should also obtain a *direction*, signed by the client, for release of the client's file to a successor paralegal or lawyer. … If the file will be collected by the client personally, the paralegal should obtain a written acknowledgement signed by the client, confirming that the client has received the file.
>
> Cooperation with the successor licensee will normally include providing any memoranda of fact or law that have been prepared by the paralegal in connection with the matter, but confidential information not clearly related to the matter should not be disclosed without the written consent of the client.

Before agreeing to represent a client of a predecessor licensee, a successor paralegal shall be satisfied that the predecessor has withdrawn or has been discharged by the client (Rule 3.08(14)).

The commentary to Rule 3.7-10 of the *Rules of Professional Conduct* notes that it is acceptable for a successor licensee to urge the client to settle or take reasonable steps toward settling any outstanding account of the former licensee, especially if the former licensee withdrew for good cause or was capriciously discharged. However, if a trial or hearing is in progress or imminent, or if the client would otherwise be prejudiced, the existence of an outstanding account should not be allowed to interfere with the successor licensee acting for the client.

CHAPTER SUMMARY

The fiduciary relationship between the paralegal and the client gives rise to a special standard of care that imposes the following duties on the paralegal: loyalty, competence, honesty and candour, confidentiality, avoidance of conflicts of interest, and accounting for client property. These duties are codified in the Rules.

A paralegal shall perform any services undertaken on a client's behalf to the standard of a competent paralegal. A competent paralegal is a paralegal who has and applies the relevant knowledge, skills, and attributes appropriate to each client matter. These include but are not limited to (1) knowledge of general legal principles and procedures and substantive law; (2) application of appropriate skills; (3) conscientious, cost-effective, and diligent representation; (4) client service and communication; (5) effective practice management; and (6) pursuing appropriate training and development to maintain or enhance knowledge and skills.

A paralegal shall be honest and candid when advising all clients. You must advise the client honestly and candidly of the applicable law, the client's options, possible outcomes, and possible risks. Your advice should enable the client to make informed decisions and give appropriate instructions in the matter.

You should always ensure that clients, including prospective clients, understand that you are a paralegal, not a lawyer. You shall never undertake or provide advice about a matter that is outside of the scope of permitted practice for paralegals.

When advising a client, you shall never knowingly assist in or encourage any dishonesty, fraud, crime, or illegal conduct. You shall not instruct a client on how to violate the law and avoid punishment.

A paralegal shall, at all times, hold in strict confidence all information concerning the business and affairs of a client that is acquired in the course of their professional relationship, and shall not disclose any such information unless expressly or implicitly authorized by the client or required by law to do so. The duty of confidentiality begins at the commencement of the paralegal–client relationship and continues indefinitely.

A paralegal shall not advise or represent opposing parties in a dispute, except as permitted by the Rules. A paralegal shall not act or continue to act in a matter when there is or is likely to be a conflicting interest unless, after disclosure adequate to make an informed decision, the client or prospective client consents. To help avoid conflicts of interest, a paralegal should consider maintaining a conflicts checking system and should carefully consider his or her obligations under Rule 3.04.

When a paralegal changes firms, a conflict of interest may arise. Rule 3.05 sets out procedures to be followed by paralegals who are transferring to a new firm and by new paralegals who are preparing to join a firm.

A paralegal should be cautious about entering with a client into any business arrangement that is unrelated to the provision of paralegal services, as this may cause a conflict of interest for the paralegal.

A paralegal is a fiduciary with respect to any client property that comes into her possession, and shall care for that property as a careful and prudent owner would when dealing with similar property. The paralegal must comply with the rules and the law about the preservation of property entrusted to a fiduciary, including maintaining a valuable property record in accordance with By-law 9.

The client may terminate the paralegal–client relationship at any time, for any reason. A paralegal shall not withdraw from representation of a client before the matter in which the paralegal was retained is concluded except for good cause and upon notice to the client appropriate in the circumstances.

Good cause for withdrawal will depend on many factors, including: the nature of the matter and the stage you are at in the matter; the relationship with the client; your expertise and experience; and any harm or prejudice to the client that may result from the withdrawal of services. These factors may also determine what appropriate notice is in the circumstances. Generally, you should try to safeguard the client from prejudice or harm. If you are at a critical procedural stage in a matter, even though grounds for withdrawal from representation may exist, you may be required to continue your representation of the client.

In certain situations, a paralegal is required to withdraw from representation, even if the paralegal or the client wishes to continue with the retainer. A paralegal shall withdraw from representation if: discharged by the client; the client's instructions require the paralegal to act contrary to the Rules or By-Laws; or the paralegal is not competent to continue to handle the matter.

Special restrictions on withdrawal from representation apply in criminal and quasi-criminal matters.

KEY TERMS

affiliated entity, 132
affiliation, 132
alternative dispute resolution, 103
beneficiary, 90
competent paralegal, 92
continuing client, 108
continuing relationship, 130
direction, 141
dispute, 119
error, 105
express (or explicit) authorization, 111
fiduciary, 90
fiduciary relationship, 90
guarantee, 137
honest and candid, 98
implied authorization, 111
independent legal advice, 124
independent legal representation, 122
justified disclosure, 112
multi-discipline practice, 131
omission, 105
permitted disclosure, 112
procedural law, 94
professional judgment, 94
serious loss of confidence, 144
substantive law, 93
surety, 138
valuable property record, 139

REFERENCES

Constitution Act, 1982, being Schedule B to the *Canada Act 1982* (U.K.), 1982, c. 11.

Courts of Justice Act, RSO 1990, c. C.43.

Criminal Code, RSC 1985, c. C-46, as amended.

Criminal Rules of the Ontario Court of Justice (July 1, 2012), http://www.ontariocourts.ca/ocj/criminal-rules/criminal-rules.

Curtis, Carole, Dealing with the Difficult Client (October 2003), http://www.practicepro.ca/practice/pdf/DealingDifficultClientCaroleCurtis.pdf.

French Language Services Act, RSO 1990, c. F.32.

Highway Traffic Act, RSO 1990, c. H.8.

Income Tax Act, RSC 1985, c. 1, as amended.

Insurance Act, RSO 1990, c. I.8.

Law Society Act, RSO 1990, c. L.8, as amended.

Law Society of Upper Canada, *By-Laws* (2007), as amended ("the By-Laws"), http://www.lsuc.on.ca/with.aspx?id=1070.

Law Society of Upper Canada, Commentary to the Rules of Professional Conduct (October 2014), http://www.lsuc.on.ca/lawyer-conduct-rules.

Law Society of Upper Canada, Continuing Professional Development Requirement, http://www.lsuc.on.ca/CPD-Requirement.

Law Society of Upper Canada, *Paralegal Professional Conduct Guidelines* (October 2014) ("the Guidelines"), http://www.lsuc.on.ca/paralegal-conduct-guidelines.

Law Society of Upper Canada, *Paralegal Rules of Conduct* (October 2014) ("the Rules"), http://www.lsuc.on.ca/paralegal/conduct/rules.

Law Society of Upper Canada, *Rules of Professional Conduct* (2014), http://www.lsuc.on.ca/lawyer-conduct-rules.

Lemieux, Tim, Is anyone listening? *LawPRO Magazine* 10:2 (Fall 2011), http://www.practicepro.ca/lawpromag/Communications-claims-causes.pdf.

Office of the Privacy Commissioner of Canada, Fact Sheet: "Complying with the *Personal Information Protection and Electronic Documents Act*" (2014), http://www.priv.gc.ca/resource/fs-fi/02_05_d_16_e.asp.

Ontario Business Corporations Act, RSO 1990, c. B.16, as amended.

Personal Information Protection and Electronic Documents Act, SC 2000, c. 5.

Provincial Offences Act, RSO 1990, c. P.33, as amended.

O. Reg. 258/98, Rules of the Small Claims Court, http://www.e-laws.gov.on.ca/html/regs/english/elaws_regs_980258_e.htm.

Residential Tenancies Act, 2006, SO 2006, c.17, as amended.

Smith v. Jones, [1999] 1 SCR 455.

REVIEW QUESTIONS

1. Your practice is restricted to Small Claims Court litigation and *Highway Traffic Act* matters. The property manager for a corporate residential landlord for whom you have done some collections work wants to retain you to defend the landlord in a *Provincial Offences Act* prosecution. The landlord has been charged with several offences contrary to the residential tenancies legislation, including harassment and interference with the tenants' enjoyment of the premises. The landlord's first court appearance is scheduled for two weeks' time. At that time, a trial date will be set. From your *Highway Traffic Act* work, you know that the earliest available trial dates are six or seven months away.

   Residential tenancies law is an area into which you are eager to expand. You would also like to accept the retainer because the matter is complex and you look forward to the challenge. You have already checked out some continuing professional development opportunities at the Law Society website, for which you will be charged.

   If the landlord is convicted, the maximum fine is $100,000.

   Should you accept the retainer?

2. A client consults you about commencing a claim for wrongful dismissal in Small Claims Court. Based on what he is telling you and the documents he has produced for you, you do not think that he has a good case. On the other hand, you could use the money, and he appears to be very eager to sue his former employer. "I don't care if I win. I just want to get these guys," he tells you. "I want to jerk them around the way they jerked me around. I can pay."

   What are some issues to consider?

3. A client has several invoices that have been outstanding for 90 days. You wish to put them in collection. What procedures should you follow and what information may you disclose to the collection agency?

4. Joseph Kutar meets with you at your office to discuss a *Highway Traffic Act* matter. While you are reviewing the certificate of offence, Joseph reads the labels on some of the client files stacked on your desk. "I know that landlord," he says, indicating one of the files. "I used to live in one of their buildings. A real slum." You move the files to the floor behind your desk. Then you ask Joseph some questions about the *Highway Traffic Act* matter, taking notes of his answers.

   Based on what he tells you of the matter and your review of the certificate of offence, you advise him to plead down to a lesser offence with fewer demerit points. When he hears this, Joseph's behaviour becomes belligerent and threatening. "I'm a courier," he says. "Any more demerit points and I can't drive. I'll find someone else who knows what they're doing!" He grabs the certificate of offence off your desk and leaves your office.

   A few days later you have some matters in traffic court. Outside the courtroom, you get into a conversation with a couple of other paralegals who do a lot of traffic court work. One of them, Alice Fisher, says jokingly to you, "I'm doing some work for a former client of yours, one J.K. He told me he had to fire you because you kept giving him bad advice. What's the real story?" You change the subject, and start talking about how difficult it is becoming to find parking near the courthouse.

   Several people are sitting or standing close by and can overhear your conversation.

   Discuss some professional and practice management issues that arise based on the facts above.

5. Theresa Santos wishes to meet with you to discuss a residential tenancies matter. She wishes to apply for an abatement of rent and other relief on grounds of non-repair of the residential premises and harassment by the landlord or the landlord's agent. You are familiar with Theresa's landlord, having acted for the landlord in the past in tenant applications similar to Theresa's, though for a different building. You have not had any work from that landlord for over a year, but you figure your experience from the previous matters will give you an advantage in this application.

   Should you accept the retainer?

6. Before agreeing to a joint retainer in which you have a continuing relationship with one client, for whom you act regularly, what steps must you take?

7. You are considering accepting a position that has just been offered to you at a new paralegal firm. You have appeared opposite this firm on several matters in the past, and you are very impressed by their advocacy skills and high standards of professionalism. What are some issues that both you and the new firm should consider?

8. Your client is Lars Larssen. On January 3, 20—, you receive a TAG Heuer sports watch valued at $7,500 from your client, which is to be held in trust pending a court order determining ownership of the property.

On February 14, 20—, pursuant to a written settlement agreement between the parties and a signed direction from your client, you deliver the watch to your client's former partner, Sigrid Gutman.

Complete the valuable property record for this item.

Schwarz and Berryman Professional Corporation
Licensed Paralegals
Valuable Property Record

Client	Description of property	Date received	Received from	Value	Delivered to	Date of delivery

Advocacy

5

LEARNING OBJECTIVES

After reading this chapter, you will understand:

- The paralegal as advocate.
- The paralegal advocate's duty to clients, tribunals, and others.
- The paralegal advocate's obligations in the tribunal process.
- Disclosure of documents.
- Disclosure of errors and omissions.
- Procedure when agreeing to a guilty plea.
- Interviewing witnesses.
- Communicating with witnesses giving testimony.
- The paralegal as witness.
- Dealing with unrepresented persons.

General (Rule 4; Guideline 12)

advocate
a person who assists, defends, or pleads for others before a tribunal

tribunal
includes courts, boards, arbitrators, mediators, administrative agencies, and bodies that resolve disputes, regardless of their function or the informality of their procedures

adjudicator
a person who hears or considers a proceeding before a tribunal and makes a decision with respect to that proceeding

An **advocate** is a someone who speaks and acts on behalf of others. One of an advocate's roles is to assist, plead for, or defend others before a tribunal.

For purposes of the *Paralegal Rules of Conduct*, the term **tribunal** includes courts, boards, arbitrators, mediators, administrative agencies, and bodies that resolve disputes, regardless of their function or the informality of their procedures (Rule 1.02). An **adjudicator** is any person who hears or considers any type of proceeding before a tribunal and renders a decision with respect to that proceeding (Guideline 12).

Rule 4 of the Rules, which governs advocacy, applies to all appearances and proceedings before all tribunals in which the paralegal may appear (Rule 4.01(2)).

The Paralegal as Advocate (Rule 4.01)

Duty to Clients, Tribunals, and Others (Rules 4.01(1)–(6), (8), (9), 6.01(1), (2))

The paralegal advocate must balance a number of duties.

> The paralegal has a duty to represent his or her client diligently and fearlessly. Generally, the paralegal has no obligation to assist an opposing party, or to advance matters harmful to the client's case. However, these general principles do not mean that, when acting as advocate for a client before a tribunal, the paralegal can behave as he or she likes or, in some cases, as his or her client may instruct. Rule 4 describes the professional obligations that a paralegal owes to opposing parties, other paralegals and lawyers, the tribunal, and the administration of justice. These obligations are paramount, and must be met by the paralegal in each and every tribunal proceeding in which the paralegal acts as advocate for a client (Guideline 12).

Rule 4.01(1) states that:

> When acting as an advocate, the paralegal shall represent the client resolutely and honourably within the limits of the law while, at the same time, treating the tribunal and other licensees with candour, fairness, courtesy and respect.

Rule 4 does not require a paralegal to assist an adversary or advance matters derogatory to the client's case, except as otherwise provided in the Rules (Rule 4.01(3)).

In addition to your duty to represent the client resolutely and honourably, when acting as a paralegal advocate, you have a duty to the administration of justice (Rules 6.01(1), (2)):

> (1) A paralegal shall encourage public respect for, and try to improve, the administration of justice.
>
> (2) A paralegal shall take care not to weaken or destroy public confidence in legal institutions or authorities by making irresponsible allegations or comments particularly when commenting on judges or members of a tribunal.

Rule 4.01(4) sets out the following requirements for paralegal advocates.

> (4) Without restricting the generality of subrule (1), the paralegal shall,
> (a) raise fearlessly every issue, advance every argument, and ask every question, however distasteful, that the paralegal thinks will help the client's case;
> (b) endeavour, on the client's behalf, to obtain the benefit of every remedy and defence authorized by law;
> (c) never waive or abandon a client's legal rights, for example, an available defence under a statute of limitations, without the client's informed consent; and
> (d) avoid and discourage the client from resorting to frivolous and vexatious objections, or from attempts to gain advantage from mistakes or oversights not going to the merits, or from tactics designed to merely delay or harass the other side.

A **remedy** is a method of enforcing a right, or preventing or compensating for a wrong.

A **statutory limitation period** is a period of time established by a statute for commencing a proceeding. After the statutory limitation period has expired, any proceeding by or against your client is **statute-barred**—that is, it is stopped by the expiry of the statutory limitation period. For example, s. 786 of the *Criminal Code* states that in a summary conviction matter, no proceedings shall be commenced more than six months after the time when the subject matter of the proceedings arose, unless the prosecutor and the defendant agree.

Informed consent is consent based on information that is sufficient to allow the client to assess the situation and make an informed decision. Consent should always be obtained or confirmed in writing.

Special rules apply to agreements on guilty pleas. See Rules 4.01(8) and (9), and the discussion at page 163 of this chapter.

An **objection** is an argument by a party that a particular piece of evidence, line of questioning, or other matter is improper or illegal and should not be allowed by the court. A **frivolous and vexatious objection** is an objection that has no legal merit and is made to annoy, harass, or embarrass the other side. The **merits of the case** are the legal principles upon which a party's assertion of rights is based. A mistake or oversight that does not go to the merits of the case does not affect a party's legal rights.

remedy
a way of enforcing a right, or preventing or compensating for a wrong

statutory limitation period
a period of time established by a statute for commencing a proceeding

statute-barred
a proceeding that is prevented by the expiry of the statutory limitation period

objection
an argument by a party that a particular piece of evidence, line of questioning, or other matter is improper or unlawful and should not be allowed by the court

frivolous and vexatious objection
an objection that has no legal merit and is made to annoy, harass, or embarrass the other side

merits of the case
the legal principles upon which a party's assertion of rights is based

Duty as Prosecutor (Rule 4.01(5.1))

When acting as a prosecutor, a paralegal shall act for the public and the administration of justice resolutely and honourably within the limits of the law while treating the tribunal with candour, fairness, courtesy, and respect (Rule 4.01(5.1)).

The role of the prosecutor is not to "win" every case by obtaining a conviction. Prosecutors have a duty to administer justice fairly and impartially, with a view to the community interest. Prosecutors are (or should be) non-partisan. They must put all the available evidence before the court, with the object of obtaining a just and fair result.

Candour, Fairness, Courtesy, and Respect (Rules 4.01(1), (4)(d), (5)(o), 7.01(3))

When acting as an advocate, a paralegal shall treat the tribunal and other licensees with candour, fairness, courtesy and respect (Rule 4.01(1)).

A paralegal shall avoid and discourage the client from resorting to frivolous and vexatious objections, or from attempts to gain advantage from mistakes or oversights not going to the merits, or from tactics designed to merely delay or harass the other side (Rule 4.01(4)(d)). A paralegal shall not, by his or her conduct, needlessly inconvenience a witness (Rule 4.01(5)(o)).

A paralegal shall not, in the course of providing legal services, communicate, in writing or otherwise, with a client, another licensee, or any other person in a manner that is abusive, offensive, or otherwise inconsistent with the proper tone of a professional communication from a paralegal (Rule 7.01(3)).

A paralegal should not engage in rude and disruptive behaviour before a tribunal, or uncivil correspondence, language, or behaviour toward opposing parties or their advocates (Guideline 12).

In *Principles of Civility for Advocates* (2006), the Advocates Society notes that

> [c]ivility amongst those entrusted with the administration of justice is central to its effectiveness and to the public's confidence in that system. Civility ensures matters before the court are resolved in an orderly way and helps preserve the role of counsel in the justice system as an honourable one.
>
> Litigation, however, whether before a court or tribunal is not a "tea party." Counsel are bound to vigorously advance their client's case, fairly and honourably. Accordingly, counsel's role is openly and necessarily partisan and nothing which follows is intended to undermine those principles. But counsel can disagree, even vigorously, without being disagreeable. Whether among counsel or before the courts, antagonistic or acrimonious behaviour is not conducive to effective advocacy. Rather, civility is the hallmark of our best counsel.

If complained of to the Law Society, lack of civility may result in disciplinary action. One of the Law Society's goals is to encourage civil conduct and respond in an appropriate and effective manner to complaints of incivility.

The Paralegal and the Tribunal Process (Rule 4.01(5))

When acting as an advocate, the paralegal shall not (Rule 4.01(5)):

- abuse the tribunal's process by instituting or continuing malicious proceedings (Rule 4.01(5)(a));
- mislead the tribunal (Rule 4.01(5)(c), (d), (f), (i), (j), (k));
- attempt to influence the tribunal by methods other than open persuasion as an advocate (Rule 4.01(5)(e), (h));
- engage in dishonest or dishonourable conduct (Rule 4.01(5)(b), (c), (f));
- harass or influence a witness (Rule 4.01(5)(g), (i), (l), (m), (n));
- needlessly inconvenience a witness (Rule 4.01(5)(o)); or

- appear before a court or tribunal while under the influence of alcohol or a drug (Rule 4.01(5)(p)).

Malicious Proceedings (Rule 4.01(5)(a))

A paralegal shall not abuse the process of the tribunal by instituting or prosecuting proceedings that, although legal in themselves, are clearly motivated by malice on the part of the client and are brought solely for the purpose of injuring the other party (Rule 4.01(5)(a)). A paralegal should not help a client to bring proceedings that have no merit. Claims that have no merit waste the time of the tribunal and its officers, and do not further the cause of justice (Guideline 12).

BOX 5.1 Abuse of Tribunal Process

Fact Situation

A prospective client consults with you about commencing a proceeding against his neighbour in Small Claims Court for damages of $2,000. According to the client, the neighbour's collection of brightly painted garden gnomes and other garden statuary has reduced the value of the client's property by at least that much. "He must have a hundred gnomes over there," the client says. "I have a barbecue in my back yard, and my guests can't believe what they're seeing. I've talked to the Property Standards people at City Hall about it. They won't do anything. There's nothing in the by-laws about garden gnomes."

Throughout the interview, the client speaks of the neighbour in angry, disparaging terms. He mentions that the neighbour makes insulting remarks and spreads malicious gossip about him in the neighbourhood. When you suggest that he consider building a fence between the two properties, he says, "That's what I'm going to do, when I get the $2,000."

Question for Discussion

Should you accept the retainer?

Threatening Criminal Proceedings (Rules 4.01(5)(n), 3.02(9), 3.08(5))

When acting as an advocate, a paralegal shall not, when representing a complainant or potential complainant, attempt to gain a benefit for the complainant by threatening the laying of a criminal charge or by offering to seek to procure the withdrawal of a criminal charge (Rule 4.01(5)(n)).

A **complainant** is a person who alleges that he was the victim of a crime, and who takes part in the prosecution of the person(s) accused of committing the crime.

complainant
a person who alleges that he was the victim of a crime, and who takes part in the prosecution of the person(s) accused of committing the crime

Subject to the direction of a tribunal, you shall withdraw from representation if your client in a litigation matter instructs you to advise another party that you will have criminal charges laid against them if they do not accede to your client's demands (Rule 3.08(5)(b)).

It is an abuse of a tribunal's process to threaten to make or to make a complaint in order to gain an advantage in a civil action, even if the client in the civil action has a legitimate claim for damages.

Misleading the Tribunal (Rules 4.01(5)(c), (d), (f), (i), (j), (k))

A paralegal must ensure that neither the paralegal nor his or her client(s) misleads the tribunal. For a tribunal to decide a matter effectively and appropriately, the tribunal must have access to everything that is relevant to the issues to be decided (Guideline 12).

A paralegal advocate shall not knowingly attempt to deceive a tribunal or influence the course of justice by offering false evidence, misstating facts or law, presenting or relying upon a false or deceptive affidavit, suppressing what ought to be disclosed, or otherwise assisting in any deception, crime, or illegal conduct (Rule 4.01(5)(c)).

BOX 5.2 What Is an Affidavit?

An **affidavit** is a written statement of facts that is confirmed under oath or by affirmation by the person making it. The person making the affidavit is called the **deponent**.

The content of an affidavit is evidence. Swearing or affirming a false or deceptive affidavit or assisting another person to do so with intent to mislead is an offence contrary to s. 131 of the *Criminal Code*.

affidavit
a written statement of facts that is confirmed under oath or by affirmation by the person making it

deponent
a person who makes an affidavit

binding authority
a judicial decision by a higher court that must be followed by lower courts; also known as a binding precedent

A paralegal advocate shall not deliberately refrain from informing the tribunal of any binding authority that the paralegal considers to be directly on point and that has not been mentioned by an opponent (Rule 4.01(5)(d)). **Binding authority** (also known as binding precedent) is a judicial decision by a higher court that must be followed by lower courts.

BOX 5.3 Binding Authority (Rule 4.01(5)(d))

Fact Situation

You represent the defendant in a Small Claims Court proceeding. During some last-minute online research before the trial, you find a Divisional Court decision dealing with issues very similar to those in your matter. The decision is unfavourable to your client's defence and favourable to the plaintiff's claim. The decision is binding on the Small Claims Court. There are some minor legal and factual differences between the matter dealt with in the appellate decision and the matter in which you are acting.

To your surprise, during submissions, the licensee representing the plaintiff does not refer to the decision.

Question for Discussion

Are you required to inform the court of a binding precedent that will almost certainly prejudice your client's defence?

A paralegal advocate shall not knowingly assert a fact as true when its truth cannot reasonably be supported by the evidence or as a matter of which notice may be taken by the tribunal (Rule 4.01(5)(f)).

BOX 5.4 Judicial Notice

What is meant by "a matter of which notice may be taken by the tribunal" (Rule 4.05(5)(f))? This is known in the courts as **judicial notice**. Adjudicators may notice, or accept as true, certain notorious facts (that is, matters of common knowledge) without hearing evidence and without inquiry. Other lesser-known facts (for example, matters that can be checked in a standard reference work and are not easily disputed) may be judicially noticed after inquiry.

judicial notice
when a tribunal notices, or accepts as true, certain notorious facts or matters of common knowledge without hearing evidence and without inquiry; other lesser-known facts may be noticed after inquiry

A paralegal advocate shall not knowingly:

- misstate the contents of a document, the testimony of a witness, the substance of an argument, or the provisions of a statute or like authority (Rule 4.01(5)(i));
- permit a witness or party to be presented in a false or misleading way or to impersonate another (Rule 4.01(5)(j)); or
- misrepresent the client's position in the litigation or the issues to be determined in the litigation (Rule 4.01(5)(k)).

You must represent your client fearlessly and resolutely, but you shall not knowingly engage in dishonest conduct that misleads the tribunal and others in order to protect your client or gain an advantage for your client.

Improperly Influencing the Tribunal (Rule 4.01(5)(e), (h))

A paralegal advocate shall not:

- appear before a judicial officer when the paralegal, a partner of the paralegal, a paralegal employed by the paralegal firm, or the client has a business or personal relationship with the officer that gives rise to, or might reasonably appear to give rise to, pressure, influence, or inducement affecting the impartiality of the officer, unless all parties consent and it is in the interests of justice (Rule 4.01(5)(e)); or
- endeavour or allow anyone else to endeavour, directly or indirectly, to influence the decision or action of the tribunal or any of its officials in any case or matter by any means other than open persuasion as an advocate (Rule 4.01(5)(h)).

Guideline 12 comments that:

> For the public to have respect for the administration of justice, tribunals must be fair, objective, independent, and neutral. There should be no personal connection between an adjudicator and any of the parties to a proceeding or their advocates.
>
> The only appropriate way to influence the tribunal's decision is through open persuasion as an advocate. This is done by making submissions based on legal principles and offering appropriate evidence before the tribunal in the presence

of, or on notice to, all parties to the proceeding, or as otherwise permitted or required by the tribunal's rules of procedure. A paralegal should not communicate directly with the adjudicator in the absence of the other parties, unless permitted to do so by the tribunal's rules of procedure.

Dishonest Conduct (Rules 4.01(5)(b), (c), (f))

A paralegal advocate shall not knowingly:

- assist or permit the client to do anything that the paralegal considers to be dishonest or dishonourable (Rule 4.01(5)(b)); or
- attempt to deceive a tribunal or influence the course of justice by offering false evidence, misstating facts or law, presenting or relying upon a false or deceptive affidavit, suppressing what ought to be disclosed, or otherwise assisting in any deception, crime, or illegal conduct (Rule 4.01(5)(c)); or
- assert a fact as true when its truth cannot reasonably be supported by the evidence or as a matter of which notice may be taken by the tribunal (Rule 4.01(5)(f)).

You must represent your client fearlessly and resolutely, but you shall not knowingly engage in dishonest conduct that misleads the tribunal and others in order to protect your client or gain an advantage for your client:

> Acting with integrity before a tribunal means being honest and acting with high ethical principles (Guideline 12).

BOX 5.5 Dishonest Conduct

Fact Situation

You are acting for the plaintiff in an unliquidated claim in Small Claims Court. The defendant failed to file a defence within the prescribed time, and has been noted in default. You have prepared a motion in writing for an assessment of damages, and a supporting affidavit.

The client provided the material in the affidavit to you during a telephone conversation just after the defendant was noted in default. You phoned her because you wanted to clarify some issues before you got started on the supporting affidavit. You took detailed notes of what she said, and went over them with her before ending the call. The statements in the affidavit accurately reflect your notes of the conversation. The statements contain information that is relevant to issues in the matter and, in particular, relevant to determination of the quantum of damages owing.

When the client reviews the supporting affidavit, she objects to several statements because they are harmful to her case. "If the judge reads this, I'll get less money," she says. "Why should I say anything that's going to take money out of my pocket? I never would have told you that stuff if I'd known you were going to use it against me. I want you to leave it out completely, or change it to say something that will get me what I'm asking for."

The client is correct that the material is harmful to her case.

Questions for Discussion

Should you follow the client's instructions to delete or alter the contents of the affidavit? If yes, why? If no, why not, and what action should you take?

Admissions by the Client (Rule 4.01(5)(b), (c), (f))

Guideline 12 states that when defending an accused person, a paralegal's duty is to protect the client from being convicted, except by a tribunal of competent jurisdiction and upon legal evidence sufficient to support a conviction for the offence with which the client is charged. Accordingly, a paralegal may properly rely upon any evidence or defences, including technicalities, as long as they are not known to be false or fraudulent.

The paralegal must advise the client that any admissions made by the client to the paralegal may impose strict limitations on how the paralegal conducts the client's defence (Guideline 12). The Rules require that the paralegal shall not:

- knowingly assist or permit the client to do anything that the paralegal considers to be dishonest or dishonourable;
- knowingly attempt to deceive the tribunal; or
- knowingly assert that a fact is true when its truth cannot be supported by the evidence.

Where the client has admitted to the paralegal any or all of the elements of the offence with which the client is charged, the paralegal must not do or say anything before the tribunal—including call any evidence, or make any arguments or submissions—that would contradict the facts admitted to the paralegal by the client (Guideline 12). This would be misleading the tribunal.

Where the client admits all of the elements of the offence to the paralegal and the paralegal is convinced that the admissions are true and voluntary, the paralegal is restricted in how he conducts the client's defence. The paralegal may object to the jurisdiction of the tribunal, or to the form or admissibility of the evidence, or may question whether the evidence is sufficient to prove beyond a reasonable doubt that the accused committed the offence (Guideline 12).

Where the client admits all the elements of the offence to the paralegal, the paralegal shall not:

- suggest that someone else committed the offence;
- try to establish a defence of alibi; or
- call any evidence that the paralegal believes is false because of the client's admissions (Guideline 12).

Where the client admits all of the elements of the offence to the paralegal, the paralegal is also limited in the extent to which he may attack the evidence for the prosecution. The paralegal may test the evidence given by each witness for the prosecution. The paralegal may argue that the evidence, as a whole, is not sufficient to prove the client guilty beyond a reasonable doubt. The paralegal should go no further than that (Guideline 12).

BOX 5.6 Elements of the Offence

elements of the offence the components of an offence that must be proven beyond a reasonable doubt by the prosecution in order to obtain a conviction

The **elements of the offence** are the legal requirements of the offence. They are the components of the offence that must be proven beyond a reasonable doubt by the prosecution in order to obtain a conviction. They are found in the statute that creates the offence, and in the jurisprudence interpreting the statute. The essential components of an offence are:

1. *Actus reus* (guilty act): the physical components of the offence, including conduct, circumstances, and consequences.
2. *Mens rea* (guilty mind): the mental component, including intention or knowledge, blameworthiness, or fault.

To obtain a conviction, the prosecution must call evidence that proves all of the elements of the offence beyond a reasonable doubt. If the defence raises a reasonable doubt in the mind of the court, the accused should be acquitted.

Witnesses (Rule 4.01(5)(g), (i), (j), (l), (m), (n), (o))

A paralegal advocate shall not:

- make suggestions to a witness recklessly or knowing them to be false (Rule 4.01(5)(g));
- knowingly misstate the testimony of a witness (Rule 4.01(5)(i));
- knowingly permit a witness or party to be presented in a false or misleading way or to impersonate another (Rule 4.01(5)(j));
- needlessly abuse, hector, harass, or inconvenience a witness (Rule 4.01(5)(l));
- improperly dissuade a witness from giving evidence or suggest that a witness be absent (Rule 4.01(5)(m));
- when representing a complainant or potential complainant, attempt to gain a benefit for the complainant by threatening the laying of a criminal charge or by offering to seek or to procure the withdrawal of a criminal charge (Rule 4.01(5)(n)); and
- needlessly inconvenience a witness (Rule 4.01(5)(o)).

Disclosure of Documents (Rule 4.01(6))

Rule 4.01(6) states that:

> (6) If the rules of a tribunal require the parties to produce documents, a paralegal, when acting as an advocate,
>
> (a) shall explain to his or her client the necessity of making full disclosure of all documents relating to any matter in issue and the duty to answer to the best of his or her knowledge, information and belief, any proper question relating to any issue in the action;
>
> (b) shall assist the client in fulfilling his or her obligation to make full disclosure; and
>
> (c) shall not make frivolous requests for the production of documents or make frivolous demands for information.

Timely, complete, and accurate disclosure helps settlement efforts and makes the hearing process more effective and fair (Guideline 12).

Disclosure requirements vary, depending on the tribunal. You should carefully review the procedure of a tribunal and any other relevant law to determine the timing and extent of required disclosure.

Errors and Omissions (Rule 4.01(7))

A paralegal who does, or fails to do, something that may involve a breach of this rule, shall, subject to Rule 3.03 relating to confidentiality, disclose the error or omission and do all that can reasonably be done in the circumstances to rectify it (Rule 4.01(7)).

Any disclosure by the paralegal when making reasonable attempts to correct the error or omission is subject to Rule 3.03 relating to confidentiality. Confidential information shall not be disclosed unless the disclosure is expressly or impliedly authorized by the client, required by law or by an order of a tribunal of competent jurisdiction, required to provide information to the Law Society, or otherwise permitted by Rule 3 (Rule 3.03(1)).

See also the discussion of Rule 3.02(21) Errors at page 105 in Chapter 4.

Agreement on Guilty Pleas (Rules 4.01(8), (9))

Unless the client instructs otherwise, a paralegal acting for an accused or a person who is about to be charged in a criminal or quasi-criminal matter may discuss with the prosecutor a possible resolution to the case (Rule 4.01(8)).

Before negotiating a guilty plea on behalf of the client, the paralegal should obtain and review disclosure and complete any investigation that is appropriate in the circumstances. The paralegal may then enter into an agreement with the prosecutor about a guilty plea if certain conditions have been met.

Rule 4.01(9) states the preconditions to a guilty plea.

> (9) A paralegal, on behalf of his or her client, may enter into an agreement with a prosecutor about a guilty plea, if, following investigation,
>
> (a) the paralegal advises the client about the prospects for an acquittal or finding of guilt;
>
> (b) the paralegal advises the client of the implications and possible consequences of a guilty plea and particularly of the sentencing authority and discretion of the court, including the fact that the court is not bound by any agreement about a guilty plea;
>
> (c) the client is prepared voluntarily to admit the necessary factual and mental elements of the offence charged; and
>
> (d) the client voluntarily instructs the paralegal to enter into an agreement as to a guilty plea.

As an advocate for a person accused in a criminal or quasi-criminal matter, the paralegal should take steps reasonable in the circumstances to satisfy herself that the client's instructions to enter into the agreement on a guilty plea are informed, voluntary, and in writing (Guideline 12).

Interviewing Witnesses (Rule 4.02)

General (Rules 4.02(1), 4.01(5)(g), (i), (j), (l), (m), (n), 4.03)

Subject to the rules on communication with a represented party at Rule 7.02, a paralegal may seek information from any potential witness, whether under subpoena or not, but shall disclose the paralegal's interest and take care not to subvert or suppress any evidence or procure the witness to stay out of the way (Rule 4.02(1)).

Guideline 12 comments that:

> As an advocate, a paralegal may contact all possible witnesses for both sides of a matter (subject to Rule 7.02 regarding communications with a represented person, corporation, or organization), but the paralegal must be fair and honest when dealing with them. This includes the paralegal speaking to the opposing party or co-accused. The paralegal must make it clear to the witness who is the paralegal's client(s) and that the paralegal is acting only in the interests of his or her client(s). As part of this disclosure, the paralegal should give the witness his or her name, tell the witness that he or she is a paralegal, the name of the client(s) he or she represents in the matter, and his or her status in the proceeding. A paralegal should make an extra effort to be clear when the witness does not have legal representation. Note that, although a paralegal may ask to speak to a potential witness, the witness does not have to speak to the paralegal.

A witness has no obligation to talk to you. If a witness tells you he does not want to speak with you, you should leave the witness alone. You are not permitted to needlessly harass or inconvenience a witness (Rule 4.01(5)(l)).

When interviewing witnesses, you shall take care not to subvert or suppress any evidence. You must not coach a witness to leave out evidence or to say things that are not completely true in order to benefit your client (Rule 4.02(1)).

When interviewing witnesses, you shall take care not to procure the witness to stay out of the way—in other words, you shall not cause or persuade a witness not to give evidence at trial (Rule 4.02(1)).

Additional restrictions on a paralegal advocate's conduct when dealing with witnesses are set out in Rule 4.01(5). Among other things, Rule 4.01(5) requires that, when acting as an advocate, a paralegal shall not:

- make suggestions to a witness recklessly or knowing them to be false;
- knowingly permit a witness or party to be presented in a false or misleading way, or to impersonate another;
- needlessly abuse, hector, harass, or inconvenience a witness; or
- improperly dissuade a witness from giving evidence, or suggest that a witness be absent.

Communication with Witnesses Giving Testimony (Rule 4.03)

When preparing for a hearing, you may contact any witness that is unrepresented, whether the witness is sympathetic to your client's cause or not. Different rules apply during a hearing. During a hearing, a paralegal's ability to speak with a witness giving testimony is limited. This ensures that the paralegal does not influence the evidence the witness will give. A comment made by the paralegal to the paralegal's own witness during court recess, for example, may result in a breach of the Rules. The witness may return to the witness box and, as a result of the communication with the paralegal, offer evidence that is slanted to benefit the paralegal's client. Such evidence is no longer neutral and could mislead the tribunal (Guideline 12).

Whether or not you may speak to a witness after the hearing has started depends upon

- whether the witness gives evidence that supports your cause or the cause of an opposing party, and
- what stage the witness is at in giving evidence.

A witness who gives evidence that supports your cause is called a **sympathetic witness**. A witness who gives evidence that supports an opposing party's cause is called an **unsympathetic witness**.

sympathetic witness
a witness who gives evidence that supports a party's cause

unsympathetic witness
a witness who gives evidence that supports an opposing party's cause

Rule 4.03 should be read in conjunction with Rule 7.02 (discussed in Chapter 6). You should not approach or communicate with a witness who has legal representation except through or with the consent of the person's legal representative.

Whether a paralegal is representing a plaintiff, a defendant, a third party, or an accused, there are certain key stages in the process during which the paralegal may have discussions with the witness. Rule 4.03(1) states:

> (1) Subject to the direction of the tribunal, a paralegal shall observe the following rules respecting communication with witnesses giving evidence:
>
> (a) During examination-in-chief, the examining paralegal may discuss with the witness any matter that has not been covered in the examination up to that point.
>
> (b) During examination-in-chief by another licensee of a witness who is unsympathetic to the paralegal's cause, the paralegal not conducting the examination-in-chief may discuss the evidence with the witness.
>
> (c) Between completion of examination-in-chief and commencement of cross-examination of the paralegal's own witness, the paralegal ought not to discuss the evidence given in chief or relating to any matter introduced or touched on during the examination-in-chief.
>
> (d) During cross-examination by an opposing licensee, the witness's own representative ought not to have any conversation with the witness about the witness's evidence or any issue in the proceeding.
>
> (e) Between completion of cross-examination and commencement of a re-examination, a paralegal who is going to re-examine the witness ought not to have any discussion about evidence that will be dealt with on re-examination.

> (f) During cross-examination by the representative of a witness unsympathetic to the cross-examiner's cause, the paralegal may discuss the witness's evidence with the witness.
>
> (g) During cross-examination by the representative of a witness who is sympathetic to that licensee's cause, any conversations ought to be restricted in the same way as communications during examination-in-chief of one's own witness.
>
> (h) During re-examination of a witness called by an opposing licensee, if the witness is sympathetic to the paralegal's cause, the paralegal ought not to discuss the evidence to be given by that witness during re-examination. The paralegal may, however, properly discuss the evidence with a witness who is adverse in interest.

With the consent of the opposing licensee or with leave of the tribunal, a paralegal may enter into discussions with a witness that might otherwise raise a question under this rule as to the propriety of the discussions (Rule 4.03(2)).

Rule 4.03(1) applies, with necessary modifications, to examinations out of court (Rule 4.03(3)). An **examination out of court** is a procedure during which a party or witness is examined under oath or affirmation by opposing parties or their representatives with a view to obtaining facts and information that will assist the parties to prepare their case. In Superior Court of Justice proceedings, examinations out of court include oral or written examinations for discovery (*Rules of Civil Procedure*, Rule 31), taking of evidence before trial (*Rules of Civil Procedure*, Rule 36.01), and cross-examination on an affidavit for use on a motion or application (*Rules of Civil Procedure*, Rule 39.02). See Rule 34.01 of the *Rules of Civil Procedure*.

examination out of court a procedure during which a party or witness is examined under oath or affirmation by opposing parties or their representatives with a view to obtaining facts and information that will assist the parties to prepare their case

The Paralegal as Witness (Rule 4.04)

Rule 4.04(1) states:

> (1) A paralegal who appears as advocate shall not testify or submit his or her own affidavit evidence before the tribunal unless
>
> (a) permitted to do so by law, the tribunal, the rules of court or the rules of procedure of the tribunal, or
>
> (b) the matter is purely formal or uncontroverted.

The role of a paralegal acting as an advocate is different from the role of a paralegal appearing as a witness.

> As an advocate, the paralegal's role is to further the client's case within the limits of the law. The role of a witness is to give evidence of facts that may or may not assist in furthering the case of any of the parties to a proceeding. Because these roles are different, a person may not be able to carry out the functions of both advocate and witness at the same time.
>
> Unless permitted by the tribunal, when acting as an advocate for his or her client before a tribunal, the paralegal should not express personal opinions or beliefs or assert as a fact anything that is properly subject to legal proof, cross-examination, or challenge, or otherwise appear to be giving unsworn testimony. This is improper and may put the paralegal's own credibility in issue.

Table 5.1 Communication with Witnesses (Paralegal Rule 4.03(1))

<table>
<tr><th>STAGE OF PROCEEDING</th><th colspan="4">PERMITTED COMMUNICATION WITH WITNESS IN STAND</th></tr>
<tr><th>You call the witness</th><th colspan="3">Sympathetic witness or unsympathetic witness*</th><th>Applicable point under Rule 4.03(1)</th></tr>
<tr><td>• Examination-in-chief conducted by you</td><td colspan="3">During an interval, you may discuss anything not covered in the examination to that point.</td><td>(a)</td></tr>
<tr><td>• After examination-in-chief
• Before cross-examination</td><td colspan="3">You shall not discuss with the witness the evidence given during examination-in-chief or relating to any matter touched on during examination-in-chief.</td><td>(c)</td></tr>
<tr><td>• Cross-examination by opposing party</td><td colspan="3">You shall have no conversation with the witness about the witness's evidence or any issue in the proceeding.</td><td>(d)</td></tr>
<tr><td>• After cross-examination
• Before re-examination</td><td colspan="3">You shall have no conversation with the witness about evidence to be dealt with on re-examination.</td><td>(e)</td></tr>
<tr><td>• Re-examination</td><td colspan="3">During an interval, you may discuss anything not covered in the re-examination to that point.</td><td>(a)</td></tr>
<tr><th>Opposing party calls the witness</th><th>Sympathetic witness</th><th>Applicable point under Rule 4.03(1)</th><th>Unsympathetic witness</th><th>Applicable point under Rule 4.03(1)</th></tr>
<tr><td>• Examination-in-chief conducted by opposing party</td><td>You may discuss the witness's evidence with the witness.</td><td>–</td><td>You may discuss the witness's evidence with the witness.</td><td>(b)</td></tr>
<tr><td>• After examination-in-chief
• Before cross-examination</td><td>You may discuss the witness's evidence with the witness.</td><td>–</td><td>You may discuss the witness's evidence with the witness.</td><td>–</td></tr>
<tr><td>• Cross-examination conducted by you</td><td>You may discuss anything not covered in the witness's evidence to that point.</td><td>(g)</td><td>You may discuss the witness's evidence with the witness.</td><td>(f)</td></tr>
<tr><td>• After cross-examination
• Before re-examination</td><td>You may discuss the witness's evidence with the witness.</td><td>–</td><td>You may discuss the witness's evidence with the witness.</td><td>–</td></tr>
<tr><td>• Re-examination by opposing party</td><td>You shall have no conversation with the witness about evidence to be dealt with on re-examination.</td><td>(h)</td><td>You may discuss the witness's evidence with the witness.</td><td>(h)</td></tr>
</table>

* A sympathetic witness gives evidence that supports your cause; an unsympathetic witness gives evidence that supports an opposing party's cause.

> Unless permitted by the tribunal, the paralegal who is a necessary witness should testify and entrust the conduct of the case to another licensee. A paralegal who has appeared as a witness on a matter should not act as an advocate or legal representative in any appeal of that matter.
>
> There are no restrictions on the advocate's right to cross-examine another licensee, however, and the paralegal who does appear as a witness should not expect to receive special treatment because of professional status (Guideline 12).

Subject to any contrary provisions of the law or the discretion of the tribunal before which you are appearing, when acting as an advocate for a client before a tribunal you shall not submit your own affidavit to the tribunal (Rule 4.04(1)). An affidavit is sworn, written evidence. If you submit an affidavit in a proceeding, you are acting as a witness.

Dealing with Unrepresented Persons (Rule 4.05)

When providing legal services, you may find yourself dealing with opposing parties or other individuals with an interest in the matter who are not represented by a paralegal or a lawyer. A conflict of interest may arise if the unrepresented person comes to believe that you are protecting his or her interests.

Rule 4.05 states:

> When a paralegal deals on a client's behalf with an unrepresented person, the paralegal shall,
>
> (a) take care to see that the unrepresented person is not proceeding under the impression that his or her interests will be protected by the paralegal; and
>
> (b) make clear to the unrepresented person that the paralegal is acting exclusively in the interests of the client and accordingly his or her comments may be partisan.

Making it clear to the unrepresented person that you are acting exclusively in the interests of your own client may require more than simply telling this to the unrepresented person. Guideline 12 recommends that, to avoid misunderstandings, you should confirm in writing to the unrepresented person the steps you have taken to fulfill the requirements of Rule 4.05.

You may be able to act for unrepresented persons who have an interest in the matter, such as a co-accused, but you must consider Rules 3.04(7) to (13), which govern joint retainers.

Withdrawal and Disclosure Obligations (Rule 3.08; Guideline 12)

If, after explanation and advice from the paralegal, the client persists in instructing the paralegal to engage in or continue a type of conduct prohibited by Rule 4, the paralegal must withdraw from representing the client in the matter (Guideline 12).

Withdrawal from representation is discussed in Chapter 4, pages 141–148.

CHAPTER SUMMARY

The paralegal advocate must balance a number of duties, as explained in Rule 4 and Guideline 12. You must represent your client honourably and resolutely within the limits of the law; treat other licensees and the tribunal before which you are appearing with candour, fairness, courtesy, and respect; and encourage public respect for, and try to improve, the administration of justice.

You have a duty to represent your client fearlessly and resolutely. You must balance that duty against the limits set by Rule 4 on how you may conduct yourself when acting as advocate for a client. Your conduct must also be governed by your professional obligations to other parties, other licensees, the tribunal, and the administration of justice.

You shall not abuse the process of the tribunal by commencing or continuing to act in proceedings that, although legal, are clearly motivated by malice on the part of the client and are brought solely for the purpose of injuring the other party.

You shall not knowingly assist or permit the client to do anything that the paralegal considers to be dishonest or dishonourable.

You shall not knowingly attempt to deceive a tribunal or influence the course of justice by offering false evidence, misstating facts or law, presenting or relying upon a false or deceptive affidavit, suppressing what ought to be disclosed, or otherwise assisting in any deception, crime, or illegal conduct.

You shall avoid and discourage the client from resorting to frivolous and vexatious objections, trying to gain advantage from mistakes or oversights made by the other side that do not go to the merits of the case, and using tactics designed merely to delay or harass the other side. You shall not knowingly assist or permit the client to do anything that you consider to be dishonest or dishonourable.

You shall not appear before an adjudicator if you, your partner, a paralegal employed by your firm, or your client has a business or personal relationship with the adjudicator that either affects the adjudicator's impartiality or may reasonably appear to affect the adjudicator's impartiality.

You must ensure that neither you nor your client misleads the tribunal. You shall not attempt, directly or indirectly, to influence the decision or action of a tribunal or its officers in any case or matter except by open persuasion as an advocate. You shall not knowingly attempt to deceive a tribunal or influence the course of justice by offering false evidence, misstating facts or law, suppressing relevant information, or otherwise assisting in any deception, crime, or illegal conduct.

Where the procedural rules of a tribunal require the parties to produce documents, you shall explain the disclosure obligation to the client and assist him to fulfill his obligation to make full and fair disclosure.

In criminal and quasi-criminal matters, you must advise the client that any admissions he makes to you may impose strict limitations on how you conduct his defence.

Before agreeing to a guilty plea on behalf of the client, you must obtain and review disclosure and complete any investigation that is appropriate in the circumstances. When entering into an agreement with the prosecutor about a guilty plea, you must comply with Rule 4.01(9) to ensure that the client's consent to the plea is informed and voluntary.

You may seek information from any potential witness in a proceeding, including witnesses appearing for opposing parties. However, a witness has no obligation to speak to you, and you are not permitted to harass a witness.

Your ability to speak to a witness who is giving testimony is restricted by the provisions in Rule 4.03(1).

When acting as an advocate for a client before a tribunal, you shall not act as a witness before the tribunal unless permitted to do so by the rules of the court or the rules of procedure of the tribunal, or unless the matter is purely formal and not subject to dispute. You shall not express personal opinions or beliefs or appear to give unsworn testimony.

When dealing on a client's behalf with an unrepresented person, you shall urge the unrepresented person to obtain independent legal representation, do nothing to make the unrepresented person think that you will protect his interests, and make it clear that you are acting exclusively in the interests of your own client, in writing if necessary.

If, after explanation and advice from you, the client persists in instructing you to engage in or continue a type of conduct prohibited by Rule 4, you shall withdraw from representing the client in the matter.

KEY TERMS

adjudicator, 154
advocate, 154
affidavit, 158
binding authority, 158
complainant, 157
deponent, 158
elements of the offence, 162
examination out of court, 166
frivolous and vexatious objection, 155
judicial notice, 159
merits of the case, 155
objection, 155
remedy, 155
statute-barred, 155
statutory limitation period, 155
sympathetic witness, 165
tribunal, 154
unsympathetic witness, 165

REFERENCES

Advocates Society, *Principles of Civility for Advocates* (2006), reprinted with permission in Canadian Bar Association, *Code of Professional Conduct* (Ottawa: Canadian Bar Association, 2009), http://www.cba.org/cba/activities/pdf/codeofconduct.pdf.

Criminal Code, RSC 1985, c. C-46, as amended.

Highway Traffic Act, RSO 1990, c. H.8, as amended.

Law Society of Upper Canada, *Paralegal Professional Conduct Guidelines* (October 2014) ("the Guidelines"), http://www.lsuc.on.ca/paralegal-conduct-guidelines.

Law Society of Upper Canada, *Paralegal Rules of Conduct* (October 2014) ("the Rules"), http://www.lsuc.on.ca/paralegal-conduct-rules.

Rules of Civil Procedure, RRO 1990, Reg. 194.

REVIEW QUESTIONS

1. Your client is the plaintiff in a Small Claims Court proceeding. The defendant is self-represented. You have told the defendant several times that you are acting solely in the interests of the plaintiff.

   A date has been set for a settlement conference. Recently, the defendant called you. He wanted information about what a settlement conference was, and what he had to do to prepare for it. "I thought you might be able to help me out here," he tells you. "You've had a lot of experience with this stuff."

   You tell him that you do not represent him and cannot assist him. Is there anything more that you need to do?

2. You represent a defendant in a *Highway Traffic Act* matter. Your client has indicated that she would like to plead down to reduce the fine and demerit points. What steps must you take?

3. You represent the accused on a charge of assault, where the Crown has elected to proceed by way of summary conviction. The accused has admitted to you that she committed the offence.

   What effect does this have on your conduct of her defence?

4. You are preparing for a trial in a Small Claims Court proceeding in which you represent the defendant.
   a. May you contact a witness for the plaintiff?
   b. When contacting witnesses, what information should you provide?
   c. What if a witness tells you she does not want to speak with you?

5. You are representing the defendant in a Small Claims Court proceeding. The plaintiff is represented by another paralegal. At the trial of the matter, the plaintiff's evidence is given by the plaintiff himself, and by another witness (Witness 2), who is unrepresented. Your client is the only witness for the defence.

   When answering the following questions, assume that both parties are individuals. Refer to any relevant rules and give reasons for your answer.
   a. During examination-in-chief of the plaintiff by the plaintiff's paralegal, may you discuss the plaintiff's evidence with the plaintiff?
   b. During your cross-examination of the plaintiff, may you discuss the plaintiff's evidence with the plaintiff?

c. During re-examination, if any, of the plaintiff by the plaintiff's paralegal, may you discuss the plaintiff's evidence with the plaintiff?

d. Witness 2 for the plaintiff is unsympathetic to your cause. During examination-in-chief of Witness 2 by the plaintiff's paralegal, may you discuss Witness 2's evidence with her?

e. During your cross-examination of Witness 2, may you discuss Witness 2's evidence with Witness 2?

f. During re-examination of Witness 2 by the plaintiff's paralegal, may you discuss Witness 2's evidence with Witness 2?

g. During your examination-in-chief of the defendant, may you discuss your client's evidence with your client?

h. During the interval between the conclusion of your examination-in-chief of the defendant and the commencement of cross-examination by the opposing licensee, may you discuss your client's evidence with your client?

i. During cross-examination of the defendant by the plaintiff's paralegal, may you discuss your client's evidence with your client?

j. During the interval between the conclusion of cross-examination by the opposing licensee and your re-examination of the defendant, may you discuss your client's evidence with your client?

6. Monica Manners is a paralegal carrying on business as MM Paralegal PC. Monica is consulted by a neighbour, Sandra Avila. Sandra has a legal basement apartment in her house. The tenant, Jack Jones, has lived there for two years. The current rent is $850.00, inclusive of utilities. Sandra recently learned that when a tenant leaves, she can raise the rent as much as she wants. "I'm too nice to this person!" she tells you. "Hydro, everything, it's going up. I can't survive with what I'm making on that apartment!" Sandra wants to evict her tenant.

When Monica asks Sandra what grounds she has for eviction, Sandra says, "What grounds do I need? It's my property! He's a zombie! A moron! I want him out! You think of some grounds!"

Monica shrugs. "OK, I'll think of something. I guarantee you we'll get rid of him. It's foolproof. But first, I need some money up front. How about $1,000?" Sandra pays by credit card.

Monica knows that Sandra has an adult daughter, Heather, who has an apartment downtown. Having considered the matter, Monica decides to terminate Jack's tenancy on grounds that the landlord requires possession of the rental unit because a family member wants to move in. She figures that they can always say that Heather changed her mind at the last minute.

Monica completes the notice of termination of tenancy and serves it on Jack. She issues the notice of application and serves a copy, along with the notice of hearing, on Jack. A few weeks later, Jack's paralegal, Hiram Barker, notifies you that his client intends to dispute the application. He also advises you that he intends to summon Heather as a witness. Monica tells Sandra that Heather should do everything she can to avoid service of the summons, and should be unavailable on the hearing date.

Prior to the hearing date, Monica phones Jack several times, urging him to pack up and move out. "I'm telling you this for your own good," she says. "If you don't leave, we'll get an eviction order and the sheriff will come and toss you and your dog into the street!"

On the morning of the hearing, Monica arrives early. She checks the list of hearings, and sees that the adjudicator is Allan Edgar. When Sandra arrives, Monica says, "Well, we lucked out on this one. This guy's so dumb he can barely read. His ten-year-old daughter writes his decisions for him."

During her opening submission, Monica addresses the adjudicator as Allan. She points out that Hiram Barker has a reputation for representing tenants without valid disputes and prolonging landlord applications needlessly just to harass landlords and drive their expenses up. "Who knows, maybe he got evicted sometime in the past, and he never got over it," she concludes.

While Hiram Barker is making his opening submissions, Monica makes faces and occasional comments to Sandra. At one point, when the adjudicator is asking Hiram Barker a question, Monica pulls out her cellphone and starts texting while the adjudicator is talking.

Several times during the hearing, when Hiram Barker is cross-examining Sandra and during direct examination of Jack Jones, Monica rolls her eyes and makes snorting noises. During cross-examination of Jack Jones, she is extremely aggressive. She often cuts off his answers before he has finished speaking.

Has Monica Manners acted ethically?

Duty to Others

LEARNING OBJECTIVES

After reading this chapter, you will understand:

- Encouraging respect for the administration of justice.
- Irresponsible allegations.
- Maintaining security of court facilities.
- Inappropriate public statements.
- Working with or employing unauthorized persons.
- Obligations of suspended paralegals.
- Obligations of paralegals who have provided undertakings to the Law Society.
- The duty of courtesy and good faith to licensees and others.
- Communication with a represented person, corporation, or organization.
- Communication with the Law Society.
- The duty to report misconduct by yourself or others.
- The duty to report certain offences to the Law Society.
- The disciplinary authority of the Law Society.
- Conduct unbecoming a paralegal.
- Professional misconduct.

Encouraging Respect for the Administration of Justice (Rule 6.01; Guideline 16)

A paralegal has a duty to provide legal services and discharge all responsibilities to clients, tribunals, the public, and other members of the legal professions honourably and with integrity (Rule 2.01(1)). As part of the duty of integrity, a paralegal shall encourage public respect for, and try to improve, the administration of justice (Rule 6.01(1)).

An important part of a paralegal's duty to act with integrity is his or her obligation to the administration of justice detailed in Rule 6. The obligation includes a paralegal's duty to assist in maintaining the security of court facilities, the duty to refrain from inappropriate public statements, and the obligation to prevent unauthorized practice (Guideline 16).

Irresponsible Allegations (Rule 6.01(2))

A paralegal shall take care not to weaken or destroy public confidence in legal institutions or authorities by making irresponsible allegations or comments, particularly when commenting on judges or members of a tribunal (Rule 6.01(2)).

Although directed to lawyers, the commentary to Rule 5.6-1 of the *Rules of Professional Conduct* may be of assistance to paralegals when considering Rule 6.01(2) of the *Paralegal Rules of Conduct*:

> **Criticizing Tribunals**—Although proceedings and decisions of tribunals are properly subject to scrutiny and criticism by all members of the public, including lawyers, judges and members of tribunals are often prohibited by law or custom from defending themselves. Their inability to do so imposes special responsibilities upon lawyers. First, a lawyer should avoid criticism that is petty, intemperate, or unsupported by a *bona fide* belief in its real merit, bearing in mind that in the eyes of the public, professional knowledge lends weight to the lawyer's judgments or criticism. Second, if a lawyer has been involved in the proceedings, there is the risk that any criticism may be, or may appear to be, partisan rather than objective. Third, where a tribunal is the object of unjust criticism, a lawyer, as a participant in the administration of justice, is uniquely able to and should support the tribunal, both because its members cannot defend themselves and because in doing so the lawyer is contributing to greater public understanding of and therefore respect for the legal system.

BOX 6.1 Irresponsible Allegations

Fact Situation

You are representing an injured worker who is the objecting party in a *Workplace Safety and Insurance Act* appeal. On the hearing date, you get to the tribunal early. While you are waiting for your client outside the hearing room, you begin chatting with a paralegal colleague who is there on another matter. Your colleague asks you if you have appeared on previous matters before the appeals resolution officer who is presiding that day. "Every time I get her, I also get a bad result," your colleague says. "That woman loves employers. She'll go to any lengths to force an injured worker to go back to work." Several people, including your client, who are standing nearby overhear your colleague's remarks.

Question for Discussion

Consider the appropriateness or otherwise of your colleague's comment, with reference to the applicable rule(s). How should you respond?

Security of Court Facilities (Rules 6.01(3), 3.03)

As part of a paralegal's duty to the justice system, the paralegal must help ensure that its facilities remain safe. Rule 6.01(3) states:

> (3) Subject to Rule 3.03 relating to confidentiality, a paralegal who has reasonable grounds for believing that a dangerous situation is likely to develop at a court facility shall inform the persons having responsibility for security at the facility and give particulars.

Guideline 16 recommends that, in a situation to which Rule 6.01(3) applies, you should consider requesting additional security at the facility and notifying other paralegals or lawyers who may be affected.

If your reasonable belief is based on information from or about someone who is not your client, you may disclose whatever information you think is necessary when advising the appropriate persons about the dangerous situation.

Imminent Risk of Death or Serious Bodily Harm (Rules 3.03(5), (9); Guideline 8)

If your reasonable belief concerns a client, when considering what action, if any, to take in order to comply with Rule 6.01(3), you must carefully consider your obligations of confidentiality under Rule 3.03. Rule 3.03(5) provides a limited exception to the general rule that a paralegal shall, at all times, hold in strict confidence all information concerning the business and affairs of a client acquired in the course of their professional relationship except as set out in Rule 3.03(1). Rule 3.03(5) permits a paralegal to disclose confidential information when the paralegal believes on reasonable grounds that there is an imminent risk of death or serious bodily harm, and disclosure is necessary to prevent the death or harm.

Guideline 8 recommends that, in assessing whether disclosure of confidential information is justified to prevent death or serious bodily harm pursuant to Rule 3.03(8), the paralegal should consider a number of factors, including:

> a) the likelihood that the potential injury will occur and its imminence;
> b) the apparent absence of any other feasible way to prevent the potential injury; and
> c) the circumstances under which the paralegal acquired the information of the client's intent or prospective course of action.

Guideline 8 also suggests that a paralegal who believes that disclosure may be warranted under Rule 3.03(5) may wish to seek legal advice. Rule 3.03(8) permits a paralegal to disclose confidential information to a lawyer or another paralegal to secure legal advice about the paralegal's proposed conduct. If it is practicable, the paralegal may consider seeking a court order for disclosure.

If confidential information is disclosed, the paralegal should record the circumstances of the disclosure as soon as possible.

The commentary to Rule 3.3-3 of the *Rules of Professional Conduct* recommends that the record of disclosure should include:

> (a) the date and time of the communication in which the disclosure is made;
>
> (b) the grounds in support of the lawyer's decision to communicate the information, including the harm intended to be prevented, the identity of the person who prompted communication of the information as well as the identity of the person or group of persons exposed to the harm; and
>
> (c) the content of the communication, the method of communication used, and the identity of the person to whom the communication was made.

When making the disclosure, the paralegal shall not disclose more information than is necessary to prevent the death or harm.

Where a paralegal discloses confidential information to prevent a dangerous situation from developing at a court facility, the paralegal should consider providing this information to the persons having responsibility for security at the facility anonymously or through another paralegal or a lawyer (Guideline 8).

Public Appearances and Statements (Rules 6.01(4), (4.1))

So long as there is no infringement of the paralegal's obligation to the client, the paralegal profession, the courts, or the administration of justice, a paralegal may communicate information to the media and may make public appearances and statements (Rule 6.01(4)).

A paralegal shall not communicate information to the media or make public statements about a matter before a tribunal if the paralegal knows or ought to know that the information or statement will have a substantial likelihood of materially prejudicing a party's right to a fair trial or hearing (Rule 6.01(4.1)).

When making statements to the media with, or on behalf of, a client, a paralegal must be mindful of his or her obligations to act in the client's best interests and within the scope of his or her instructions from the client (Guideline 16).

The comments below are adapted from the commentary to Rule 7.5-1 of the *Rules of Professional Conduct* for lawyers.

- Public communications about a client's affairs should not be used for the purpose of publicizing the paralegal and should be free from any suggestion that the paralegal's real purpose is self-promotion or self-aggrandizement.
- Paralegals should be aware that when they make a public appearance or give a statement they will ordinarily have no control over any editing that may follow or the context in which the appearance or statement may be used, or under what headline it may appear.

Working with or Employing Unauthorized Persons (Rules 6.01(5), (6))

When carrying out its regulatory functions under the *Law Society Act*, one of the principles that the Law Society shall have regard to is its duty to protect the public interest (*Law Society Act*, s. 4.2).

Section 26.1 of the Act requires that any person who provides legal services or practises law in Ontario shall be licensed by the Law Society, unless they are exempt from licensing or are deemed not to be providing legal services or practising law by the By-laws.

Rules 6.01(5) and (6) state:

> (5) A paralegal shall assist in preventing the unauthorized practice of law and the unauthorized provision of legal services.
>
> (6) Without the express approval of a committee of Convocation appointed for the purpose, a paralegal shall not retain, occupy office space with, use the services of, partner or associate with, or employ in any capacity having to do with the provision of legal services any person who, in Ontario or elsewhere,
>
> (a) is disbarred and struck off the Rolls,
>
> (b) is a person whose licence to practise law or to provide legal services is revoked,
>
> (c) as a result of disciplinary action, has been permitted to resign his or her membership in the Law Society or to surrender his or her licence to practise law or to provide legal services, and has not had his or her licence restored,
>
> (d) is suspended,
>
> (e) is a person whose licence to practise law or to provide legal services is suspended, or
>
> (f) is subject to an undertaking not to practise law or to provide legal services.

Guideline 16 notes that the obligations found in Rules 6.01(5) and (6) stem from a paralegal's obligation to the administration of justice and from the regulatory scheme for paralegals and lawyers set out in the *Law Society Act*.

Under the Act, anyone who provides legal services or practises law must be licensed by the Law Society, unless they are exempt from this requirement, or deemed not to be providing legal services or practising law. A person who is not a lawyer or a licensed paralegal is subject neither to a professional code of conduct nor the Law Society's jurisdiction, which exist to protect the public. Only clients of regulated service providers have important protections, such as the following:

- adherence to a mandatory code of professional conduct,
- maintenance and operation of a trust account in accordance with strict mandatory guidelines,
- mandatory professional liability insurance coverage, and
- the Law Society's Compensation Fund for persons who have been harmed by dishonest licensees (Guideline 16).

BOX 6.2 Speaking to the Media

The following material has been adapted from "Speaking to the Media," an online publication available at the Lawyers' Professional Indemnity Company website (http://www.practicepro.ca). The material at the LawPRO website addresses matters that give rise to errors and omissions claims. An error or omission may, but does not always, constitute a breach of an ethical duty.

- Obtain your client's consent in advance if you are speaking about a particular client matter. If the retainer agreement contains terms about public communications and statements to the media, review them carefully. If the retainer agreement is silent about public communications and statements to the media, obtain your client's voluntary, informed consent in writing before you make a public statement.
- If the matter is ongoing, do not discuss any confidential information or information about the strategy of your client's case or position.
- Avoid taking questions in the heat of the moment, before you have had a chance to think.
- Ask the reporter to provide you with a copy of the questions or discuss the reporter's objectives for the interview ahead of time. Emphasize that you are asking for this only because you want to come to the interview fully prepared with all the information the reporter seeks.
- Try to control the interview. Identify your key messages ahead of time and rehearse different ways to communicate this message. Look for an opportunity to work your key message into every answer that you provide.
- Ensure that you understand the question or point. If you do not or the question is too broad, ask for clarification before responding.
- If you do not know the answer to a question, say so. If appropriate, offer to find the information needed and get back to the reporter with the answer. Do not be lured into guessing or speculating.
- When you do provide an answer, keep your remarks brief. Resist the temptation to expand your answer to fill dead air time.
- Ask to review a draft of the written article so that you can verify the facts and avoid having to seek a correction at a later date. Understand that if the reporter agrees to this request, you cannot expect to make any editorial changes (you cannot change quotations, the tone of the article, descriptions, etc.).
- Leave your emotions outside of the interview. Be courteous but recognize the duties imposed by the *Paralegal Rules of Conduct* that you owe to your client, to opposing counsel, and to courts and tribunals.

Practice by Suspended Paralegals Prohibited (Rule 6.01(7))

Rule 6.01(7) states that:

> (7) A paralegal whose licence to provide legal services is suspended shall comply with the requirements of the By-laws and shall not
>
> (a) provide legal services; or
>
> (b) represent or hold himself or herself out as a person entitled to provide legal services.

A suspended paralegal shall comply with By-law 7.1 (Part II) and By-law 9 (Part II.1).

By-Law 7.1 (Part II)

By-law 7.1, s. 8 states that the following definitions apply for purposes of Part II:

> "existing client" means,
> (a) a person who is a client of a suspended licensee when a suspension order is made against the licensee, or
> (b) a person who becomes a client of the suspended licensee after the suspension order is made but before the suspension begins;
>
> "former client" means a person who was a client of a suspended licensee before a suspension order was made against the licensee but who was not a client when the order was made;
>
> "prospective client" means a person who seeks to retain a suspended licensee after the suspension order is made [against] the licensee but before the suspension begins;
>
> "suspended licensee" means a licensee who is the subject of a suspension order;
>
> "suspension order" means an order made under the Act suspending a licensee's licence to practise law in Ontario as a barrister and solicitor or to provide legal services in Ontario, regardless of whether the suspension begins when the order is made or thereafter.

BOX 6.3 Working with or Employing Unauthorized Persons

Fact Situation

You are a licensed paralegal with a large office space. To reduce your business expenses, you decide to enter into a space-sharing arrangement with a possibility of referrals. One of the people who responds to your advertisement tells you that she is a lawyer who has been running a consulting service for small business start-ups for several years. She seems like a very nice person who would be perfect for your space-sharing arrangement. After she leaves, you search her name at the Law Society website. To your surprise, her name does not appear. When you call to check her status, you are informed that she was disbarred.

Question for Discussion

May you enter into a space-sharing arrangement with this person?

Notice Requirements and Other Obligations Before Suspension Begins

A suspended paralegal shall, before the suspension begins, but not later than the date on which the suspension begins:

(a) notify every existing client, on whose matters the work will not be completed by the suspended paralegal before the suspension begins, of the suspension order, and that
  (i) the suspended paralegal will be unable to complete the work,
  (ii) the client will need to retain another licensee to complete the work, and
  (iii) the suspended paralegal, subject to any rights that the suspended paralegal may have over the client's file, will transfer the file to a licensee, if any, retained by the client to complete the work, or will return the file to the client (s. 9(1)).

The notice requirements above do not apply if the only work remaining to be completed on the client's matter is a final report to the client, or the fulfillment of one or more undertakings given by the suspended paralegal. In such a case, the suspended paralegal shall, before the suspension begins, notify the client of the name and contact information of the licensee retained by the suspended paralegal to complete the work (s. 9(2)). See the discussion of ss. 12 and 13 below.

If, on the date the suspension begins, the only work remaining for a suspended paralegal to complete on a client's matter is a final report to the client, the suspended paralegal shall, before the suspension begins, retain another licensee who is authorized to do so to review the client's file and to complete and send the final report to the client (s. 12).

If, on the date the suspension begins, the only work remaining for a suspended licensee to complete on a client's matter is the fulfillment of one or more undertakings given by the suspended licensee, the suspended licensee shall retain another licensee or person, who is authorized to do so, to take all steps necessary to fulfill the undertakings (s. 13).

A suspended licensee, at the time a prospective client seeks to retain the suspended licensee, shall notify the prospective client of the suspension order (s. 11).

A suspended licensee shall, before the suspension begins:

(a) return to the client all original documents; or
(b) transfer the client's file, including all original documents, to another licensee who is authorized to perform any requisite work (s. 14(2)).

A suspended licensee shall, on or before the date the suspension begins, return to the Law Society any photo identification card issued to her or him by the Society (s. 16).

Notice Requirements and Other Obligations During Suspension

A suspended paralegal shall, during the suspension,

(a) notify all persons who contact the suspended paralegal's place of business of the suspension order; and
(b) notify any existing client or former client who contacts the suspended paralegal's place of business of the name and contact information of another licensee who has been given possession of the clients' documents and files (s. 10).

A suspended paralegal shall, not later than 30 days after the suspension begins, complete and file with the Society, in a form provided by the Society, a report confirming and providing details of the suspended paralegal's compliance with By-law 7.1, Part II (s. 18).

A suspended paralegal may apply in writing to the Society for an exemption from or a modification of a requirement mentioned in Part II, and the Society may exempt the suspended paralegal from or modify the requirement, subject to such terms and conditions as the Society may impose (s. 19).

By-Law 9 (Part II.1)

By-law 9 sets out special requirements for record-keeping and handling of client money and other client property by licensees.

At a minimum, a paralegal firm should maintain two bank accounts: a general account and a mixed trust account. A mixed trust account is a trust account that holds client money for many different client matters.

The general account is the firm's operating account. This is the account you use to:

- deposit payments from clients you have billed for completed legal services;
- pay your office expenses, such as rent, office supplies, staff salaries, bank charges, and so on; and
- pay yourself.

No money belonging to clients should be in the general account.

Client money, such as a money retainer, remains the property of the client and must be held for the benefit of the client. A money retainer is paid to you for future legal services. You must hold the money retainer for the benefit of the client until the legal services contracted for have been provided and the client has been properly invoiced for them.

Whenever you receive a money retainer, or other money to be held on behalf of a client, you must deposit the money to your trust account. Trust accounts are the accounts you use to:

- deposit money you receive from your clients to be paid to another party;
- deposit money you receive from other parties on behalf of your clients;
- deposit money you receive from clients for future legal services and disbursements;
- disburse money as directed by your clients;
- reimburse your practice for proper expenses you have made on behalf of your clients; and
- transfer money to your general account for fees *after* you have sent a bill to your client for completed legal services.

By-law 9, Part II.1 sets out restrictions on the handling of client money or other client property by a suspended paralegal.

Part II.1 Definitions (s. 2.1)

For the purposes of By-law 9, Part II.1,

> "suspended licensee" means a licensee who is the subject of a suspension order;
>
> "suspension order" means an order made under the Act suspending a licensee's licence to practise law in Ontario as a barrister and solicitor or to provide legal services in Ontario, regardless of whether the suspension begins when the order is made or thereafter.

Handling of Client Money or Other Property

Subject to ss. 2.2(2) and 2.3, a suspended paralegal shall not, during the suspension, receive from or on behalf of a person or groups of persons any money or other property and shall not otherwise handle money or other property that is held in trust for a person or group of persons (s. 2.2(1)).

EXCEPTIONS

A suspended paralegal may receive, from or on behalf of a person or group of persons, money:

(a) in payment of fees for services performed by the suspended paralegal for the person or group; or
(b) in reimbursement for money properly spent, or for expenses properly incurred, on behalf of the person or group (s. 2.2(2)).

Trust Account (s. 2.3)

A suspended paralegal shall, within 30 days of the beginning of the suspension, withdraw from every trust account kept in the name of the suspended paralegal, or in the name of the firm of licensees of which the suspended paralegal is a partner or by which the suspended paralegal is employed, and, as required, pay to the appropriate person,

(i) money properly required for payment to a person on behalf of a client;
(ii) money required to reimburse the suspended paralegal for money properly expended, or for expenses properly incurred, on behalf of a client;
(iii) money required for or toward payment of fees for services performed by the suspended paralegal; and
(iv) all other money that belongs to the suspended paralegal or to a person other than the client (s. 2.3(1)(a)).

A suspended paralegal shall, within 30 days of the beginning of the suspension, after complying with s. 2.3(1)(a), withdraw from every trust account kept in the name of the suspended paralegal, or in the name of the firm of licensees of which the suspended paralegal is a partner or by which the suspended paralegal is employed, all money belonging to a client and pay the money to,

(i) the client,
(ii) another licensee to whom the client has directed the suspended paralegal to make payment, or
(iii) another licensee who has agreed with the suspended paralegal to accept payment in the event that the suspended paralegal is unable to pay the money to the client or as directed by the client (s. 2.3(1)(b)).

A suspended paralegal shall, within 30 days of the beginning of the suspension, after complying with ss. 2.3(1)(a) and (b),

(i) close every trust account that was kept in the name of the suspended paralegal, and
(ii) cancel or cause to be cancelled the suspended paralegal's signing authority on every trust account that was kept in the name of the firm of licensees of which the suspended paralegal is a partner or by which the suspended paralegal is employed (s. 2.3(1)(c)).

A suspended paralegal is not required to comply with s. 2.3(1)(b) if the client's file is transferred, in accordance with Part II of By-law 7.1, to another licensee in the firm of licensees of which the suspended paralegal is a partner or by which the suspended paralegal is employed (s. 2.3(2)).

Report to Law Society on Compliance with Part II.1 (s. 2.3(4))

A suspended licensee shall, not later than 30 days after the suspension begins, complete and file with the Society, in a form provided by the Society, a report confirming and providing details of the suspended licensee's compliance with this section (s. 2.3(4)).

Permission to Be Exempt from Requirement (s. 2.4)

A suspended paralegal may apply in writing to the Society for an exemption from or a modification of a requirement mentioned in Part II.1, and the Society may exempt the suspended paralegal from or modify the requirement, subject to such terms and conditions as the Society may impose.

BOX 6.4 How Does By-Law 9, Part II.1 Work?

Elizabeth May is a paralegal sole practitioner. She uses two bank accounts in her firm: a general account and a mixed trust account.

Elizabeth is suspended effective April 1. As of April 1, she is holding $8,000 in trust on account of settlement funds paid by another party for the benefit of Client A. In the period from her last interim invoice to Client A until April 1, Elizabeth has provided unpaid legal services worth $600 in Client A's matter.

Question

Is Elizabeth permitted to invoice Client A and pay the invoice from the funds held in trust for Client A?

Discussion

Yes, if there is a term in Elizabeth's retainer agreement with the client that she may pay her fees from settlement funds, and if she does so on or before April 30. Section 2.3(1)(a)(iii) permits a suspended paralegal to withdraw money from trust for payment of proper fees and disbursements within 30 days of the beginning of the suspension.

After she has invoiced Client A, Elizabeth may properly withdraw funds from the trust account and transfer them to her general (operating) account. The invoice received by the client will show the transfer from trust and a balance owing of zero, because it has been paid in full out of trust.

Question

What about the balance of the settlement funds that Elizabeth is holding in her trust account for the benefit of Client A?

Discussion

Having paid herself, Elizabeth must now pay the balance of the money in trust to the client or to another licensee as directed by the client (s. 2.3(1)(b)). Any direction by the client with respect to payment of the funds should be in writing.

On or before the end of the 30-day period, all funds held in Elizabeth's trust account must be properly disbursed in accordance with Part II.1. The mixed trust account must be closed. Elizabeth must provide to the Law Society an accounting of all transactions carried out during the 30-day period (s. 2.3(4)).

Undertakings Not to Provide Legal Services (Rules 6.01(8), (9))

A paralegal who gives an undertaking to the Law Society not to provide legal services shall not:

(a) provide legal services, or
(b) represent or hold himself or herself out as a person entitled to provide legal services (Rule 6.01(8)).

A paralegal who gives an undertaking to the Law Society to restrict her provision of legal services shall comply with the undertaking (Rule 6.01(9)).

Guidelines for Paralegals Who Are Suspended or Who Have Undertaken Not to Provide Legal Services

The Law Society has published a document outlining general guidelines for paralegals who are suspended or who have given an undertaking not to provide legal services or to restrict legal services. The following is excerpted from "Guidelines for Paralegals Who Are Suspended or Who Have Given an Undertaking Not to Provide Legal Services," which is available online at the Law Society website (http://www.lsuc.on.ca).

Mandatory Activities

2(1) Before the effective date of the suspension or undertaking not to provide legal services, the suspended paralegal shall:

a) Remove any sign from his or her door, building, premises, window, building directory, property, vehicle or any other location designating it as a "paralegal office," "law office," or "legal office" or designating the former paralegal as being able to provide legal services or to be a "paralegal," "law clerk," "court agent," "Licensee of the Law Society of Upper Canada," "Licensed by the Law Society of Upper Canada," or "notary public" or similar words giving the impression, in English or any other language, that he or she is able to provide legal services;

b) Remove or cross out the words or terms set out in (a) from all stationery, letterhead, business cards, forms, stamps, accounts, electronic mail forms, internet sites and any other advertisements or publications bearing his or her name;

c) Disconnect his or her telephone and facsimile lines or arrange for a voice message to advise callers that his or her professional business is closed until further notice and provide callers with the name and number of another licensee to call for information regarding their files; and

d) Suspended paralegals under a definite suspension may leave a message advising when the office will reopen.

A **definite suspension** is a suspension for a fixed period of time.

definite suspension
a suspension for a fixed period of time imposed upon a licensee by the Law Society

Prohibited Activities

3(1) Effective from the date of suspension or undertaking not to provide legal services, the suspended paralegal shall not:

a) Accept legal work for new clients;

b) Accept new legal work for existing clients;

c) Notarize documents pursuant to the *Notaries Act*, RSO 1990, c. N.6, or commission affidavits or statutory declarations pursuant to the *Commissioners for taking Affidavits Act*, RSO 1990, c. C.17;

d) Report to clients, other than to:

i) inform them of the suspension or the undertaking not to provide legal services; and

ii) deliver an account for services rendered in the period before the suspension or undertaking not to provide legal services began;

e) Give to another licensee or receive on behalf of a client, other individual, corporation or other entity, any undertaking with respect to any legal matter;

f) Occupy or share office space with a licensee in contravention of Subrule 6.01(6) of the *Paralegal Rules of Conduct*; and

g) Provide services to a licensee, in relation to that licensee's professional business in contravention of Subrule 6.01(6) of the *Paralegal Rules of Conduct*.

(2) The suspended paralegal shall not resume the provision of legal services upon termination of a suspension or undertaking not to practise until the suspended paralegal receives written confirmation of the termination of the suspension or undertaking not to provide legal services from the Law Society. This confirmation will be promptly given.

Permitted Activities

4(1) During the term of the suspension or undertaking not to provide legal services, the suspended paralegal may only:

a) See clients for the limited purpose of assisting them in transferring their past or present legal work to another licensee;

b) If requested by the client, suggest a referral to a particular licensee to continue work on the client's file. The ultimate choice of who is retained rests with the client and not with the suspended paralegal;

c) Collect accounts receivable;

d) Render accounts for work completed before the effective date of the suspended paralegal's suspension or undertaking not to provide legal services; and

e) Make arrangements with the licensee whom the suspended paralegal has retained to complete outstanding reporting letters and undertakings for his or her remuneration.

Duty to Licensees and Others: Courtesy and Good Faith (Rule 7.01; Guideline 17)

A paralegal's general duty of courtesy and good faith is set out in Rule 2.01(3): "A paralegal shall be courteous and civil, and shall act in good faith with all persons with whom he or she has dealings in the course of his or her practice." You should guard against letting your personal dislike of another licensee, or a client's animosity toward another party, cloud your judgment in a matter. Guideline 17 comments that:

> Discourteous and uncivil behaviour between paralegals or between a paralegal and a lawyer will lessen the public's respect for the administration of justice and may harm the clients' interests. Any ill feeling that may exist between parties, particularly during adversarial proceedings, should never be allowed to influence paralegals or lawyers in their conduct and demeanour toward each other or the parties. Hostility or conflict between representatives may impair their ability to focus on their respective clients' interests and to have matters resolved without undue delay or cost.

Rule 7.01 sets out various types of conduct that are prohibited. If a complaint is made about a paralegal whose conduct does not comply with Rule 7.01, the Law Society will review that conduct and may discipline the paralegal complained of.

Sharp Practice (Rule 7.01(1))

A paralegal shall avoid sharp practice and shall not take advantage of or act without fair warning on slips, irregularities, or mistakes on the part of other licensees if these do not go to the merits of the matter and do not involve any diminution of the client's rights (Rule 7.01(1)).

sharp practice dishonourable taking of advantage; trickery

Sharp practice is the dishonourable taking of advantage. Guideline 17 comments that:

Sharp practice occurs when a paralegal obtains, or tries to obtain, an advantage for the paralegal or client(s) by using dishonourable means. This would include, for example, lying to another paralegal or a lawyer, trying to trick another paralegal or a lawyer into doing something, or making an oral promise to another paralegal or lawyer with the intention of reneging on the promise later. As another example, if an opposing paralegal were under a mistaken belief about the date of an upcoming trial, a paralegal would be obligated to tell the opposing representative about the error, rather than ignoring the matter in the hope the opposing representative would not appear at the trial.

BOX 6.5 Sharp Practice

Fact Situation

You are a paralegal licensee in your first year of practice. Your client is the plaintiff in a Small Claims Court action for $9,000 based on damage to property. The defendant is represented by a paralegal with fifteen years of experience. The defence was served two weeks ago.

The defendant's paralegal phones you one day and says, "Why don't we settle on the terms that my guy will pay your client $7,000?" Your client has told you that, to avoid the expense of a trial, she is prepared to settle for less than the full amount claimed. There was no proposal of terms of payment in the defence.

Question for Discussion

How should you respond?

BOX 6.6 Taking Advantage of an Innocent Mistake

Fact Situation

Your client is the defendant in a Small Claims Court action. There is a lot of animosity between your client and the plaintiff. The plaintiff is represented by a paralegal whom you dislike and distrust.

A date has been scheduled for a settlement conference for October 15. The plaintiff's paralegal sends you what is, in your opinion, a completely unnecessary and mildly insulting letter reminding you of your disclosure obligations under Small Claims Court Rule 13.03. You note that, according to the letter, she thinks the settlement conference is scheduled for November 15.

When you advise your client of the error, he is delighted. "If they don't show up, they'll look like clowns, and maybe we'll get some costs," he comments. He tells you to act as though you did not notice the incorrect date.

Question for Discussion

Should you follow your client's instructions?

Reasonable Requests (Rule 7.01(2))

A paralegal shall agree to reasonable requests by other licensees concerning trial dates, adjournments, waiver of procedural formalities, and similar matters that do not prejudice the rights of the client.

Abusive Communication (Rule 7.01(3))

When providing legal services, a paralegal shall not communicate with a client, another licensee, or any other person in a manner that is abusive, offensive, or otherwise inconsistent with the proper tone of a professional communication from a paralegal. This rule applies to written and spoken communications.

Unfounded Criticism of Other Licensees (Rule 7.01(4))

A paralegal shall not engage in ill-considered or uninformed criticism of the competence, conduct, advice, or charges of other licensees. However, a paralegal should be prepared to represent a client in a complaint involving another licensee when requested to do so.

Prompt Communication (Rule 7.01(5))

A paralegal shall answer with reasonable promptness all professional letters and communications from other licensees that require an answer. A paralegal shall be punctual in fulfilling all commitments.

Recording Conversations (Rule 7.01(6))

A paralegal shall not use any device to record a conversation between the paralegal and a client or another licensee, even if lawful, without first informing the other person of the intention to do so.

Documents Sent in Error (Rule 7.01(7))

A paralegal who receives a document relating to the representation of the paralegal's client and knows or reasonably should know that the document was inadvertently sent shall promptly notify the sender.

BOX 6.7 Courtesy and Good Faith

Fact Situation

Your client is the plaintiff in a Small Claims Court matter. There is a lot of animosity between your client and the defendant. The defendant is represented by another paralegal.

A date has been set for trial. One week before the trial date, the defendant's paralegal phones you in a panic. He has just discovered that he has an out-of-town hearing in another court on the date set for the Small Claims trial. It will be impossible for him to appear on both matters.

You have provided full disclosure, reviewed the defendant's disclosure, and interviewed and summoned witnesses. "I can't believe that anyone—even you—can just forget a trial until one week before it's supposed to happen," you tell him. "I have to wonder how you manage to get dressed in the morning. Or does your wife have to dress you?" You say this in a pleasant, even tone of voice. The other paralegal cuts off the call.

You telephone your client to discuss the situation with her. "The man's a cretin," you tell her in the course of the conversation. "They're handing out licences like popcorn these days."

Question for Discussion

Have you acted ethically?

Communication with a Represented Person, Corporation, or Organization (Rule 7.02)

You shall not approach or deal with a person who is represented by a legal practitioner except in accordance with Rule 7.02. Rule 7.02(1) states that:

> (1) Subject to subrules (2) and (3), if a person is represented by a legal practitioner in respect of a matter, a paralegal shall not, except through or with the consent of the legal practitioner,
> (a) approach or communicate or deal with the person on the matter, or
> (b) attempt to negotiate or compromise the matter directly with the person.

Rule 7.02 applies to communications with any person, whether or not a party to a formal adjudicative proceeding, contract, or negotiation, who is represented by a licensee concerning the matter to which the communication relates (Rule 7.02(7)).

The prohibition on communications with a represented person applies if the paralegal has direct knowledge of the representation or if he should be able to infer the representation from the circumstances (Rule 7.02(8)).

Exceptions to Rule 7.02(1)

Limited Scope Retainer (Rule 7.02(2))

A limited scope retainer is a retainer where a legal practitioner provides part, but not all, of the legal services required in a client matter.

Subject to subrule (3), if a person is receiving legal services from a legal practitioner under a limited scope retainer on a particular matter, a paralegal may, without the consent of the legal practitioner, approach, communicate, or deal directly with the person on the matter, unless the paralegal receives written notice of the limited nature of the legal services being provided by the legal practitioner and the approach, communication, or dealing falls within the scope of the limited scope retainer (Rule 7.02(2)). Guideline 17 comments that:

> Where notice as described in Rule 7.02(2) has been provided to a paralegal, the paralegal is required to communicate with the legal practitioner who is representing the person under a limited scope retainer, but only to the extent of the matter(s) within the limited scope retainer as identified by the legal practitioner. The paralegal may communicate with the person on matters outside the limited scope retainer.

Second Opinion (Rule 7.02(3))

A paralegal who is not otherwise interested in a matter may give a second opinion to a person who is represented by a legal practitioner with respect to that matter (Rule 7.02(3)).

Communication with Corporation or Organization

Rule 7.02(4) states that:

> (4) A paralegal retained to act on a matter involving a corporation or organization that is represented by a legal practitioner in respect of that matter shall not, without the legal practitioner's consent or unless otherwise authorized or required by law, communicate, facilitate communication with or deal with a person
>
> (a) who is a director or officer, or another person who is authorized to act on behalf of the corporation or organization,
>
> (b) who is likely involved in decision-making for the corporation or organization or who provides advice in relation to the particular matter,
>
> (c) whose act or omission may be binding on or imputed to the corporation or organization for the purposes of its liability, or
>
> (d) who supervises, directs or regularly consults with the legal practitioner and who makes decisions based on the legal practitioner's advice.

For purposes of Rule 7.02(4), "organization" includes a partnership, limited partnership, association, union, fund, trust, co-operative, unincorporated association, or sole proprietorship, and a government department, agency, or regulatory body (Rule 7.02(6)).

If a person described in subrule (4)(a), (b), (c), or (d) is represented in the matter by a legal practitioner, the consent of the legal practitioner is sufficient to allow a paralegal to communicate, facilitate communication with, or deal with the person (Rule 7.02(5)).

BOX 6.8 Communication with Represented Persons

Fact Situation

You are representing the plaintiff in a Small Claims Court action. The defendant, who is represented by another paralegal, is anxious to settle the matter. He has been contacting your client directly to discuss terms of settlement. Your client has indicated that she does not feel comfortable about this, and would prefer that the defendant stop approaching her directly. You have notified the defendant's paralegal of this in writing.

One morning, the defendant calls you. He tells you he wants to discuss the case and propose terms of settlement. "This way we'll get things done faster, and it will cost me less," he says.

Question for Discussion

May you discuss the matter with the defendant?

Figure 6.1 Represented Parties: Permitted and Prohibited Communication (Rule 7.02)

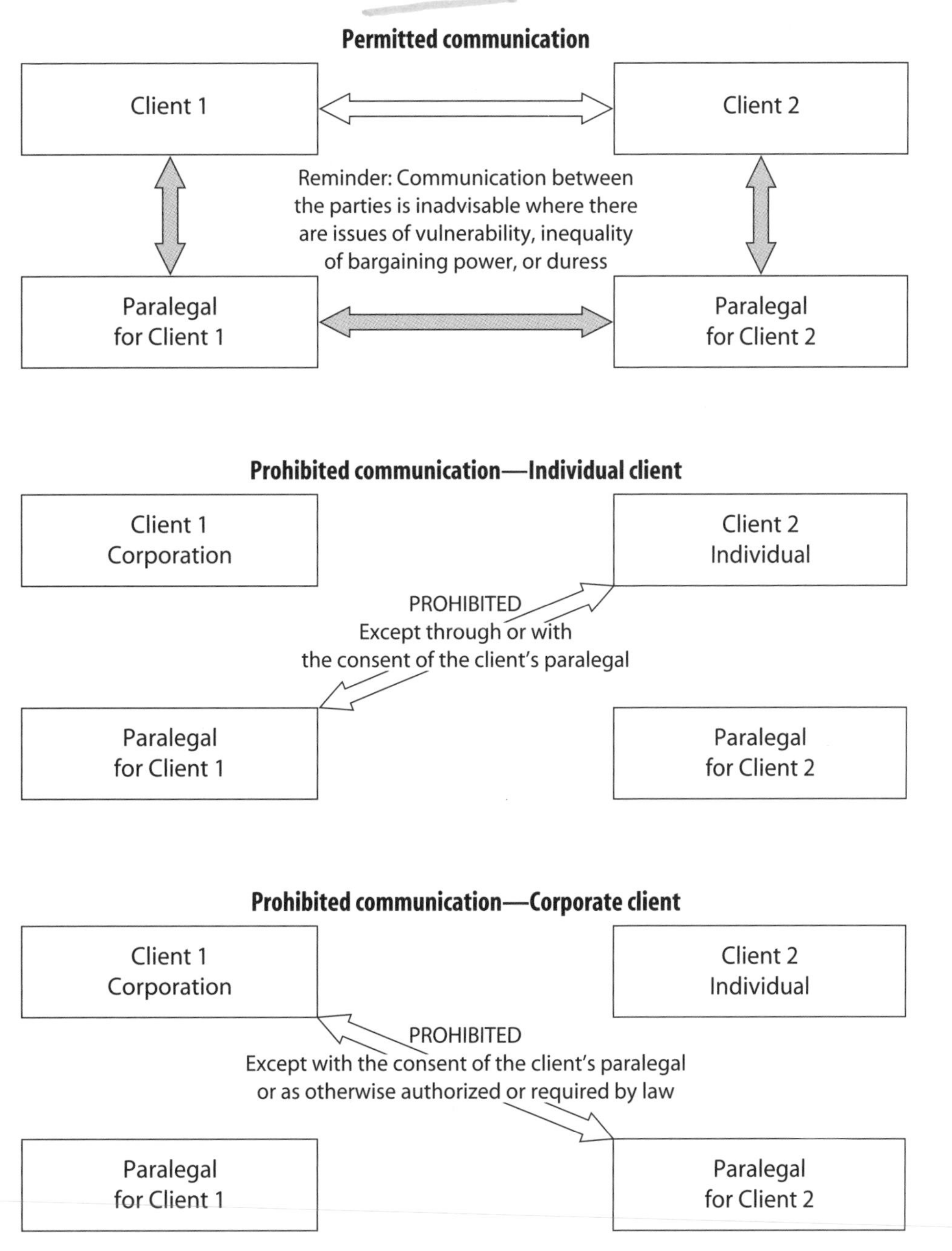

Responsibility to the Law Society (Rule 9; Guideline 21)

The Law Society is the governing body for all persons licensed to practise law or provide legal services in Ontario.

> All paralegals and lawyers owe a duty to their governing body, the Law Society, so that it can effectively and efficiently carry out its mandate to govern the legal professions in the public interest. Rule 9 details various obligations owed to the Law Society, many of which focus on measures to protect the public from inappropriate paralegal or lawyer conduct (Guideline 21).

Communications from the Law Society

A paralegal shall reply promptly and completely to any communication from the Law Society, and shall provide a complete response to any request from the Law Society (Rule 9.01(1)).

The Law Society is mandated to protect the public interest. The Law Society will investigate a complaint against you if the complaint raises any genuine regulatory issues—in the case of a complaint by a client, any issues of whether your conduct may harm the public.

> In addition to the obligation to reply promptly and completely to communication from the Law Society, which is set out in Rule 9.01(1), a paralegal also has a duty to cooperate with a person conducting an investigation under the [*Law Society*] *Act*. A paralegal who fails to respond promptly and completely to a Law Society inquiry about a complaint, or who fails to cooperate with a Law Society investigation, may be disciplined on that issue, regardless of the merits or outcome of the original complaint (Guideline 21).

Duty to Report Misconduct

A paralegal must assist the Law Society in upholding the integrity of the paralegal profession by reporting professional misconduct in accordance with Rule 9.01(2):

> (2) A paralegal shall report to the Law Society, unless to do so would be unlawful or would involve a breach of confidentiality between the paralegal and his or her client,
>
> (a) the misappropriation or misapplication of trust monies by a licensee;
>
> (b) the abandonment of a law practice by a lawyer or a legal services practice by a paralegal;
>
> (c) participation in serious criminal activity related to a licensee's practice;
>
> (d) the mental instability of a licensee if it is of such a serious nature that the licensee's clients are likely to be materially prejudiced; and
>
> (e) any other situation where a licensee's clients are likely to be severely prejudiced.

Nothing in Rule 9.01(2) is intended to interfere with the paralegal's duty to the client (Rule 9.01(3)). A report under Rule 9.01(2) must be made in good faith and without malice or ulterior motive (Rule 9.01(4)).

Guideline 21 notes that:

> Unless a paralegal or lawyer who departs from proper professional conduct is checked at an early stage, loss or damage to clients and others may ensue. As such, a paralegal must assist the Law Society in upholding the integrity of the profession by reporting professional misconduct of the type outlined in Rule 9.01(2).
>
> Evidence of seemingly isolated events, or "less serious" breaches of the *Rules*, may, under investigation, disclose a more serious situation or may indicate the commencement of a course of conduct that may lead to serious breaches in the future. It is proper therefore (unless it is confidential or otherwise unlawful) for a paralegal to report to the Law Society any instance involving a breach of the *Rules* or the *Rules of Professional Conduct*.
>
> The obligation to report misconduct applies to the paralegal's own conduct, as well as that of other paralegals and lawyers.
>
> The onus is on the paralegal to take the necessary steps to carry out his or her obligations to the Law Society and to protect both himself or herself and his or her client. If a paralegal is unsure as to whether to report another paralegal's or lawyer's conduct, the paralegal should consider seeking the advice of the Law Society directly (through the Practice Management Helpline at 416-947-3315 or 1-800-668-7380 extension 3315) or indirectly (through another paralegal or lawyer).

Encouraging a Client to Report Dishonest Conduct (Rules 9.01(5)–(8))

A paralegal shall encourage a client who has a claim or complaint against an apparently dishonest licensee to report the facts to the Law Society as soon as reasonably practicable (Rule 9.01(5)).

If the client refuses to report a claim against an apparently dishonest licensee to the Law Society, the paralegal shall obtain instructions in writing to proceed with the client's private remedies without notice to the Law Society (Rule 9.01(6)).

A paralegal shall inform the client of the provision of the *Criminal Code* that deals with the concealment of an indictable offence in return for an agreement to obtain valuable consideration (Rule 9.01(7)).

If the client wishes to pursue a private agreement with the apparently dishonest licensee, the paralegal shall not continue to act if the agreement constitutes a breach of s. 141 of the *Criminal Code* (Rule 9.01(8)).

Section 141(1) of the *Criminal Code* is excerpted below.

> **Compounding indictable offence**
>
> 141(1) Everyone who asks for or obtains or agrees to receive or obtain any valuable consideration for himself or any other person by agreeing to compound or conceal an indictable offence is guilty of an indictable offence and liable to imprisonment for a term not exceeding two years.

Duty to Report Certain Offences

If a paralegal is charged with an offence described in By-law 8 of the Law Society, he or she shall inform the Law Society of the charge and of its disposition in accordance with the By-law (Rule 9.01(9)).

> All paralegals have a duty to report themselves to the Law Society if certain charges (identified in By-law 8, s. [2]) have been laid against them.
>
> The By-law only requires the paralegal to self-report the above-mentioned criminal charges or convictions. A paralegal is only required to report another paralegal or lawyer who is involved in criminal activity in certain circumstances (Guideline 21).

Section 2(1) of By-law 8 is excerpted below.

> 2(1) Every licensee shall inform the Society in writing of,
> (a) a charge that the licensee committed,
> (i) an indictable offence under the *Criminal Code* (Canada),
> (ii) an offence under the *Controlled Drugs and Substances Act* (Canada),
> (iii) an offence under the *Income Tax Act* (Canada) or under an Act of the legislature of a province or territory of Canada in respect of the income tax law of the province or territory, where the charge alleges, explicitly or implicitly, dishonesty on the part of the licensee or relates in any way to the professional business of the licensee,
> (iv) an offence under an Act of the legislature of a province or territory of Canada in respect of the securities law of the province or territory, where the charge alleges, explicitly or implicitly, dishonesty on the part of the licensee or relates in any way to the professional business of the licensee, or
> (v) an offence under another Act of Parliament, or under another Act of the legislature of a province or territory of Canada, where the charge alleges, explicitly or implicitly, dishonesty on the part of the licensee or relates in any way to the professional business of the licensee; and
> (b) the disposition of a charge mentioned in clause (a).

A licensee shall report a charge to the Law Society as soon as reasonably practicable after she receives notice of the charge, and shall report the disposition of the charge as soon as reasonably practicable after she receives notice of the disposition (By-law 8, s. 2(3)).

Requirement to Report; Private Prosecution

By-law 8, s. 2(2) states that:

> (2) Despite subsection (1), a licensee is only required to inform the Society of a charge contained in an information laid under section 504 of the *Criminal Code* (Canada), other than an information referred to in subsection 507(1) of the *Criminal Code* (Canada), and of the disposition of the charge, if the charge results in a finding of guilt or a conviction.

Section 504 of the *Criminal Code* permits anyone (other than a peace officer, a public officer, the attorney general, or the attorney general's agent) who, on reasonable grounds, believes that a person has committed an indictable offence, to appear before a justice and lay an information in writing and under oath. A licensee who has been charged under s. 504 is only required to inform the Society of the charge and of its outcome if there is a finding of guilt or a conviction (By-law 8, s. 2(2)). If the licensee is acquitted, there is no obligation under By-law 8 to report the private prosecution to the Law Society.

In a private prosecution, a licensee shall report a charge and the disposition of the charge as soon as reasonably practicable after he or she receives notice of the disposition (By-law 8, s. 2(4)).

Disciplinary Authority of the Law Society (Rules 9.01(10)–(13); Guideline 22)

Section 33 of the *Law Society Act* states that a licensee shall not engage in professional misconduct or conduct unbecoming a licensee.

The Law Society may discipline a paralegal for **professional misconduct** (Rule 9.01(11)) or for **conduct unbecoming a paralegal** (Rule 9.01(12)).

Rule 9.01(13) states that:

> (13) In subrules (11) and (12),
>
> "conduct unbecoming a paralegal" means conduct in a paralegal's personal or private capacity that tends to bring discredit upon the paralegal profession including,
>
> (a) committing a criminal act that reflects adversely on the paralegal's honesty, trustworthiness, or fitness as a paralegal,
>
> (b) taking improper advantage of the youth, inexperience, lack of education, unsophistication, ill health, vulnerability or unbusinesslike habits of another, or
>
> (c) engaging in conduct involving dishonesty;
>
> "professional misconduct" means conduct in a paralegal's professional capacity that tends to bring discredit upon the paralegal profession, including,
>
> (a) violating or attempting to violate one of these Rules, or a requirement of the *Law Society Act* or its regulations or by-laws,
>
> (b) knowingly assisting or inducing another licensee to violate or attempt to violate these Rules, a requirement of the *Law Society Act* or its regulations or by-laws,
>
> (c) knowingly assisting or inducing a non-licensee partner or associate of a multi-discipline practice to violate or attempt to violate the rules in the *Paralegal Rules of Conduct* or a requirement of the *Law Society Act* or its regulations or by-laws,
>
> (d) misappropriating or otherwise dealing dishonestly with a client's or a third party's money or property,
>
> (e) engaging in conduct that is prejudicial to the administration of justice,

professional misconduct
conduct in a paralegal's professional capacity that tends to bring discredit upon the paralegal profession

conduct unbecoming a paralegal
conduct in a paralegal's personal or private capacity that tends to bring discredit upon the paralegal profession

> (f) stating or implying an ability to influence improperly a government agency or official, or
>
> (g) knowingly assisting a judge or judicial officer in conduct that is a violation of applicable rules of judicial conduct or other law.

A paralegal is subject to the disciplinary authority of the Law Society regardless of where the paralegal's conduct occurs (Rule 9.01(10)). If you engage in conduct unbecoming while on vacation in British Columbia, and it comes to the Law Society's attention, you may be disciplined. Guideline 22 comments that:

> Dishonourable or questionable conduct on the part of a paralegal in either private life or while providing legal services will reflect adversely upon the integrity of the profession and the administration of justice. Whether within or outside the professional sphere, if the conduct is such that knowledge of it would be likely to impair a client's trust in the paralegal, the Law Society may be justified in taking disciplinary action.
>
> Generally, however, the Law Society will not be concerned with the purely private or extra-professional activities of a paralegal that do not bring into question the paralegal's professional integrity.
>
> The *Rules* cannot address every situation. As such, a paralegal is required to follow both the "letter" and the "spirit" of the *Rules*. The "letter" of the rule is the meaning of the rule as it is written. The "spirit" of the rule is the sense of the rule or the meaning or importance of the rule, even though it may not be explicit or stated in the written version of the Rule.

CHAPTER SUMMARY

A paralegal has a duty to provide legal services and discharge all responsibilities to clients, tribunals, the public, and other members of the legal profession honourably and with integrity (Rule 2.01(1)). Rule 6 sets out a paralegal's duties to the administration of justice. A paralegal shall encourage public respect for, and try to improve, the administration of justice. You shall take care not to undermine or destroy public confidence in legal institutions or authorities by making irresponsible allegations or comments, particularly when commenting on judges or members of a tribunal.

As part of your duty to the justice system, you must help to ensure that its facilities remain safe. A paralegal who has reasonable grounds for believing that a dangerous situation is likely to develop at a court facility shall inform persons having responsibility for security at the facility and give particulars. If your belief is based on information from or about a client, you must consider your obligations to the client under Rule 3.03 regarding confidentiality when deciding what action to take.

So long as there is no infringement of the paralegal's obligation to the client, the paralegal profession, the courts, or the administration of justice, a paralegal may communicate information to the media and may make public appearances and statements.

You shall not communicate information to the media or make public statements about a matter before a tribunal if you know or ought to know that there is a substantial likelihood that the information or statement will materially prejudice a party's right to a fair trial or hearing.

As a member of the Law Society, you shall assist in preventing the unauthorized practice of law and the unauthorized provision of legal services. You shall not retain, share office space with, use the services of, partner or associate with, or employ in any capacity having to do with the provision of legal services any person who, in Ontario or elsewhere, is not a member in good standing of the Law Society.

A paralegal whose licence to provide legal services is suspended shall not provide legal services or represent or hold himself out as a person entitled to provide legal services. He shall also comply with the By-law 7.1 (Part II) and By-law 9 (Part II.1) requirements regarding notice requirements and other obligations during suspension, and restrictions on handling of client money or other property by a suspended paralegal.

A paralegal who gives an undertaking to the Law Society not to provide legal services shall not provide legal services or represent or hold himself out as a person entitled to provide legal services. A paralegal who gives an undertaking to the Law Society to restrict his provision of legal services shall comply with the undertaking.

As a paralegal, you have a general duty of courtesy and good faith. You shall be courteous and civil, and shall act in good faith with all persons with whom you have dealings in the course of your practice (Rule 7).

You should guard against letting your personal dislike of another licensee cloud your judgment in a matter, or allowing a client's animosity toward other parties in an adversarial proceeding to influence your conduct and demeanour toward those parties or their licensees.

Rule 7.01 sets out various types of prohibited conduct. If a complaint is made about a paralegal whose conduct does not comply with Rule 7.01, the Law Society will review that conduct and may discipline the paralegal complained of.

Licensees owe various duties to the Law Society, including the duty to respond promptly and completely to a Law Society communication; to report misconduct; to report certain offences; and to submit to the disciplinary authority of the Law Society (Rule 9).

The *Law Society Act* prohibits a paralegal from engaging in professional misconduct or conduct unbecoming a licensee. The Law Society may discipline a paralegal for such conduct if it tends to bring discredit upon the paralegal profession and to raise issues of the paralegal's professional integrity, regardless of whether the paralegal is acting as a paralegal or in a personal capacity and regardless of where the conduct occurs.

KEY TERMS

conduct unbecoming a paralegal, 195
definite suspension, 185
professional misconduct, 195
sharp practice, 186

REFERENCES

Abrahams, Dan, *Mostly Common Sense: Staying Out of Trouble with the Law Society* (May 2008), Law Society of Upper Canada, http://www.lsuc.on.ca//WorkArea/DownloadAsset.aspx?id=11528&langtype=1033.

Commissioners for Taking Affidavits Act, RSO 1990, c. C.17.

Criminal Code, RSC 1985, c. C-46.

Law Society Act, RSO 1990, c. L.8, as amended.

Law Society of Upper Canada, *By-Laws* (2007), as amended ("the By-laws"), http://www.lsuc.on.ca/with.aspx?id=1070.

Law Society of Upper Canada, Guidelines for Paralegals Who are Suspended or Who have Given an Undertaking Not to Provide Legal Services, http://www.lsuc.on.ca/For-Paralegals/About-Your-Licence/Paralegal-Discipline-and-Complaints.

Law Society of Upper Canada, *Paralegal Professional Conduct Guidelines* (October 2014) ("the Guidelines"), http://www.lsuc.on.ca/paralegal-conduct-guidelines.

Law Society of Upper Canada, *Paralegal Rules of Conduct* (October 2014) ("the Rules"), http://www.lsuc.on.ca/paralegal-conduct-rules.

Law Society of Upper Canada, *Rules of Professional Conduct* (2014), http://www.lsuc.on.ca/lawyer-conduct-rules.

Law Society of Upper Canada, Working or Associating with a Former or Suspended Licensee, http://www.lsuc.on.ca/For-Paralegals/Manage-Your-Practice/Practice-Arrangements/Working-or-Associating-with-a-Former-or-Suspended-Licensee.

Lawyers' Professional Indemnity Company, Speaking to the Media, http://www.practicepro.ca/information/speakingtomedia.asp.

Notaries Act, RSO 1990, c. N.6.

O. Reg. 258/98, Rules of the Small Claims Court, http://www.e-laws.gov.on.ca/html/regs/english/elaws_regs_980258_e.htm.

Workplace Safety and Insurance Act, SO 1997, c. 16, Sched. A.

REVIEW QUESTIONS

1. You are attending at court on a summary conviction matter. While waiting outside the courtroom for your matter to be called, your client starts talking with some other people. "These judges," he says in a loud voice. "As far as I can see, they're all in the prosecutor's pocket." The others grin and nod. "You've got that right," one of them comments. Your client looks over at you and says, in a loud, argumentative voice, "Am I right? You're the expert. What's your opinion?"

   How should you respond?

2. In the course of a court proceeding, your client's conduct, both in and out of the courtroom, has become increasingly erratic and hostile to the judge. She has made several comments in your presence about how she would like to "kill that judge." You are getting very concerned, because she has a history of becoming violent when she doesn't take her medication regularly.

   What should you do?

3. You have been approached by the local media to participate in a press conference about a client matter that is ongoing. Your client is enthusiastic. She wants to get her message out to the press. You are flattered, because you believe that the publicity will be good for you and your firm, and may bring in a lot of new business.

   What are some issues that you need to consider?

4. "A suspended paralegal may continue to advertise her legal services during the period of the suspension." True or false? Give reasons for your answer.

5. "A suspended paralegal may continue to receive money in payment of outstanding invoices after commencement of the suspension." Please comment.

6. You are attempting to negotiate settlement in a client matter. The opposing paralegal has called you several times to discuss settlement. During the course of several telephone conversations, she has made statements and later denied them. Sometimes she claims that she said something else, or that you misunderstood what she said. You have taken copious notes of your conversations with the opposing paralegal. You are beginning to find her conduct very annoying and a waste of time. To produce a verifiable record, you would like to start taping your conversations with her. May you do so?

7. You have just received a request for information from the Law Society concerning a client complaint. In your opinion, the client is motivated purely by malice, and the complaint is trivial, silly, and a complete waste of your time. You are very busy in your practice at the moment, and would rather use your time and energy to provide good service to your clients. You figure you will get back to the Law Society when your workload lightens up a bit. Discuss.
8. You are representing a client in a Small Claims Court matter. The opposing paralegal is Jonathon Meissen. At the settlement conference, the judge made an order that Jonathon's client was to provide additional disclosure by a stated date. The deadline for the additional disclosure has now passed, and you have received nothing. You have left several voicemails but have received no response. You are getting very frustrated, because you need the disclosure to prepare for trial. You decide to send your field placement student to pick up the disclosure in person. You leave Jonathon a voicemail to that effect.

   When the field placement student arrives at Jonathon's office to pick up the disclosure, he calls you on his cell phone. "The door's locked, there's no one here, and the lights are off," he tells you. "The sign is gone, and the guy down the hall told me the place is empty. It's been empty for at least three weeks. The guy said that's how long people have been coming around asking about him." You hang up and call Jonathon's business number. It has been disconnected.

   You are very concerned that Jonathon has just walked away from his practice. What are your obligations?

Practice Management 7

LEARNING OBJECTIVES

After reading this chapter, you will understand:

- Reasonable fees and disbursements.
- Contingency fees.
- Fee splitting.
- Referral fees.
- Professional responsibility.
- Financial obligations.
- Supervisory responsibility.
- Delegation.
- Making legal services available.
- Marketing of legal services.
- Advertising of fees.
- Errors and omissions insurance.

Fees and Retainers (Rule 5; Guidelines 13, 14)

What Are Fees?

Fees are what a client pays to a paralegal for legal services provided by the paralegal to the client, including advice, correspondence, drafting pleadings and other documents, and appearances before tribunals.

Fees may be determined in a variety of ways, including:

- An *hourly rate*, charging for the actual time spent on the client matter;
- A *block, fixed, or flat fee*, charging a fixed amount for performing a particular task;
- *Fees by stages*, charging for a matter that is broken down into stages, and an estimate is given as to the fee for each stage or step in the matter; or
- *Contingency fees*, where payment of part or all of the paralegal's fee depends upon the successful disposition or completion of the matter for which your services are provided (Guideline 13).

The paralegal should consider which method best suits the circumstances and the client.

fees based on an hourly rate an arrangement whereby a paralegal is paid for actual time spent on the client matter; calculated by multiplying the paralegal's hourly rate (or that of others who have completed work on the file) by the amount of time spent on the client matter to the date of the invoice

docket a manual or electronic record of all time spent on a client matter

docketed time the total time recorded to a client matter

billable time time that is charged to the client on an invoice

to write off time to not bill a client for time that was spent on the client matter

non-billable time time that is docketed to a client matter but is not billed to the client

Fees Based on an Hourly Rate

When you charge **fees based on an hourly rate**, you are paid for actual time spent on the client matter. In order to calculate this kind of fee, you must establish an hourly rate that is reasonable in the circumstances, and you must keep track of time spent on the client matter by you and anyone to whom you delegate work. When you bill the client, you determine the fee owing to the date of the invoice by multiplying your hourly rate (and that of others who have completed work on the file) by the amount of time spent on the client matter to the date of the invoice.

You may wish to consider establishing different hourly rates for yourself for different types of matters, depending on their complexity, the time and effort required, and so on.

For a client matter where you are charging an hourly rate, you should **docket**, or record, your time for all tasks completed on the file. Time records may be maintained manually or by using accounting or practice management software. The time record should state the client name, the client matter number or code, the name of the person performing the task, details of the task, and the amount of time spent on the task.

Your **docketed time**—the total time you record to a client matter—may not necessarily turn into **billable time**, or the time that you actually charge to the client on an invoice. In certain situations, you may determine that it is reasonable **to write off time**—that is, not to include some time when calculating your fee. Or you may designate certain tasks on the file as **non-billable time**. You should consider keeping complete time records of all time spent on a client matter, whether the time is billed to the client or not. These records provide a useful tool for determining what activities are unproductive or inefficient.

Fixed, Flat, or Block Fees

A **fixed, flat, or block fee** is a fixed amount charged for a particular task or client matter. Regardless of how much time is spent on a matter, the fee charged to the client does not change.

Fixed fees may be used in high-volume practice areas with routine procedures, such as *Highway Traffic Act* matters and civil collections.

As a tool for determining whether the fixed fee you are charging is appropriate in all of the circumstances, you should consider docketing time spent on fixed fee matters by you and the persons under your supervision.

fixed, flat, or block fee
a fixed amount charged for a particular task or client matter

Fees by Stages

With **fees by stages**, you break the matter down into stages and charge the client based on a reasonable estimate of the fee for each stage or step in the matter. When estimating fees, you should consider advising the client of any facts or circumstances that form the basis of the estimate, and any facts or circumstances that may result in an increase or decrease in the estimate.

fees by stages
an arrangement whereby the client matter is broken down into stages and the client is charged based on a reasonable estimate of the fee for each stage or step in the matter

Contingency Fees

In a **contingency fee** arrangement, payment of your fee in whole or in part is contingent upon the successful disposition or completion of the matter for which your services are provided. The amount of your fee may be calculated as a percentage of any amount recovered by the client.

Contingency fees are discussed in more detail below on pages 206–207.

contingency fee
a fee that is contingent, in whole or in part, on the successful disposition or completion of the matter for which the paralegal's services are to be provided

What Are Disbursements?

Disbursements are expenses related to the client matter that are paid by the paralegal on behalf of the client and for which the paralegal is entitled to be reimbursed. Some examples of disbursements are charges for:

- research, such as Quicklaw charges or research conducted by third-party professionals;
- mileage;
- postage, photocopying, faxing documents, or sending documents by courier;
- long-distance phone calls;
- expert reports;
- transcripts or certified documents; and/or
- tribunal or court filing fees related to the client matter (Guideline 13).

A paralegal cannot charge more than the actual cost of the disbursement. A paralegal cannot make a profit from disbursements at the client's expense.

Reasonable Fees and Disbursements

A paralegal shall not charge or accept any amount for a fee or disbursement unless it is fair and reasonable and has been disclosed in a timely fashion (Rule 5.01(1)).

Guideline 13 comments that:

> Too often, misunderstandings about fees and disbursements result in disputes over legal bills and complaints from unhappy clients. Since these disputes reflect badly on the paralegal profession and the administration of justice, it is important that a paralegal discuss with his or her client(s) the amount of fees and disbursements that will likely be charged. It will be to the benefit of all concerned if the paralegal ensures that the client has a clear understanding not only of what legal services the paralegal will provide, but [also of] how much those services are likely to cost.

Fair and Reasonable Fee

Factors to be considered when deciding what is a fair and reasonable fee are set out at Rule 5.01(2):

> (2) What is a fair and reasonable fee will depend upon such factors as,
> (a) the time and effort required and spent;
> (b) the difficulty of the matter and importance of the matter to the client;
> (c) whether special skill or service was required and provided;
> (d) the amount involved or the value of the subject matter;
> (e) the results obtained;
> (f) fees authorized by statute or regulation;
> (g) special circumstances, such as the loss of other retainers, postponement of payment, uncertainty of reward, or urgency;
> (h) the likelihood, if made known to the client, that acceptance of the retainer will result in the paralegal's inability to accept other employment;
> (i) any relevant agreement between the paralegal and the client;
> (j) the experience and ability of the paralegal;
> (k) any estimate or range of fees given by the paralegal; and
> (l) the client's prior consent to the fee.

Hidden Fees (Rule 5.01(3))

No fee, reward, costs, commission, interest, rebate, agency or forwarding allowance, or other compensation related to his or her employment may be taken by the paralegal from anyone other than the client without full disclosure to, and the consent of, the client (Rule 5.01(3)). The client's consent shall be fully informed and voluntary after disclosure, and shall be in writing or, if spoken, shall be confirmed in writing (Rule 1.02).

The relationship between paralegal and client is based on trust. The client must be able to rely on the paralegal's honesty and ability to act in the client's best interests. This means that the paralegal cannot hide from the client any financial dealings in his or her matter (Guideline 13).

Timely Disclosure

Along with the other terms of the paralegal–client retainer, you should discuss your fee for a client matter with the client at the outset of the retainer, and confirm the discussion in writing, by a retainer agreement or engagement letter. You will find samples of a retainer agreement and an engagement letter in Chapter 3 at Appendixes 3.1 and 3.2.

The following are steps that will assist a paralegal in meeting his or her obligations under Rule 5.01(1):

(a) A paralegal should provide to the client in writing, before or within a reasonable time after commencing a representation, as much information regarding fees and disbursements, and interest as is reasonable and practical in the circumstances, including the basis on which fees will be determined;

(b) A paralegal should confirm with the client in writing the substance of all fee discussions that occur as a matter progresses. The paralegal may revise the initial estimate of fees and disbursements.

(c) A paralegal should openly disclose and discuss with clients all items that will be charged as disbursements and how those amounts will be calculated. If an administrative charge forms part of the amount charged as a disbursement, disclosure of such charge should be made to the client(s) in advance (Guideline 13).

When discussing fees and disbursements with the client, you should provide a reasonable estimate of the total cost based on the services to be provided under the retainer. It is inappropriate to provide an unreasonable estimate (for example, quoting a fee that you know is unrealistically low) in order to obtain the client's business. It is also inappropriate to manipulate fees and disbursements in order to provide a lower fee estimate (Guideline 13).

Sometimes something happens in a client matter that you could not foresee at the outset of the retainer. If the result is higher costs than you originally estimated, you must advise the client, explain why the original estimate has changed, provide a revised estimate, and obtain the client's instructions based on the new information. The revised estimate, along with the change of circumstances giving rise to it, should be confirmed in writing. Any new client instructions based on the new information should be confirmed in writing (Guideline 13).

Statement of Account (Rule 5.01(4))

A **statement of account** tells the client how much she owes the paralegal on account of fees and disbursements as of the date of the account. It is also called an invoice or a bill.

statement of account
a statement (that is, an invoice or bill) that tells the client how much is owed to the paralegal for fees, disbursements, and HST as of the date of the account

In a statement of account delivered to a client, you shall clearly and separately detail amounts charged as fees and as disbursements (Rule 5.01(4)).

In addition to detailing fees and disbursements, the *statement of account* or bill delivered to the client by the paralegal should detail clearly and separately the amount the paralegal has charged for Harmonized Sales Tax (HST). The HST applies to fees and some disbursements, as outlined by the Canada Revenue Agency (CRA) guidelines. The paralegal should review and sign the statement of account before it is sent to the client.

Should a dispute arise about the statement of account, the paralegal should discuss the matter openly and calmly with the client in an effort to resolve the matter. Civility and professionalism must govern all discussions, including discussions relating to fee disputes with clients (Guideline 13).

Lawyers are permitted to charge interest on outstanding accounts in accordance with s. 33 of the *Solicitors Act*. Interest on unpaid fees, charges, and disbursements is calculated from a date that is one month after the bill is delivered (s. 33(1)). The rate of interest chargeable shall be shown on the bill delivered (s. 33(3)).

Paralegals are not prohibited from charging interest on outstanding accounts. Paralegals may wish to consider s. 33 of the *Solicitors Act* and any other applicable law when doing so.

You will find sample invoices in Appendixes 7.1 and 7.2.

Assessment of Accounts

If a client disputes a paralegal's account, the dispute must be adjudicated by a court.

If the account has not been paid, the paralegal will be entitled to collect the amount owing in accordance with the court decision.

If the account has been paid, from the trust account or otherwise, then the paralegal must comply with Rule 5.01(6), which states that if the amount of fees or disbursements charged by a paralegal is reduced by a court order, the paralegal must repay the money owing to the client pursuant to the court order as soon as is practicable.

Joint Retainers (Rule 5.01(10))

If a paralegal is acting for two or more clients in the same matter, the paralegal shall divide the fees and disbursements equitably between them, unless there is an agreement by the clients otherwise.

Where fees and disbursements are divided between or among joint clients, each joint client should receive a separate statement of account.

Division of Fees (Rule 5.01(11))

Fees for a matter may be divided between licensees who are not in the same firm if the client consents and the fees are divided in proportion to the work done and the responsibilities assumed.

The client's consent shall be fully informed and voluntary after disclosure, and shall be in writing or, if spoken, shall be confirmed in writing (Rule 1.02).

Contingency Fees (Rules 5.01(7)–(9))

A contingency fee is a fee that is contingent, in whole or in part, on the successful disposition or completion of the matter for which the paralegal's services are to be provided (Rule 5.01(7); Guideline 13).

Except in quasi-criminal or criminal matters, a paralegal may enter into a written agreement that provides that the paralegal's fee is contingent, in whole or in part, on the successful disposition or completion of the matter for which the paralegal's services are to be provided (Rule 5.01(7)).

A contingency fee is often, but not always, stated as a percentage of any amount recovered by the client. In determining the appropriate percentage or other basis of a contingency fee, the paralegal shall advise the client on the factors that are being taken into account in determining the percentage or other basis for the fee, including:

- the likelihood of success;
- the nature and complexity of the claim;
- the expense and risk of pursuing the claim;
- the amount of the expected recovery;
- who is to receive an award of costs; and
- the amount of costs awarded (Rule 5.01(8)).

The percentage or other basis of a contingency fee agreed upon under subrule (7) shall be fair and reasonable, taking into consideration all of the circumstances and the factors listed in subrule (8) (Rule 5.01(9)).

The contingency fee agreement must be clear about how the fee will be calculated. Guideline 13 recommends that you refer to Regulation 195/04 to the *Solicitors Act*, which applies to contingency fees for lawyers, for guidance regarding the terms to be included in a paralegal contingency fee agreement.

Fee Splitting and Referrals (Rules 5.01(11), (12), (13), (14))

Fee Splitting

Fee splitting occurs when a paralegal shares or splits her fee with another person.

Fee splitting is permitted between licensees who are not in the same firm if the client consents and the fees are divided in proportion to the work done and the responsibilities assumed (Rule 5.01(11)). The client's consent shall be fully informed and voluntary after disclosure, and it must be in writing or confirmed as soon as is practicable (Rule 1.02).

fee splitting
an arrangement where a paralegal shares or splits a client fee with another person

Fee splitting is not permitted if the person(s) with whom the fee is to be divided are non-licensees (Rule 5.01(12)):

> (12) A paralegal shall not,
> (a) directly or indirectly share, split, or divide his or her fees with any person who is not a licensee, including an affiliated entity; or
> (b) give any financial or other reward to any person who is not a licensee, including an affiliated entity for the referral of clients or client matters.

Rule 5.01(12) does not apply to multi-discipline practices of paralegal and non-licensee partners where the partnership agreement provides for the sharing of fees, cash flows, or profits among members of the firm.

Referral Fees

Guideline 13 defines a **referral fee** as:

- a fee paid by a paralegal to another paralegal or lawyer for referring a client to the paralegal, or

referral fee
a fee paid by a paralegal to another licensee for referring a client to the paralegal, or a fee paid to a paralegal by another licensee for the paralegal's referral of a person to the other licensee

- a fee paid to a paralegal by another paralegal or lawyer for his or her referral of a person to another paralegal or lawyer.

Referral fees are permitted in the following circumstances (Rule 5.01(14)):

> (14) A paralegal who refers a matter to another licensee because of the expertise and ability of the other licensee to handle the matter may accept, and the other licensee may pay, a referral fee if,
> (a) the referral was not made because of a conflict of interest,
> (b) the fee is reasonable and does not increase the total amount of the fee charged to the client, and
> (c) the client is informed and consents.

The client's consent shall be fully informed and voluntary after disclosure, and shall be in writing or, if spoken, shall be confirmed in writing (Rule 1.02).

The Rules do not prohibit a paralegal from:

(a) making an arrangement respecting the purchase and sale of a professional business when the consideration payable includes a percentage of revenues generated from the business sold;
(b) entering into a lease under which a landlord directly or indirectly shares in the fees or revenues generated by the provision of legal services; or
(c) paying an employee for services, other than for referring clients, based on the revenue of the paralegal's firm or professional business (Guideline 13).

BOX 7.1 Reminder: Affiliated Entities and Multi-Discipline Practices

An affiliated entity is any person or group of persons other than a person or group authorized to provide legal services in Ontario. An affiliation is an arrangement where a paralegal services firm provides legal services to the public jointly with a non-legal entity whose members practise a profession, trade, or occupation that supports or supplements the paralegal's provision of legal services.

A multi-discipline practice is a business arrangement that permits paralegal licensees to enter into a partnership or association that is not a corporation with non-licensees to provide to clients the services of a non-licensee who practises a profession, trade, or occupation that supports or supplements the provision of legal services. Multi-discipline practices are governed by By-law 7, Part III, and Rules 3.04(14) and 8.01. They are discussed in Chapter 4 on pages 131–132.

BOX 7.2 Fee Splitting and Referrals

Fact Situation

You are a paralegal licensee. You have been approached by Sandra Hobbins. Sandra is a property manager whose portfolio includes a number of multi-unit residential buildings. She tells you that she will refer all her residential tenancy matters to you, in return for 15 percent of your fee for each file. "It's a good deal for both of us," she says. "I can guarantee you around thirty L1s per month, and there are usually one or two other applications as well." (An L1 is application for termination of a residential tenancy for non-payment of rent.) Sandra also tells you that she will require a payment of $500 as a referral fee before she starts sending you any files.

Question for Discussion

May you enter into this arrangement?

Retainers (Rule 5.01; Guideline 14; By-law 9)

BOX 7.3 Reminder: What Is a Retainer?

In a legal services context, the word "retainer" has several meanings.

- A paralegal–client retainer (referred to in Guideline 14 as a retainer) is the contractual relationship between the client and the paralegal whereby the client agrees to hire the paralegal and the paralegal agrees to provide legal services to the client in a particular matter.
- A retainer agreement is a written contract between the paralegal and the client that sets out the scope of the legal services to be provided in a particular client matter and the likely cost of those services to the client, as well as the other terms of the paralegal–client retainer.
- A money retainer is money paid by the client to the paralegal for future legal services in a particular client matter.

The Retainer Agreement

If the client decides to retain you, you should discuss, at the initial consultation or as soon as possible thereafter, the scope of the legal services to be provided, and the likely cost of those services (Guideline 14).

When estimating fees, you should consider advising the client of any facts or circumstances that form the basis of the estimate, and, if practicable, any facts or circumstances that may result in an increase or decrease in the estimate.

Other terms that you should discuss with the client include but are not limited to:

- how fees will be calculated;
- anticipated cost of disbursements;
- HST exigible on fees and disbursements;
- your billing practices—that is, how frequently the client will be billed for fees and disbursements;
- the circumstances in which a money retainer will be required to be replenished; and
- how settlement funds payable to or by the client are to be handled.

You must ensure that the client understands the scope of the legal services to be provided; how fees, disbursements, and HST will be charged; and any other terms of the paralegal–client retainer.

It is advisable to confirm the terms of the retainer in writing. Depending on the nature of the client matter, confirmation in writing may be done by:

- a retainer agreement signed back by the client;
- an engagement letter delivered by the paralegal to the client; or
- a confirming memo delivered to the client by mail, email, or fax.

You should consider including a term in the written confirmation of the retainer that any settlement funds payable to the client by another person, or payable by the client to another person, be paid to you in trust. If the settlement funds are payable to the client, and the client has agreed that any outstanding fees or disbursements that have been invoiced may be paid from settlement funds payable to the client and received in trust before paying the balance out of trust to the client, the written confirmation of the retainer should contain a term to that effect. You shall not pay any amounts from settlement funds held in trust to any person until full and final waivers have been signed by all parties.

BOX 7.4 Reminder: Retainer Agreements

The retainer agreement is a valuable tool for managing client expectations about all aspects of the paralegal–client retainer. See the discussion of retainer agreements in Chapter 3 on pages 55–56 and in Chapter 4 on page 95. You will find a sample retainer agreement, adapted for a paralegal firm, at Appendix 3.1. Sample retainer agreements are also available at the Lawyers' Professional Indemnity Company website (http://www.practicepro.ca).

A retainer agreement must be adapted to reflect the terms of the agreement between the paralegal and the client in a particular client matter.

Money Retainers (Rule 5.01; By-law 9, Part IV)

A money retainer is a payment made by the client to the paralegal for future legal services and disbursements in the client matter.

> If practical, the paralegal should obtain a money retainer from the client at the beginning of the relationship. When determining the amount of the money retainer, the paralegal should consider the circumstances of each case, the circumstances of the client and the anticipated fees, disbursements, and HST. Many of the factors are the same as those used in deciding whether a fee is fair and reasonable.
>
> The client should be advised at the outset if and when further retainers will be required. There may also be circumstances where a money retainer is not appropriate, for example, when a client and the paralegal have entered into a contingency fee agreement (Guideline 14).

A money retainer shall be deposited to your trust account as soon as possible upon receipt, and by no later than close of business on the next bank day (By-law 9, ss. 1(3), 7(1)). Trust money shall be held for the benefit of the client until part or all the services agreed upon have been provided and invoiced to the client. Proper disbursements and expenses paid from the general (operating) account in the client matter may be reimbursed to the operating account from client funds held in trust (By-law 9, s. 9(1)2).

> To avoid disagreements in circumstances where a disbursement will be particularly substantial, a paralegal may want to obtain the client's approval prior to the expense being incurred (Guideline 14).

The Trust Account (Rule 5.01(5); Guideline 15; By-law 9, Part IV)

Client money, such as a money retainer or settlement funds, remains the property of the client. It must be deposited to your trust account and held for the benefit of the client.

Generally, a paralegal practice will have one general (operating) bank account and one mixed trust bank account. A mixed trust bank account is a trust account that holds money for more than one client matter. By-law 9 requires you to keep special trust records for the mixed trust account so that you can keep track of what money belongs to which client matter. Where you are retained on more than one matter for a client, you must also keep track of the trust funds to be credited to each active matter for that client. The tracking process is facilitated by assigning a unique client matter number to every new client matter opened. Where a client has several different matters ongoing at the same time, each client matter should be assigned a unique client matter number for file management and accounting purposes.

A paralegal shall not appropriate any funds of the client held in trust, or otherwise under the paralegal's control, for or on account of fees, except as permitted by the By-Laws under the *Law Society Act* (Rule 5.01(5)).

> The *Rules* are not intended to be an exhaustive statement of the considerations that apply to payment of a paralegal's account from trust. The handling of trust money is generally governed by the by-laws of the Law Society.
>
> Refusing to reimburse any portion of advance fees for work that has not been carried out when the contract of professional services with the client has terminated is a breach of the obligation to act with integrity (Guideline 13).

By-law 9, Part IV, s. 9(1) states that a licensee may withdraw from a trust account only the following money:

1. Money properly required for payment to a client or to a person on behalf of a client.
2. Money required to reimburse the licensee for money properly expended on behalf of a client or for expenses properly incurred on behalf of a client.
3. Money properly required for or toward payment of fees for services performed by the licensee for which a billing has been delivered.
4. Money that is directly transferred into another trust account and held on behalf of a client.
5. Money that under this Part should not have been paid into a trust account but was through inadvertence paid into a trust account.

You shall never disburse from trust an amount in excess of the amount actually held in trust in a particular client matter. You are personally responsible for reimbursing the trust account from your operating account for any amount paid out of a client trust account in error.

After you have prepared an invoice (called a "statement of account" in Rule 5.01) and delivered it to a client, you may transfer funds held in trust to the credit of that client matter out of the trust account into your general (operating) account, in payment of the invoice. The payment from trust must be stated in a separate line on the invoice. Any amount still owing after payment has been made from trust must also be stated in a separate line on the invoice. If the amount invoiced was paid in full out of trust, the amount owing on the invoice will be stated in a separate line as zero.

You will find sample invoices at Appendixes 7.1 and 7.2 on pages 228–229.

If the funds held in trust to the credit of the client matter are not adequate to pay the total amount of the invoice, you may deduct only the amount actually held in trust from the invoice, and transfer only the amount actually held in trust to the general account. The client is responsible for paying any balance still owing after the funds held in trust to the credit of the client matter are deducted from the client's bill and transferred to your general account. Where the client pays an outstanding balance on an invoice, any payment may be deposited directly to your general (operating) account, because it is for legal services that have been performed and for reasonable disbursements and expenses that have been incurred and billed to the client.

interim invoice an invoice that is delivered to the client before the client matter is completed, for fees and disbursements to the date of the interim invoice

You do not have to wait until a client matter is concluded to bill the file. An **interim invoice** is an invoice that is delivered to the client before the client matter is completed, for fees and disbursements to the date of the interim invoice. Presenting interim accounts at reasonable intervals in a lengthy client matter is an effective way of managing client expectations about the cost of a matter. You should consider interim billing in any client matter that is ongoing over a period of time. Interim billing should take place at reasonable intervals. If interim billing depletes the funds held in trust to the credit of the client matter, you may require additional money retainers at reasonable intervals as well. You should advise the client of your billing practices at the outset of the retainer, and confirm that advice in writing in the retainer agreement or engagement letter.

When determining the frequency and amount of the money retainers required of clients, you should consider your obligation to continue to represent clients in certain circumstances, despite non-payment of fees. You may not withdraw from representing a non-paying client if serious prejudice to the client would result. Refer to Rule 3.08, Withdrawal from Representation, discussed in Chapter 4 on pages 141–148.

BOX 7.5 Billing the Client

You are holding money in your mixed trust bank account as follows:

Client	Matter number	Amount
A	001	$500
B	002	$1,000
C	003	$400
D	004	$600
Total monies held in trust:		$2,500

Assume that all matters are being billed at an hourly rate.

Fact Situation 1

You have completed legal services in Matter 001 for Client A. The total of fees, disbursements, and HST is $650. You have $2,500 in your mixed trust account.

Questions for Discussion

Can you pay the total amount owing from trust? What information should be stated on the invoice?

Fact Situation 2

You have completed legal services in Matter 004. The amount of the final invoice is $400.

Question for Discussion

Can you pay the total amount owing from trust?

Fact Situation 3

Matter 002 is ongoing. You have completed several steps in the proceeding, including the settlement conference. To date, your legal services total $850 including HST. A trial date has been set for four months' time. For the trial, you will need to interview and obtain statements from three witnesses for your client, and serve a summons upon an opposing party's witness whom you wish to cross-examine. You will also require an expert's report, which will cost $500.

Question for Discussion

What are your next steps?

Trust Controls (By-law 9; Guideline 15)

A paralegal must be in control of her or his trust account. He or she should review the trust ledger accounts for all client matters where money is held in trust on a monthly basis.

Non-licensees are not permitted by By-law 9 to disburse funds from trust. There is a very limited exception in By-law 9, s. 11(b):

> 11. A cheque drawn on a trust account shall not be …
>
> (b) signed by a person who is not a licensee except in exceptional circumstances and except when the person has signing authority on the trust account on which a cheque will be drawn and is bonded in an amount at least equal to the maximum balance on deposit during the immediately preceding fiscal year of the licensee in all the trust accounts on which signing authority has been delegated to the person.

The Law Society has found appropriate exceptional circumstances to be very rare.

Signing authority on the trust account should be limited to senior paralegals. If paralegal associates are given signing authority on the trust account, there should be a limit on the amount that they can sign for.

> If there is only one paralegal with signing authority on the trust account(s) it would be prudent to make arrangements for another paralegal or a lawyer to have signing authority on the trust account(s) in case of an unexpected emergency (i.e. illness or accident) or planned absence (i.e. vacation). The paralegal may arrange this through his or her financial institution through a power of attorney. The chosen paralegal or lawyer must be insured and entitled to provide legal services or to practise law.
>
> To ensure that no unauthorized withdrawals from trust are being made, the paralegal should limit access to blank trust account cheques and electronic banking software. A paralegal should never sign blank trust cheques. The paralegal should use pre-numbered trust cheques and keep them locked up when not in use (Guideline 15).

If trust money has been wrongfully withdrawn from a client matter account, you shall reimburse the client matter account from your general (operating) account immediately upon discovery of the error.

Retention of Financial Records (By-law 9)

A paralegal shall retain the following records for at least the six-year period immediately preceding the paralegal's most recent fiscal year end (s. 23(1)):

- general receipts and disbursements journals, and
- fees book or chronological record of billings.

Note that By-law 9, which is a minimum standard and concerns itself principally with trust accounts, does not require that a client's general ledger be maintained. You should consider retaining your client's general ledger, which tracks client receivables, for at least the six-year period immediately preceding your most recent fiscal year end. A **client receivable** is money that is owed to a paralegal by a client for an unpaid balance on an invoice for legal services that have been rendered and reasonable expenses and disbursements that have been incurred in a client matter.

client receivable
money that is owed to a paralegal by a client for an unpaid balance on an invoice for legal services that have been rendered and reasonable expenses and disbursements that have been incurred in a client matter

A paralegal shall retain the following records for at least the ten-year period immediately preceding the paralegal's most recent fiscal year end (s. 23(2)):

- trust receipts and disbursements journals;
- clients' trust ledger;
- trust comparisons;
- valuable property record; and
- trust bank statements or pass books, cashed cheques and detailed duplicate deposit slips for all trust accounts, and signed electronic trust transfer requisitions and signed printed confirmations of electronic transfers of trust funds.

Practice Management (Rule 8)

Running an effective paralegal practice involves a range of responsibilities. You must make decisions about what procedures and systems you need to have in place to make the business successful, while ensuring compliance with and being responsible for your professional obligations under the Rules and By-Laws.

Delegation and Supervision (Rules 8.01(1), (3)–(5); By-law 7.1, Part I; Guideline 18)

Delegation

A paralegal shall, in accordance with the By-Laws, assume complete professional responsibility for all business entrusted to her or him (Rule 8.01(1)).

In appropriate circumstances, a paralegal should consider providing legal services with the assistance of competent non-licensees. For purposes of By-law 7.1, Part I,

> "non-licensee" means an individual who,
>
> (a) in the case of the assignment of tasks and functions by a person licensed to practise law in Ontario as a barrister and solicitor, is not a person licensed to practise law in Ontario as a barrister and solicitor and, in the case of the assignment of tasks and functions by a person licensed to provide legal services in Ontario, is not a licensee,

(b) is engaged by a licensee to provide her or his services to the licensee, and
(c) expressly agrees with the licensee that the licensee shall have effective control over the individual's provision of services to the licensee.

For the purposes of subsection 1, a licensee has effective control over an individual's provision of services to the licensee when the licensee may, without the agreement of the individual, take any action necessary to ensure that the licensee complies with the *Law Society Act*, the By-Laws, the Society's rules of professional conduct, and the Society's policies and guidelines (By-law 7.1, s. 1(2)).

A paralegal may, in accordance with Part I of By-law 7.1, assign to a non-licensee tasks and functions in connection with the paralegal's provision of legal services in relation to the affairs of the licensee's client (s. 3(1)). Guideline 18 comments that:

> A paralegal may, in appropriate circumstances, provide services with the assistance of persons of whose competence the paralegal is satisfied. Proper use of support staff allows the paralegal to make efficient use of the time he or she has for providing legal services, and may result in savings to the client. Under By-Law 7.1, some tasks may be delegated to persons who are not licensed and other tasks may not. Though certain tasks may be delegated, the paralegal remains responsible for all services rendered and all communications by and prepared by his or her employees.
>
> The extent of supervision required will depend on the task, including the degree of standardization and repetitiveness of the task and the experience of the employee. Extra supervisory care may be needed if there is something different or unusual in the task. The burden rests on the paralegal to educate the employee concerning the tasks that may be assigned and then to supervise the manner in which these tasks are completed.
>
> A paralegal should ensure that employees who are not licensed clearly identify themselves as such when communicating with clients, prospective clients, courts or tribunals, or the public. This includes both written and verbal communications.

A paralegal who is affiliated with an entity under By-law 7 may, in accordance with Part I of By-law 7.1, assign to the entity or its staff tasks and functions in connection with the provision of legal services in relation to the affairs of the licensee's client only if the client consents to the licensee doing so (By-law 7.1, s. 3(2)). The client's consent shall be fully informed and voluntary after disclosure, and shall be in writing or, if spoken, shall be confirmed in writing (Rule 1.02).

Multi-Discipline Practice (Rules 3.04(15), 8.01(1), (5))

A multi-discipline practice is a business arrangement that permits paralegal licensees to provide to clients the services of a non-licensee who practises a profession, trade, or occupation that supports or supplements the provision of legal services (By-law 7, s. 18(1)). The paralegal licensee must have effective control over the non-legal professional's provision of services to clients of the multi-discipline practice (By-law 7, s. 18(2)2).

A paralegal in a multi-discipline practice shall, in accordance with the By-Laws, assume complete professional responsibility for all business entrusted to him or her (Rule 8.01(1)). A paralegal in a multi-discipline practice shall ensure that non-licensee partners and associates comply with the Rules and all ethical principles that govern a paralegal in the discharge of his or her professional obligations (Rule 8.01(5)).

A paralegal in a multi-discipline practice must ensure that the client understands that legal services are provided by the paralegal, and supplemented by the non-legal professional services of non-licensee partners and associates.

Assignment of Tasks or Functions—Direct Supervision (Rule 8.01(3); By-law 7.1, s. 4)

A paralegal shall, in accordance with the By-Laws, directly supervise staff and assistants to whom particular tasks and functions are delegated (Rule 8.01(3)).

A paralegal shall assume complete professional responsibility for her or his provision of legal services in relation to the affairs of the paralegal's clients and shall directly supervise any non-licensee to whom are assigned particular tasks and functions in connection with the paralegal's provision of legal services in relation to the affairs of each client (By-law 7.1, s. 4(1)).

By-law 7.1, s. 4(2) states that,

> (2) Without limiting the generality of subsection (1),
>
> (a) the licensee shall not permit a non-licensee to accept a client on the licensee's behalf;
>
> (b) the licensee shall maintain a direct relationship with each client throughout the licensee's retainer;
>
> (c) the licensee shall assign to a non-licensee only tasks and functions that the non-licensee is competent to perform;
>
> (d) the licensee shall ensure that a non-licensee does not act without the licensee's instruction;
>
> (e) the licensee shall review a non-licensee's performance of the tasks and functions assigned to her or him at frequent intervals;
>
> (f) the licensee shall ensure that the tasks and functions assigned to a non-licensee are performed properly and in a timely manner;
>
> (g) the licensee shall assume responsibility for all tasks and functions performed by a non-licensee, including all documents prepared by the non-licensee; and
>
> (h) the licensee shall ensure that a non-licensee does not, at any time, act finally in respect of the affairs of the licensee's client.

Assignment of Tasks or Functions—Express Instruction and Authorization (By-law 7.1, s. 5(1))

By-law 7.1, s. 5(1) requires that a paralegal give a non-licensee written instructions and authorization before the non-licensee performs certain tasks.

(1) A licensee shall give a non-licensee express instruction and authorization prior to permitting the non-licensee,

(a) to give or accept an undertaking on behalf of the licensee;

(b) to act on behalf of the licensee in respect of a scheduling or other related routine administrative matter before an adjudicative body; or

(c) to take instructions from the licensee's client.

Assignment of Tasks or Functions—Prior Consent and Approval (By-law 7.1, s. 5(2))

A paralegal shall obtain a client's consent to permit a non-licensee to conduct routine negotiations with third parties in relation to the affairs of the paralegal's client and shall approve the results of the negotiations before any action is taken following from the negotiations.

The client's consent shall be fully informed and voluntary after disclosure, and shall be in writing or, if spoken, shall be confirmed in writing (Rule 1.02).

Tasks and Functions That May Not Be Assigned (Rule 8.01(4); By-law 7.1, s. 6)

Certain tasks and functions cannot be assigned by a paralegal to a non-licensee. Rule 8.01(4) states that:

(4) A paralegal shall not permit a non-licensee;

(a) to provide legal services;

(b) to be held out as a licensee; or

(c) to perform any of the duties that only paralegals may perform or do things that paralegals themselves may not do.

By-law 7.1, s. 6(1) states that:

(1) A licensee shall not permit a non-licensee,

(a) to give the licensee's client legal advice;

(b) to act on behalf of a person in a proceeding before an adjudicative body, other than on behalf of the licensee in accordance with subsection 5(1), unless the non-licensee is authorized under the *Law Society Act* to do so;

(c) to conduct negotiations with third parties, other than in accordance with subsection 5(2);

(d) to sign correspondence, other than correspondence of a routine administrative nature; or

(e) to forward to the licensee's client any document, other than a routine document, that has not been previously reviewed by the licensee.

In your supervisory role, as the person responsible for all business entrusted to you, you shall not permit an employee to do anything that paralegals may not do, including engaging in unauthorized practice. If a paralegal employs a lawyer, the lawyer employee cannot practise law, because the paralegal employer does not have the

Table 7.1 Delegation to Non-Licensee Employees (Rule 8.01; By-law 7.1)

TASK, FUNCTION, OR CONDUCT	IS AN EMPLOYEE PERMITTED TO PERFORM THE TASK OR FUNCTION?	AUTHORITY
Accept a client on the paralegal's behalf	No	By-law 7.1, s. 4
Act without the paralegal's instruction	No	By-law 7.1, s. 4
Act finally in a client's affairs	No	By-law 7.1, s. 4
Give or accept an undertaking on behalf of the paralegal	Yes, with the paralegal's express instruction and authorization permitting the employee to do so	By-law 7.1, s. 5(1)
	No, in any other circumstances	
Appear before an adjudicative body	Yes, on scheduling or other routine administrative matters and with the paralegal's express instruction and authorization permitting the employee to do so	By-law 7.1, s. 5(1)
	Yes, if non-licensee falls within the exemptions	*Law Society Act*, s. 1(8) By-law 4
	No, in any other circumstances	By-law 7.1, s. 6
Give a client legal advice	No	By-law 7.1, s. 6
Take instructions from a client	Yes, with the paralegal's express instruction and authorization permitting the employee to do so	By-law 7.1, s. 5(1)
	No, in any other circumstances	
Conduct negotiations with third parties	Yes, in routine negotiations, with the client's prior consent and with the paralegal's approval of the results of the negotiations before any further action following from the negotiations	By-law 7.1, s. 5(2)
	No, if it is not a routine negotiation	By-law 7.1, s. 6
Sign correspondence	Yes, if correspondence is of a routine administrative nature	By-law 7.1, s. 6
	No, in any other circumstances	
Forward a document to the client without review by the paralegal	Yes, if it is a routine document	By-law 7.1, s. 6
	No, in any other circumstances	
Provide legal services	No	Rule 8.01(4)
Hold himself out as a licensee	No	Rule 8.01(4)
Perform any duty that only a paralegal may perform	No	Rule 8.01(4)
Do anything that a paralegal may not do	No	Rule 8.01(4)

education, training, and knowledge to supervise someone engaged in the practice of law. A paralegal employer may supervise a lawyer employee if the lawyer employee practises within the permitted scope of practice for paralegals.

Collection Letters (By-law 7.1, s. 7)

Special restrictions apply to collection letters. By-law 7.1, s. 7 states that:

> (7) A licensee shall not permit a collection letter to be sent to any person unless,
>
> (a) the letter is in relation to the affairs of the licensee's client;
>
> (b) the letter is prepared by the licensee or by a non-licensee under the direct supervision of the licensee;
>
> (c) if the letter is prepared by a non-licensee under the direct supervision of the licensee, the letter is reviewed and approved by the licensee prior to it being sent;
>
> (d) the letter is on the licensee's business letterhead; and
>
> (e) the letter is signed by the licensee.

Hiring and Training of Staff (Guideline 18)

Hiring Staff

In order to run your practice efficiently and to comply with your obligations to clients under the Rules and By-Laws, you must take steps to hire trustworthy, competent staff and train them properly. Proper hiring and training of staff will assist you to manage your practice effectively, as required by Rule 3.01(4)(h). Guideline 18 comments that:

> In order to fulfill his or her responsibilities to clients under the Rules and By-Laws, a paralegal should take care to properly hire and train staff. A paralegal should obtain information about a potential employee to inform himself or herself about the employee's competence and trustworthiness. If the position involves handling money, the paralegal may ask for the applicant's consent to check his or her criminal record and credit reports. A paralegal must comply with privacy legislation and should refer to the Rules to review questions that can and cannot be asked of an applicant, as outlined in the *Human Rights Code*. A paralegal should confirm the information contained in a candidate's resume, consult references, and verify previous employment experiences before offering employment to a candidate.

Training Staff

A paralegal shall assume complete professional responsibility for all business entrusted to her or him (Rule 8.01(1)). You cannot make legal services available to the public in an efficient and convenient way if you do not have trained, competent staff. Training ensures that staff have the knowledge, skills, and attributes to perform their employment duties effectively. It also ensures that they are aware of their professional obligations in a legal services practice.

Proper hiring and training of non-licensees will assist you in managing your practice effectively, as required by Rules 3.01(4)(c) and (h). Since you are responsible for the professional business, it will help you to fulfill this responsibility if you educate your staff regarding

- the types of tasks that will and will not be delegated;
- the need to act with courtesy and professionalism;
- the definition of discrimination and harassment, and the prohibition against any conduct that amounts to discrimination and harassment;
- the duty to maintain client confidentiality and methods used to protect confidential client information (e.g., avoiding gossip inside and outside of the office);
- the definition of a conflict of interest, the duty to avoid conflicts, and how to use a conflicts checking system;
- proper handling of client property, including money; and
- proper record keeping (Guideline 18).

An office procedures manual is a valuable tool for assisting staff to perform their duties effectively and professionally.

Financial Obligations (Rule 8.01(2); Guideline 23)

A paralegal shall promptly meet financial obligations incurred in the course of practice on behalf of clients unless, before incurring such an obligation, the paralegal clearly indicates in writing to the person to whom it is to be owed that it is not to be a personal obligation of the paralegal (Rule 8.01(2)).

The duty to promptly meet financial obligations established by Rule 8.01 is a professional duty. A paralegal should be aware that failure to meet financial responsibilities contemplated by Rule 8.01 may also have legal consequences. Guideline 23 comments that:

> The business of providing legal services often requires that a paralegal incur financial obligations to others on behalf of clients. Such obligations include charges for medical reports, disbursements payable to government registries, fees charged by expert witnesses, sheriffs, special examiners, registrars, court reporters and public officials, and the accounts of agents retained in other jurisdictions.
>
> To assist in avoiding disputes about payment of accounts, where a paralegal retains a person on behalf of a client, the paralegal should clarify the terms of the retainer in writing. This includes specifying the fees, the nature of the services to be provided, and the person responsible for payment. If the paralegal is not responsible for the payment of the fees, the paralegal should help in making satisfactory arrangements for payment if it is reasonably possible to do so.
>
> If there is a change of representative, the paralegal who originally retained the person to whom the financial obligation will be owed should advise him or her about the change and provide the name, address, telephone number, fax number and email address of the new paralegal or lawyer.

To avoid misunderstandings, a paralegal should consider discussing anticipated expenses and disbursements (including extraordinary disbursements such as medical reports) with the client at the initial consultation, and clarifying with the client who is responsible for payment. The arrangement should be confirmed in writing in the retainer agreement or engagement letter.

Making Legal Services Available (Rule 8.02; Guideline 19)

A paralegal shall make legal services available to the public in an efficient and convenient way (Rule 8.02(1)). This does not mean that you must accept every retainer that is offered. Guideline 19 comments that:

> A paralegal has a general right to decline a particular representation (except when assigned as representative by a tribunal), but it is a right that should be exercised prudently, particularly if the probable result would be to make it difficult for a person to obtain legal advice or representation. Generally, the paralegal should not exercise the right merely because a person seeking legal services or that person's cause is unpopular or notorious, or because powerful interests or allegations of misconduct or malfeasance are involved, or because of the paralegal's private opinion about the guilt of the accused. A paralegal declining representation should assist in obtaining the services of a lawyer or another licensed paralegal qualified in the particular field and able to act.
>
> A person who is vulnerable or who has suffered a traumatic experience and has not yet had a chance to recover may need the professional assistance of a paralegal. A paralegal is permitted to provide assistance to a person if a close relative or personal friend of the person contacts the paralegal for this purpose, and to offer assistance to a person with whom the paralegal has a close family or professional relationship.

A person requiring legal services should be able to find a qualified paralegal with minimum delay and inconvenience. A paralegal assists in this process by promoting his or her legal services to the public. A paralegal's promotional strategies must comply with the Rules. They must be in the best interests of the public, and consistent with a high standard of professionalism.

Rule 8.02(2) imposes restrictions upon the manner in which a paralegal offers legal services:

> (2) In offering legal services, a paralegal shall not use means
>
> (a) that are false or misleading,
>
> (b) that amount to coercion, duress or harassment,
>
> (c) that take advantage of a person who is vulnerable or who has suffered a traumatic experience and has not yet had a chance to recover,
>
> (d) that are intended to influence a person who has retained another paralegal or a lawyer for a particular matter to change his or her representative for that matter, unless the change is initiated by the person or the other representative, or
>
> (e) that otherwise bring the paralegal profession or the administration of justice into disrepute.

A paralegal shall not advertise services that are beyond the permissible scope of paralegal practice (Rule 8.02(3)).

Marketing Legal Services (Rules 8.02, 8.03)

marketing includes advertisements and similar communications in various media, as well as firm names (including trade names), letterhead, business cards, and logos (Rule 8.03(1))

For the purposes of Rule 8.03, **marketing** includes advertisements and similar communications in various media, as well as firm names (including trade names), letterhead, business cards, and logos (Rule 8.03(1)).

Rule 8.03(2) sets out parameters for the marketing of legal services.

> (2) A paralegal may market legal services if the marketing
> (a) is demonstrably true, accurate and verifiable,
> (b) is neither misleading, confusing or deceptive, nor likely to mislead, confuse or deceive, and
> (c) is in the best interests of the public and is consistent with a high standard of professionalism.

When advertising fees, a paralegal shall comply with Rule 8.03(3).

> (3) A paralegal may advertise fees charged for legal services by the paralegal for legal services if
> (a) the advertising is reasonably precise as to the services offered for each fee quoted,
> (b) the advertising states whether other amounts, such as disbursements and taxes, will be charged in addition to the fee, and
> (c) the paralegal strictly adheres to the advertised fee in every applicable case.

Rules 8.02 and 8.03 are intended to ensure that a paralegal does not market his or her services in a way that misleads clients or the public, while still permitting the paralegal to differentiate his or her services from those of other licensees. A paralegal's marketing and advertising should not suggest that the paralegal is a lawyer. A paralegal should take steps to correct any misapprehension on the part of a client or prospective client in that respect (Guideline 19).

Guideline 19 provides examples of marketing practices that may contravene Rule 8.03. These practices include those that:

- state an amount of money that the paralegal has recovered for a client or refer to the paralegal's degree of success in past cases, unless such statement is accompanied by a further statement that past results are not necessarily indicative of future results and that the amount recovered and other litigation outcomes will vary according to the facts in individual cases;
- suggest qualitative superiority to lawyers or other paralegals;
- raise expectations unjustifiably;
- suggest or imply that the paralegal is aggressive;
- disparage or demean other persons, groups, organizations, or institutions;
- take advantage of a vulnerable person or group;
- use testimonials or endorsements that contain emotional appeals.

BOX 7.6 Marketing a Paralegal Firm

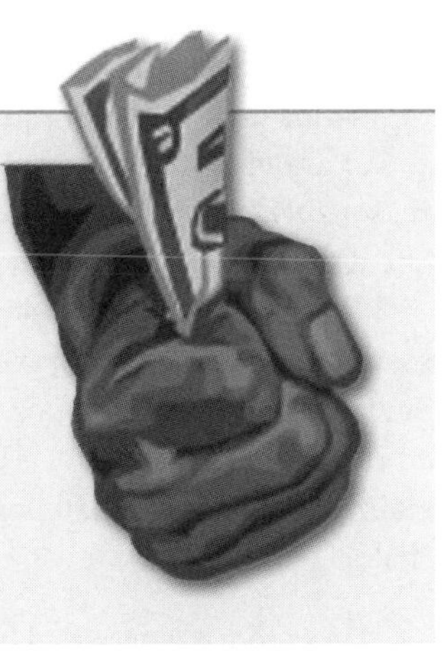

Fact Situation

Your paralegal firm does a lot of work for multi-unit residential landlords. Most of the matters involve terminating tenancies and evicting tenants for non-payment of rent. You are designing a brochure to advertise your firm to potential landlord clients. You want to use this logo on your brochure:

Question for Discussion

Is the logo an acceptable marketing strategy?

Internet Marketing

Advertising by paralegals that uses electronic media, such as websites, social media, and email, is governed by the Rules.

In addition to the Rules, paralegals who are contemplating marketing their services using electronic media should review and consider the Canadian Bar Association's "Practising Ethically with Technology," along with any material relating to this issue that is posted from time to time in the Practice Management Topics on the Law Society website.

Internet advertising is not limited to a particular geographic area, and access is not confined to a particular group of users. Anyone anywhere in the world who has Internet access can view your website.

To prevent confusion in the minds of users as to your identity, location, and qualifications, you should provide the following information:

- your name;
- your status as a licensed paralegal;
- the name of your paralegal firm;
- your mailing address;
- your licensed jurisdiction of practice; and
- the email address of at least one paralegal responsible for communication.

You should consider stating the areas of law in which paralegals are authorized to provide legal services in Ontario, in accordance with Rule 8.02(3).

Any information about you or your firm posted at a website shall comply with Rule 8.03(2).

Compulsory Errors and Omissions Insurance (Rule 8.04; By-law 6, Part II; Guideline 20)

Errors and omissions insurance is professional liability insurance intended to reimburse clients for any damage or loss suffered as a result of a paralegal's negligence or wrongdoing when working on a client matter.

All paralegals practising in Ontario shall obtain and maintain adequate errors and omissions insurance as required by the Law Society (Rule 8.04(1)).

A paralegal shall give prompt notice of any circumstance that the paralegal may reasonably expect to give rise to a claim to an insurer or other indemnitor so that the client's protection from that source will not be prejudiced (Rule 8.04(2)).

When a claim of professional negligence is made against a paralegal, she or he shall assist and cooperate with the insurer or other indemnitor to the extent necessary to enable the claim to be dealt with promptly (Rule 8.04(3)).

In cases where liability is clear and the insurer is prepared to pay its portion of the claim, the paralegal shall pay the balance (Rule 8.04(4)). Guideline 20 recommends that:

> As soon as a paralegal discovers an error or omission that is or may reasonably be expected to involve liability to his or her client, the paralegal should take the following steps, in addition to those required by Rule 8.04:
>
> - immediately arrange an interview with the client and advise the client that an error or omission may have occurred that may form the basis of a claim against the paralegal by the client;
> - advise the client to obtain an opinion from an independent paralegal or lawyer and that, in the circumstances, the paralegal may not be able to continue acting for the client; and
> - subject to the rules about confidentiality, inform the insurer of the facts of the situation.
>
> While the introduction of compulsory insurance imposes additional obligations upon a paralegal, those obligations must not impair the relationship between the paralegal and client or the duties owed to the client.

CHAPTER SUMMARY

A paralegal shall not charge or accept any amount for a fee or disbursement unless it is fair and reasonable and has been disclosed in a timely fashion. At the outset of the paralegal–client retainer, you should discuss with the client the scope of the legal services to be provided and the likely cost of those services. You should also discuss the money retainer, billing practices, and other important terms of the paralegal–client retainer.

You must ensure that the client understands the scope of the legal services to be provided; how fees, disbursements, and HST will be charged; and any other terms of the retainer. The terms of the paralegal–client retainer in a client matter should be confirmed in writing, by a retainer agreement or engagement letter.

No fee, reward, costs, commission, interest, rebate, agency or forwarding allowance, or other compensation related to his employment may be taken by the paralegal from anyone other than the client, without full disclosure to, and consent of, the client.

In a statement of account to a client, you shall clearly and separately detail amounts charged as fees, amounts charged as disbursements, and the amount payable for HST. You should review and sign the statement of account before it is delivered to the client.

If a client disputes a paralegal's account, the dispute must be adjudicated by a court. If the amount of fees or disbursements charged is reduced by a court order, the paralegal must repay the monies to the client as soon as is practicable.

Except in quasi-criminal or criminal matters, you may enter into a written agreement that provides that your fee is contingent, in whole or in part, on the successful disposition or completion of the matter for which your services are to be provided.

If you are acting for two or more clients in a joint retainer arrangement, you shall divide the fees and disbursements equitably between or among them, unless the clients have agreed to another arrangement. Each joint client shall receive a separate statement of account.

Fees for a matter may be divided between licensees who are not in the same firm if the client consents and the fees are divided in proportion to the work done and the responsibilities assumed.

You shall not share, split, or divide your fees with any person who is not a licensee, including an affiliated entity.

You shall not give any financial or other reward to any person who is not a licensee, including an affiliated entity, for the referral of clients or client matters.

If you refer a matter to another licensee because of her expertise and ability to handle the matter, you may accept, and the other licensee may pay, a referral fee if the referral was not made because of a conflict of interest, the fee is reasonable and does not increase the total amount of the fee charged to the client, and the client is informed and consents.

Client money, such as a money retainer or settlement funds, remains the property of the client. It must be deposited to your trust account and held for the benefit of the client. A paralegal shall not appropriate any funds of the client held in trust or otherwise under the paralegal's control, for or on account of fees, except as permitted by the By-Laws under the *Law Society Act*.

A paralegal shall, in accordance with the By-Laws, assume complete professional responsibility for all business entrusted to her or him. In appropriate circumstances, a paralegal should consider providing legal services with the assistance of competent non-licensees. A paralegal may assign to a non-licensee tasks and functions in connection with the paralegal's provision of legal services in relation to the affairs of the licensee's client. When doing so, you shall ensure compliance with Rule 8.01(4) and By-law 7.1, Part I.

In order to run your practice efficiently and effectively, you must take steps to hire trustworthy, competent staff, and ensure that they receive appropriate training before you delegate tasks or functions to them. You shall, in accordance with the By-Laws, directly supervise staff and assistants to whom particular tasks and functions are delegated.

A paralegal shall promptly meet financial obligations incurred in the course of practice on behalf of clients unless, before incurring the obligation, the paralegal clearly indicates in writing to the person to whom it is to be owed that it is not to be a personal obligation of the paralegal.

A paralegal shall make legal services available to the public in an efficient and convenient way. A paralegal must be able to market his services to the public in a way that differentiates those services from services provided by other licensees, including lawyers. A paralegal shall not use marketing strategies that are false or misleading, not in the best interests of the public, or inconsistent with high standards of professionalism.

The Rules govern marketing by paralegals that uses electronic media.

All paralegals practising in Ontario shall obtain and maintain adequate errors and omissions insurance as required by the Law Society.

KEY TERMS

billable time, 202
client receivable, 214
contingency fee, 203
docket, 202
docketed time, 202
fees based on an hourly rate, 202
fees by stages, 203
fee splitting, 207
fixed, flat, or block fee, 203
interim invoice, 212
marketing, 222
non-billable time, 202
referral fee, 207
statement of account, 205
to write off time, 202

REFERENCES

Canadian Bar Association, Ethics and Responsibility Committee, *Practising Ethically with Technology* (August 2014), http://www.cba.org/CBA/activities/pdf/guidelines-eng.pdf.

Highway Traffic Act, RSO 1990, c. H.8.

Human Rights Code, RSO 1990, c. H.19, as amended.

Law Society Act, RSO 1990, c. L.8, as amended.

Law Society of Upper Canada, *By-Laws* ("the By-Laws") (2005), http://www.lsuc.on.ca/with.aspx?id=1070.

Law Society of Upper Canada, *Ethical Considerations and Technology*, http://rc.lsuc.on.ca/pdf/pmg/tech_guidelines.pdf.

Law Society of Upper Canada, *Paralegal Professional Conduct Guidelines* (October 2014) ("the Guidelines"), http://www.lsuc.on.ca/paralegal-conduct-guidelines.

Law Society of Upper Canada, *Paralegal Rules of Conduct* (October 2014) ("the Rules"), http://www.lsuc.on.ca/paralegal-conduct-rules.

Law Society of Upper Canada, *Practice Management Guidelines* (2008), http://www.lsuc.on.ca/with.aspx?id=2147490535.

Law Society of Upper Canada, *Rules of Professional Conduct* (2014), http://www.lsuc.on.ca/lawyer-conduct-rules.

O. Reg. 195/04, Contingency Fee Agreements, http://www.e-laws.gov.on.ca/html/regs/english/elaws_regs_040195_e.htm.

Solicitors Act, RSO 1990, c. S-15.

REVIEW QUESTIONS

1. You are going through a slow period in your paralegal practice. A client approaches you about an assault charge, where the Crown has elected to proceed by way of summary conviction. Ordinarily, you would charge an hourly rate of $100 for your fees in such a matter, but you need the business, so you give the client an estimate of the total cost based on an hourly rate of $70. You figure you can always adjust your fee later, pleading unforeseen circumstances. You also plan to make a little extra by padding the disbursements.

   Discuss, referring to the applicable rule(s) and other authorities, if any.

2. Henrietta Stackpole is a licensed paralegal. Henrietta is retained by Stephen Foster to represent him in a Small Claims Court action for damages for a minor personal injury. The initial consultation is brief, as Henrietta is very busy at the time. She quotes an hourly rate of $100, and requests a money retainer of $500. She never does get around to confirming the paralegal–client retainer in writing.

   The matter fails to settle, and a trial date is scheduled. At trial, Henrietta intends to rely upon a medical report from Stephen's treating physician. The fee for the report is $400. The deadline for service of the medical report on the other parties is fast approaching. Henrietta pays for the report from the funds in trust. She moves the balance in trust into her general account to pay for some disbursements incurred at the commencement of the matter, including $75 for issuing the claim.

   At trial, Stephen is awarded $12,000 plus costs. He is very disappointed with this result.

   Henrietta arranges with the paralegal for the defendant for the settlement funds to be paid to her in trust. She invoices Stephen for $3,000, and remits the balance to him. Stephen is outraged. "I already paid you $500!" he says. "I thought that was your fee! Now you turn around and give yourself a bonus for doing a lousy job?" He says he is going to complain to the Law Society and he is also going to go to court to dispute the account.

   What steps could Henrietta have taken to avoid this outcome?

3. Robert Miller is a paralegal licensee who specializes in defending persons charged with *Highway Traffic Act* offences.

   Robert has grown his practice by approaching police officers who appear as witnesses on his own or other matters at the courthouse, asking them to direct to him the people they charge, and offering to pay the officers a fee for every defendant who retains Robert to defend them. He gives each officer who agrees to this arrangement a set of his business cards, telling the officer to mark it in a particular manner and give it to the defendant at the time the charge is made, with instructions to present it to Robert, who will give the defendant a "special price."

   Many officers refuse to agree to the arrangement, but several do. Robert keeps a list of the officers' names and the special marks made on their cards so that he knows whom to pay and how much. He charges the clients who are referred to him in this manner a higher fee than he charges his other clients because he factors in the referral fee.

   All defendants who are referred to Robert in this manner are required to swear an affidavit at the time of retaining him that states one of the following: "I learned of the licensed paralegal in the following manner: From a friend / By observing him in court / Through advertising." Robert tells them that the affidavits are totally confidential and that he uses them to formulate marketing strategies.

   Has Robert behaved ethically?
4. You specialize in residential tenancies matters. A landlord whom you have never represented telephones you seeking legal services. When you perform a conflicts check, you discover a conflicting interest. You refer the landlord to another paralegal, who is also a residential tenancies specialist. The other paralegal wishes to pay you a referral fee. She has her client's consent. May she pay, and may you accept, the referral fee?
5. You have just received a money retainer from a new client. You have some bills you need to pay, and you are running short of cash in the general account. You would like to deposit the new client's money retainer directly to the general account and use it to pay the bills. You plan to replace it later.

   Discuss.
6. A client sends you a cheque for payment of an outstanding invoice. What do you do with the money?
7. You are holding $800 in trust in a client matter. You have completed the preliminary steps in the matter, and have delivered an interim invoice for $600 to the client. May you use the money held in trust to pay the invoice?
8. Eugene Onegin is a licensed paralegal with a specialization in *Highway Traffic Act* offences. Aleksandr Pushkin consults with Eugene about a careless driving charge. Aleksandr has several previous convictions. He tells Eugene that he can't afford to pay the fine.

   "Don't worry!" Eugene tells Aleksandr. "If you get convicted, you pay the fine, but you don't pay me!!"

   Discuss, referring to any rules or other authorities upon which you are relying.
9. Pamela Okker is a licensed paralegal. To market her firm, she is setting up a website. At the website, below her name, is the statement: "Highway Traffic Act offences: 100% acquittals. We are quite simply THE BEST!! We are AWESOME!!" She is described as "Duly licensed by the Law Society of Upper Canada."

   Discuss, referring to any rules or other authorities upon which you are relying.

APPENDIX 7.1 Sample Invoice—No Money Retainer

Judith N. Black, Licensed Paralegal
123 Radiant Way, Suite 200
Brampton, Ontario X1X 2Y3
TEL: 905 122 3333 FAX: 905 123 4444 email: jblack@paralegal.emp.ca

HST Registration No.:	12568 8777 RT
Client matter No.:	01328
Invoice No.:	859
Date:	June 30, 20—

Sylvia Cisco
1234 Pleasant Valley Crescent
Mississauga, Ontario X1X 3Y4

Re: Sylvia Cisco v. 880345 Ontario Inc.

For Professional Services Rendered:

[Description of legal services in the client matter for the period ending June 30, 20—]

MY FEE:	$400.00
TOTAL FEE:	$400.00

DISBURSEMENTS	Disbursements
Photocopies	56.25
Court work*	37.00
Issue claim*	75.00
Service*	50.00
Default judgment*	35.00

Total disbursements	$253.25

* HST exempt

TOTAL FEES AND DISBURSEMENTS	$653.25
13% HST on account	59.31
	$712.56
Transferred from trust	0.00
Balance in trust	0.00
Previous balance	0.00
Previous payments	0.00
BALANCE DUE AND OWING	$712.56

THIS IS MY ACCOUNT HEREIN

Judith Black

Judith N. Black
Licensed Paralegal

Interest will be charged on accounts not paid within 30 days at a rate of
3.0% per annum from the date of the account until any outstanding balance is paid in full.

APPENDIX 7.2 Sample Invoice—Money Retainer

Judith N. Black, Licensed Paralegal
123 Radiant Way, Suite 200
Brampton, Ontario X1X 2Y3
TEL: 905 122 3333 FAX: 905 123 4444 email: jblack@paralegal.emp.ca

HST Registration No.:	12568 8777 RT
Client matter No.:	01315
Invoice No.:	860
Date:	June 30, 20—

Frances Ciccone
88 Hayward Boulevard
Georgetown, Ontario X1X 4Z5

Re: Ciccone—Careless driving charge

For Professional Services Rendered:

[Description of legal services in the client matter for the period ending June 30, 20—]

		MY FEE:	$600.00
		TOTAL FEE:	$600.00
DISBURSEMENTS	Disbursements		
Photocopies	42.50		
* HST exempt			
Total disbursements			$ 42.50
TOTAL FEES AND DISBURSEMENTS			$642.50
13% HST on account			$ 83.53
			$726.03
Transferred from trust			726.03
Balance in trust			73.97
Previous balance			0.00
Previous payments			0.00
BALANCE DUE AND OWING			0.00

THIS IS MY ACCOUNT HEREIN

Judith Black

Judith N. Black
Licensed Paralegal

Interest will be charged on accounts not paid within 30 days at a rate of
3.0% per annum from the date of the account until any outstanding balance is paid in full.

Appendixes

Paralegal Rules of Conduct

Adopted by Convocation March 29, 2007, effective May 1, 2007
Amendments based on the Federation of Law Societies
Model Code of Professional Conduct adopted by Convocation
February 27, 2014, effective October 1, 2014
Amendments current to October 1, 2014

RULE 1 CITATION AND INTERPRETATION

1.01 CITATION

1.01 (1) These Rules may be cited as the *Paralegal Rules of Conduct*.

1.02 INTERPRETATION

Definitions

1.02 In these Rules,

"affiliated entity" means any person or group of persons other than a person or group authorized to provide legal services in Ontario;

"affiliation" means the joining on a regular basis of a paralegal or group of paralegals with an affiliated entity in the delivery or promotion and delivery of the legal services of the paralegal or group of paralegals and the non-legal services of the affiliated entity;

[New—October 2008]

"associate" includes:

(a) a licensee who provides legal services in a firm of licensees through an employment or other contractual relationship; and

(b) a non-licensee employee of a multi-discipline practice providing services that support or supplement the practice of law or provision of legal services.

[Amended October 2014]

"client" means a person who:

(a) consults a paralegal and on whose behalf the paralegal provides or agrees to provide legal services; or

(b) having consulted the paralegal, reasonably concludes that the paralegal has agreed to provide legal services on his or her behalf

and includes a client of the firm of which the paralegal is a partner or associate, whether or not the paralegal handles the client's work;

"conflict of interest" means the existence of a substantial risk that a paralegal's loyalty to or representation of a client would be materially and adversely affected by the paralegal's own interest or the paralegal's duties to another client, a former client or a third person. The risk must be more than a mere possibility; there must be a genuine, serious risk to the duty of loyalty or to client representation arising from the retainer.

"consent" means fully informed and voluntary consent after disclosure:

(a) in writing, provided that where more than one person consents, each signs the same or a separate document recording the consent, or

(b) orally, provided that each person consenting receives a separate written communication recording their consent as soon as practicable;

[Amended October 2014]

"Law Society" means the Law Society of Upper Canada;

"licensee" means,

(a) a person licensed to practise law in Ontario as a barrister and solicitor, or

(b) a person licensed to provide legal services in Ontario;

"legal practitioner" means a person

(a) who is a licensee;

(b) who is not a licensee but who is a member of the bar of a Canadian jurisdiction, other than Ontario, and who is authorized to practise law as a barrister and solicitor in that other jurisdiction.

[Amended October 2014]

"limited scope retainer" means the provision of legal services by a paralegal for part, but not all, of a client's legal matter by agreement between the paralegal and the client.

[Amended October 2014]

"paralegal" means a paralegal licensee of the Law Society;

"paralegal firm" includes one or more paralegals practising in a sole proprietorship, partnership or professional corporation;

"Rules" means the *Paralegal Rules of Conduct*;

"tribunal" includes courts, boards, arbitrators, mediators, administrative agencies, and bodies that resolve disputes, regardless of their function or the informality of their procedures.

RULE 2 PROFESSIONALISM

2.01 INTEGRITY AND CIVILITY

Integrity

2.01 (1) A paralegal has a duty to provide legal services and discharge all responsibilities to clients, tribunals, the public and other members of the legal professions honourably and with integrity.

(2) A paralegal has a duty to uphold the standards and reputation of the paralegal profession and to assist in the advancement of its goals, organizations and institutions.

Civility

(3) A paralegal shall be courteous and civil, and shall act in good faith with all persons with whom he or she has dealings in the course of his or her practice.

Outside Interests and Public Office

(4) A paralegal who engages in another profession, business, occupation or other outside interest or who holds public office concurrently with the provision of legal services, shall not allow the outside interest or public office to jeopardize the paralegal's integrity, independence, or competence.

(5) A paralegal shall not allow involvement in an outside interest or public office to impair the exercise of his or her independent judgment on behalf of a client.

Acting as Mediator

(6) A paralegal who acts as a mediator shall, at the outset of the mediation, ensure that the parties to it understand fully that the paralegal is not acting as a representative for either party but, as mediator, is acting to assist the parties to resolve the issues in dispute.

[Amended October 2014]

2.02 UNDERTAKINGS AND TRUST CONDITIONS

2.02 (1) A paralegal shall fulfil every undertaking given and shall not give an undertaking that cannot be fulfilled.

(2) Except in exceptional circumstances, a paralegal shall give his or her undertaking in writing or confirm it in writing as soon as practicable after giving it.

(3) Unless clearly stated in the undertaking, a paralegal's undertaking is a personal promise and it is his or her personal responsibility.

(4) A paralegal shall honour every trust condition once accepted.

[Amended October 2014]

2.03 HARASSMENT AND DISCRIMINATION

Application of *Human Rights Code*

2.03 (1) The principles of the Ontario *Human Rights Code* and related case law apply to the interpretation of this rule.

(2) A term used in this rule that is defined in the *Human Rights Code* has the same meaning as in the *Human Rights Code*.

Harassment

(3) A paralegal shall not engage in sexual or other forms of harassment of a colleague, a staff member, a client or any other person on the ground of race, ancestry, place of origin, colour, ethnic origin, citizenship, creed, sex, sexual orientation, gender identity, gender expression, age, record of offences, marital status, family status or disability.

Discrimination

(4) A paralegal shall respect the requirements of human rights laws in force in Ontario and without restricting the generality of the foregoing, a paralegal shall not discriminate on the grounds of race, ancestry, place of origin, colour, ethnic origin, citizenship, creed, sex, sexual orientation, gender identity, gender expression, age, record of offences, marital status, or disability with respect to the employment of others or in dealings with other licensees or any other person.

(5) The right to equal treatment without discrimination because of sex includes the right to equal treatment without discrimination because a woman is or may become pregnant.

Services

(6) A paralegal shall ensure that no one is denied services or receives inferior service on the basis of the grounds set out in this rule.

Employment Practices

(7) A paralegal shall ensure that his or her employment practices do not offend this rule.

[Amended October 2014]

RULE 3 DUTY TO CLIENTS

3.01 COMPETENCE

Required Standard

3.01 (1) A paralegal shall perform any services undertaken on a client's behalf to the standard of a competent paralegal.

(2) A paralegal is required to recognize a task for which the paralegal lacks competence and the disservice that would be done to the client by undertaking that task. A paralegal shall not undertake a matter without being competent to handle it or being able to become competent without undue delay or expense to the client.

(3) If a paralegal discovers that he or she lacks the competence to complete the task for which he or she has been retained, the paralegal shall:

(a) decline to act;

(b) obtain the client's consent to retain, consult or collaborate with another licensee who is competent and licensed to perform that task; or

(c) obtain the client's consent for the paralegal to become competent without undue delay, risk or expense to the client.

Who is Competent

(4) For the purposes of this rule, a competent paralegal is one who has and applies the relevant knowledge, skills, and attributes appropriate to each matter undertaken on behalf of a client including,

(a) knowing general legal principles and procedures and the substantive law and procedures for the legal services that the paralegal provides;

(b) investigating facts, identifying issues, ascertaining client objectives, considering possible options, and developing and advising clients on appropriate courses of action;

(c) implementing, as each matter requires, the chosen course of action through the application of appropriate skills, including,

(i) legal research,

(ii) analysis,

(iii) application of the law to the relevant facts,

(iv) writing and drafting,

(v) negotiation,

(vi) alternative dispute resolution,

(vii) advocacy, and

(viii) problem-solving;

(d) representing the client in a conscientious, diligent, and cost-effective manner;

(e) communicating with the client at all relevant stages of a matter in a timely and effective manner;

(f) answering reasonable client requests in a timely and effective manner;

(g) ensuring that all applicable deadlines are met;

(h) managing one's practice effectively;

(i) applying intellectual capacity, judgment, and deliberation to all functions;

(j) pursuing appropriate training and development to maintain and enhance knowledge and skills;

(k) adapting to changing requirements, standards, techniques and practices; and

(l) complying in letter and in spirit with all requirements pursuant to the *Law Society Act*.

[Amended October 2014]

3.02 ADVISING CLIENTS

Quality of Service

3.02 (1) A paralegal has a duty to provide courteous, thorough and prompt service to clients. The quality of service required of a paralegal is service that is competent, timely, conscientious, diligent, efficient and civil.

(2) A paralegal shall be honest and candid when advising clients.

(3) A paralegal shall not undertake or provide advice with respect to a matter that is outside his or her permissible scope of practice.

[Amended October 2014]

Dishonesty, Fraud, etc. by Client or Others

(4) A paralegal shall not knowingly assist in or encourage any dishonesty, fraud, crime, or illegal conduct or advise a client or any other person on how to violate the law and avoid punishment.

(5) When retained by a client, a paralegal shall make reasonable efforts to ascertain the purpose and objectives of the retainer and to obtain information about the client necessary to fulfill this obligation.

(6) A paralegal shall not use his or her trust account for purposes not related to the provision of legal services.

[Amended October 2014]

(7) A paralegal shall not act or do anything or omit to do anything in circumstances where he or she ought to know that, by acting, doing the thing or omitting to do the thing, he or she is being used by a client, by a person associated with a client or by any other person to facilitate dishonesty, fraud, crime or illegal conduct.

[New—May 2012]

(8) A paralegal who is employed or retained by an organization to act in a matter in which the paralegal knows that the organization has acted, is acting or intends to act dishonestly, fraudulently, criminally, or illegally shall do the following, in addition to their obligations under subrule (4):

(a) advise the person from whom the paralegal takes instructions and the chief legal officer, or both the chief legal officer and the chief executive officer, that the conduct is, was or would be dishonest, fraudulent, criminal, or illegal and should be stopped,

(b) if necessary because the person from whom the paralegal takes instructions, the chief legal officer, or the chief executive officer refuses to cause the conduct to be stopped, advise progressively the next highest persons or groups, including ultimately, the board of directors, the board of trustees, or the appropriate committee of the board, that the conduct was, is or would be dishonest, fraudulent, criminal, or illegal and should be stopped, and

(c) if the organization, despite the paralegal's advice, continues with or intends to pursue the wrongful conduct, withdraw from acting in the matter in accordance with rule 3.08.

[Amended October 2014]

Threatening Criminal Proceedings

(9) A paralegal shall not, in an attempt to gain a benefit for a client, threaten, or advise a client to threaten:

(a) To initiate or proceed with a criminal or quasi-criminal charge; or

(b) To make a complaint to a regulatory authority.

(10) Subrule (9)(b) does not apply to an application made in good faith to a regulatory authority for a benefit to which a client may be legally entitled.

Settlement and Dispute Resolution

(11) A paralegal shall advise and encourage a client to compromise or settle a dispute whenever it is possible to do so on a reasonable basis, and shall discourage the client from commencing or continuing useless legal proceedings.

(12) The paralegal shall consider the use of alternative dispute resolution (ADR) when appropriate, inform the client of ADR options, and, if so instructed, take steps to pursue those options.

Client with Diminished Capacity

(13) If a client's ability to make decisions is impaired because of minority, mental disability or for some other reason, the paralegal shall, as far as reasonably possible, maintain a normal professional relationship with that client.

(14) If the disability of the client is such that the client no longer has the legal capacity to manage his or her legal affairs, the paralegal shall take such steps as are appropriate to have a lawfully authorized representative appointed.

Providing Legal Services Under a Limited Scope Retainer

(15) Before providing legal services under a limited scope retainer, a paralegal shall advise the client honestly and candidly about the nature, extent and scope of the services that the paralegal can provide and, where appropriate, whether the services can be provided within the financial means of the client.

[Amended October 2014]

(16) When providing legal services under a limited scope retainer, a paralegal shall confirm the services in writing and give the client a copy of the written document when practicable to do so.

[New—September 2011]

(17) Subrule (16) does not apply to a paralegal if the legal services are

(a) legal services provided by a licensed paralegal in the course of his or her employment as an employee of Legal Aid Ontario;

(b) summary advice provided in community legal clinics, student clinics or under the *Legal Aid Services Act, 1998*;

(c) summary advice provided through a telephone-based service or telephone hotline operated by a community-based or government funded program.

(d) summary advice provided by the paralegal to a client in the context of an introductory consultation, where the intention is that the consultation, if the client so chooses, would develop into a retainer for legal services for all aspects of the legal matter; or

(e) *pro bono* summary legal services provided in a non-profit or court-annexed program.

[New—September 2011]

Medical-Legal Reports

(18) A paralegal who receives a medical-legal report from a physician or health professional that is accompanied by a proviso that it not be shown to the client, shall return the report immediately to the physician or health professional, without making a copy, unless the paralegal has received specific instructions to accept the report on that basis.

(19) A paralegal who receives a medical-legal report from a physician or health professional containing opinions or findings that, if disclosed, might cause harm or injury to the client, shall attempt to dissuade the client from seeing the report but, if the client insists, the paralegal shall produce the report.

(20) If a client insists on seeing a medical-legal report about which the paralegal has reservations for the reasons noted in subrule (11), the paralegal shall recommend that the client attend at the office of the physician or health professional to see the report, in order that the client will have the benefit of the expertise of the physician or health professional in understanding the significance of the conclusions contained in the medical-legal report.

Errors

(21) If, in connection with a matter for which a paralegal is responsible, the paralegal discovers an error or omission that is or may be damaging to the client and that cannot be rectified readily, the paralegal shall,

(a) promptly inform the client of the error or omission, being careful not to prejudice any rights of indemnity that either of them may have under an insurance, client's protection or indemnity plan, or otherwise;

(b) recommend that the client obtain legal advice elsewhere concerning any rights the client may have arising from the error or omission; and

(c) advise the client that in the circumstances, the paralegal may no longer be able to act for the client.

Official Language Rights

(22) A paralegal shall, where appropriate, advise a client who speaks French of the client's language rights, including the right of the client to be served by a paralegal who is competent to provide legal services in the French language.

[Amended October 2014]

3.03 CONFIDENTIALITY

Confidential Information

3.03 (1) A paralegal shall, at all times, hold in strict confidence all information concerning the business and affairs of a client acquired in the course of their professional relationship and shall not disclose any such information unless:

(a) expressly or impliedly authorized by the client;

(b) required by law or by order of a tribunal of competent jurisdiction to do so;

(c) required to provide the information to the Law Society, or

(d) otherwise permitted by this rule.

(2) The duty of confidentiality under subrule (1) continues indefinitely after the paralegal has ceased to act for the client, whether or not differences have arisen between them.

(3) The paralegal shall keep the client's papers and other property out of sight, as well as out of reach, of those not entitled to see them.

Justified or Permitted Disclosure

(4) A paralegal shall disclose confidential information when required by law or by order of a tribunal of competent jurisdiction.

(5) A paralegal may disclose confidential information when the paralegal believes on reasonable grounds that there is an imminent risk of death or serious bodily harm, and disclosure is necessary to prevent the death or harm.

(6) In order to defend against the allegations, a paralegal may disclose confidential information if it is alleged that the paralegal or his or her employees,

(a) have committed a criminal offence involving a client's affairs;

(b) are civilly liable with respect to a matter involving a client's affairs; or

(c) have committed acts of professional negligence; or

(d) have engaged in acts of professional misconduct or conduct unbecoming a paralegal.

(7) A paralegal may disclose confidential information in order to establish or collect his or her fees.

(8) A paralegal may disclose confidential information to a lawyer or another paralegal to secure legal advice about the paralegal's proposed conduct.

(9) A paralegal shall not disclose more information than is necessary when he or she discloses confidential information as required or permitted by subrules (4), (5), (6) and (7).

[Amended October 2014]

3.04 CONFLICTS OF INTEREST—GENERAL

Avoidance of Conflicts of Interest

(1) A paralegal shall not act or continue to act for a client where there is a conflict of interest, except as permitted under this rule.

(2) A paralegal shall not advise or represent opposing parties in a dispute.

(3) A paralegal shall not represent a client in a matter when there is a conflict of interest unless

(a) there is express or implied consent from all clients; and

(b) it is reasonable for the paralegal to conclude that he or she is able to represent each client without having a material adverse effect upon the representation of or loyalty to the other client.

(4) For the purpose of this rule:

(a) Express consent must be fully informed and voluntary after disclosure.

(b) Consent may be implied and need not be in writing where all of the following apply:

(i) the client is a government, financial institution, publicly traded or similarly substantial entity, or an entity with in-house counsel,

(ii) the matters are unrelated,

(iii) the paralegal has no relevant confidential information from one client that might reasonably affect the representation of the other client, and

(iv) the client has commonly consented to lawyers acting for and against it in unrelated matters.

Acting Against Former Clients

(5) Unless the former client consents, a paralegal shall not act against a former client in,

(a) the same matter;

(b) any related matter; or

(c) except as provided by subrule (6), in any new matter, if the paralegal has relevant confidential information arising from the representation of the former client that may prejudice that client.

(6) If a paralegal has acted for a client and obtained confidential information relevant to a matter, the paralegal's partner or employee may act in a subsequent matter against that client, provided that:

(a) the former client consents to the paralegal's partner or employee acting; or

(b) the paralegal's firm establishes that it has taken adequate measures on a timely basis to ensure that there will be no risk of disclosure of the former client's confidential information to the other licensee having carriage of the new matter.

Joint Retainers

(7) Before agreeing to act for more than one client in a matter or transaction, a paralegal shall advise the clients that,

(a) the paralegal has been asked to act for both or all of them;

(b) no information received in connection with the matter from one client can be treated as confidential so far as any of the others are concerned; and

(c) if a conflict develops that cannot be resolved, the paralegal cannot continue to act for both or all of them and may have to withdraw completely.

(8) If a paralegal has a continuing relationship with a client for whom he or she acts regularly, before agreeing to act for that client and another client in a matter or transaction, the paralegal shall advise the other client of the continuing relationship and recommend that the client obtain independent legal advice about the joint retainer.

(9) If a paralegal has advised the clients, as provided under subrules (8) and (9), and the parties are content that the paralegal act for both or all of them, the paralegal shall obtain their consent.

(10) Consent to a joint retainer must be obtained from each client in writing, or recorded through a separate written communication to each client.

(11) Although all parties concerned may consent, a paralegal shall avoid acting for more than one client if it is likely that an issue contentious between them will arise or their interests, rights, or obligations will diverge as the matter progresses.

(12) Except as provided by subrule (13) if a contentious issue arises between two clients who have consented to a joint retainer, the paralegal must not advise either of them on the contentious issue and the following rules apply:

(a) The paralegal shall

(i) refer the clients to other licensees for that purpose; or

(ii) if not legal advice is required and the clients are sophisticated, advise them of their option to settle the contentious issue by direct negotiation in which the paralegal does not participate.

(b) If the contentious issue is not resolved, the paralegal shall withdraw from the joint representation.

(13) If a paralegal's clients consent to a joint retainer and also agree that if a contentious issue arises the paralegal may continue to advise one of them and a contentious issue

does arise, the paralegal may advise the one client about the contentious matter and shall refer the other or others to another licensee for that purpose.

Multi-Discipline Practices

(14) A paralegal in a multi-discipline practice shall ensure that non-licensee partners and associates observe this rule for the provision of legal services and for any other business or professional undertaking carried on by them outside the professional business.

Affiliations

(15) Where there is an affiliation, before accepting a retainer to provide legal services to a client jointly with non-legal services of an affiliated entity, a paralegal shall disclose to the client

(a) any possible loss of confidentiality because of the involvement of the affiliated entity, including circumstances where a non-licensee or staff of the affiliated entity provide services, including support services, in the paralegal's office,

(b) the paralegal's role in providing legal services and in providing non-legal services or in providing both legal and non-legal services, as the case may be,

(c) any financial, economic or other arrangements between the paralegal and the affiliated entity that may affect the independence of the paralegal's representation of the client, including whether the paralegal shares in the revenues, profits or cash flows of the affiliated entity; and

(d) agreements between the paralegal and the affiliated entity, such as agreements with respect to referral of clients between the paralegal and the affiliated entity, that may affect the independence of the paralegal's representation of the client.

(16) Where there is an affiliation, after making the disclosure as required by subrule (15), a paralegal shall obtain the client's consent before accepting a retainer under that subrule.

(17) Where there is an affiliation, a paralegal shall establish a system to search for conflicts of interest of the affiliation.

[Amended October 2014]

3.05 CONFLICTS OF INTEREST—TRANSFERS

Application of Rule

3.05 (1) This rule applies where a paralegal transfers from one paralegal firm ("former paralegal firm") to another ("new paralegal firm"), and either the transferring paralegal or the new paralegal firm is aware at the time of the transfer or later discovers that,

(a) the new paralegal firm represents a client in a matter that is the same as or related to a matter in which the former paralegal firm represents its client ("former client");

(b) the interests of those clients in that matter conflict; and

(c) the transferring paralegal actually possesses relevant information respecting that matter.

Paralegal Firm Disqualification

(2) If a transferring paralegal actually possesses information respecting a former client that is confidential and that, if disclosed to a paralegal in the new paralegal firm, may prejudice the former client, the new paralegal firm shall cease representation of its client unless the former client consents to the new paralegal firm's continued representation or the new paralegal firm establishes that it is in the interests of justice that it continue to represent the client.

(3) In deciding whether or not it is appropriate to continue to act for a client, the new paralegal firm shall consider all the circumstances including,

(a) the adequacy and timing of the measures taken to ensure that no disclosure to any paralegal of the new paralegal firm of the former client's confidential information will occur;

(b) the availability of suitable alternative representation;

(c) the measures taken to ensure that no disclosure of the former client's confidential information, to any paralegal in the new paralegal firm, will occur;

(d) the extent of any prejudice to any party;

(e) the good faith of the parties; and

(f) issues affecting the public interest.

(4) If a transferring paralegal actually possesses relevant information respecting a former client but that information is not confidential information as described in subrule (2), the paralegal shall execute an affidavit or solemn declaration to that effect, and the new paralegal firm shall,

(a) notify its client and the former client, or if the former client is represented in that matter by a licensee, notify that licensee, of the relevant circumstances and its intended action under this rule; and

(b) deliver to the persons referred to in clause (a) a copy of the paralegal's affidavit or solemn declaration executed under this subrule.

Transferring Paralegal Disqualification

(5) A transferring paralegal described in subrule (2) or (4) shall not, unless the former client consents,

(a) participate in any manner in the new paralegal firm's representation of its client in that matter; or

(b) disclose any confidential information respecting the former client.

(6) No paralegal in the new paralegal firm shall, unless the former client consents, discuss with a transferring paralegal described in subrule (2) or (4) the new paralegal

firm's representation of its client or the former paralegal firm's representation of the former client in that matter.

(7) Anyone who has an interest in, or who represents a party in, a matter referred to in this rule may apply to a tribunal of competent jurisdiction for a determination of any aspect of this rule.

3.06 DOING BUSINESS WITH A CLIENT

3.06 (1) A paralegal must not enter into a transaction with a client unless the transaction is fair and reasonable to the client, the client consents to the transaction and the client has independent legal representation with respect to the transaction.

Transactions with Clients

(2) Subject to subrule (3), if a client intends to enter into a transaction with a paralegal who is representing the client, or with a corporation or other entity in which the paralegal has an interest other than a corporation or other entity whose securities are publicly traded, the paralegal, before accepting any retainer,

(a) shall disclose and explain the nature of the conflicting interest to the client, or, in the case of a potential conflict, how and why it might develop later;

(b) shall recommend independent legal representation and shall require that the client receive independent legal advice; and

(c) if the client requests the paralegal to act, shall obtain the client's written consent.

(3) If a client intends to pay for legal services by transferring to a paralegal a share, participation or other interest in property or in an enterprise, the paralegal shall recommend, but need not require, that the client receive independent legal advice before agreeing to act for the client.

(4) This rule does not apply to a transfer of a non-material interest in a publicly traded enterprise.

(5) If the paralegal does not choose to make disclosure of the conflicting interest or cannot do so without breaching a confidence, the paralegal shall decline the retainer.

Borrowing from Clients

(6) A paralegal shall not borrow money from a client unless,

(a) the client is a lending institution, financial institution, insurance company, trust corporation or any similar institution whose business includes lending money to members of the public; or

(b) the client is a related person as defined in section 251 of the *Income Tax Act* (Canada) and the paralegal is able to discharge the onus of proving that the client's interests were fully protected by the nature of the case and by independent legal advice or independent legal representation.

Guarantees by Paralegal

(7) Subject to subrule (8), a paralegal shall not guarantee personally, or otherwise provide security for, any indebtedness in respect of which a client is a borrower or lender.

(8) A paralegal may give a personal guarantee if,

(a) the lender is a lending institution, financial institution, insurance company, trust company or any similar corporation whose business includes lending money to members of the public, and the lender is directly or indirectly providing funds solely for the paralegal, the paralegal's spouse, parent or child;

(b) the transaction is for the benefit of a non-profit or charitable institution where the paralegal as a member or supporter of such institution is asked, either individually or together with other members or supporters of the institution to provide a guarantee; or

(c) the paralegal has entered into a business venture with a client and the lender requires personal guarantees from all participants in the venture as a matter of course and,

(i) the paralegal has complied with the requirements of these Rules regarding the avoidance of conflicts of interest, and

(ii) the lender and the participants in the venture who are or were clients of the paralegal have received independent legal representation.

Judicial Interim Release

(9) Subject to subrule (10), a paralegal shall not in respect of any accused person for whom the paralegal acts

(a) act as a surety for the accused;

(b) deposit with a court the paralegal's own money or that of any firm in which the paralegal is a partner to secure the accused's release;

(c) deposit with any court other valuable security to secure the accused's release; or

(d) act in a supervisory capacity to the accused.

(10) A paralegal may do any of the things referred to in subrule (9) if the accused is in a family relationship with the paralegal and the accused is represented by the paralegal's partner or associate.

[Amended October 2014]

3.07 CLIENT PROPERTY

Preservation of Client's Property

3.07 (1) A paralegal shall care for a client's property as a careful and prudent owner would when dealing with like property and shall observe all relevant rules and law about the preservation of property entrusted to a fiduciary.

Notification of Receipt of Property

(2) A paralegal shall promptly notify the client of the receipt of any money or other property of the client, unless satisfied that the client is aware they have come into the paralegal's custody.

Identification of Property

(3) A paralegal shall clearly label and identify the client's property and place it in safekeeping, distinguishable from the paralegal's own property.

(4) A paralegal shall maintain such records as necessary to identify a client's property that is in the paralegal's custody.

Accounting and Delivery

(5) A paralegal shall account promptly for a client's property that is in the paralegal's custody and upon request, shall deliver it to the order of the client or, if appropriate, at the conclusion of the retainer.

(6) If a paralegal is unsure of the proper person to receive a client's property, the paralegal shall apply to a tribunal of competent jurisdiction for direction.

[Amended October 2014]

3.08 WITHDRAWAL FROM REPRESENTATION

Withdrawal from Representation

3.08 (1) A paralegal shall not withdraw from representation of a client except for good cause and on reasonable notice to the client.

Optional Withdrawal

(2) Subject to subrules (7), (8) and (9) and the direction of the tribunal, a paralegal may withdraw if there has been a serious loss of confidence between the paralegal and the client.

(3) Without limiting subrule (2), a paralegal may withdraw if the client deceives the paralegal or refuses to accept and act upon the paralegal's advice on a significant point.

(4) A paralegal shall not use the threat of withdrawal as a device to force a hasty decision by the client on a difficult question.

Mandatory Withdrawal

(5) Subject to subrules (7), (8) and (9) and the direction of the tribunal, a paralegal shall withdraw if,

(a) discharged by the client;

(b) the client's instructions require the paralegal to act contrary to the Rules, or by-laws; or

(c) the paralegal is not competent to continue to handle the matter.

Non-payment of Fees

(6) Subject to subrules (7), (8) and (9) and the direction of the tribunal, unless serious prejudice to the client would result, a paralegal may withdraw from a case if, after reasonable notice, the client fails to provide a retainer or funds on account of disbursements or fees.

Withdrawal from Quasi-Criminal and Criminal Cases

(7) A paralegal who has agreed to act in a quasi-criminal or criminal case may withdraw because the client has not paid the agreed fee or for other adequate cause if the interval between the withdrawal and the date set for the trial of the case is sufficient to enable the client to obtain alternate representation and to allow such other licensee adequate time for preparation and if the paralegal,

(a) advises the client, preferably in writing, that the paralegal is withdrawing and the reason for the withdrawal;

(b) accounts to the client for any monies received on account of fees and disbursements;

(c) notifies the prosecution in writing that the paralegal is no longer acting;

(d) in a case where the paralegal's name appears in the records of the court as acting for the accused, notifies the clerk or registrar of the appropriate court in writing that the paralegal is no longer acting; and

(e) complies with the applicable rules of the tribunal or court.

(8) A paralegal who has agreed to act in a quasi-criminal or criminal case may not withdraw because of non-payment of fees if the date set for the trial of the case is not far enough removed to enable the client to obtain the services of another licensee or to enable the other licensee to prepare adequately for trial and if an adjournment of the trial date cannot be obtained without adversely affecting the client's interests.

(9) If,

(a) a paralegal is justified in withdrawing from a quasi-criminal or criminal case for reasons other than non-payment of fees; and

(b) there is not a sufficient interval between a notice to the client of the paralegal's intention to withdraw and the date when the case is to be tried to enable the client to obtain the services of another licensee and to enable the new licensee to prepare adequately for trial, the paralegal, unless instructed otherwise by the client, shall attempt to have the trial date adjourned and may withdraw from the case only with permission of the court before which the case is to be tried.

Manner of Withdrawal

(10) When a paralegal withdraws, he or she shall try to minimize expense and avoid prejudice to the client and shall do all that can reasonably be done to facilitate the orderly transfer of the matter to the successor licensee.

(11) Upon discharge or withdrawal, a paralegal shall,

(a) deliver to the client or to the order of the client, all papers and property to which the client is entitled, (subject to the paralegal's right to a lien);

(b) subject to any applicable trust conditions, give the client all information that may be required in connection with the case or matter;

(c) account for all funds of the client then held or previously dealt with, including the refunding of any monies not earned during the representation;

(d) promptly render an account for outstanding fees and disbursements; and

(e) cooperate with the successor licensee so as to minimize expense and avoid prejudice to the client; and

(f) comply with the applicable rules of court.

(12) In addition to the obligations set out in subrule (11), upon withdrawal, a paralegal shall notify the client in writing, stating:

(a) the fact that the paralegal has withdrawn;

(b) the reasons, if any, for the withdrawal; and

(c) in the case of litigation, that the client should expect that the hearing or trial will proceed on the date scheduled and that the client should retain a new legal practitioner promptly.

(13) If the paralegal who is discharged or withdraws is a member of a firm, the client shall be notified that the paralegal and the firm are no longer acting for the client.

Duties of Successor Paralegal

(14) Before agreeing to represent a client of a predecessor licensee, a successor paralegal shall be satisfied that the predecessor has withdrawn or has been discharged by the client.

[Amended October 2014]

RULE 4 ADVOCACY

4.01 THE PARALEGAL AS ADVOCATE

Duty to Clients, Tribunals and Others

4.01 (1) When acting as an advocate, the paralegal shall represent the client resolutely and honourably within the limits of the law while, at the same time, treating the tribunal and other licensees with candour, fairness, courtesy and respect.

(2) This rule applies to appearances and proceedings before all tribunals in which the paralegal may appear.

(3) This rule does not require a paralegal, except as otherwise provided in these Rules, to assist an adversary or advance matters derogatory to the client's case.

(4) Without restricting the generality of subrule (1), the paralegal shall,

(a) raise fearlessly every issue, advance every argument, and ask every question, however distasteful, that the paralegal thinks will help the client's case;

(b) endeavour, on the client's behalf, to obtain the benefit of every remedy and defence authorized by law;

(c) never waive or abandon a client's legal rights, for example, an available defence under a statute of limitations, without the client's informed consent; and

(d) avoid and discourage the client from resorting to frivolous and vexatious objections, or from attempts to gain advantage from mistakes or oversights not going to the merits, or from tactics designed to merely delay or harass the other side.

The Paralegal and the Tribunal Process

(5) When acting as an advocate, the paralegal shall not,

(a) abuse the process of the tribunal by instituting or prosecuting proceedings which, although legal in themselves, are clearly motivated by malice on the part of the client and are brought solely for the purpose of injuring the other party;

(b) knowingly assist or permit the client to do anything that the paralegal considers to be dishonest or dishonourable;

(c) knowingly attempt to deceive a tribunal or influence the course of justice by offering false evidence, misstating facts or law, presenting or relying upon a false or deceptive affidavit, suppressing what ought to be disclosed, or otherwise assisting in any deception, crime or illegal conduct;

(d) deliberately refrain from informing the tribunal of any binding authority that the paralegal considers to be directly on point and that has not been mentioned by an opponent;

(e) appear before a judicial officer when the paralegal, a partner of the paralegal, a paralegal employed by the paralegal firm or the client has a business or personal relationship with the officer that gives rise to, or might reasonably appear to give rise to, pressure, influence or inducement affecting the impartiality of the officer, unless all parties consent and it is in the interests of justice;

(f) knowingly assert as true, a fact when its truth cannot reasonably be supported by the evidence or as a matter of which notice may be taken by the tribunal;

(g) make suggestions to a witness recklessly or knowing them to be false;

(h) endeavour or allow anyone else to endeavour, directly or indirectly, to influence the decision or action of the tribunal or any of its officials in any case or matter by any means other than open persuasion as an advocate;

(i) knowingly misstate the contents of a document, the testimony of a witness, the substance of an argument or the provisions of a statute or like authority;

(j) knowingly permit a witness or party to be presented in a false or misleading way or to impersonate another;

(k) knowingly misrepresent the client's position in the litigation or the issues to be determined in the litigation;

(l) needlessly abuse, hector, harass or inconvenience a witness;

(m) improperly dissuade a witness from giving evidence or suggest that a witness be absent;

(n) when representing a complainant or potential complainant, attempt to gain a benefit for the complainant by threatening the laying of a criminal charge or by offering to seek or to procure the withdrawal of a criminal charge;

(o) needlessly inconvenience a witness and

(p) appear before a court or tribunal while under the influence of alcohol or a drug.

[Amended October 2014]

Duty as Prosecutor

(5.1) When acting as a prosecutor, a paralegal shall act for the public and the administration of justice resolutely and honourably within the limits of the law while treating the tribunal with candour, fairness, courtesy, and respect.

[New—May 2010]

Disclosure of Documents

(6) If the rules of a tribunal require the parties to produce documents, a paralegal, when acting as an advocate,

(a) shall explain to his or her client the necessity of making full disclosure of all documents relating to any matter in issue and the duty to answer to the best of his or her knowledge, information and belief, any proper question relating to any issue in the action;

(b) shall assist the client in fulfilling his or her obligation to make full disclosure; and

(c) shall not make frivolous requests for the production of documents or make frivolous demands for information.

Errors and Omissions

(7) A paralegal who does, or fails to do, something which may involve a breach of this rule, shall, subject to rule 3.03 relating to confidentiality, disclose the error or omission and do all that can reasonably be done in the circumstances to rectify it.

Agreement on Guilty Pleas

(8) Before a charge is laid or at any time after a charge is laid, a paralegal acting for an accused or potential accused may discuss with the prosecutor the possible disposition of the case, unless the client instructs otherwise.

(9) A paralegal, on behalf of his or her client, may enter into an agreement with a prosecutor about a guilty plea, if, following investigation,

(a) the paralegal advises the client about the prospects for an acquittal or finding of guilt;

(b) the paralegal advises the client of the implications and possible consequences of a guilty plea and particularly of the sentencing authority and discretion of the court, including the fact that the court is not bound by any agreement about a guilty plea;

(c) the client is prepared voluntarily to admit the necessary factual and mental elements of the offence charged; and

(d) the client voluntarily instructs the paralegal to enter into an agreement as to a guilty plea.

4.02 INTERVIEWING WITNESSES

Interviewing Witnesses

4.02 (1) Subject to the rules on communication with a represented party at Rule 7.02, a paralegal may seek information from any potential witness, whether under subpoena or not, but shall disclose the paralegal's interest and take care not to subvert or suppress any evidence or procure the witness to stay out of the way.

[Amended October 2014]

4.03 COMMUNICATION WITH WITNESSES GIVING TESTIMONY

Communication with Witnesses Giving Testimony

4.03 (1) Subject to the direction of the tribunal, a paralegal shall observe the following rules respecting communication with witnesses giving evidence:

(a) During examination-in-chief, the examining paralegal may discuss with the witness any matter that has not been covered in the examination up to that point.

(b) During examination-in-chief by another licensee of a witness who is unsympathetic to the paralegal's cause, the paralegal not conducting the examination-in- chief may discuss the evidence with the witness.

(c) Between completion of examination-in-chief and commencement of cross- examination of the paralegal's own witness, the paralegal ought not to discuss the evidence given in chief or relating to any matter introduced or touched on during the examination-in-chief.

(d) During cross-examination by an opposing licensee, the witness's own representative ought not to have any conversation with the witness about the witness's evidence or any issue in the proceeding.

(e) Between completion of cross-examination and commencement of a re-examination, a paralegal who is going to re-examine the witness ought not to have any discussion about evidence that will be dealt with on re-examination.

(f) During cross-examination by the representative of a witness unsympathetic to the cross-examiner's cause, the paralegal may discuss the witness's evidence with the witness.

(g) During cross-examination by the representative of a witness who is sympathetic to that licensee's cause, any conversations ought to be restricted in the same way as communications during examination-in-chief of one's own witness.

(h) During re-examination of a witness called by an opposing licensee, if the witness is sympathetic to the paralegal's cause, the paralegal ought not to discuss the evidence to be given by that witness during re-examination. The paralegal may, however, properly discuss the evidence with a witness who is adverse in interest.

(2) With the consent of the opposing licensee or with leave of the tribunal, a paralegal may enter into discussions with a witness that might otherwise raise a question under this rule as to the propriety of the discussions.

(3) This rule applies, with necessary modifications, to examinations out of court.

4.04 THE PARALEGAL AS WITNESS

The Paralegal as Witness

4.04 (1) A paralegal who appears as advocate shall not testify or submit his or her own affidavit evidence before the tribunal unless

(a) permitted to do so by law, the tribunal, the rules of court or the rules of procedure of the tribunal, or

(b) the matter is purely formal or uncontroverted.

[Amended October 2014]

4.05 DEALING WITH UNREPRESENTED PERSONS

4.05 When a paralegal deals on a client's behalf with an unrepresented person, the paralegal shall,

(a) take care to see that the unrepresented person is not proceeding under the impression that his or her interests will be protected by the paralegal; and

(b) make clear to the unrepresented person that the paralegal is acting exclusively in the interests of the client and accordingly his or her comments may be partisan.

[Amended October 2014]

RULE 5 FEES AND RETAINERS

5.01 FEES AND RETAINERS

Reasonable Fees and Disbursements

5.01 (1) A paralegal shall not charge or accept any amount for a fee or disbursement unless it is fair and reasonable and has been disclosed in a timely fashion.

(2) What is a fair and reasonable fee will depend upon such factors as,

(a) the time and effort required and spent;

(b) the difficulty of the matter and importance of the matter to the client;

(c) whether special skill or service was required and provided;

(d) the amount involved or the value of the subject matter;

(e) the results obtained;

(f) fees authorized by statute or regulation;

(g) special circumstances, such as the loss of other retainers, postponement of payment, uncertainty of reward, or urgency;

(h) the likelihood, if made known to the client, that acceptance of the retainer will result in the paralegal's inability to accept other employment;

(i) any relevant agreement between the paralegal and the client;

(j) the experience and ability of the paralegal;

(k) any estimate or range of fees given by the paralegal; and

(l) the client's prior consent to the fee.

(3) No fee, reward, costs, commission, interest, rebate, agency or forwarding allowance, or other compensation related to his or her employment may be taken by the paralegal from anyone other than the client, without full disclosure to, and the consent of, the client.

(4) In a statement of account delivered to the client, a paralegal shall clearly and separately detail amounts charged as fees and as disbursements.

(5) A paralegal shall not appropriate any funds of the client held in trust, or otherwise under the paralegal's control, for or on account of fees, except as permitted by the by-laws under the *Law Society Act*.

(6) If the amount of fees or disbursements charged by a paralegal is reduced by a Court Order, the paralegal must repay the monies to the client as soon as is practicable.

Contingency Fees

(7) Except in quasi-criminal or criminal matters, a paralegal may enter into a written agreement that provides that the paralegal's fee is contingent, in whole or in part, on the successful disposition or completion of the matter for which the paralegal's services are to be provided.

(8) In determining the appropriate percentage or other basis of a contingency fee under subrule (7), the paralegal shall advise the client on the factors that are being taken into account in determining the percentage or other basis, including the likelihood of success, the nature and complexity of the claim, the expense and risk of pursuing it, the amount of the expected recovery, who is to receive an award of costs and the amount of costs awarded.

(9) The percentage or other basis of a contingency fee agreed upon under subrule (7) shall be fair and reasonable, taking into consideration all of the circumstances and the factors listed in subrule (8).

Joint Retainers

(10) If a paralegal is acting for two or more clients in the same matter, the paralegal shall divide the fees and disbursements equitably between them, unless there is an agreement by the clients otherwise.

Division of Fees

(11) Fees for a matter may be divided between licensees who are not in the same firm if the client consents and the fees are divided in proportion to the work done and the responsibilities assumed.

[Amended October 2014]

Fee Splitting

(12) A paralegal shall not,

(a) directly or indirectly share, split, or divide his or her fees with any person who is not a licensee, including an affiliated entity; or

(b) give any financial or other reward to any person who is not a licensee, including an affiliated entity for the referral of clients or client matters.

(13) Subrule (11) does not apply to multi-discipline practices of paralegal and non-licensee partners where the partnership agreement provides for the sharing of fees, cash flows or profits among members of the firm.

[Amended October 2014]

Referral Fees

(14) A paralegal who refers a matter to another licensee because of the expertise and ability of the other licensee to handle the matter may accept, and the other licensee may pay, a referral fee if,

(a) the referral was not made because of a conflict of interest,

(b) the fee is reasonable and does not increase the total amount of the fee charged to the client; and

(c) the client is informed and consents.

[Amended October 2014]

RULE 6 DUTY TO THE ADMINISTRATION OF JUSTICE

6.01 ENCOURAGING RESPECT FOR THE ADMINISTRATION OF JUSTICE

General Duty

6.01 (1) A paralegal shall encourage public respect for, and try to improve, the administration of justice.

(2) A paralegal shall take care not to weaken or destroy public confidence in legal institutions or authorities by making irresponsible allegations or comments particularly when commenting on judges or members of a tribunal.

Security of Court Facilities

(3) Subject to Rule 3.03 relating to confidentiality, a paralegal who has reasonable grounds for believing that a dangerous situation is likely to develop at a court facility shall inform the persons having responsibility for security at the facility and give particulars.

Public Appearances and Statements

(4) So long as there is no infringement of the paralegal's obligation to the client, the paralegal profession, the courts, or the administration of justice, a paralegal may communicate information to the media and may make public appearances and statements.

(4.1) A paralegal shall not communicate information to the media or make public statements about a matter before a tribunal if the paralegal knows or ought to know that the information or statement will have a substantial likelihood of materially prejudicing a party's right to a fair trial or hearing.

[Amended October 2014]

Working With or Employing Unauthorized Persons

(5) A paralegal shall assist in preventing the unauthorized practice of law and the unauthorized provision of legal services.

(6) Without the express approval of a committee of Convocation appointed for the purpose, a paralegal shall not retain, occupy office space with, use the services of, partner or associate with, or employ in any capacity having to do with the provision of legal services any person who, in Ontario or elsewhere,

(a) is disbarred and struck off the Rolls,

(b) is a person whose license to practice law or to provide legal services is revoked,

(c) as a result of disciplinary action, has been permitted to resign his or her membership in the Law Society or to surrender his or her licence to practise law or to provide legal services, and has not had his or her license restored,

(d) is suspended,

(e) is a person whose license to practise law or to provide legal services is suspended, or

(f) is subject to an undertaking not to practise law or to provide legal services.

[Amended—January 2008]

Practice by Suspended Paralegal Prohibited

(7) A paralegal whose license to provide legal services is suspended shall comply with the requirements of the by-laws and shall not

(a) provide legal services; or

(b) represent or hold himself or herself out as a person entitled to provide legal services.

[New—January 2008]

Undertakings Not to Provide Legal Services

(8) A paralegal who gives an undertaking to the Law Society not to provide legal services shall not,

(a) provide legal services; or

(b) represent or hold himself or herself out as a person entitled to provide legal services.

[New—January 2008]

Undertakings to Provide Legal Services Subject to Restrictions

(9) A paralegal who gives an undertaking to the Law Society to restrict his or her provision of legal services shall comply with the undertaking.

[New—January 2008]

RULE 7 DUTY TO LICENSEES AND OTHERS

7.01 COURTESY AND GOOD FAITH

(1) A paralegal shall avoid sharp practice and shall not take advantage of or act without fair warning on slips, irregularities or mistakes on the part of other licensees not going to the merits or involving the sacrifice of a client's rights.

(2) A paralegal shall agree to reasonable requests concerning trial dates, adjournments, waiver of procedural formalities and similar matters that do not prejudice the rights of the client.

(3) A paralegal shall not, in the course of providing legal services, communicate, in writing or otherwise, with a client, another licensee, or any other person in a manner that is abusive, offensive, or otherwise inconsistent with the proper tone of a professional communication from a paralegal.

(4) A paralegal shall not engage in ill-considered or uninformed criticism of the competence, conduct, advice or charges of other licensees, but should be prepared, when requested, to represent a client in a complaint involving another licensee.

(5) A paralegal shall answer with reasonable promptness, all professional letters and communications from other licensees that require an answer, and a paralegal shall be punctual in fulfilling all commitments.

(6) A paralegal shall not use any device to record a conversation between the paralegal and a client or another licensee, even if lawful, without first informing the other person of the intention to do so.

(7) A paralegal who receives a document relating to the representation of the paralegal's client and knows or reasonably should know that the document was inadvertently sent shall promptly notify the sender.

[Amended October 2014]

7.02 COMMUNICATION WITH A REPRESENTED PERSON, CORPORATION OR ORGANIZATION

(1) Subject to subrules (2) and (3), if a person is represented by a legal practitioner in respect of a matter, a paralegal shall not, except through or with the consent of the legal practitioner,

(a) approach or communicate or deal with the person on the matter, or

(b) attempt to negotiate or compromise the matter directly with the person.

(2) Subject to subrule (3), if a person is receiving legal services from a legal practitioner under a limited scope retainer on a particular matter, a paralegal may, without the consent of the legal practitioner, approach, communicate or deal directly with the person on the matter, unless the paralegal receives written notice of the limited nature of the legal services being provided by the legal practitioner and the approach, communication or dealing falls within the scope of the limited scope retainer.

(3) A paralegal who is not otherwise interested in a matter may give a second opinion to a person who is represented by a legal practitioner with respect to that matter.

(4) A paralegal retained to act on a matter involving a corporation or organization that is represented by a legal practitioner in respect of that matter shall not, without the legal practitioner's consent or unless otherwise authorized or required by law, communicate, facilitate communication with or deal with a person

(a) who is a director or officer, or another person who is authorized to act on behalf of the corporation or organization,

(b) who is likely involved in decision-making for the corporation or organization or who provides advice in relation to the particular matter,

(c) whose act or omission may be binding on or imputed to the corporation or organization for the purposes of its liability, or

(d) who supervises, directs or regularly consults with the legal practitioner and who makes decisions based on the legal practitioner's advice.

(5) If a person described in subrule (4) (a), (b), (c) or (d) is represented in the matter by a legal practitioner, the consent of the legal practitioner is sufficient to allow a paralegal to communicate, facilitate communication with or deal with the person.

(6) In subrule (4), "organization" includes a partnership, limited partnership, association, union, fund, trust, co-operative, unincorporated association, sole proprietorship and a government department, agency, or regulatory body.

(7) This rule applies to communications with any person, whether or not a party to a formal adjudicative proceeding, contract, or negotiation, who is represented by a licensee concerning the matter to which the communication relates.

(8) The prohibition on communications with a represented person applies if the paralegal has direct knowledge of the representation or if he or she should be able to infer the representation from the circumstances.

[New—October 2012]

RULE 8 PRACTICE MANAGEMENT

8.01 GENERAL OBLIGATIONS

Professional Responsibility

8.01 (1) A paralegal shall, in accordance with the by-laws, assume complete professional responsibility for all business entrusted to him or her.

[Amended—October 2008]

Financial Responsibility

(2) A paralegal shall promptly meet financial obligations incurred in the course of practice on behalf of clients unless, before incurring such an obligation, the paralegal clearly indicates in writing to the person to whom it is to be owed that it is not to be a personal obligation of the paralegal.

[Amended—January 2009]

Supervisory Responsibility

(3) A paralegal shall, in accordance with the by-laws, directly supervise staff and assistants to whom particular tasks and functions are delegated.

[Amended—October 2008]

Delegation

(4) A paralegal shall not permit a non-licensee,

(a) to provide legal services;

(b) to be held out as a licensee; or

(c) to perform any of the duties that only paralegals may perform or do things that paralegals themselves may not do.

(5) A paralegal in a multi-discipline practice shall ensure that non-licensee partners and associates comply with these rules and all ethical principles that govern a paralegal in the discharge of his or her professional obligations.

[New—October 2008]

8.02 MAKING LEGAL SERVICES AVAILABLE

8.02 (1) A paralegal shall make legal services available to the public in an efficient and convenient way.

Restrictions

(2) In offering legal services, a paralegal shall not use means

(a) that are false or misleading,

(b) that amount to coercion, duress or harassment,

(c) that take advantage of a person who is vulnerable or who has suffered a traumatic experience and has not yet had a chance to recover,

(d) that are intended to influence a person who has retained another paralegal or a lawyer for a particular matter to change his or her representative for that matter, unless the change is initiated by the person or the other representative, or

(e) that otherwise bring the paralegal profession or the administration of justice into disrepute.

(3) A paralegal shall not advertise services that are beyond the permissible scope of practice of a paralegal.

[Amended—November 2008]

8.03 MARKETING OF LEGAL SERVICES

(1) In this Rule, "marketing" includes advertisements and other similar communications in various media as well as firm names (including trade names), letterhead, business cards and logos.

(2) A paralegal may market legal services if the marketing

(a) is demonstrably true, accurate and verifiable,

(b) is neither misleading, confusing, or deceptive, nor likely to mislead, confuse or deceive, and

(c) is in the best interests of the public and is consistent with a high standard of professionalism.

Advertising of Fees

(3) A paralegal may advertise fees charged by the paralegal for legal services if

(a) the advertising is reasonably precise as to the services offered for each fee quoted,

(b) the advertising states whether other amounts, such as disbursements and taxes will be charged in addition to the fee, and

(c) the paralegal strictly adheres to the advertised fee in every applicable case.

[Amended—November 2008]

8.04 COMPULSORY ERRORS AND OMISSIONS INSURANCE

Duty to Obtain and Maintain Insurance

8.04 (1) All paralegals practising in Ontario shall obtain and maintain adequate errors and omissions insurance as required by the Law Society.

(2) A paralegal shall give prompt notice of any circumstance that the paralegal may reasonably expect to give rise to a claim to an insurer or other indemnitor so that the client's protection from that source will not be prejudiced.

(3) When a claim of professional negligence is made against a paralegal, he or she shall assist and cooperate with the insurer or other indemnitor to the extent necessary to enable the claim to be dealt with promptly.

(4) In cases where liability is clear and the insurer or other indemnitor is prepared to pay its portion of the claim, the paralegal shall pay the balance.

[Amended—January 2010]

RULE 9 RESPONSIBILITY TO THE LAW SOCIETY

9.01 RESPONSIBILITY TO THE LAW SOCIETY

Communications from the Law Society

9.01 (1) A paralegal shall reply promptly and completely to any communication from the Law Society and shall provide a complete response to any request from the Law Society.

Duty to Report Misconduct

(2) A paralegal shall report to the Law Society, unless to do so would be unlawful or would involve a breach of confidentiality between the paralegal and his or her client,

(a) the misappropriation or misapplication of trust monies by a licensee;

(b) the abandonment of a law practice by a lawyer or a legal services practice by a paralegal;

(c) participation in serious criminal activity related to a licensee's practice;

(d) the mental instability of a licensee of such a serious nature that the licensee's clients are likely to be materially prejudiced; and

(e) any other situation where a licensee's clients are likely to be severely prejudiced.

(3) Nothing in subrule (2) is meant to interfere with the paralegal's duty to the client.

(4) A report under subrule (2) must be made in good faith and without malice or ulterior motive.

(5) A paralegal shall encourage a client who has a claim or complaint against an apparently dishonest licensee to report the facts to the Law Society as soon as reasonably practicable.

(6) If the client refuses to report a claim against an apparently dishonest licensee to the Law Society, the paralegal shall obtain instructions in writing to proceed with the client's private remedies without notice to the Law Society.

(7) A paralegal shall inform the client of the provision of the *Criminal Code of Canada* dealing with the concealment of an indictable offence in return for an agreement to obtain valuable consideration. (section 141).

(8) If the client wishes to pursue a private agreement with the apparently dishonest licensee, the paralegal shall not continue to act if the agreement constitutes a breach of section 141 of the *Criminal Code of Canada*.

Duty to Report Certain Offences

(9) If a paralegal is charged with an offence described in By-Law 8 of the Law Society, he or she shall inform the Law Society of the charge and of its disposition in accordance with the By-law.

Disciplinary Authority

(10) A paralegal is subject to the disciplinary authority of the Law Society regardless of where the paralegal's conduct occurs.

Professional Misconduct

(11) The Law Society may discipline a paralegal for professional misconduct.

Conduct Unbecoming a Paralegal

(12) The Law Society may discipline a paralegal for conduct unbecoming a paralegal.

Definitions

(13) In subrules (11) and (12),

"conduct unbecoming a paralegal" means conduct in a paralegal's personal or private capacity that tends to bring discredit upon the paralegal profession including,

> (a) committing a criminal act that reflects adversely on the paralegal's honesty, trustworthiness, or fitness as a paralegal,
>
> (b) taking improper advantage of the youth, inexperience, lack of education, unsophistication, ill health, vulnerability or unbusinesslike habits of another, or
>
> (c) engaging in conduct involving dishonesty;

"professional misconduct" means conduct in a paralegal's professional capacity that tends to bring discredit upon the paralegal profession, including,

(a) violating or attempting to violate one of these Rules, or a requirement of *Law Society Act* or its regulations or by-laws,

(b) knowingly assisting or inducing another licensee to violate or attempt to violate these Rules, a requirement of the *Law Society Act* or its regulations or by-laws,

(c) knowingly assisting or inducing a non-licensee partner or associate of a multi-discipline practice to violate or attempt to violate the rules in the *Paralegal Rules of Conduct* or a requirement of the *Law Society Act* or its regulations or by-laws,

[Amended October 2014]

(d) misappropriating or otherwise dealing dishonestly with a client's or a third party's money or property,

(e) engaging in conduct that is prejudicial to the administration of justice,

(f) stating or implying an ability to influence improperly a government agency or official, or

(g) knowingly assisting a judge or judicial officer in conduct that is a violation of applicable rules of judicial conduct or other law.

Paralegal Professional Conduct Guidelines

B

Effective October, 2008
Amendments based on the Federation of Law Societies Model Code of Professional Conduct effective October 1, 2014
Amendments current to October 1, 2014

INTRODUCTION TO THE *PARALEGAL PROFESSIONAL CONDUCT GUIDELINES*

Purpose

1. Under the *Law Society Act*, the Law Society has the right to make rules and regulations to govern the professional conduct of lawyers and paralegals. The *Act* also gives the Society the ability to discipline those lawyers or paralegals who do not adhere to the rules. Regulations include the By-Laws under the *Act* and the *Paralegal Rules of Conduct,* which were adopted to govern the professional conduct of licensed paralegals.
2. The *Paralegal Professional Conduct Guidelines* ("Guidelines") have been created to assist paralegals with the interpretation and application of the *Paralegal Rules of Conduct* ("*Rules*"). The Guidelines should be considered along with the *Rules*, the *Law Society Act* (the "*Act*"), the By-Laws made under the *Act* and any other relevant case law or legislation. Neither the *Rules* nor the Guidelines can cover every situation; they should be interpreted and applied with common sense and in a manner consistent with the public interest and the integrity of the profession. It is expected that a paralegal will exercise his or her professional judgment in interpreting the Guidelines, keeping in mind the paralegal's obligations to the client, the court or tribunal and the Law Society.

Accessing the Guidelines

3. The Guidelines are available in electronic form. They are cross-referenced to the *Rules* and are linked directly to the *Rules* on the Law Society's website.

Terminology

4. For the purposes of these Guidelines, the word
   - "*Act*" refers to the *Law Society Act*,
   - "Guidelines" refers to the *Paralegal Professional Conduct Guidelines*,
   - "*Rules*" refers to the *Paralegal Rules of Conduct*,
   - "paralegal" refers to paralegals licensed to provide legal services by the Law Society of Upper Canada, and
   - "lawyer" refers to lawyers licensed to practise law by the Law Society of Upper Canada.

5. The following may be of assistance in interpreting the Guidelines:
   - The terms "shall" or "must" are used in those instances where compliance is mandated by either the by-laws made pursuant to the *Law Society Act* or the *Rules*.
   - The term "should" and the phrase "should consider" indicate a recommendation. These terms refer to those practices or policies that are considered by the Law Society to be a reasonable goal for maintaining or enhancing professional conduct.
   - The term "may" and the phrase "may consider" convey discretion. After considering suggested policies or procedures preceded by "may" or "may consider", a paralegal has discretion whether or not to follow the suggestions, depending upon the paralegal's particular circumstances, areas of professional business or clientele, or the circumstances of a particular client or matter.

GUIDELINE 1: PROFESSIONALISM—INTEGRITY & CIVILITY

General

Rule Reference: Rule 2.01(1) & (2)

1. A paralegal should inspire the respect, confidence and trust of clients and the community.
2. Public confidence in the administration of justice and in the paralegal profession may be eroded by a paralegal's unprofessional conduct. A paralegal's conduct should reflect favourably on the legal professions, inspire the confidence, respect and trust of clients and of the community, and avoid even the appearance of impropriety.
3. A paralegal has special responsibilities by virtue of the privileges afforded the paralegal profession and the important role it plays in a free and democratic society and in the administration of justice. This includes a special responsibility to recognize the diversity of the Ontario community, to protect the dignity of individuals and to respect human rights laws in force in Ontario.

Integrity and Civility

Rule Reference: Rule 2.01(1) & (2)

4. Acting with ***integrity*** means that a paralegal will be honest and will act with high ethical and moral principles. ***Integrity*** is the fundamental quality of any person who seeks to provide legal services. If integrity is lacking, the paralegal's usefulness to the client and reputation within the profession will be destroyed regardless of how competent the paralegal may be.
5. Acting with ***civility*** means that a paralegal will communicate politely and respectfully and act in a manner that does not cause unnecessary difficulty or harm to another.
6. The obligation to show courtesy and good faith extends to clients, opposing parties, other paralegals and lawyers, support staff, adjudicators, court and tribunal officers and staff and representatives of the Law Society. This obligation applies regardless of where the paralegal may be appearing or at what stage of the process the matter may be.

GUIDELINE 2: OUTSIDE INTERESTS

General

Rule Reference: Rule 2.01(3) & (4)

1. The term "outside interest" covers the widest range of activities. It includes activities that may overlap or be connected with provision of legal services, for example, acting as a director of a corporation or writing on legal subjects, as well as activities less connected such as, for example, a career in business, politics, broadcasting or the performing arts.
2. When participating in community activities, a paralegal should be mindful of the possible perception that the paralegal is providing legal services and a paralegal-client relationship has been established. A paralegal should not carry on, manage or be involved in any outside interest in such a way that makes it difficult to distinguish in which capacity the paralegal is acting, or that would give rise to a conflict of interest or duty to a client.
3. It is the paralegal's responsibility to consider whether the outside interest may impair his or her ability to act in the best interest of his or her client(s). If so, the paralegal must withdraw, either from representation of the client or from the outside interest.
4. When acting in another role, the paralegal must continue to fulfill his or her obligations under the *Rules*, for example, to
   - act with integrity,
   - be civil and courteous,
   - be competent in providing legal services,
   - avoid conflicts of interest, and
   - maintain confidentiality.

Acting as a Mediator

Rule Reference: Rule 2.01(5)

5. A mediator works with disputing parties to help them resolve their dispute. A paralegal acting as a mediator is not providing legal services to either party—the relationship is not a paralegal-client relationship. This does not preclude the mediator from giving information on the consequences if the mediation fails.
6. When acting as a mediator, the paralegal should guard against potential conflicts of interest. For example, neither the paralegal nor the paralegal's partners or associates should provide legal services to the parties. Further, a paralegal-mediator should suggest and encourage the parties to seek the advice of a qualified paralegal or a lawyer before and during the mediation process if they have not already done so. Refer to Guideline 9: Conflicts of Interest for more information on how a paralegal's outside interests may conflict with the paralegal's duty to his or her clients.

GUIDELINE 3: UNDERTAKINGS AND TRUST CONDITIONS

General

Rule Reference: Rule 2.02

1. Money and property change hands in most legal transactions. A paralegal may be required to hold documents and property in trust until the performance of particular conditions. These conditions are called ***trust conditions***. Promises to carry

out specific tasks and/or fulfill specific conditions are called ***undertakings***. Rule 2.02 sets out a paralegal's obligations in relation to undertakings and trust conditions.

Undertakings

Rule Reference: Rule 2.02(1), (2) & (3)

2. An undertaking is a personal promise. A paralegal could, for example, give an undertaking to complete a task or provide a document. Fulfilling that promise is the responsibility of the paralegal giving the undertaking.
3. The person who accepts the paralegal's undertaking is entitled to expect the paralegal to carry it out personally. Using the phrase "on behalf of my client," even in the undertaking itself, may not release the paralegal from the obligation to honour the undertaking. If a paralegal does not intend to take personal responsibility, this should be clearly outlined in the written undertaking. In those circumstances, it may only be possible for the paralegal to personally undertake to make "best efforts."
4. A court or a tribunal may enforce an undertaking. The paralegal may be brought before a court or tribunal to explain why the undertaking was not fulfilled. The court or tribunal may order the paralegal to take steps to fulfill the undertaking and/or pay damages caused by the failure to fulfill the undertaking.
5. To avoid misunderstandings and miscommunication, a paralegal should remember the following points about undertakings. A paralegal
   - should ensure that the wording of the undertaking is clear. If a paralegal is the recipient of an undertaking given by another paralegal or a lawyer, the paralegal should ensure that the wording is clear and consistent with his or her understanding of the undertaking. The paralegal should contact the other paralegal or lawyer to clarify the issue as soon as possible if this is not the case.
   - should consider specifying a deadline for fulfilling the undertaking.
   - should ensure that the undertaking provides for contingencies (e.g. if the obligations in the undertaking rely on certain events occurring, the paralegal should indicate what will happen if these events do not occur).
   - should confirm whether or not the individual providing the undertaking is a paralegal or a lawyer.

Trust Conditions

Rule Reference: Rule 2.02(4)

6. Once a trust condition is accepted, it is binding upon a paralegal, whether imposed by another legal practitioner or by a lay person.
7. Trust conditions should be clear, unambiguous and explicit and should state the time within which the conditions must be met. Trust conditions should be imposed and accepted in writing. Trust conditions may be varied with the consent of the person imposing them, and the variation should be confirmed in writing,
8. A paralegal should not impose or accept trust conditions that are unreasonable, nor accept trust conditions that cannot be fulfilled personally. When a paralegal accepts property subject to trust conditions, the paralegal must fully comply with such conditions, even if the conditions subsequently appear unreasonable.
9. A paralegal may seek to impose trust conditions upon a non-licensee, but great caution should be exercised in so doing since such conditions would be enforceable only through the courts as a matter of contract law.

GUIDELINE 4: HARASSMENT AND DISCRIMINATION

The Human Rights Code

Rule Reference: Rule 2.03

1. A paralegal's obligations regarding harassment and discrimination are outlined in the *Rules*, the *Human Rights Code* and related case law.
2. The *Human Rights Code* gives everyone equal rights and opportunities without discrimination relating to matters such as employment, housing and services. The purpose of the Code is to prevent discrimination or harassment on the grounds of
   - race or colour,
   - citizenship, ancestry , place of origin or ethnic origin,
   - creed,
   - sex (including pregnancy),
   - sexual orientation,
   - age (means an age that is 18 or more),
   - record of offences (in the context of employment only),
   - marital or family status,
   - disability,
   - gender identity or gender expression or
   - the receipt of public assistance (in the context of housing only).
3. More information about obligations under the *Human Rights Code* may be found at http://www.ohrc.on.ca/.

Discrimination

Rule Reference: Rule 2.03(4) & (5)

4. ***Discrimination*** means treating another person in the context, for example, of employment, services or housing, differently and less than others, because of any of the Code's prohibited grounds.
5. A paralegal should review and become familiar with human rights laws to ensure that the paralegal is meeting his or her legal and ethical obligations to others.

Harassment

Rule Reference: Rule 2.03(3)

6. ***Harassment*** is a form of discrimination. Harassment means vexatious comments or actions that are unwelcome to the person receiving the comments or actions, or comments or actions that ought reasonably be known to be unwelcome. Generally speaking, harassment is a "course of conduct" or a pattern of behaviour where more than one incident has occurred. Even one incident however, may constitute harassment if the incident is serious in nature.
7. ***Sexual harassment*** is defined in the *Human Rights Code* as an incident or series of incidents involving unwelcome sexual advances, requests for sexual favours or other verbal or physical conduct of a sexual nature when one or more of the following circumstances are present:
   - such conduct might reasonably be expected to cause insecurity, discomfort, offence or humiliation to the recipient(s) of the conduct,
   - giving in to such conduct is a condition for the supply of legal services by the paralegal, whether this condition was spoken or unspoken by the paralegal,

- giving in to such conduct is a condition of employment by the paralegal, whether this condition was spoken or unspoken by the paralegal,
- giving in to or rejecting such conduct affects the paralegal's employment decisions regarding his or her employee (which may include assigning file work to the employee, matters of promotion, raise in salary, job security, and employee benefits, among other things),
- such conduct is intended to or results in interfering with an employee's work performance, or
- such conduct creates an uncomfortable, unfriendly or unpleasant work environment.

8. Examples of behaviour considered as harassment include, but are not limited to
   - sexist jokes causing embarrassment or offence,
   - the display of offensive material, such as racial graffiti,
   - the use of sexually degrading words to describe a person,
   - the use of derogatory or degrading remarks directed at one's sex or one's sexual orientation,
   - the use of sexually suggestive or obscene comments or gestures,
   - unwelcome comments or inquiries about one's sex life,
   - repeated racial slurs directed at language or accent of a particular group,
   - unwelcome sexual flirtations, advances or propositions,
   - leering,
   - persistent unwanted contact or attention after the end of a consensual relationship,
   - requests for sexual favours,
   - unwanted touching,
   - verbal abuse or threats, or
   - sexual assault.

Promoting Equity and Diversity

9. The Law Society's Equity Initiatives department has developed a series of best practices and model policies to guide paralegals and lawyers in promoting equity and diversity in all areas of their professional business. All paralegals should consider adopting model policies to assist them in meeting their legal and professional conduct responsibilities. Model policies cover practices relating to employment and the provision of services to clients and include
   - preventing and responding to workplace harassment and discrimination,
   - promoting equity in the workplace,
   - parental and pregnancy leaves and benefits,
   - accommodation in the workplace, flexible work arrangements, and
   - issues relating to creed and religious beliefs, to gender and sexual orientation, and to individuals with disabilities.
10. Equity Initiatives has also developed a professional development program to design and deliver education and training to legal service providers regarding these equity and diversity issues. A paralegal may contact the Law Society to discuss available training sessions, which may be offered as seminars, workshops or informal meetings. Full information regarding these initiatives is available on the Equity section of the Law Society website at www.lsuc.on.ca.

Discrimination and Harassment Counsel

11. The Law Society provides the services of ***Discrimination and Harassment Counsel*** to anyone who may have experienced discrimination by a paralegal or a lawyer, or within a paralegal or lawyer's professional business. This service is funded by the Society but is completely independent of the Society. The service is free to the Ontario public, including paralegals and lawyers, and is strictly confidential.
12. The Discrimination and Harassment Counsel can provide advice and support and will review options with the individual using the service, which may include
    - filing a complaint with the Law Society,
    - filing a complaint with the Ontario Human Rights Commission, and
    - allowing the Discrimination and Harassment Counsel to mediate a resolution if all parties agree.
13. More information is available at www.dhcounsel.on.ca/.

GUIDELINE 5: CLIENTS

General

Rule Reference: Rule 1.02
Rule 3

1. One of the most important duties of a paralegal is the duty of service to his or her ***client***.

   This duty includes obligations to be competent, maintain confidentiality, avoid conflicts of interest and continue to represent the client unless the paralegal has good reason for withdrawing. As a result, it is important for the paralegal to know exactly who is a client because it is to the client that most of the duties outlined in the *Rules* are owed. ***Client*** is defined in Rule 1.02.
2. The courts have made a distinction between a solicitor-client relationship and a solicitor-client retainer. This jurisprudence may be used by the courts to define the paralegal-client relationship and paralegal-client retainer in future. The ***relationship*** is established when the prospective client has his or her first consultation with the lawyer or law firm about retaining services. The relationship may be established without formality. The ***retainer*** is established once the lawyer agrees (expressly or implied by the lawyer's conduct) to provide legal services. The solicitor-client relationship, with all of its important duties, for example, confidentiality, continues after the retainer is established.
3. In most cases, it is clear who is the ***client***. However, there may be situations where it is difficult to determine who is the client from whom the paralegal should be receiving instructions. Problems may develop in situations involving ***joint clients***, ***authorized representatives***, ***organizations***, ***"phantom" clients*** or ***unrepresented opposing parties***.

Joint Clients

Rule Reference: Rule 3.04(7)–(13)

4. A ***joint retainer*** occurs where a paralegal agrees to represent two or more clients in the same matter. As with any retainer, the paralegal should clearly identify the clients to whom legal services will be provided, to ensure that the paralegal fulfills his or her duties to those clients.

Authorized Representatives

Rule Reference: Rule 3.02(13) & (14)
Rule 3.04(7)–(13)

5. Identifying who is the client and whose instructions should be followed can be difficult where a client representative is involved. The paralegal should consider, determine and clearly outline these matters at the start of the relationship. If a paralegal is acting for both the individual and the individual's authorized representative, the paralegal must comply with the rules regarding joint retainers.

Acting for an Organization

Rule Reference: Rule 3.04(7)–(13)

6. When acting for a client that is an organization, it is in the paralegal's interests to clarify which officers, employees or agents of the organization may properly give instructions on the organization's behalf. The paralegal should confirm with those individuals that the paralegal acts for the organization and not for the individuals who act as its instructing agents.
7. If a paralegal is retained by both the organization and one or more of its officers, employees, or agents in the same matter, the paralegal must comply with Rule 3.04(8)–(14) regarding joint retainers.

"Phantom" Clients

8. An individual may believe that he or she is represented by a paralegal, though he or she has not formally retained or hired the paralegal. In these cases, the paralegal may be unaware that the individual considers himself or herself the paralegal's client. These types of individuals are sometimes referred to as "phantom" clients.
9. Phantom clients are problematic because they may in fact be clients or prospective clients to whom the paralegal owes duties, yet they are phantoms that the paralegal does not see. This situation may arise when something the paralegal has done or a conversation the paralegal has had, had led a person to believe that the paralegal represents that person. One of the common ways in which phantom clients are created is through a person who consults with the paralegal on a matter but does not clearly indicate whether he or she wants to hire the paralegal or pursue the matter.
10. To avoid the problem of phantom clients, it is helpful for the paralegal to clearly identify who is the client, what is the client's matter, and who is to provide instructions. To avoid collecting phantom clients, a paralegal should also clearly communicate his or her role with anyone the paralegal deals with as a paralegal. It may be helpful for the paralegal to
    - confirm in writing whether or not the paralegal will provide legal services for a person who has consulted with him or her and refer to any limitation periods (i.e. retainer agreement, engagement or non-engagement letter),
    - inform third party individuals who attend meetings with a client that the paralegal represents the client only, and not the third party,
    - discourage clients from relaying legal advice to third parties, and
    - avoid discussing legal matters outside the working environment or a working relationship.

GUIDELINE 6: COMPETENCE AND QUALITY OF SERVICE

General

Rule Reference: Rule 3.01
Rule 3.02(1)

1. A licensed paralegal is held out to be knowledgeable, skilled and capable in his or her permissible area of practice. A client hires a legal service provider because the client does not have the knowledge and skill to deal with the legal system on his or her own. When a client hires a paralegal, the client expects that the paralegal is competent and has the ability to properly deal with the client's case.
2. A paralegal should not undertake a matter without honestly feeling competent to handle it, or being able to become competent without undue delay, risk, or expense to the client. This is an ethical consideration and is distinct from the standard of care that a tribunal would invoke for purposes of determining negligence.

Limited Scope Retainers

3. A paralegal may provide legal services under a limited scope retainer, but must carefully assess in each case whether, under the circumstances, it is possible to render those services in a competent manner. Although an agreement for such services does not exempt a paralegal from the duty to provide competent representation, the limitation is a factor to be considered when determining the legal knowledge, skill, thoroughness and preparation reasonably necessary for the representation. The paralegal should ensure that the client is fully informed of the nature of the arrangement and clearly understands the scope and limitation of the services.

   Cross reference Rule 3.02(15)–(17)

The Required Standard of Competence

Rule Reference: Rule 3.01(1)
Rule 3.01(4)

Knowledge

Rule Reference: Rule 3.01(4)(a) & (b)

4. Competence is founded upon both ethical and legal principles. Competence involves more than an understanding of legal principles; it involves an adequate knowledge of the practice and procedures by which such principles can be effectively applied. To accomplish this, the paralegal should keep abreast of developments in all areas of law in which the paralegal provides legal services.
5. The competent paralegal will ensure that only after all necessary information has been gathered, reviewed and considered does he or she advise the client as to the course(s) of action that will most likely meet the client's goals, taking care to ensure that the client is made aware of all foreseeable risks and/or costs associated with the course(s) of action.
6. Unless the client instructs otherwise, the paralegal should investigate the matter in sufficient detail to be able to express an opinion, even where the paralegal has been retained to provide services under a limited scope retainer. If the circumstances

do not justify an exhaustive investigation with consequent expense to the client, the paralegal should so state in the opinion.

Client Service and Communication

Rule Reference: Rule 3.01(4)(d), (e), (f) & (g)

7. Client service is an important part of competence. Most of the complaints received by the Law Society relate to client service, such as not communicating with a client, delay, not following client instructions and not doing what the paralegal or lawyer was retained to do.
8. Rule 3.01(4) contains important requirements for paralegal-client communication and service. In addition to those requirements, a paralegal can provide more effective client service by
   - keeping the client informed regarding his or her matter, through all relevant stages of the matter and concerning all aspects of the matter,
   - managing client expectations by clearly establishing with the client what the paralegal will do or accomplish and at what cost, and
   - being clear about what the client expects, both at the beginning of the retainer and throughout the retainer.
9. A paralegal should meet deadlines, unless the paralegal is able to offer a reasonable explanation and ensure that no prejudice to the client will result. Whether or not a specific deadline applies, a paralegal should be prompt in prosecuting a matter, responding to communications and reporting developments to the client. In the absence of developments, contact with the client should be maintained to the extent the client reasonably expects.

Providing Services Under a Limited Scope Retainer

Rule Reference: Rule 3.02(15)–(17)

10. Where a paralegal provides services under a limited scope retainer to a client, it is very important to clearly identify the scope of the retainer, such as identifying the services that the paralegal will and will not be providing to the client. It is advisable that the limits of the paralegal's retainer are clearly stated in a written retainer agreement.

Practice Management

Rule Reference: Rule 3.01(4)(h)
By-Law 9

11. In a busy office, practice management includes ensuring that there is sufficient staff to assist the paralegal in fulfilling his or her professional responsibilities, for example, ensuring that communications from clients, other paralegals or lawyers are responded to and that financial records are kept in accordance with the requirements of By-Law 9.
12. Competent practice management requires that the paralegal effectively manage his or her staff, time, finances and client information. A paralegal should consider the following practice management tools:
   - workplace policies and business procedures for staff,
   - planning and reminder systems, and time docketing systems for time management, and

- filing organizational and storage systems for management of client information and a system for effectively identifying and avoiding conflicts.

Applying Skills & Judgment

Rule Reference: Rule 3.01(4)(c), (i) & (l)

13. When serving clients, or otherwise acting in a professional capacity, a competent paralegal should understand the legal concepts, issues and facts, give careful consideration to the matters he or she handles and make decisions that are reasoned and make sense in the client's circumstances.
14. A competent paralegal knows the *Rules* and understands why each *Rule* is important. The paralegal uses this knowledge and understanding to guide his or her own conduct.

Continuing Education / Professional Development

Rule Reference: Rule 3.01(4)(j) & (k)

15. A paralegal is responsible for remaining competent throughout his or her career. A competent paralegal understands that maintaining competence is an ongoing professional commitment that requires the paralegal to constantly assess his or her knowledge and skills.

Failing to Be Competent

Rule Reference: Rule 3.01

16. The *Rules* do not require a standard of perfection. An error or omission, even though it might be actionable for damages in negligence or contract, will not necessarily constitute a breach of Rule 3.01. Conversely, incompetent professional practice may constitute professional misconduct whether or not the error or omission is actionable through the courts for professional negligence. While damages may be awarded for negligence, incompetence can give rise to the additional sanction of disciplinary action.

GUIDELINE 7: ADVISING CLIENTS

Honesty and Candour

Rule Reference: 3.02(2)

1. A paralegal has a duty of candour with the client on matters relevant to the retainer. A paralegal is required to inform the client of information known to the paralegal that may affect the interests of the client in the matter.
2. A paralegal must honestly and candidly advise the client regarding the law and the client's options, possible outcomes and risks of his or her matter, so that the client is able to make informed decisions and give the paralegal appropriate instructions regarding the case. Fulfillment of this professional responsibility may require a difficult but necessary conversation with a client and/or delivery of bad news. It can be helpful for advice that is not well-received by the client to be given or confirmed by the paralegal in writing.

   When advising a client, a paralegal

   - should explain to and obtain agreement from the client about what legal services the paralegal will provide and at what cost. Subject to any specific

instructions or agreement, the client does not direct every step taken in a matter. Many decisions made in carrying out the delivery of legal services are the responsibility of the paralegal, not the client, as they require the exercise of professional judgment. However, the paralegal and the client should agree on the specific client goals to be met as a result of the retainer. This conversation is particularly important in the circumstances of a limited scope retainer.
- should explain to the client under what circumstances he or she may not be able to follow the client's instructions (for example, where the instructions would cause the paralegal to violate the *Rules*).
- should ensure that clients understand that the paralegal is not a lawyer and should take steps to correct any misapprehension on the part of a client, or prospective client.

3. In some limited circumstances, it may be appropriate to withhold information from a client. For example, with client consent, a paralegal may act where the paralegal receives information in the course of representing the client on the basis that the paralegal is not permitted to share the information with the client. However, it would not be appropriate to act for a client where the paralegal has relevant material information about that client received through a different retainer. In those circumstances the paralegal cannot be honest and candid with the client and should not act.

Dishonesty, Fraud or Crime by Client or Others

Rule Reference: Rule 3.02(4), (5), (6), (7) & (8)
Rule 3.08
By-Law 9

4. A paralegal must be alert to the warning signs that may indicate dishonesty or illegal conduct by a client or any other person. The paralegal may need to, or be forced to, withdraw from representing a client where the client takes part in this type of dishonourable conduct.
5. The requirement in subrule (5) is especially important where a paralegal has suspicions or doubts about whether he or she might be assisting a client in crime or fraud. For example, if a paralegal is consulted by a prospective client who requests the paralegal to deposit an amount of cash into the paralegal's trust account but is vague about the purpose of the retainer, the paralegal has an obligation to make further inquiries about the retainer. (The paralegal should also have regard to the provisions of By-Law 9 regarding cash transactions). The paralegal should make a record of the results of these inquiries.
6. A client or another person may attempt to use a paralegal's trust account for improper purposes, such as hiding funds, money laundering or tax sheltering. These situations highlight the fact that when handling trust funds, it is important for a paralegal to be aware of his or her obligations under the Rules and the Law Society's By-laws regulating the handling of trust funds.
7. Rule 3.02(8) speaks of conduct that is dishonest, fraudulent, criminal or illegal, and this conduct would include acts of omission as well as acts of commission. Conduct likely to result in substantial harm to the organization, as opposed to genuinely trivial misconduct by an organization, would invoke these rules.

Settlement and Dispute Resolution

Rule Reference: Rule 3.02(11) & (12)

8. A paralegal has an important role to play in both commencing and settling legal proceedings.
9. The paralegal should assist the client in his or her decision about commencing legal proceedings by reviewing the reasons for and against starting the proceeding, and explaining the potential consequences of a decision to commence litigation.
10. In the course of the proceedings, the paralegal should seek the client's instructions to make an offer of settlement to the other party as soon as reasonably possible. As soon as possible after receipt of an offer of settlement from the other party, the paralegal must explain to the client the terms of the offer, the implications of accepting the offer and the possibility of making a counter-offer. When making an offer of settlement, a paralegal should allow the other party reasonable time for review and acceptance of the offer. The paralegal should not make, accept or reject an offer of settlement without the client's clear and informed instructions. To avoid any misunderstandings, the paralegal should confirm the client's instructions in writing.

Client with Diminished Capacity

Rule Reference: Rule 3.02(13) & (14)
Rule 2.03

11. A paralegal must be particularly sensitive to the individual needs of a client under a disability. The paralegal should maintain a good professional relationship with the client, even if the client's ability to make decisions is impaired because of minority, mental disability or some other reason. The paralegal should also be aware of his or her duty to accommodate a client with a disability.
12. A paralegal who is asked to provide services under a limited scope retainer to a client under a disability should carefully consider and assess in each case how, under the circumstances, it is possible to render those services in a competent manner.

MEDICAL-LEGAL REPORTS

Rule Reference: Rule 3.02(18), (19) & (20)

13. On occasion, in the course of representing and advising a client, a paralegal may need to obtain a report from an expert to help the client's case. Since a medical-legal report may contain information sensitive to the client, a paralegal has special responsibilities where such reports are concerned.
14. After an expert has been hired, but before the report has been prepared, the paralegal should speak to the expert to see if the findings in the report will advance the client's cause. If the findings do not, and subject to any legal requirements, the paralegal may decide not to obtain a *written* report.

Errors

Rule Reference: Rule 3.02(21)

15. When providing legal services, the paralegal may make a mistake or fail to do something he or she should have done. When the paralegal realizes this has happened, he or she must fulfill specific duties to the client.

Official Language Rights

Rule Reference: Rule 3.02(22)

16. When advising French-speaking clients, a paralegal should advise a client of his or her French language rights under each of the following (where appropriate):
    - Subsection 19(1) of the *Constitution Act, 1982* on the use of French or English in any court established by Parliament,
    - Section 530 of the *Criminal Code* (Canada) on an accused's right to a trial before a court that speaks the official language of Canada that is the language of the accused,
    - Section 126 of the *Courts of Justice Act* that requires that a proceeding in which the client is a party be conducted as a bilingual (English and French) proceeding, and
    - Subsection 5(1) of the *French Language Services Act* for services in French from Ontario government agencies and legislative institutions.

Multi-Discipline Practices

Rule Reference: Rule 3.04(14)
Rule 8.01(5)
Rule 1.01 definitions of "associate" and "professional misconduct"
By-Law 7

17. In a multi-discipline practice, a paralegal should be particularly alert to ensure that the client understands that he or she is receiving legal services only from the paralegal. If advice or service is sought from non-licensed members of the firm, it should be sought and provided independently of and outside the scope of the retainer for the provision of legal services. A paralegal should also be aware that advice or services provided by a non-licensed member of the firm will be subject to the constraints outlined in the relevant by-laws and rules governing multi-discipline practices. One way to distinguish the advice or services of non-licensed members of the firm is to ensure that such advice or services is provided from a location separate from the premises of the multi-discipline practice.

Affiliations

Rule Reference: Rule 3.04(15), (16) & (17)
Rule 1.01 definitions of "affiliated entity" and "affiliation"
By-Law 7

18. Before accepting a retainer, the *Rules* impose certain disclosure and consent requirements on a paralegal providing legal services jointly with non-legal services of an affiliated entity.

GUIDELINE 8: CONFIDENTIALITY

General

Rule Reference: Rule 3.03(1)

1. A paralegal cannot render effective professional service to a client, unless there is full and unreserved communication between them. The client must feel completely

secure that all matters discussed with the paralegal will be held in strict confidence. The client is entitled to proceed on this basis, without any express request or stipulation.

2. A paralegal's duty of loyalty to a client prohibits the paralegal from using any client information for a purpose other than serving the client in accordance with the terms of the retainer. A paralegal cannot disclose client information to serve another client or for his or her own benefit.

What Information Must Be Protected?

Rule Reference: Rule 3.03(1)

3. The obligation to protect client information extends to information whether or not it is relevant or irrelevant to the matter for which the paralegal is retained. The source of the information does not matter. The information could be received from the client or from others. The information may come in any form—the spoken word, paper, computer documents, e-mails, audio or video recordings. The obligation also extends to the client's papers and property, the client's identity and the fact that the client has consulted or retained the paralegal.
4. A paralegal should be cautious in accepting confidential information on an informal or preliminary basis from anyone, since possession of the information may prevent the paralegal from subsequently acting for another party in the same or a related matter.
5. Generally, unless the nature of the matter requires such disclosure, a paralegal should not disclose having been retained by a person about a particular matter; or consulted by a person about a particular matter, whether or not a paralegal–client relationship has been established between them.

How Long Does the Duty Last?

Rule Reference: Rule 3.03(2)

6. The Rules provide that the duty of confidentiality lasts indefinitely. The duty continues, even after the client or former client dies.
7. Problems can arise when information is provided to a paralegal or a paralegal firm by a prospective client. For lawyers, the duty to protect confidential information begins when a prospective client first contacts the lawyer or law firm. The courts may determine that a paralegal also owes a duty of confidentiality to prospective clients, even if the paralegal is never actually retained by the prospective client.

Who Owes the Duty?

Rule Reference: Rule 3.03(1) & (3)
Rule 8.01(1)

8. The paralegal, and all other employees of the paralegal firm, owe the duty of confidentiality to every client. A paralegal must ensure that his or her employees, and anyone involved with the client's matter, understand the duty of confidentiality as set out in the *Rules*. The paralegal is ultimately responsible, if someone employed by the paralegal discloses confidential information without client authorization or as permitted by the *Rules*.

When, If Ever, Is Disclosure of Confidential Information Permitted? Disclosure With Client Authority

Rule Reference: Rule 3.03(1)

9. Disclosure of confidential information may be authorized by the client. This authorization may be express or implied. For example, where a paralegal is retained to represent a client in a Small Claims Court matter, the paralegal has the client's implied authority to disclose enough information to complete the necessary forms.
10. When disclosing confidential information on the express authority of the client, the paralegal should consider
    - whether the client understands his or her right to confidentiality,
    - whether the client understands the potential implications of disclosure,
    - whether the client has shown a clear, informed and voluntary intention to forego the right to confidentiality, and
    - whether, in the particular circumstances, it would be prudent to obtain the client's written authorization to disclose.

Disclosure Without Client Authority: General

Rule Reference: Rule 3.03(4), (5), (6), (7) (8) & (9)

11. Rule 3.03 identifies a number of situations in which a paralegal ***shall*** or ***may*** disclose confidential client information, whether or not the client consents to the disclosure.
12. This rule does not permit the paralegal to reveal confidential information about past criminal conduct, or to prevent future illegal or criminal conduct that does not involve death or serious bodily harm.

Disclosure Without Client Authority to Prevent Serious Bodily Harm

Rule Reference: Rule 3.03(5), (8) & (9)

13. Serious psychological harm may constitute serious bodily harm if it substantially interferes with the health or well-being of an individual.
14. A paralegal who believes that disclosure may be warranted may wish to seek legal advice. In assessing whether disclosure of confidential information is justified to prevent death or serious bodily harm, the paralegal should consider a number of factors, including:
    a) the likelihood that the potential injury will occur and its imminence;
    b) the apparent absence of any other feasible way to prevent the potential injury; and
    c) the circumstances under which the paralegal acquired the information of the client's intent or prospective course of action.
15. If confidential information is disclosed, the paralegal should record the circumstances of the disclosure as soon as possible.

Disclosure Without Client Authority to Establish or Collect Fees

Rule Reference: Rule 3.03(7) & (9)

16. If a paralegal wishes to use a collection agency for an outstanding account, the information provided to the collection agency should be limited to that necessary to collect the fees. Information contained in documents that is not necessary to enforce payment should either be deleted or blocked out.

Other Obligations Relating to Confidential Information— Security of Court Facilities and Misconduct

Rule Reference: Rule 3.03
Rule 6.01(3)
Rule 9.01(2)

17. The *Rules* require a paralegal to disclose confidential client information in other circumstances—for the security of court facilities, and to report certain acts of misconduct to the Law Society.
18. Where a paralegal discloses confidential information to prevent a dangerous situation from developing at a court facility, the paralegal should consider providing this information to the persons having responsibility for security at the facility anonymously or through another paralegal or a lawyer.

Avoiding Inadvertent Disclosure

Rule Reference: Rule 3.03(1)

19. The following steps may assist a paralegal in meeting his or her obligation to protect confidential client information:
    - not disclosing having been consulted or retained by a particular person unless the nature of the matter requires disclosure,
    - taking care not to disclose to one client confidential information about another client and declining any retainer that might require such disclosure,
    - being mindful of the risk of disclosure of confidential information when the paralegal provides legal services in association with other licensees in cost-sharing, space- sharing or other arrangements, and taking steps to minimize the risk,
    - avoiding indiscreet conversations about a client's affairs, even with the paralegal's spouse or family,
    - shunning any gossip about a client's affairs, even though the client is not named or otherwise identified,
    - not repeating any gossip or information about a client's business or affairs that is overheard or recounted to the paralegal, and
    - avoiding indiscreet shop-talk between colleagues that may be overheard by third parties.

Office Procedures

Rule Reference: Rule 3.03(1) & (3)
Rule 8.01(1)

20. A paralegal should establish office procedures to ensure that the confidentiality of client information is protected, such as:
    - recording the identity and particulars of every client or potential client,
    - screening for conflicts of interest when a potential client first contacts the firm, and prior to his or her disclosure of confidential information to the paralegal,
    - establishing a communication policy with each client outlining how communications between the client and firm will be conducted,
    - keeping file cabinets away from the reception area, placing computer screens so they cannot be viewed by people not in the firm, keeping client files out of sight, locking file cabinets when no one is in the office, limiting access to client

files only to staff who work on the matter, shredding confidential information before discarding, ensuring appropriate security for off-site storage of files,
- taking steps to protect confidential information obtained and sent in an electronic form,
- ensuring that all staff understand their obligations with respect to confidentiality and,
- limiting access to confidential information by outside service providers.

GUIDELINE 9: CONFLICTS OF INTEREST

GENERAL

Definition

Examples of Conflicts of Interest

Rule Reference: Rule 1.02

1. Conflicts of interest are defined in Rule 1.02.
2. Conflicts of interest can arise in many different circumstances. The following are examples of situations in which conflicts of interest commonly arise requiring a paralegal to take particular care to determine whether a conflict of interest exists:
   (a) A paralegal acts as an advocate in one matter against a person when the paralegal represents that person on some other matter.
   (b) A paralegal, an associate, a partner or a family member has a personal financial interest in a client's affairs or in a matter in which the paralegal is requested to act for a client.
   (c) A paralegal has a sexual or close personal relationship with a client.
   (d) A paralegal or the paralegal's firm acts for a public or private corporation and the paralegal serves as a director of the corporation. These two roles may result in a conflict of interest or other problems.

DUTY TO AVOID CONFLICTS OF INTEREST

The Duty

Rule Reference: Rule 3.04(1) & (2)

3. The duty to avoid conflicts of interest is found in Rule 3.04(1) and (2).

To Whom Is the Duty Owed—Current Clients and Prospective Clients

Rule Reference: Rule 1.02 definition
Rule 3.04(1), (3), & (4)

4. A paralegal owes the duty of avoiding conflicts of interest to all clients, including prospective clients. A paralegal should identify potential conflicts of interest at the first contact with a prospective client. A ***prospective client*** can be described as one who has consulted with a paralegal or paralegal firm to see if the firm will take on his or her matter or to see if he or she would like to hire the paralegal or firm.
5. Conflicts of interest may arise at any time. A paralegal should use a conflicts checking system to assist in managing conflicts of interest. The paralegal should examine whether a conflict of interest exists not only at the outset, but throughout the duration of a retainer because new circumstances or information may establish or reveal a conflict of interest.

6. At the time that a paralegal becomes aware of a conflict, or potential conflict, the paralegal should consider whether to accept the retainer, or to continue to act. This applies even where the client consents or where the retainer would not, in the paralegal's opinion, breach the *Rules*. The paralegal should consider the delay, expense and inconvenience that would arise for the client and/or the paralegal, should the paralegal be required to withdraw from the matter at a later stage in the proceedings.

To Whom Is the Duty Owed—the Firm's Clients

Rule Reference: Rule 1.02 definition of "client"

7. Since every client of a paralegal firm is also the client of every other paralegal employed at the firm, if one paralegal in the firm has a conflict of interest in a matter, then all paralegals in the firm have a conflict in that matter. As a result, when checking for conflicts, the paralegal should review the names of all current and former clients of the firm and not just the clients personally served by the individual paralegal.

DEALING WITH A CONFLICT OF INTEREST

Disclosing All Information

Rule Reference: Rule 3.04(3) & (4)

8. Disclosure is an essential element to obtaining a client's consent. The client needs to know of anything that may influence the paralegal's judgment or loyalty. Once the paralegal has provided the client with all the details, the paralegal must allow the client time to consider them or to ask for further clarification.
9. There may be situations where it is impossible for a paralegal to give a client or prospective client all necessary information. This may happen when the details about the conflict involve another client or a former client. Since a paralegal cannot reveal confidential information regarding another client, the paralegal may only say that there is a conflict and that he or she cannot continue with or accept the retainer.

Obtaining Consent

Rule Reference: Rule 1.02 definition of "consent"
Rule 3.04(3) & (4)

10. The client may only consent after being given all information required to make an informed decision. This is called ***informed consent***.
11. A paralegal may be able to request that a client consent in advance to conflicts that might arise in the future. The effectiveness of such consent is generally determined by the extent to which the client understands the material risks involved. A paralegal may wish to recommend that the client obtain independent legal advice before deciding whether to provide consent. Advance consent should be recorded in writing.
12. The *Rules* permit consent to be implied in some circumstances.

Independent Legal Advice/Legal Representation

Rule Reference: Rules 3.04(8), 3.06(2)(b) and 3.06(4)(b), 3.06(6)(c)

13. There are situations where the client's informed and written consent is not enough to allow the paralegal to accept or continue with a matter. In some circumstances, the client must receive advice from an independent legal advisor regarding the matter or transaction before the paralegal may taken any further steps in the client's matter.
14. An independent legal advisor is another paralegal or lawyer, who can provide the client with ***independent legal advice***. This advisor is unrelated to the client's matter, associated parties or the paralegal. He or she is unbiased and objective and does not have a conflict of interest.
15. In circumstances where the paralegal is prohibited from acting for a client or prospective client, the paralegal must suggest that the individual obtain his or her own independent legal representation. ***Independent legal representation*** means that the individual has retained a legal representative, either a paralegal or lawyer, to act as his or her own representative in the matter. This retained representative is objective and does not have any conflicting interest with regards to the matter.

Refusal to Act, Withdrawal of Services

Rule Reference: Rules 3.04(1) and 3.08

16. In some cases, the only way to deal with the conflict is to refuse to act. The paralegal may have to decline the retainer at the outset or may have to terminate the retainer and withdraw from representing the client at a later time. A paralegal may need to take this step even where the client wants the paralegal to accept the retainer, or to continue to act.

JOINT CLIENTS

General

Rule Reference: Rule 3.04(8)–(14)

17. A paralegal may be asked to represent more than one client in a matter or transaction. This is referred to as a ***joint retainer***.
18. Acting in a joint retainer places the paralegal in a potential conflict of interest. A paralegal has an obligation to all clients and in a joint retainer, the paralegal must remain loyal and devoted to all clients equally—the paralegal cannot choose to serve one client more carefully or resolutely than any other. If the interests of one client change during the course of the retainer, the paralegal may be in a conflict of interest.

Before Accepting the Joint Retainer

Rule Reference: Rule 3.04(7)–(13)
Rule 3.02(13) & (14)

19. In cases where one of the joint clients is not sophisticated or is vulnerable, the paralegal should consider the provisions of Rule 3.02(13) and (14) regarding clients under a disability. The paralegal may want to recommend that the client obtain independent legal advice prior to agreeing to the joint retainer. This will

ensure that the client's consent to the joint retainer is informed, genuine not obtained through coercion.

If a Conflict Develops Between Joint Clients

Rule Reference: Rule 3.04(12)–(13)

20. Subrules 3.04(12)–(13) set out the steps a paralegal must take in the event that a conflict develops between joint clients.

ACTING AGAINST CLIENTS

Acting Against Former Clients in the Same or Related Matters

Rule Reference: Rule 3.04(2), (5)(a) & (b)

21. A paralegal is not permitted to act against a former client in the same or related matters, except with the former client's informed consent.

Acting Against Former Clients in New Matters

Rule Reference: Rule 3.04(5)(c), (6)

22. A paralegal is permitted to act against a former client in a new matter, except in accordance with subrules 3.04(5)(c) and (6).
23. Even where the *Rules* do not prohibit a paralegal from acting against a client or former client, the paralegal should consider whether to accept the retainer (or continue acting). To act against a client or former client may damage the paralegal–client relationship, may result in court proceedings or a complaint to the Law Society.

PARALEGAL TRANSFER BETWEEN FIRMS

General

Rule Reference: Rule 3.05

24. Problems concerning confidential information may arise when a paralegal changes firms and the firms act for opposing clients in the same or a related matter. The potential risk is that confidential information about the client from the paralegal's former office may be revealed to the members of the new firm and used against that client. A paralegal should carefully review the *Rules* when transferring to a new office or when a new paralegal is about to join the paralegal firm.

DEALING WITH UNREPRESENTED PERSONS

General

Rule Reference: Rule 4.05
Rule 3.04(7)–(13)

25. When a paralegal deals on a client's behalf with an unrepresented person, there is a potential danger to the paralegal that the unrepresented person may think that the paralegal is looking after his or her interests. Rule 4.05 provides specific requirements aimed at minimizing this risk.
26. If an unrepresented person who is the opposite party requests the paralegal to advise or act in the matter, the paralegal is not permitted to accept the retainer. If

the unrepresented party otherwise has an interest in the matter, such as a co-accused, the paralegal may be permitted to act, but should be governed by the considerations outlined in Rule 3.04(7)–(13) about joint retainers.

FINANCIAL INTERESTS

Doing Business with a Client

Rule Reference: Rule 3.06(1)–(3)

27. A paralegal should be cautious about entering into a business arrangement with his or her client(s) that is unrelated to the provision of paralegal services. This includes any transaction with a client, including lending or borrowing money, buying or selling property, accepting a gift, giving or acquiring ownership, security or other pecuniary interest in a company or other entity, recommending an investment and entering into a common business venture.
28. Since the paralegal is or was the client's advisor, the paralegal may have a conflict of interest. The paralegal may unknowingly influence the client to agree to an arrangement that may be unfair or unreasonable to the client. This danger is present when the client wants to invest with the paralegal.

Borrowing from Clients

Rule Reference: Rule 3.06(5)

29. A paralegal must not borrow from clients except in accordance with Rule 3.06(4).

Guaranteeing Client Debts

Rule Reference: Rule 3.06(5)–(6)

30. A paralegal must not guarantee client debts except in accordance with Rule 3.06(5) and (6).

PERSONAL INTERESTS

Conflicts of Interest Arising from Personal Relationships

Rule Reference: Rule 3.04(1)

31. The *Rules* do not prohibit a paralegal from providing legal services to friends or family members, but they do require the paralegal to avoid existing or potential conflicts of interest.
32. A conflict of interest may arise when a paralegal provides legal services to a friend or family member, or when the client and the paralegal have a sexual or intimate personal relationship. In these circumstances, the paralegal's personal feelings for the client may impede the paralegal's ability to provide objective, disinterested professional advice to the client. Before accepting a retainer from or continuing a retainer with a person with whom the paralegal has a sexual or intimate personal relationship, a paralegal should consider the following factors:
    - The vulnerability of the client, both emotional and economic;
    - The fact that the paralegal and client relationship may create a power imbalance in favour of the paralegal or, in some circumstances, in favour of the client;
    - Whether the sexual or intimate personal relationship may jeopardize the client's right to have all information concerning the client's business and affairs held in

strict confidence. For example, the existence of the personal relationship may obscure whether certain information was acquired by the paralegal in the course of the paralegal and client relationship;

- Whether such a relationship may require the paralegal to act as a witness in the proceedings;
- Whether such a relationship may interfere with the paralegal's fiduciary obligations to the client, including his or her ability to exercise independent professional judgment and his or her ability to fulfill obligations to the administration of justice.

33. Generally speaking, there is no conflict of interest if another paralegal or lawyer at the firm who does not have a sexual or intimate personal relationship with the client, handles the client's matter.

Conflicts of Interest Arising from a Paralegal's Outside Interests

Rule Reference: **Rule 1.02 definition of "conflict of interest"**
Rule 2.01(4) & (5)

34. A conflict of interest may arise from the paralegal's outside interests. Outside interests covers the widest possible range of activities and includes those that may overlap with the business of providing legal services, as well as activities that have no connection to the law or working as a paralegal. If a paralegal has other businesses or interests separate from his or her paralegal firm, those interests may influence the way the paralegal serves clients. Whatever the outside interest, a paralegal must guard against allowing those outside interests to interfere or conflict with his or her duties to clients. (Also refer to Guideline 2: Outside Interests).
35. If a paralegal is in public office while still providing legal services to clients, the paralegal must not allow his or her duties as a public official to conflict with his or her duties as a paralegal. If there is a possibility of a conflict of interest, the paralegal should avoid it either by removing himself or herself from the discussion and voting in the public capacity or by withdrawing from representation of the client.

MULTI-DISCIPLINE PRACTICE

Conflicts of Interest Arising from Multi-Discipline Practice

Rule Reference: **3.04(14)**
By-Law 7

36. A paralegal should be alert to conflicts of interest arising from a multi-discipline practice, as he or she is subject to the requirements of Rule 3.04(14).

AFFILIATIONS

Conflicts of Interest Arising from Paralegals and Affiliated Entities

Rule Reference: **Rule 1.02 definition of "conflict of interest"**
Rule 3.04(15), (16) & (17)
By-Law 7

37. A conflict of interest may arise from a paralegal's, or his or her associate's, interest in an affiliated firm of non-licensees where that interest conflicts with the paralegal's duties to a client. Rule 3.04(15) and (16) impose disclosure and consent requirements on a paralegal in an affiliation.

38. Conflicts of interest arising out of a proposed retainer by a client should be addressed as if the paralegal's practice and the practice of the affiliated entity were one where the paralegal accepts a retainer to provide legal services to that client jointly with non-legal services of the affiliated entity.
39. The affiliation is subject to the same conflict of interest rules as apply to paralegals.

GUIDELINE 10: DEALING WITH CLIENT PROPERTY

General

Rule Reference: Rule 3.07
By-Law 9

1. The term ***client property*** covers a wide range of items such as money or other valuables, physical items and information. For proper receipt, handling and disbursement of monies received from or on behalf of a client, refer to By-Law 9 and Guideline 15: Trust Accounts.

The Valuable Property Record

Rule Reference: By-Law 9, section 18.9

2. The valuable property record documents the paralegal's receipt, storage and delivery of client property. Client property may include, for example:
   - stocks, bonds or other securities in bearer form,
   - jewelry, paintings, furs, collector's items or any saleable valuables, and
   - any property that a paralegal can convert to cash on his or her own authority.
3. The valuable property record should not include items that cannot be sold or negotiated by the paralegal, for example, wills, securities registered in the client's name, corporate records or seals. A paralegal should maintain a list of these items, but that list should be separate from the valuable property record.

The Client File

Rule Reference: Rule 3.07
Rule 3.03(3)

4. The duty to preserve client property also applies to the documents that a client may give to the paralegal at the beginning of the paralegal-client relationship and documents that are created or collected by the paralegal for the client's benefit during the relationship.
5. The courts have developed law on the issue of the client file as between lawyers and clients. This jurisprudence may be applied to define the paralegal's client file in future. Generally, documents provided to a lawyer at the start of the retainer and those created during the retainer as part of the services provided, would belong to the client. These include
   - originals of all documents prepared for the client,
   - all copies of documents for which copies the client has paid,
   - a copy of letters from a lawyer to third parties or from a lawyer to third parties,
   - originals of letters from a lawyer to the client (presumably these would have already been sent to the client in the course of the retainer),
   - copies of case law,
   - briefs,

- memoranda of law, where the client paid for preparation of the memoranda,
- notes or memoranda of meetings with opposing parties or their representatives, court or tribunal conferences, interviews of witnesses, etc.,
- trial preparation documents, trial briefs, document briefs, trial books,
- copies of vouchers and receipts for disbursements a lawyer made on the client's behalf,
- experts' reports,
- photographs, and
- electronic media such as computer discs.

6. Documents belonging to a lawyer (for example, notes or memoranda of meetings or telephone calls with the client) would not need to be provided to the client.
7. A paralegal should consider retaining copies of client documents, at his or her own cost, to defend against complaints or claims that may be made against the paralegal in future.

GUIDELINE 11: WITHDRAWAL FROM REPRESENTATION

General

Rule Reference: Rule 3.08

1. A client may end the paralegal-client relationship at any time and for any reason. A paralegal is subject to certain restrictions in ending the paralegal-client relationship. The Rule requires reasonable notice; an essential element of reasonable notice is notification to the client, unless the client cannot be located after reasonable efforts.
2. Whether the paralegal has good cause for withdrawal will depend on many factors, including
   - the nature and stage of the matter,
   - the relationship with the client,
   - the paralegal's expertise and experience, and
   - any harm or prejudice to the client that may result from the withdrawal.
3. Rule 3.08 specifies a paralegal's obligations when withdrawing legal services. It sets out situations in which the paralegal
   - may choose to withdraw (***optional withdrawal***),
   - must withdraw (***mandatory withdrawal***), and
   - must comply with special rules (***withdrawal from quasi-criminal and criminal cases***).
4. To avoid misunderstandings, it will be helpful for the paralegal to explain to the client, at the beginning of the relationship
   - that all documents to which the client is entitled will be returned to the client when their relationship ends or the matter concludes, and
   - which documents in the file will belong to the paralegal, so that they will be kept by the paralegal when their relationship ends or the matter is finished.
5. To ensure that the client understands these details, the paralegal should consider including them in his or her engagement letter or retainer agreement.
6. Every effort should be made to ensure that withdrawal occurs at an appropriate time in the proceedings in keeping with the paralegal's obligations. The tribunal, opposing parties and others directly affected should also be notified of the withdrawal.

7. When the paralegal withdraws, he or she is subject to restrictions relating to the disclosure of client information. This would restrict the paralegal from revealing the reason for withdrawing to a ***successor*** (a paralegal or lawyer who accepts the client's matter after the original paralegal has withdrawn). Refer to Guideline 8: Confidentiality for further information on this subject.
8. Cooperation with the successor licensee will normally include providing any memoranda of fact or law that have been prepared by the paralegal in connection with the matter, but confidential information not clearly related to the matter should not be disclosed without the written consent of the client.

Optional Withdrawal

Rule Reference: Rule 3.08(2), (3), (4), (6), (7), (8) & (9)

9. During a retainer, a situation may arise that will allow the paralegal to withdraw from representing the client.
10. A ***serious loss of confidence*** means that the paralegal and the client can no longer trust and rely on each other, making it impossible to have a normal paralegal–client relationship. An example would be where the client deceives or lies to the paralegal. Another example would be where the client refuses unreasonably to accept and act on the paralegal's advice on an important point.
11. If the retainer relates to a criminal or quasi-criminal matter, the paralegal must ensure that he or she complies with the special rules relating to withdrawal in those types of cases (refer to section entitled "Withdrawal from Quasi-Criminal and Criminal Cases" at Rule 3.08(7)).

Mandatory Withdrawal

Rule Reference: Rule 3.08(5), (7), (8) & (9)

12. In certain situations, a paralegal is required to withdraw from representing a client, even if the paralegal or the client wishes to continue with the retainer.

Withdrawal from Criminal or Quasi-Criminal Matters

Rule Reference: Rule 3.08(7), (8) & (9)

13. Whether a paralegal may withdraw in these types of matters has to do with the amount of time between ***the withdrawal*** (the date and time the paralegal intends to stop representing the client) and ***the trial*** (the date and time the client's trial begins).
14. Generally, the amount of time between the withdrawal and trial must be sufficient to allow the client to hire another representative and the new representative to prepare properly for trial.
15. While the *Rules* do not require the paralegal to make an application to be removed as the client's representative, most tribunal rules do. Therefore, the paralegal should consult the rules of the tribunal to determine what process is to be followed. The paralegal must not tell the tribunal or the prosecutor the reasons for withdrawal, unless disclosure is justified in accordance with the *Rules*.
16. The paralegal may seek to adjourn the trial to give the client or the new representative more time to prepare, as long as the adjournment does not prejudice the client.

Manner of Withdrawal

Rule Reference: Rules 3.08(10), (11), (12) & (13)

17. Where a paralegal withdraws from representation of a client, the required manner of withdrawal is set out in subrules 3.08(10), (11), (12) and (13).

Duties of the Successor Paralegal

Rule Reference: Rule 3.08(14)

18. If a client who was represented by another paralegal or a lawyer contacts a paralegal, that paralegal has obligations as the ***successor paralegal***.

Written Confirmation

19. If a paralegal's services are terminated while the client's matter is ongoing and the client requests that the matter be transferred to a new paralegal or lawyer, the paralegal should confirm, in writing, the termination of the retainer. The paralegal should also obtain a ***direction***, signed by the client, for release of the client's file to a successor paralegal or lawyer. A ***direction*** is a written document instructing the paralegal to release the file to the successor paralegal or lawyer. If the file will be collected by the client personally, the paralegal should obtain a written acknowledgement signed by the client, confirming that the client has received the file.

GUIDELINE 12: ADVOCACY

Definitions

Rule Reference: Rule 4
Rule 1.02 definition of "tribunal"

1. An ***advocate*** is someone who speaks and acts on behalf of others. Rule 4 outlines a paralegal's duties when appearing as an advocate before a tribunal. Rule 4 applies to all appearances and all proceedings before all tribunals. A ***tribunal*** can be either an administrative board or a court of law. An ***adjudicator*** is any person who hears or considers any type of proceeding before a tribunal and renders a decision with respect to that proceeding.

General

Rule Reference: Rule 4

2. The paralegal has a duty to represent his or her client diligently and fearlessly. Generally, the paralegal has no obligation to assist an opposing party, or to advance matters harmful to the client's case. However, these general principles do not mean that, when acting as advocate for a client before a tribunal, the paralegal can behave as he or she likes or, in some cases, as his or her client may instruct. Rule 4 describes the professional obligations that a paralegal owes to opposing parties, other paralegals and lawyers, the tribunal and the administration of justice. These obligations are paramount, and must be met by the paralegal in each and every tribunal proceeding in which the paralegal acts as advocate for a client.

Candour, Fairness, Courtesy and Respect

Rule Reference: Rule 4.01(1), 4.01(4)(d)
Rule 4.01(5)(o)
Rule 7.01(3)

3. A paralegal should not engage in rude and disruptive behaviour before a tribunal, or uncivil correspondence, language or behaviour towards opposing parties or their advocates.

Malicious Proceedings

Rule Reference: Rule 4.01(5)(a)

4. A paralegal should not help a client to bring proceedings that have no merit. Claims that have no merit waste the time of the tribunal and its officers, and do not further the cause of justice.

Misleading the Tribunal

Rule Reference: Rule 4.01(5)(c), (d), (f), (i), (j) & (k)

5. A paralegal must ensure that neither the paralegal nor his or her client(s) misleads the tribunal. For a tribunal to decide a matter effectively and appropriately, the tribunal must have access to everything that is relevant to the issues to be decided.

Improperly Influencing the Tribunal

Rule Reference: Rule 4.01(5)(e) & (h)

6. For the public to have respect for the administration of justice, tribunals must be fair, objective, independent and neutral. There should be no personal connection between an adjudicator and any of the parties to a proceeding or their advocates.
7. The only appropriate way to influence the tribunal's decision is through open persuasion as an advocate. This is done by making submissions based on legal principles and offering appropriate evidence before the tribunal in the presence of, or on notice to, all parties to the proceeding, or as otherwise permitted or required by the tribunal's rules of procedure. A paralegal should not communicate directly with the adjudicator in the absence of the other parties, unless permitted to do so by the tribunal's rules of procedure.

Dishonest Conduct

Rule Reference: Rule 4.01(5)(b), (c) & (f)

8. Acting with integrity before a tribunal means being honest and acting with high ethical principles.

Admissions by the Client

Rule Reference: Rule 4.01(5)(b), (c) & (f)

9. When defending an accused person, a paralegal's duty is to protect the client from being convicted, except by a tribunal of competent jurisdiction and upon legal evidence sufficient to support a conviction for the offence with which the client is charged. Accordingly, a paralegal may properly rely on any evidence or defences, including "technicalities", as long as they are not known to be false or fraudulent.

10. However, admissions made by a client to a paralegal may impose strict limitations on the paralegal's conduct of the client's defence. The client should be made aware of this by the paralegal. Where the client has admitted to the paralegal any or all of the elements of the offence with which the client is charged, a paralegal must not do or say anything before the tribunal, including calling any evidence, that would contradict the facts admitted by the client to the paralegal. This would be misleading the court.
11. Where the client has admitted to the paralegal all the elements of the offence, and the paralegal is convinced that the admissions are true and voluntary, the paralegal may properly take objection to the jurisdiction of the tribunal, or to the form, admissibility or sufficiency of the evidence. The paralegal could not suggest that someone else committed the offence, try to establish an alibi or call any evidence which, by reason of the admissions, the paralegal believes to be false. Admission by the client to the paralegal of all of the elements of the offence with which the paralegal is charged also limits the extent to which the paralegal may attack the evidence for the prosecution. The paralegal may test the evidence given by each witness for the prosecution and may argue that the evidence, as a whole, is not enough to prove the client guilty. The paralegal should go no further than that.

Witnesses

Rule Reference: Rule 4.01(5) (g), (i), (j), (l), (m) & (n)
Rule 4.02
Rule 4.03
Rule 7.01(6)

12. As an advocate, a paralegal may contact all possible witnesses for both sides of a matter, (subject to Rule 7.02 regarding communications with a represented person, corporation, or organization,) but the paralegal must be fair and honest when dealing with them. This includes the paralegal speaking to the opposing party or co-accused. The paralegal must make it clear to the witness who is the paralegal's client(s) and that that the paralegal is acting only in the interests of his or her client(s). As part of this disclosure, the paralegal should give the witness his or her name, tell the witness that he or she is a paralegal, the name of the client(s) he or she represents in the matter, and his or her status in the proceeding. A paralegal should make an extra effort to be clear when the witness does not have legal representation. Note that, although a paralegal may ask to speak to a potential witness, the witness does not have to speak to the paralegal.
13. During a hearing, a paralegal's ability to speak with a witness giving testimony is limited. This ensures that the paralegal does not influence the evidence the witness will give. A comment made by the paralegal to the paralegal's own witness during court recess, for example, may result in a breach of the *Rules*. The witness may return to the witness box and, as a result of the communication with the paralegal, offer evidence that is slanted to benefit the paralegal's client. Such evidence is no longer neutral and could mislead the tribunal.

Disclosure of Documents

Rule Reference: Rule 4.01(6)

14. The rules of procedure of the tribunal may require parties to produce documents and information to the tribunal or to the other parties in the matter. Timely, complete and accurate disclosure helps settlement efforts and makes the hearing process more effective and fair.

Agreement on Guilty Pleas

Rule Reference: Rule 4.01(8) & (9)

15. As an advocate for a person accused in a criminal or quasi-criminal matter, the paralegal should take steps reasonable in the circumstances to satisfy himself or herself that the client's instructions to enter into the agreement on a guilty plea is informed and voluntary. The paralegal should ensure the client's instructions to enter into an agreement on a guilty plea are in writing.

The Paralegal as Witness

Rule Reference: Rule 4.04

16. As an advocate, the paralegal's role is to further the client's case within the limits of the law. The role of a witness is to give evidence of facts that may or may not assist in furthering the case of any of the parties to a proceeding. Because these roles are different, a person may not be able to carry out the functions of both advocate and witness at the same time.

17. Unless permitted by the Tribunal, when acting as an advocate for his or her client before a tribunal, the paralegal should not express personal opinions or beliefs or assert as a fact anything that is properly subject to legal proof, cross-examination, or challenge, or otherwise appear to be giving unsworn testimony. This is improper and may put the paralegal's own credibility in issue.

17.1 Unless permitted by the tribunal, the paralegal who is a necessary witness should testify and entrust the conduct of the case to another licensee. A paralegal who has appeared as a witness on a matter should not act as an advocate or legal representative in any appeal of that matter.

17.2 There are no restrictions on the advocate's right to cross-examine another licensee, however, and the paralegal who does appear as a witness should not expect to receive special treatment because of professional status.

Dealing with Unrepresented Persons

Rule Reference: Rule 4.05

18. The paralegal has a special duty when representing a client and an opposing party is not represented by a paralegal or a lawyer.

19. To avoid misunderstandings, it will be helpful for the paralegal to confirm in writing the steps he or she takes to fulfill the requirements of Rule 4.05.

Withdrawal and Disclosure Obligations

Rule Reference: Rule 4.01(7)
Rule 3.08

20. If, after explanation and advice from the paralegal, the client persists in instructing the paralegal to engage in or continue a type of conduct prohibited by Rule 4, the paralegal must withdraw from representing the client in the matter. (See Guideline 11: Withdrawal of Representation).

GUIDELINE 13: FEES

Introduction

Rule Reference: Rule 5.01(1)

1. Too often, misunderstandings about fees and disbursements result in disputes over legal bills and complaints from unhappy clients. Since these disputes reflect badly on the paralegal profession and the administration of justice, it is important that a paralegal discuss with his or her client(s) the amount of fees and disbursements that will likely be charged. It will be to the benefit of all concerned if the paralegal ensures that the client has a clear understanding not only of what legal services the paralegal will provide, but how much those services are likely to cost.

Fees and Disbursements

2. Generally, a ***fee*** refers to the paralegal's wage. Clients pay fees for the legal services provided by the paralegal. Fees may be billed in a variety of ways, including:
   - An *hourly rate*, charging for the actual time spent on the client matter,
   - A *block, fixed or flat fee*, charging a fixed amount for performing a particular task,
   - *Fees by stages*, charging for a matter which is broken down into stages, and an estimate is given as to the fee for each stage or step in the matter, or
   - *Contingency fees*, where part or all of the paralegal's fee depends on the successful completion of the matter, and the amount may be expressed as a percentage of the client's recovery in the matter.
3. The paralegal should consider which method best suits the circumstances and the client.
4. A ***disbursement*** refers to any expense that the paralegal pays on behalf of the client for which the paralegal is entitled to be reimbursed by the client. Common disbursements include charges for
   - research, such as Quicklaw charges or research conducted by third party professionals,
   - mileage,
   - postage, photocopying, faxing documents or sending documents by courier,
   - long-distance phone calls,
   - expert reports,
   - transcripts or certified documents, and/or
   - tribunal or court filing fees related to the client matter.
5. A paralegal cannot charge more than the actual cost of the disbursement. A paralegal cannot make a profit from disbursements at the client's expense.

Discussing Fees and Disbursements

Rule Reference: Rule 5.01(1)

6. The following are steps that will assist a paralegal in meeting his or her obligations under Rule 5.01(1).
   (a) A paralegal should provide to the client in writing, before or within a reasonable time after commencing a representation, as much information regarding fees and disbursements, and interest as is reasonable and practical in the circumstances, including the basis on which fees will be determined;
   (b) A paralegal should confirm with the client in writing the substance of all fee discussions that occur as a matter progresses. The paralegal may revise the initial estimate of fees and disbursements.
   (c) A paralegal should openly disclose and discuss with clients all items that will be charged as disbursements and how those amounts will be calculated. If an administrative charge forms part of the amount charged as a disbursement, disclosure of such charge should be made to the client(s) in advance.
7. In discussing fees and disbursements with clients, it is appropriate for a paralegal to
   - provide a reasonable estimate of the total cost as opposed to an unreasonable estimate designed to garner the client's business, and
   - not manipulate fees and disbursements in a manner as to provide a lower fee estimate.
8. When something happens in the matter that the paralegal or client did not expect, resulting in costs that are higher than the paralegal's original estimate, the paralegal should immediately give the client a revised estimate of cost, and an explanation of why the original estimate has changed. The client can then instruct the paralegal based on the new information. The new understanding should be confirmed in writing.

Hidden Fees

Rule Reference: Rule 5.01(3)

9. The relationship between paralegal and client is based on trust. The client must be able to rely on the paralegal's honesty and ability to act in the client's best interests. This means that the paralegal cannot hide from the client any financial dealings in his or her matter.

Payment and Appropriation of Funds

Rule Reference: Rule 5.01(5)
Rule 2.01(1)

10. The *Rules* are not intended to be an exhaustive statement of the considerations that apply to payment of a paralegal's account from trust. The handling of trust money is generally governed by the by-laws of the Law Society.
11. Refusing to reimburse any portion of advance fees for work that has not been carried out when the contract of professional services with the client has terminated is a breach of the obligation to act with integrity.

Fee Splitting and Referral Fees

Rule Reference: Rule 5.01(11), (12) & (13)
By-Law 7 (Multi-Discipline Practices)

12. ***Fee splitting*** occurs when a paralegal shares or divides his or her fee with another person.

    Where a client consents, a paralegal and another paralegal or lawyer who are not at the same firm may divide between them the fees for a matter, so long as the fees are split relative to the work done and the responsibility assumed by each paralegal and/or lawyer. Multi-discipline practices are exempt from the prohibition against fee-splitting in certain circumstances.
13. A ***referral fee*** is
    - a fee paid by a paralegal to another paralegal or lawyer for referring a client to the paralegal, or
    - a fee paid to the paralegal by another paralegal or lawyer for his or her referral of a person to another paralegal or lawyer.
14. The *Rules* do not prohibit a paralegal from:
    (a) Making an arrangement respecting the purchase and sale of a professional business when the consideration payable includes a percentage of revenues generated from the business sold;
    (b) Entering into a lease under which a landlord directly or indirectly shares in the fees or revenues generated by the provision of legal services;
    (c) Paying an employee for services, other than for referring clients, based on the revenue of the paralegal's firm or professional business.

The Statement of Account

Rule Reference: Rule 5.01(4)

15. In addition to detailing fees and disbursements, the ***statement of account*** or bill delivered to the client by the paralegal should detail clearly and separately the amount the paralegal has charged for Harmonized Sales Tax (HST). The HST applies to fees and some disbursements, as outlined by the Canada Revenue Agency (CRA) guidelines. The paralegal should review and sign the statement of account before it is sent to the client.
16. Should a dispute arise about the statement of account, the paralegal should discuss the matter openly and calmly with the client in an effort to resolve the matter. Civility and professionalism must govern all discussions, including discussions relating to fee disputes with clients.

Contingency Fees

Rule Reference: Rule 5.01(6)–(8)

17. A ***contingency fee*** is a fee that is paid when and if a particular result is achieved in a client's matter.
18. Rule 5.01(7) outlines the factors to be considered in determining the appropriate percentage (or other basis) of the contingency fee agreement. Regardless of which factors are used to determine the fee and the other terms of the contingency fee agreement, the ultimate fee must still be fair and reasonable.

19. The contingency fee agreement should be clear about how the fee will be calculated.
20. It may be helpful for a paralegal to refer to *Regulation 195/04* to the *Solicitor's Act* (which applies to contingency fees for lawyers) for guidance as to what terms should be included in a paralegal contingency fee agreement.

GUIDELINE 14: RETAINERS

General

1. In the context of providing legal services, the word ***retainer*** may mean any or all of the following:
   - the client's act of hiring the paralegal to provide legal services (i.e., a ***retainer***),
   - the contract that outlines the legal services the paralegal will provide to the client and the fees and disbursements and HST to be paid by the client (i.e., a ***retainer agreement***), or
   - monies paid by the client to the paralegal in advance to secure his or her services in the near future and against which future fees will be charged (i.e., a ***money retainer***).

The Retainer Agreement

Rule Reference: Rule 5.01(1)

2. Once the paralegal has been hired by a client for a particular matter, it is advisable that the paralegal discuss with the client two essential terms of the paralegal's retainer by the client: the scope of the legal services to be provided and the anticipated cost of those services. The paralegal should ensure that the client clearly understands what legal services the paralegal is undertaking to provide. It is helpful for both the paralegal and client to confirm this understanding in writing by
   - a written retainer agreement signed by the client,
   - an engagement letter from the paralegal, or
   - a confirming memo to the client (sent by mail, e-mail or fax).

Rule Reference: Rule 3.02(15)

2.1 A written retainer agreement is particularly helpful in the circumstances of a limited scope retainer.

3. This written confirmation should set out the scope of legal services to be provided and describe how fees, disbursements and HST will be charged (see Guideline 13: Fees).

The Money Retainer

Rule Reference: By-Law 9, part IV
Rule 5.01

4. If practical, the paralegal should obtain a money retainer from the client at the beginning of the relationship. When determining the amount of the money retainer, the paralegal should consider the circumstances of each case, the circumstances of the client and the anticipated fees, disbursements and HST. Many of the factors are the same as those used in deciding if a fee is fair and reasonable.
5. The client should be advised at the outset if and when further retainers will be required. There may also be circumstances where a money retainer is not

appropriate, for example, when a client and the paralegal have entered into a contingency fee agreement.

6. A money retainer must be deposited into a paralegal's trust account. After the paralegal has delivered to the client a statement of account or bill, the paralegal pays the amount of his or her statement of account from the money retainer held in trust. Disbursements and expenses paid on behalf of the client to others may be paid directly from the money retainer in the paralegal's trust account. To avoid disagreements in circumstances where a disbursement will be particularly substantial, a paralegal may want to obtain the client's approval prior to the expense being incurred.

GUIDELINE 15: TRUST ACCOUNTS

General

Rule Reference: By-Law 9

1. A paralegal has special obligations when handling client funds. When a paralegal receives money that belongs to a client or is to be held on behalf of a client, the funds must be deposited to a ***trust account***. Because client funds must be held in trust by the paralegal, they are also known as ***trust funds***.
2. By-Law 9 outlines a paralegal's responsibilities regarding financial transactions and record-keeping, including the operation of a trust account.

Authorization to Withdraw from Trust

Rule Reference: By-Law 9

3. A paralegal must be in control of his or her trust account. Although a person who is not a licensed paralegal or lawyer may be permitted to disburse trust funds alone in exceptional circumstances, the Law Society has found appropriate exceptional circumstances to be very rare.
4. If there is only one paralegal with signing authority on the trust account(s) it would be prudent to make arrangements for another paralegal or a lawyer to have signing authority on the trust account(s) in case of an unexpected emergency (i.e. illness or accident) or planned absence (i.e. vacation). The paralegal may arrange this through his or her financial institution through a power of attorney. The chosen paralegal or lawyer must be insured and entitled to provide legal services or to practise law.
5. To ensure that no unauthorized withdrawals from trust are being made, the paralegal should limit access to blank trust account cheques and electronic banking software. A paralegal should never sign blank trust cheques. The paralegal should use pre-numbered trust cheques and keep them locked up when not in use.

GUIDELINE 16: DUTY TO THE ADMINISTRATION OF JUSTICE

General

Rule Reference: Rule 6.01

1. An important part of a paralegal's duty to act with integrity is his or her obligation to the administration of justice detailed in Rule 6. The obligation includes a paralegal's duty to assist in maintaining the security of court facilities, to refrain from

inappropriate public statements, and the obligation to prevent unauthorized practice.

Security of Court Facilities

Rule Reference: Rule 6.01(3)
Rule 3.03

2. An aspect of supporting the justice system is ensuring that its facilities remain safe. Where appropriate, a paralegal in the situation covered by Rule 6.01(3) should consider requesting additional security at the facility and notifying other paralegals or lawyers who may be affected. In considering what, if any, action to take with respect to this obligation, the paralegal must consider his or her obligations under Rule 3.03.

Public Appearances and Statements

Rule Reference: Rule 6.01(1), (2), (4) & (4.1)
Rule 3.03, 3.04
Rule 4.01(1)
Rule 7.01(4)

3. When making statements to the media with, or on behalf of, a client, a paralegal must be mindful of his or her obligations to act in the client's best interests and within the scope of his or her instructions from the client. It is also important that a person's, particularly an accused person's, right to a fair trial or hearing not be impaired by inappropriate public statements made before a case has concluded.

Provision of Legal Services Without a Licence / Practice of Law Without a Licence

Rule Reference: Rule 6.01(5) & (6)

4. The obligations found in subrules 6.01(5) & (6) stem from a paralegal's obligation to the administration of justice and from the regulatory scheme for paralegals and lawyers set out in the *Act* and discussed below.
5. Under the *Act*, anyone who provides legal services or practices law must be licensed by the Law Society, unless they are exempt from this requirement, or deemed not to be providing legal services or practicing law. A person who is not a lawyer or a licensed paralegal is subject neither to a professional code of conduct nor the Law Society's jurisdiction, which exist to protect the public. Only clients of regulated service providers have important protections, such as the following:
   - adherence to a mandatory code of professional conduct,
   - maintenance and operation of a trust account in accordance with strict mandatory guidelines,
   - mandatory professional liability insurance coverage, and
   - the Law Society's Compensation Funds.

GUIDELINE 17: DUTY TO PARALEGALS, LAWYERS AND OTHERS

General

Rule Reference: Rule 2.01(3)
Rule 7.01

1. Discourteous and uncivil behaviour between paralegals or between a paralegal and a lawyer will lessen the public's respect for the administration of justice and may harm the clients' interests. Any ill feeling that may exist between parties, particularly during adversarial proceedings, should never be allowed to influence paralegals or lawyers in their conduct and demeanour toward each other or the parties. Hostility or conflict between representatives may impair their ability to focus on their respective clients' interests and to have matters resolved without undue delay or cost.

Prohibited Conduct

Rule Reference: Rule 7.01

2. The presence of personal animosity between paralegals or between a paralegal and a lawyer involved in a matter may cause their judgment to be clouded by emotional factors and hinder the proper resolution of the matter. To that end, Rule 7.01 outlines various types of conduct that are specifically prohibited.
3. One of the prohibitions in Rule 7.01(1) refers to sharp practice. Sharp practice occurs when a paralegal obtains, or tries to obtain, an advantage for the paralegal or client(s), by using dishonourable means. This would include, for example, lying to another paralegal or a lawyer, trying to trick another paralegal or a lawyer into doing something or making an oral promise to another paralegal or lawyer with the intention of reneging on the promise later. As another example, if an opposing paralegal were under a mistaken belief about the date of an upcoming trial, a paralegal would be obligated to tell the opposing representative about the error, rather than ignoring the matter in the hope the opposing representative would not appear at the trial.

Limited Scope Retainer

Rule Reference: Rule 7.02(2)

3.1 Where notice as described in Rule 7.02(2) has been provided to a paralegal, the paralegal is required to communicate with the legal practitioner who is representing the person under a limited scope retainer, but only to the extent of the matter(s) within the limited scope retainer as identified by the legal practitioner. The paralegal may communicate with the person on matters outside the limited scope retainer.

GUIDELINE 18: SUPERVISION OF STAFF

General

Rule Reference: **By-Law 7.1**
Rule 8.01(1), (3), (4) & (5)
By-Law 7 (Multi-Discipline practices)

1. A paralegal may, in appropriate circumstances, provide services with the assistance of persons of whose competence the paralegal is satisfied. Proper use of support staff allows the paralegal to make efficient use of the time he or she has for providing legal services, and may result in savings to the client. Under By-Law 7.1, some tasks may be delegated to persons who are not licensed and other tasks may not. Though certain tasks may be delegated, the paralegal remains responsible for all services rendered and all communications by and prepared by his or her employees.
2. The extent of supervision required will depend on the task, including the degree of standardization and repetitiveness of the task and the experience of the employee. Extra supervisory care may be needed if there is something different or unusual in the task. The burden rests on the paralegal to educate the employee concerning the tasks that may be assigned and then to supervise the manner in which these tasks are completed.
3. A paralegal should ensure that employees who are not licensed clearly identify themselves as such when communicating with clients, prospective clients, courts or tribunals, or the public. This includes both written and verbal communications.
4. A paralegal in a multi-discipline practice is responsible the actions of his or her non- licensee partners and associates as set out in Rule 8.01(5).

Hiring & Training Staff

Rule Reference: **Rule 8.01(1)**
Rule 3.01(4)(c)(h)

5. In order to fulfill his or her responsibilities to clients under the *Rules* and By-Laws, a paralegal should take care to properly hire and train staff. A paralegal should obtain information about a potential employee to inform himself or herself about the employee's competence and trustworthiness. If the position involves handling money, the paralegal may ask for the applicant's consent to check his or her criminal record and credit reports. A paralegal must comply with privacy legislation and should refer to the *Rules* to review questions that can and cannot be asked of an applicant, as outlined in the *Human Rights Code*. A paralegal should confirm the information contained in a candidate's resume, consult references and verify previous employment experiences before offering employment to a candidate.
6. Proper hiring and training of persons who are not licensed will assist the paralegal in managing his or her practice effectively, as required by Rule 3.01(4)(c)(h). Since the paralegal is responsible for the professional business, it will assist the paralegal in fulfilling this responsibility if the paralegal educates staff regarding
   - the types of tasks which will and will not be delegated,
   - the need to act with courtesy and professionalism,
   - the definition of discrimination and harassment, and the prohibition against any conduct that amounts to discrimination and harassment,

- the duty to maintain client confidentiality and methods used to protect, confidential client information (e.g. avoiding gossip inside and outside of the office),
- the definition of a conflict of interest, the duty to avoid conflicts and how to use a conflict checking system,
- proper handling of client property, including money, and
- proper record keeping.

GUIDELINE 19: MAKING LEGAL SERVICES AVAILABLE AND MARKETING OF LEGAL SERVICES

Making Legal Services Available

Rule Reference: Rule 8.02
Rule 8.03

1. Rule 8.02(1) describes the paralegal's obligation to make legal services available and the manner in which he or she must do so. A paralegal has a general right to decline a particular representation (except when assigned as representative by a tribunal), but it is a right that should be exercised prudently, particularly if the probable result would be to make it difficult for a person to obtain legal advice or representation. Generally, the paralegal should not exercise the right merely because a person seeking legal services or that person's cause is unpopular or notorious, or because powerful interests or allegations of misconduct or malfeasance are involved, or because of the paralegal's private opinion about the guilt of the accused. A paralegal declining representation should assist in obtaining the services of a lawyer or another licensed paralegal qualified in the particular field and able to act.
2. A person who is vulnerable or who has suffered a traumatic experience and has not yet had a chance to recover may need the professional assistance of a paralegal. A paralegal is permitted to provide assistance to a person if a close relative or personal friend of the person contacts the paralegal for this purpose, and to offer assistance to a person with whom the paralegal has a close family or professional relationship. Rules 8.02 and 8.03 prohibit the paralegal from using unconscionable or exploitive or other means that bring the profession or the administration of justice into disrepute.

Marketing of Legal Services

Rule Reference: Rule 8.02
Rule 8.03

3. In presenting and promoting a paralegal practice, a paralegal must comply with the *Rules* regarding the marketing of legal services.
4. Rules 8.02 and 8.03 impose certain restrictions and obligations on a paralegal who wishes to market and/or advertise his or her legal services. The *Rules* help to ensure that a paralegal does not mislead clients or the public while still permitting the paralegal to differentiate himself or herself and his or her services from those of lawyers or other paralegals. A paralegal should ensure that his or her marketing and advertising does not suggest that the paralegal is a lawyer and should take steps to correct any misapprehension on the part of a client or prospective client in that respect.

5. Examples of marketing practices that may contravene Rule 8.03(1) include:
   - Stating an amount of money that the paralegal has recovered for a client or refer to the paralegal's degree of success in past cases, unless such statement is accompanied by a further statement that past results are not necessarily indicative of future results and that the amount recovered and other litigation outcomes will vary according to the facts in individual cases.
   - Suggesting qualitative superiority to lawyers or other paralegals
   - Raising expectations unjustifiably
   - Suggesting or implying the paralegal is aggressive
   - Disparaging or demeaning other persons, groups, organizations or institutions
   - Taking advantage of a vulnerable person or group
   - Using testimonials or endorsements which contain emotional appeals.

GUIDELINE 20: INSURANCE

General

Rule Reference: Rule 8.04(1)–(3)

1. As soon as a paralegal discovers an error or omission that is or may reasonably be expected to involve liability to his or her client, the paralegal should take the following steps, in addition to those required by Rule 8.04:
   - immediately arrange an interview with the client and advise the client that an error or omission may have occurred that may form the basis of a claim against the paralegal by the client;
   - advise the client to obtain an opinion from an independent paralegal or lawyer and that, in the circumstances, the paralegal may not be able to continue acting for the client; and
   - subject to the rules about confidentiality, inform the insurer of the facts of the situation.
2. While the introduction of compulsory insurance imposes additional obligations upon a paralegal, those obligations must not impair the relationship between the paralegal and client or the duties owed to the client.

GUIDELINE 21: DUTY TO THE LAW SOCIETY

General

Rule Reference: Rule 9

1. All paralegals and lawyers owe a duty to their governing body, the Law Society, so that it can effectively and efficiently carry out its mandate to govern the legal professions in the public interest. Rule 9 details various obligations owed to the Law Society, many of which focus on measures to protect the public from inappropriate paralegal or lawyer conduct.

Duty to Respond Promptly and to Co-operate with an Investigation

Rule Reference: Rule 9.01(1)

2. In addition to the obligation to reply promptly and completely to communication from the Law Society which is set out in Rule 9.01(1), a paralegal also has a duty to cooperate with a person conducting an investigation under the *Act*. A paralegal who fails to respond promptly and completely to a Law Society inquiry about a

complaint, or who fails to cooperate with a Law Society investigation, may be disciplined on that issue, regardless of the merits or outcome of the original complaint.

Duty to Report Misconduct

Rule Reference: Rule 9.01(2)–(8)

3. Unless a paralegal or lawyer who departs from proper professional conduct is checked at an early stage, loss or damage to clients and others may ensue. As such, a paralegal must assist the Law Society in upholding the integrity of the profession by reporting professional misconduct of the type outlined in Rule 9.01(2).
4. Evidence of seemingly isolated events, or "less serious" breaches of the *Rules*, may, under investigation, disclose a more serious situation or may indicate the commencement of a course of conduct that may lead to serious breaches in the future. It is proper therefore (unless it is confidential or otherwise unlawful) for a paralegal to report to the Law Society any instance involving a breach of the *Rules* or the *Rules of Professional Conduct*.
5. The obligation to report misconduct applies to the paralegal's own conduct, as well as that of other paralegals and lawyers.
6. The onus is on the paralegal to take the necessary steps to carry out his or her obligations to the Law Society and to protect both himself or herself and his or her client. If a paralegal is unsure as to whether to report another paralegal's or lawyer's conduct, the paralegal should consider seeking the advice of the Law Society directly (through the Practice Management Helpline at 416-947-3315 or 1-800-668-7380 extension 3315) or indirectly (through another paralegal or lawyer).

Duty to Report Certain Offences

Rule Reference: By-Law 8, subsection 3
Rule 9.01(9)

7. All paralegals have a duty to report themselves to the Law Society if certain charges (identified in By-Law 8, subsection 3) have been laid against them.
8. The By-Law only requires the paralegal to self-report the above-mentioned criminal charges or convictions. A paralegal is only required to report another paralegal or lawyer who is involved in criminal activity in certain circumstances.

GUIDELINE 22: THE LAW SOCIETY AND ITS DISCIPLINARY AUTHORITY

General

Rule Reference: Rule 9.01(10)–(13)

1. A paralegal may be disciplined by the Law Society for either professional misconduct or for conduct unbecoming a paralegal.
2. Examples of conduct unbecoming a paralegal include a paralegal's conviction of a criminal offence or a finding or sanction imposed on the paralegal by a tribunal or licensing body.
3. Dishonourable or questionable conduct on the part of a paralegal in either private life or while providing legal services will reflect adversely upon the integrity of the profession and the administration of justice. Whether within or outside the professional sphere, if the conduct is such that knowledge of it would be likely to impair a client's trust in the paralegal, the Law Society may be justified in taking disciplinary action.

4. Generally, however, the Law Society will not be concerned with the purely private or extra-professional activities of a paralegal that do not bring into question the paralegal's professional integrity.
5. The *Rules* cannot address every situation. As such, a paralegal is required to follow both the "letter" and the "spirit" of the *Rules*. The "letter" of the rule is the meaning of the rule as it is written. The "spirit" of the rule is the sense of the rule or the meaning or importance of the rule, even though it may not be explicit or stated in the written version of the *Rule*.

GUIDELINE 23: FINANCIAL OBLIGATIONS

General

Rule Reference: Rule 8.01(2)

1. Rule 8.01 establishes a professional duty (apart from any legal liability) regarding financial obligations incurred in the course of providing legal services on behalf of a client.
2. The business of providing legal services often requires that a paralegal incur financial obligations to others on behalf of clients. Such obligations include charges for medical reports, disbursements payable to government registries, fees charged by expert witnesses, sheriffs, special examiners, registrars, court reporters and public officials and the accounts of agents retained in other jurisdictions.
3. To assist in avoiding disputes about payment of accounts, where a paralegal retains a person on behalf of a client, the paralegal should clarify the terms of the retainer in writing. This includes specifying the fees, the nature of the services to be provided, and the person responsible for payment. If the paralegal is not responsible for the payment of the fees, the paralegal should help in making satisfactory arrangements for payment if it is reasonably possible to do so.
4. If there is a change of representative, the paralegal who originally retained the person to whom the financial obligation will be owed should advise him or her about the change and provide the name, address, telephone number, fax number and e-mail address of the new paralegal or lawyer.

Glossary

A

accommodation an action taken or a change made to allow a person or group protected by the Ontario *Human Rights Code* to engage in any of the activities covered by the Code—for example, employment

accredited legal services program a paralegal program in Ontario that is approved by the Ministry of Training, Colleges and Universities and accredited by the Law Society of Upper Canada

acting in good faith making legitimate and honest efforts to meet your obligations in a given situation, without trying to gain an unfair advantage over or mislead other persons or parties through legal technicalities or otherwise

acting with civility being polite, respectful, and considerate of others

adjudicative body a body—such as a federal or provincial court, an administrative tribunal, a statutory board, or an arbitrator—that hears evidence or legal argument and makes a decision affecting the legal interests, rights, or responsibilities of a person (*Law Society Act*, s. 1)

adjudicator a person who hears or considers a proceeding before a tribunal and makes a decision with respect to that proceeding

adverse impact discrimination *see* constructive discrimination

advocate a person who assists, defends, or pleads for others before a tribunal

affidavit a written statement of facts that is confirmed under oath or by affirmation by the person making it

affiliated entity any person or group of persons other than a person or group authorized to provide legal services in Ontario; a non-licensee or group of non-licensees

affiliation an arrangement whereby a paralegal services firm provides legal services to the public jointly with a non-legal entity whose members practise a profession, trade, or occupation that supports or supplements the paralegal's provision of legal services

alternative dispute resolution resolution of a dispute through negotiation, mediation, arbitration, or similar means, instead of litigation

ancestry family descent

B

beneficiary a person who benefits from the efforts of another

best efforts a paralegal's effort to do what he can to ensure that an undertaking is fulfilled, without assuming personal responsibility

billable time time that is charged to the client on an invoice

binding authority a judicial decision by a higher court that must be followed by lower courts; also known as a binding precedent

breach of undertaking failure to fulfill an undertaking

C

client a person who consults a paralegal and on whose behalf the paralegal provides or agrees to provide legal services; or, having consulted the paralegal, reasonably concludes that the paralegal has agreed to provide legal services on his or her behalf; includes a client of the firm of which the paralegal is a partner or associate, whether or not the paralegal handles the client's work

client identification information that By-law 7.1 requires a licensee to obtain from a client about who the client is and what he does

client receivable money that is owed to a paralegal by a client for an unpaid balance on an invoice for legal services that have been rendered and reasonable expenses and disbursements that have been incurred in a client matter

client verification information that By-law 7.1 requires a licensee to obtain in order to confirm that the client is who he says he is

client with diminished capacity a client whose capacity to make decisions is impaired because of minority, mental disability, illiteracy, or for some other reason

competent paralegal a paralegal who has and applies the relevant skills, attributes, and values appropriate to each matter undertaken on behalf of a client

complainant a person who alleges that he was the victim of a crime, and who takes part in the prosecution of the person(s) accused of committing the crime

conduct unbecoming a paralegal conduct in a paralegal's personal or private capacity that tends to bring discredit upon the paralegal profession

confidential information any information touching on the business and affairs of a client acquired in the course of the paralegal–client relationship; a paralegal has a duty to hold all such information in strictest confidence and not to disclose it to any other person, unless authorized to do so by the client or required to do so by law (Rule 3.03(1))

conflict of interest an interest, financial or otherwise, that may negatively affect a paralegal's ability to fulfill her professional and ethical obligations to a client

conflicts checking system a list of all clients (including prospective clients), opposing parties, and related parties, if any, that is checked to ensure that there are no conflicts of interest on any client files

constructive discrimination a requirement, qualification, or factor that is not discrimination on a prohibited ground but that results in the exclusion, restriction, or preference of a group of persons who are identified by a prohibited ground of discrimination (*Human Rights Code*, s. 11(1)); also known as adverse impact discrimination

contingency fee a fee that is contingent, in whole or in part, on the successful disposition or completion of the matter for which the paralegal's services are to be provided

continuing client a client for whom a paralegal acts in several different matters or transactions over a period of time

continuing professional development the maintenance and enhancement of a licensee's knowledge, skills, attitudes, and professionalism throughout the licensee's career

continuing relationship a paralegal–client relationship where a paralegal acts for the same client in several different matters or transactions over a period of time

Convocation the governing body of the Law Society of Upper Canada

creed religion or faith

D

definite suspension a suspension for a fixed period of time imposed upon a licensee by the Law Society

deponent a person who makes an affidavit

diarize to note a deadline or other important date in your tickler system, along with a series of bring-forward dates to remind you that the deadline is approaching

direction a written document, signed by the client, that instructs a paralegal to take a particular course of action in a client matter

disbursements expenses related to the client matter that are paid by the paralegal on behalf of the client and for which the paralegal is entitled to be reimbursed

discrimination unfair treatment by one person of another person or group on any of the prohibited grounds under the *Human Rights Code*

dispute an argument or disagreement between two or more parties in which the interest of one side is adverse to that of the other side

docket a manual or electronic record of all time spent on a client matter

docketed time the total time recorded to a client matter

due diligence in a legal context, exercising prudence and vigilance in determining the facts

duty of loyalty *see* duty of service

duty of service the paralegal's duty to be competent, maintain confidentiality, avoid conflicts of interest, and continue to represent the client unless the paralegal has good reason to withdraw; also known as the duty of loyalty

E

elected bencher a licensee who is elected to sit on Convocation

elements of the offence the components of an offence that must be proven beyond a reasonable doubt by the prosecution in order to obtain a conviction

engagement letter a letter to the client from the paralegal that confirms the retainer and the terms of the retainer

error an action by a legal representative that may cause harm to a client

errors and omissions insurance insurance intended to reimburse clients for loss or damage suffered as a result of negligence or wrongdoing by a legal representative

ethnic origin cultural background

examination out of court a procedure during which a party or witness is examined under oath or affirmation by opposing parties or their representatives with a view to obtaining facts and information that will assist the parties to prepare their case

express (or explicit) authorization fully informed and voluntary written or spoken authorization given by the client to the paralegal permitting disclosure of confidential information to specified third parties; if spoken, then the client shall receive a written confirmation of the consent as soon as is practicable

F

family status parent and child relationships (*Human Rights Code*, s. 10(1)); a parent may be a biological parent, an adoptive parent, or a legal guardian

fee splitting an arrangement where a paralegal shares or splits a client fee with another person

fees the amount charged to a client by a paralegal for legal services provided by the paralegal to the client, including advice, correspondence, drafting pleadings and other documents, and time spent in court

fees based on an hourly rate an arrangement whereby a paralegal is paid for actual time spent on the client matter; calculated by multiplying the paralegal's hourly rate (or that of others who have completed work on the file) by the amount of time spent on the client matter to the date of the invoice

fees by stages an arrangement whereby the client matter is broken down into stages and the client is charged based on a reasonable estimate of the fee for each stage or step in the matter

fiduciary a person who must act with scrupulous good faith, honesty, and candour for the benefit of another person, who places absolute trust and confidence in the fiduciary

fiduciary relationship a relationship of trust and confidence between two persons in which one person (the fiduciary) is required to act with scrupulous good faith, honesty, and candour for the benefit of the other person

fixed, flat, or block fee a fixed amount charged for a particular task or client matter

fresh evidence evidence of something that has happened since the first hearing, or that has come to the knowledge of the applicant since the hearing and could not by reasonable means have come to her knowledge before that time

frivolous and vexatious objection an objection that has no legal merit and is made to annoy, harass, or embarrass the other side

fulfill (or answer) an undertaking to complete the requirements of the undertaking

funds cash, currency, securities, negotiable instruments, and other financial instruments that indicate a person's title or interest in them

G

guarantee an agreement to make oneself liable or responsible to a lender for the payment of a debt if the debtor defaults in payment

H

harassment engaging in a course of vexatious comment or conduct that is known or ought reasonably to be known to be unwelcome (*Human Rights Code*, s. 10(1))

honest and candid being truthful, forthright, and sincere, and looking at both sides of each issue without bias

I

implied authorization client authorization to reveal confidential information that is not spoken or written down, but is implied by the paralegal–client relationship and the nature of the client matter

independent legal advice impartial, confidential advice obtained from a competent licensee with no personal interest in the matter; also called ILA

independent legal representation legal advice and assistance from a competent paralegal or lawyer with no personal interest in the matter

instructions directions or authorizations from a client to a paralegal with respect to a particular course of action to be taken in a matter

interim invoice an invoice that is delivered to the client before the client matter is completed, for fees and disbursements to the date of the interim invoice

J

joint clients the clients in a joint retainer

joint retainer an arrangement whereby a paralegal is hired to represent more than one client in a matter or transaction

judicial notice when a tribunal notices, or accepts as true, certain notorious facts or matters of common knowledge without hearing evidence and without inquiry; other lesser-known facts may be noticed after inquiry

justified disclosure mandatory disclosure of confidential information without the client's authority

L

Law Society of Upper Canada a self-governing body that regulates the legal and paralegal professions in Ontario in the public interest, according to Ontario law and the rules, regulations, and guidelines of the Law Society

lay bencher a non-licensee who sits on Convocation

legal practitioner a person who is a member of the bar in a Canadian jurisdiction other than Ontario, and is authorized to practise law as a barrister and solicitor in that jurisdiction; a lawyer

limited scope retainer a retainer where the client hires a paralegal to perform one specific task, such as drafting a demand letter

M

marital status for purposes of the Ontario *Human Rights Code*, the status of being married, single, widowed, divorced, separated, or living with a person in a conjugal relationship outside of marriage

marketing includes advertisements and similar communications in various media, as well as firm names (including trade names), letterhead, business cards, and logos (Rule 8.03(1))

material change in circumstances a change in the applicant's circumstances that has occurred since the previous hearing and that may justify a variation of the original order

mediation a non-adversarial process in which a qualified and impartial third party (the mediator) helps the parties to a dispute resolve their differences

mediator a qualified and impartial third party who helps the parties to a dispute resolve their differences through mediation

merits of the case the legal principles upon which a party's assertion of rights is based

misrepresentation a statement or conduct by a person that is misleading or false, and that is intended to deceive another person; includes a deliberate failure to disclose correct information

mixed trust bank account a trust account that holds money for more than one client matter; also referred to as "mixed trust account" and "trust account"

money retainer payment for future legal services, which must be held in trust for the benefit of the client until part or all of those services have been provided and invoiced to the client

multi-discipline practice a business arrangement that permits paralegal licensees to provide to clients the services of a non-licensee who practises a profession, trade, or occupation that supports or supplements the provision of legal services; also called MDP

N

negotiable instrument an unconditional order or promise to pay an amount of money, which can be transferred—for example, cheques or banknotes (paper money)

nepotism favouritism based on family relationships

non-billable time time that is docketed to a client matter but is not billed to the client

non-engagement failure to enter into a contract or agreement for legal services

non-engagement letter a letter written by a paralegal to a client confirming that, in a particular matter, the paralegal has declined to provide legal services to the client, or that the client has declined to retain the paralegal

O

objection an argument by a party that a particular piece of evidence, line of questioning, or other matter is improper or unlawful and should not be allowed by the court

omission a failure to act by a legal representative that may cause harm to a client

outside interest any profession, business, occupation, or other outside interest, including holding public office, engaged in by a paralegal concurrently with the provision of legal services

P

paralegal in Ontario, a non-lawyer agent who provides legal services to the public and who must be licensed to do so unless he falls within one of the categories of exemptions; the paralegal profession is governed by the Law Society of Upper Canada

paralegal–client relationship the professional relationship between a paralegal and a client that gives rise to a range of duties that include the duties of competence, confidentiality, and avoidance of conflicts of interest, and the duty to continue to represent the client unless the paralegal has good reason for withdrawing

paralegal–client retainer the contractual relationship between the client and the paralegal, which establishes the scope of the retainer, what the client will be charged for the legal services provided, and other terms of the agreement; also called retainer

paralegal licensee a person licensed to provide legal services in Ontario

Paralegal Standing Committee a committee of five paralegal licensees who are benchers, five lawyer licensees who are benchers, and three lay (non-licensee) benchers, which is responsible for developing policy on all issues affecting paralegal practice in Ontario

permitted disclosure discretionary disclosure of confidential information by a paralegal without the client's authority

permitted scope of paralegal practice areas of law in which licensed paralegals may provide legal services, as prescribed by the Law Society and the By-Laws

person any entity that is recognized by law as the subject of legal rights and obligations, including the right to sue and be sued

phantom client a person who believes that a paralegal is representing him, even though the paralegal has not been formally retained and may be unaware of the person's belief

place of origin for purposes of the Ontario *Human Rights Code*, a person's country or region of birth, including a region in Canada

private company a corporation whose shares are not publicly traded; also called a closely held company

procedural law the rules for judicial enforcement of a person's legal rights and obligations as set out in substantive law

professional judgment the competent paralegal's capacity to assess situations or circumstances carefully and to make sensible decisions about client matters and her own conduct

professional misconduct conduct in a paralegal's professional capacity that tends to bring discredit upon the paralegal profession

prohibited grounds grounds upon which discrimination is prohibited by the Ontario *Human Rights Code* (s. 1)—race or colour, ancestry, place of origin, ethnic origin, citizenship, creed, sex, sexual orientation, gender identity, gender expression, age, marital or family status, or disability; for purposes of employment, record of offences is also a ground of discrimination

prospective client a person who consults a paralegal regarding a legal issue but has not yet retained the paralegal and for whom the paralegal has not yet agreed to provide legal representation

provide legal services to engage in conduct involving the application of legal principles and legal judgment to the circumstances or objectives of another person

public company a corporation whose shares are for sale to the general public and that is subject to rigorous disclosure requirements under securities legislation

R

record of offence for purposes of the Ontario *Human Rights Code*, a *Criminal Code* conviction that has been pardoned, or a provincial offence

referral fee a fee paid by a paralegal to another licensee for referring a client to the paralegal, or a fee paid to a paralegal by another licensee for the paralegal's referral of a person to the other licensee

remedy a way of enforcing a right, or preventing or compensating for a wrong

representing a person in a proceeding representation includes making decisions about service and filing of documents relating to a proceeding; deciding what persons to serve a document on or with whom to file a document; deciding when, where, or how to serve or file a document; and/or engaging in any other conduct necessary to the conduct of the proceeding

retained hired to represent a person in a legal matter

retainer *see* paralegal–client retainer

retainer agreement a written agreement between the client and the paralegal that confirms that the paralegal has been hired to provide legal services to the client, and confirms the terms upon which she has been hired

S

scope of the retainer the nature and extent of the legal services to be provided by the paralegal pursuant to the paralegal–client retainer

serious loss of confidence a situation in which the paralegal and the client no longer trust and rely on each other, making it impossible to have a normal paralegal–client relationship

sharp practice dishonourable taking of advantage; trickery

statement of account a statement (that is, an invoice or bill) that tells the client how much is owed to the paralegal for fees, disbursements, and HST as of the date of the account

statute-barred a proceeding that is prevented by the expiry of the statutory limitation period

statutory limitation period a period of time established by a statute for commencing a proceeding

substantive law the statutory law and jurisprudence that creates, defines, and interprets the rights and obligations of those who are subject to it

surety a person who is responsible for an accused, and exercises supervisory functions over the defendant; the surety must ensure that the accused attends court as required until the case is concluded and abides by any conditions of judicial interim release

sympathetic witness a witness who gives evidence that supports a party's cause

T

tickler system a paper or electronic system that gives notice of upcoming deadlines (including limitation periods) or tasks to be completed

to write off time to not bill a client for time that was spent on the client matter

tribunal includes courts, boards, arbitrators, mediators, administrative agencies, and bodies that resolve disputes, regardless of their function or the informality of their procedures

trust condition a condition or conditions that must be performed before a paralegal may release certain documents and/or property held in trust by the paralegal

U

undertaking an unequivocal, personal promise by a paralegal to perform a certain act

unsympathetic witness a witness who gives evidence that supports an opposing party's cause

V

valuable property record a record of all property, other than money, held in trust for clients, as required by By-law 9, s. 18(9)

Index

A

B

C

O

P

R

S

T

Credits

Guidelines for Paralegals Who Are Suspended or Who Have Given an Undertaking Not to Provide Legal Services. Copyright 2008, The Law Society of Upper Canada. Reprinted with permission of The Law Society of Upper Canada.

Paralegal Professional Conduct Guidelines. Copyright 2008–2014, The Law Society of Upper Canada. Reprinted with permission of The Law Society of Upper Canada.

Paralegal Rules of Conduct. Copyright 2007–2014, The Law Society of Upper Canada. Reprinted with permission of The Law Society of Upper Canada.

Paralegal Standing Committee Report to Convocation. Copyright 2014, The Law Society of Upper Canada. Reprinted with permission of The Law Society of Upper Canada.

Policy on Preventing Sexual and Gender-Based Harassment. © Queen's Printer for Ontario, 2013. Reproduced with permission.

Report to the Attorney General of Ontario: Report of Appointee's Five-Year Review of Paralegal Regulation in Ontario Pursuant to Section 63.1 of the Law Society Act, by David J. Morris. © Queen's Printer for Ontario, 2012. Reproduced with permission.

Rules of Professional Conduct. Copyright 2000, The Law Society of Upper Canada. Reprinted with permission of The Law Society of Upper Canada.

Treasurer's Report to Convocation. Copyright 2012, The Law Society of Upper Canada. Reprinted with permission of The Law Society of Upper Canada.